Praise for Gregory Rodriguez's

Mongrels,
Bastards,
Orphans,
and
Vagabonds

"Shrewd. . . . Fascinating. . . . The conclusion of this excellent book is surely right."
                                                            —*The Economist*

"Brilliant. . . . Politically savvy and enchanting."
                                                            —*Los Angeles Times*

"Crisp. . . . Well-written."
                                                            —*Tucson Citizen*

"In the midst of a narrow, polemical debate on immigration, Gregory Rodriguez has written a generous, sweeping, prodigiously researched, and judicious history of Mexican Americans that helps us understand their long-term influence on American society. Smart, fun, and eminently readable, *Mongrels, Bastards, Orphans, and Vagabonds* explores five centuries of cultural collisions and convergences, and dares us to imagine a new way of thinking about the future of America."   —Bill Richardson, governor of New Mexico and former United States Ambassador to the United Nations

"Rodriguez has pulled off not one but two stunning coups—a thoroughly original history and a penetrating commentary on what race means and will mean in our era and beyond. From 1519 to the front page of today's newspaper, from the Virgin of Guadalupe to the National Council of La Raza—the sweep alone is breathtaking. But every chapter also drills deep, and they build to an important new argument about the future of the American melting pot. By turns learned, fascinating, deeply felt (this is no academic history), completely contemporary, and, in its picture of where we're heading, as persuasive as it is provocative. A tour de force." —Tamar Jacoby, author of *Someone Else's House: America's Unfinished Struggle for Integration*

"Passionately argued, thoroughly researched. . . . Draws a far more complex portrait of Mexican Americans and Mexicans in America than is found in our media. Rodriguez's book provides a welcome interjection of sanity and complexity into a debate that so far has been largely characterized by ignorance, ideology, and hysteria." —Eric Alterman, author of *Why We're Liberals: A Political Handbook for Post-Bush America*

"Trailblazing. . . . Rodriguez examines the complex racial and ethnic heritage of Mexican Americans with a sweeping historical insight that demolishes widespread prevalent myths. . . . A vital contribution to understanding the role of Mexican Americans in U.S. society." —Lou Cannon, author of *President Reagan: The Role of a Lifetime*

"An indispensable guide to America's future—and an optimistic one, too." —Adrian Wooldridge, coauthor of *The Right Nation: Conservative Power in America*

Gregory Rodriguez

Mongrels, Bastards, Orphans, and Vagabonds

Gregory Rodriguez is director of the California Fellows Program and an Irvine Senior Fellow at the New America Foundation, a nonpartisan public policy institute. He is also an op-ed columnist for the *Los Angeles Times*. He lives in Los Angeles.

Mongrels, Bastards, Orphans, and Vagabonds

Mexican Immigration and the Future of Race in America

Gregory Rodriguez

Vintage Books
A Division of Random House, Inc.
New York

For my dad

FIRST VINTAGE BOOKS EDITION, OCTOBER 2008

Copyright © 2007 by Gregory Rodriguez

All rights reserved. Published in the United States by Vintage Books, a division of Random House, Inc., New York, and in Canada by Random House of Canada Limited, Toronto. Originally published in hardcover in the United States by Pantheon Books, a division of Random House, Inc., New York, in 2007.

Vintage and colophon are registered trademarks of Random House, Inc.

The Library of Congress has cataloged the Pantheon edition as follows:
Rodriguez, Gregory.
Mongrels, bastards, orphans, and vagabonds: Mexican immigration and the future of race in America / Gregory Rodriguez.
p. cm.
Includes bibliographical references and index.
1. Mexican Americans—History. 2. Mexican Americans—Ethnic identity.
3. Chicano movement. 4. Mexico—Emigration and immigration—History.
5. United States—Emigration and immigration—History. I. Title.
E184.M5R587 2007
973'.046872—dc22 2007017464

Vintage ISBN: 978-0-375-71320-0

Author photograph © John Nelson
Book design by M. Kirsten Bearse

www.vintagebooks.com

Printed in the United States of America
10 9 8 7 6 5 4 3 2 1

Contents

Preface

On June 30, 1993, Carlos A. Fernández, a lawyer and activist from San Francisco, California, testified before the House Subcommittee on Census, Statistics, and Postal Personnel on behalf of the Association of MultiEthnic Americans, an organization whose goal was "to promote a positive awareness of interracial and multiethnic identity."[1] Fernández proposed that Directive No. 15, the federal government's guidelines for categorizing Americans by race and ethnicity, be "changed in order to allow the accurate counting of multiracial/ethnic people."[2] Although he did not testify to it, Fernández's worldview had been informed by both his own mixed background and the Hispanic Catholic view of race. In a 1992 essay, Fernández, the son of a Mexican father and an Anglo mother, speculated that the greatest contribution that Mexican Americans would give to America was "the reshaping of our attitudes about race and especially about race mixture."[3] He believed that the adoption of the Latin American concept of *mestizaje*—racial and cultural synthesis—would help Americans deal more effectively with the nation's growing diversity. According to Fernández, the official acknowledgment of intermediate racial categories would be a "crucial step" in "breaking down traditional lines of social separation" and potentially provide "the basis for a unifying national identity."[4]

Fernández's testimony and the lobbying of the Association of MultiEthnic Americans were instrumental in encouraging the federal government to allow Americans to identify themselves as members of more than one race on the 2000 census questionnaire. Fernández was not the only Mexican American intellectual to embrace Mexico's mixed racial and cultural heritage and to weigh its effect on both Mexican American identity and U.S. society. Indeed, even amid the heated rhetoric of the late 1960s pioneering Mexican American intellectuals, Ernesto Galarza, Herman Gallegos, and Julian Samora considered the heterogeneity implicit in the Mexican American experience to be an advantage. "What he lost in cultural compactness, in political hardening, even in defensive angers, he gained in range of social experience, in wider understanding of the kind of new society he was in, and in exposure to the tests and temptations of making one's way toward a beckoning American way of life."[5] In 1970, during the high point of the Chicano Movement, Galarza warned activists of the pitfalls of defining themselves too narrowly both culturally and politically. "To me the notable thing [about the conquest of Mexico] is that the indigenous Mexican survived and multiplied until he put his genetic and cultural stamp on the mixed society that emerged. But this is not altogether what the [Chicano] activists are emphasizing currently. Out of the period of servitude they abstract something else, the brand of bondage, 'We are a conquered people,' they are saying."[6] Galarza knew that the rhetoric of ethnic separatism carried with it "an insidious danger" of becoming "the very racism" that Chicano activists were combating.[7]

In 1978, historian Manuel A. Machado, Jr., complained that "the academic advocates of chicanismo constantly point out the Indian heritage of the Mexican-American," but refused to "deal with cultural hybridization for fear that it might negate the purity of the mythical Indian background."[8] He argued that "the cultural mestizaje that occurred in Mexico also blended with the Anglo to produce a value system within the Mexican-American community that is itself hybridized. Therefore, rejection of Anglo values by the Chicanos is really a rejection of one element of the Chicano culture."[9]

By the mid-1970s, Chicano Movement intellectuals were grappling with the tension between their rhetoric of ethnic nationalism and the Mexican history of *mestizaje*. In 1976, writer Federico A. Sánchez published an essay in which he declared that Mexican Americans should "devote concentrated efforts toward resolving that dilemma that has afflicted Mexico for so long, mainly the conflict that is implicit in mestizaje. . . . It is time for us to affirm the fact that we are a hybrid culture, assimilate our past, and begin the arduous task of describing the Chicano cultural configurations."[10] But whereas Mexicans grappled with the tension between their Indian and Spanish heritages, Sánchez contended that Mexican Americans had yet another culture in the mix, the Anglo American. "The original conflict, altered now by time and geography, has taken on a third dimension," he wrote.[11]

In 1979, anthropologist Carlos G. Vélez-Ibáñez suggested that mixture lay at the heart of the Mexican American culture. "We are a synthesis of myriad experiences—pan-human, multicultural, and multisocial. During the course of history, such experiences and continuing experiences are added as layers of meaning, layers of orders, layers of different and similar shared understandings, and, as a result of such experiences and the discarding of layers, we constantly 'become.' This is another way of saying that culturally we are neither Mexican nor Anglo-American, but we are of the American continent in a technologically complex society, with a complexity of experiences of moral orders."[12] In the same volume, Spanish professor Roberto R. Bacalski-Martínez described Mexican American culture in the Southwest as "incredibly ancient on the one hand, and surprisingly new on the other. Indian, Spanish, Mexican, and Anglo elements have gone into its formation, and they continue to affect it. In each case, the introduction of new elements began as a clash between two peoples which eventually resulted in a newer, richer culture."[13]

In 1980, anthropologist James Diego Vigil attempted to meld the notions of *Chicanismo*, the ideology of the Chicano movement, and *mestizaje* into the concept of *Chicanozaje*. "Generally, Chicanozaje includes a historical awareness of the Chicanos' role as oppressed members of a society," he wrote. At the same time, he argued that Mexican Americans "now realize that their past is a complex one of multiple heritages . . . [and] because of this background a whole range of cultural variation is possible. Some can favor the European side, others the Indian, or they can move in between seeking the cultural style that fits them. Chicanozaje thus expands the boundaries of the age-old mestizaje tradition of Mexico. It is a fluid, dual cultural membership that gives a deeper meaning to the term 'Chicano.' "[14]

Perhaps the most eloquent explorations of the meaning of *mestizaje* for both Mexican Americans and U.S. society were published in the 1990s. In 1992, essayist Richard Rodríguez reinterpreted the Indians' role in the conquest of Mexico as triumphant:

The Indian stands in the same relationship to modernity as she did to Spain—willing to marry, to breed, to disappear in order to ensure her inclusion in time; refusing to absent herself from the future. The Indian has chosen to survive, to consort with the living, to live in the city, to crawl on her hands and knees, if need be, to Mexico City or L.A. I take it as an Indian achievement that I am alive, that I am Catholic, that I speak English, that I am an American. My life began, it did not end, in the sixteenth century.[15]

Rodríguez also turned Chicano-era racial rhetoric on its head by declaring that "the essential beauty and mystery of the color brown is that it is a mixture of colors."[16]

In 2004, writer John Phillip Santos employed the idea of *mestizaje* to understand the effects of globalization as well as advances in molecular biology. He describes DNA as "a vast mestizo codex of our origins and diasporas across the planet going back to the beginning in unicellular biology," and asks audiences whether they can "imagine [their] progeny remaining culturally the same as [them] for 10,000 years more?"[17] As numbers and cultural confidence have grown, more Mexican American writers have speculated on the meaning of *mestizaje*. It was they who first rejected the English term "miscegenation"— with all its negative overtones—in favor of the more neutral—or has it become celebratory?—Spanish word. But none of them owned or originated the idea.

In fact, Mexico, a nation that has been grappling with the collision of cultures and races since its birth, has produced a remarkable body of thinking on the significance, challenges, and value of widespread racial and cultural mixture. While many other Latin American nations and cultures were the products of conquest and colonization, "Mexico alone is truly mestizo: it is the only nation in the hemisphere where religious and political—as well as racial—mestizaje took place."[18] As Mexican historian Enrique Krauze has written, *mestizaje* has been "absolutely central" to its history.[19]

By the early twentieth century, a wide range of intellectuals agreed that for better or worse "mestizaje was the essence of Mexican-ness."[20] In 1950, poet Octavio Paz famously wrote that "the strange permanence of Cortés and [his translator and mistress] La Malinche in the Mexican's imagination and sensibilities reveals that they are something more than historical figures: They are symbols of a secret conflict that we have still not resolved."[21] According to Paz, at the heart of Mexicanness is a "form of orphanhood, an obscure awareness that we have been torn from the All and an ardent search: a flight and a return, an effort to re-establish the bonds that unite us with the universe."[22]

After the Mexican Revolution, intellectuals like Manuel Gamio helped turn the mestizo into the "ideological symbol of the new regime."[23] According to Gamio, the mestizo was the bearer of "the national culture of the future."[24] In 1916 he wrote that it was time for Mexico's leaders to "grab hold of the blacksmith's hammer and don his leather apron to forge from the miraculous anvil the new nation of blended bronze and iron."[25] But the most influential "cultist of mestizaje" was writer, philosopher, and politician José Vasconcelos.[26] Challenging contemporary European notions that held that mixed people were inferior to "pure" races, Vasconcelos considered the mestizo to be the "bridge to the future."[27] "I have said that humanity is going back to Babel and by this I mean that the day of the isolated civilization is over. In this new coming-together of all the races we ought not to repeat the methods of the past, the methods that transformed Babel into a curse."[28]

Though he denied it, Vasconcelos sought to create a mythology for a people who had suffered from feelings of inferiority. He wanted mestizos to know their place in history:

> We are a new product, a new breed, not yet entirely shaped. . . . Many of our failings arise from the fact that we do not know exactly what we want. . . . Democracy and equal opportunities for every man has been the motto of the great American nation. Broadness, universality of sentiment and thought, in order to fulfill the mission of bringing together all the races of the earth and with the purpose of creating a new type of civilization, is, I believe, the ideal that would give us in Latin America strength and vision.[29]

Despite Vasconcelos's efforts, by the start of the twenty-first century, Mexico still had not fully come to terms with its mixed heritage.

As journalist Alan Riding observed, even today "Mexico searches endlessly for an identity, hovering ambivalently between ancient and modern, traditional and fashionable, Indian and Spanish."[30] On the one hand, noted anthropologist Claudio Lomnitz-Adler, "Mexico is a society where Indian ancestry has been proudly acknowledged," and on the other, it "clearly values whiteness as both a status symbol and as an aesthetic."[31] Nonetheless, rampant *mestizaje* and the legacy of the colonial caste system had "created a society where people manipulated their ethnic identity in order to scale the status hierarchy."[32] As a result, Mexicans developed—in the words of Mexican American poet Gloria Anzaldúa—"a tolerance for contradictions, a tolerance for ambiguity," particularly in the realm of race and culture.[33]

Of course, Mexican Americans are not the only Latin American–origin people in the United States, but at two-thirds of all Latinos, they are by far the largest Hispanic group and with the deepest historical roots.[34] They long have made up the second-largest minority in the United States, and within a few decades they will become the majority in the two most populous states in the country, California and Texas. Cumulatively over time, Mexicans have surpassed Germans to become the largest immigrant group in the history of the United States.

Because Mexican history has been characterized by widespread *mestizaje*—both cultural and racial—the Mexican American experience cannot be understood through the dichotomy of cultural resistance versus assimilation. Nor can the Latinization of the United States be viewed as the mere addition of a new color to the multicultural rainbow. For much of Mexican American history, advocates fought to be included on one side or the other of the American racial divide. Before 1970, they sought to be recognized as whites, while afterward they insisted on being "people of color." But the mass demographic shift of the late twentieth century has facilitated the resurgence of the Hispanic Catholic view of race in the Southwest, which is subsuming the region's entire color spectrum. Not only are Mexican Americans freer to insist on their racial "otherness," but by creating a racial climate in which intermarriage is more acceptable they are breaking down the barriers that have traditionally served to separate whites and nonwhites in the United States. It is not a coincidence that "the southwestern United States is more permissive of intermarriage"—of all types—"than the rest of the U.S."[35] In 1990 Los Angeles County had an intermarriage rate five times the national average.[36] More than two-thirds of the county's intermarriages involved Latinos.[37] Similarly, in 1997, two-thirds of multiracial and multiethnic births in California involved a Latino parent.[38] Anglo-Latino children are, by far, the most common mixture for interracial/interethnic children in the state.

As had occurred in the mid-nineteenth century, contemporary Mexican-Anglo marriages serve to ease tensions between the groups. The children of such marriages are symbols of the convergence of cultures. Today, many of those children are brought up with a Latino identity. Indeed, whereas only 43 percent of children born to Hispanic/non-Hispanic couples were reported as Hispanic in 1970, nearly two-thirds were identified as Latinos in 2000.[39] As it has for centuries, Hispanicity continues to absorb rather than exclude the cultures it encounters and thus redefines itself as it moves northward. Both biological and cultural *mestizaje* remain an essential characteristic of the Mexican experience in the United States. In the 1990s, 32 percent of second-generation and 57 percent of third-generation Latinos married outside their ethnic group.[40] Barry Edmonston at the Population Research Bureau in Portland, Oregon, projects that by the year 2100, the number of Latinos claiming mixed ancestry will be more than two times the number claiming a single background.[41] "Through this process of blending by marriage in the U.S.," says economist and immigration scholar James P. Smith, "Latino identity becomes something even more nuanced."[42]

Of course, the immigrant generation continues to live largely apart from mainstream American society. Today as always, immigrant communities serve, in the words of scholar Milton M. Gordon, "as a kind of decompression chamber in which the newcomers [can], at their own pace, make a reasonable adjustment to the new forces of a society vastly different from that which they had known in the Old World."[43] Particularly for noncitizens, Mexican immigrants tend to limit their civic participation to activities organized around language or country of origin. But latter-generation Mexican Americans, according to one study on voluntarism, "are more likely to be involved with mainstream groups than with Hispanic organizations."[44] In 1992, the Latino National Political Survey revealed that less than 5 percent of Mexican American respondents had either joined or contributed money to any ethnic-based organizations.[45] Indeed, with the exception of some scattered homegrown social service organizations and political groups, Mexican Americans have developed very little parallel ethnic infrastructure. There is no private Mexican American college in the United States. In Los Angeles, there is no ethnic-Mexican hospital, cemetery, college, or broad-based charity organization.

As they have throughout their history, Mexican Americans continue to seek a balance between continuity and change. In 2000, a national poll found that 89 percent of Latinos considered it important "for Latinos to maintain their distinct cultures." The same survey also revealed that 84 percent believed it was important "for Latinos to change so that they blend into the larger society as in the idea of the melting pot."[46]

At the start of the twenty-first century, the pull toward the mainstream has grown stronger than ever. The late 1990s and early 2000s saw a growing number of Mexican American politicians and entertainers gain national prominence. These political and cultural icons help normalize the image of Mexican Americans and strip them of their foreignness. In 2003, Lieutenant General Ricardo Sánchez, of Starr County, Texas, which is 98 percent Mexican American, became the commander of the allied forces in Iraq. Two years later, Alberto Gonzales, former White House legal counsel to President George W. Bush, became the first Mexican American U.S. attorney general. After building a broad electoral coalition, in July 2005 former California Assembly Speaker Antonio Villaraigosa became the first Mexican American mayor of Los Angeles since 1872. His inaugural address signaled the triumph of the ethnic over the racial narrative for Mexican Americans. His speech included four lines in Spanish, presumably designed to reach recent immigrants. "How beautiful this country is!" he said. "I am proof that the United States is a country of opportunities and freedom. In what other country in the world could I stand before you as the mayor of a great city?"[47]

In one form or the other, the notion of the melting pot has been at the center of America's national mythology since the eighteenth century. In 1782, J. Hector St. John de Crèvecoeur famously described America as a land where individuals from across Europe were melted into "a new race of man, whose labors and posterity will one day cause great changes in the world."[48] In the early twentieth century, playwright Israel Zangwill helped promote the civic faith that the fusion of ethnicities created a stronger American nation. In his 1908 drama, *The Melting Pot,* about a Jewish immigrant rejecting his faith's prohibition against intermarriage, Zangwill depicted the United States as both a safe harbor and a crucible that melted Old World ethnics into a distinctly new American culture. At the same time, however, Zangwill agreed that whites were justified in avoiding intermarriage with blacks. He would recognize only that "spiritual miscegenation" between black and white had enriched American culture.[49] In other words, throughout U.S. history access to the melting pot has been implicitly understood as being limited to ethnic whites.

Mexican Americans are forcing the United States to reinterpret the concept of the melting pot to include racial as well as ethnic mixing. Rather than abetting the segregationist ethos of a country divided into mutually exclusive groups, Mexican Americans continue to blur the lines between "us" and "them." Just as the emergence of the mestizos undermined the Spanish racial system in colonial Mexico, Mexican Americans, who have always confounded the Anglo American racial system, will ultimately destroy it, too.

Mongrels,
Bastards,
Orphans,
and
Vagabonds

One

The Birth of a People

On February 10, 1519, Hernán Cortés, along with a crew of roughly five hundred men and a handful of women, sailed west from Cuba to explore the Mexican mainland. Two previous Spanish expeditions had already reached the eastern coast of Mexico where they had heard stories of a wealthy Indian kingdom in the interior of the country. Hoping to discover great riches, Governor Diego Velázquez of Cuba had commissioned Cortés to explore and conquer new territories.

After weathering several days on stormy seas, Cortés and his eleven-ship squadron made landfall on the island of Cozumel. There a friendly band of Mayans informed Cortés that some years before two Christians had been taken captive in the neighboring land of Yucatán. The chief of Cozumel rejected the Spanish captain's request that he send a search party to locate the captured Europeans. He feared that, "were he to do that, his messenger would be captured and eaten."[1] Undeterred, Cortés dispatched his own messengers to bargain for the captives' release. The scouts took trinkets for ransom and a letter from Cortés that one man concealed in his hair.

The messengers found the two men—Jerónimo de Aguilar and Gonzalo Guerrero—living in very different conditions. The two had been the only survivors of a group of men whose boat ran aground in 1511. They had taken to the boat when their ship, which was sailing from the coast of Panamá to Santo Domingo, struck shoals on some islands near Jamaica. Their boat eventually caught a westward current that cast them ashore in Yucatán. By that time, half the men were dead.

The eighteen survivors were soon captured by Mayans. Five were sacrificed, their bodies eaten in a religious ceremony. The remaining thirteen were imprisoned to be fattened up for another day. Somehow they managed to escape their captors and took refuge with another Mayan chief, Xamanzana, who enslaved them. Before long, all died except for Aguilar and Guerrero.

When Cortés's messengers found Aguilar, he was still a slave desperately trying to hold on to Spanish ways. "He concentrated his mind by counting the days but, by the time he was liberated . . . he thought that it was a Wednesday, not a Sunday."[2] After he "read the letter and received the ransom, he carried the beads delightedly to his master . . . and begged leave to depart. The *Cacique* [local chief] gave him permission to go wherever he wished."[3] He then set out to find Guerrero, who lived some fifteen miles away. Guerrero not only was no longer being held captive, he had married the daughter of Na Chan Can, a Mayan nobleman. Guerrero's response to Cortés's letter and to Aguilar's entreaties astounded his would-be liberator. Guerrero had assimilated so thoroughly into Mayan life that he no longer felt he would be accepted by his Spanish countrymen. His face was tattooed and his ears were pierced. "What would the Spaniards say if they saw me like this?" he asked.[4]

Guerrero's Mayan wife angrily interrupted her husband's conversation with Aguilar. She demanded to know why "this slave" had "come here to call my husband away?"[5] Before Aguilar left, Guerrero explained to him the primary reason he could not leave. "Brother Aguilar," he said. "I am married and have three children, and they look at me as Cacique here, and a captain in time of war."[6] He then pointed to his children and said, "*Ya veis estos mis tres hijitos [que bonitos] son*" ("Now look at my three children, how beautiful they are!").[7] Guerrero was describing Mexico's first mestizos, its first mixed Indian/European people.

News of Guerrero's refusal to join his expedition angered Cortés. Like most Spaniards of the era, the captain could not fathom why a European would choose to live the life of a pagan. According to historian Hugh Thomas, at the time of the conquest of Mexico, "The Spanish had unbounded confidence in their own qualities, in the political wisdom of their imperial mission, and in the spiritual superiority of the Catholic Church."[8] The recently completed *reconquista*, the expulsion of the Muslims and Jews from the Iberian Peninsula, had forged a militant Christianity that played an integral role in

Spanish expansionism in the early sixteenth century. Indeed, religious conversion served as the legal justification for Spain's overseas adventures.

But this religious motive was not mere legal window dressing. Evangelization was a vital part of the sixteenth-century Spanish worldview. According to historian Lewis Hanke, "Between the two poles—the thirst for gold and the winning of souls . . . a variety of mixed motives appeared."[9] Some friars were as greedy as the most rapacious conquistadors, while some conquistadors were as sincere in their efforts to Christianize the Indians as the most devout priests. However, for many Spaniards, the spiritual and material motives were inextricably intertwined. As conquistador and chronicler Bernal Díaz del Castillo put it: "We came here to serve God, and also to get rich."[10] The early Spanish expeditions were "missions of discovery, conquest, settlement, and conversion," all in one.[11]

The religious imperative of the conquest of Mexico, however imperfectly and unevenly applied, led the Spaniards to engage intimately in the social, cultural, material, and spiritual lives of the Indians they encountered. After a contentious debate over the nature of the Indian, in 1537, Pope Paul III issued a bull, *Sublimus Dei,* which declared that "Indians are truly men" and "capable of understanding the Catholic Faith."[12] While this in no way meant that Indians would not suffer abuse at the hands of Spaniards, it did mean that the Spanish, the only European empire that openly debated the "purposes of their expansion," would ultimately seek to incorporate Indians into their Christian civilization.[13] Through the centuries, Catholics had already borrowed and absorbed a huge number of rituals and symbols from the peoples they had converted. This willingness to accept blending in the theological realm presaged a relative tolerance of racial mixing. Indeed, the large-scale mixing that would occur in Mexico over the next several centuries was due, according to historian C. E. Marshall, "in no small degree to a humanitarian spirit which found its roots in the tenets of the Catholic religion."[14]

The instructions that Governor Velázquez had drawn up for Cortés's expedition prohibited blasphemy, the playing of cards, and sleeping with—and even teasing—native women. But from the very first landing at Cozumel, the rules were broken. There, Cortés reprimanded his incorrigible friend Pedro de Alvarado for seizing "turkeys, men, women, and ornaments from the temple."[15] Hoping to avoid confrontations with the Mayans in Yucatán, Cortés directed the expedition to proceed toward the coast of the present-day Mexican state of Tabasco, where they anchored at Potonchan. It was there (probably near the present-day town of Frontera) that Cortés and his men had their first major battles with the Indians. It was also there that it became evident that the subjugation of Mexico would involve an "amorous" as well as a military conquest.[16]

After a bloody struggle with Mayan warriors in Potonchan, Cortés sent 250 men to the village of Centla to seek food. There, for the first time in the Americas, the Spaniards used horses in battle. Though outnumbered by a significant margin, the Spaniards lost not a single man in either battle, although dozens were wounded. The Indians suffered hundreds of losses. After their warriors withdrew, thirty finely dressed emissaries approached the Spaniards with "fowls, fruit, and maize cakes."[17] Later, the lord of Potonchan came and offered more food and gifts, including objects of turquoise and gold. According to Bernal Díaz, however, those "gifts were nothing . . . compared to the twenty women whom they gave us."[18] Before Cortés distributed the women among his captains, one of the two priests on the expedition, Father Bartolomé de Olmedo, baptized them. They were the first women in New Spain, the name the Spaniards would later give conquered Mexico, to become Christians.

The young woman whom Cortés presented initially to his good friend Alonso Hernández Puertocarrero was christened Doña Marina. Bernal Díaz described her as "good looking, intelligent, and self-assured."[19] Her original name was Malinali, which was also the word for the twelfth month in the Aztec calendar. She was born on the boundary between areas controlled by the Chontal Mayans and the Aztecs, and therefore spoke both Chontal Mayan and Nahuatl, the lingua franca of the Aztec empire, which stretched from central Mexico to present-day Guatemala and from the Pacific Ocean to the Gulf coast. Her father had been tlatoani—"leader" in Nahuatl—of Painala, a village near the present-day city of Coatzacoalcos in the state of Veracruz. Her mother ruled Xaltipan, a small village nearby. But when her father died, Marina's mother remarried another local leader and gave birth to a son whom they chose to be their heir. Marina was then sold to some merchants from Xicallanco, a nearby port, and declared dead. Her first owners then traded her to Mayan merchants, who, in turn, sold her to the people of Potonchan.

Marina's bilingualism and her talent for languages made her indispensable to the Spaniards from early on. Indeed, the expedition would first encounter the Nahuatl language not far from Potonchan on the coast of Veracruz. Up to that point, Cortés had depended on Jerónimo de Aguilar, the shipwrecked man whose freedom the Spaniards had bought in Yucatán. "Aguilar, who had served the party well in Yucatan and Tabasco, was suddenly faced with an unfamiliar language. It was then that Marina was observed speaking with the most recently encountered [Indians]."[20] Once Cortés learned of her bilingualism, he appointed her his interpreter and gave Hernández Puertocarrero another Indian woman. Marina's knowledge of Nahuatl as well as Mayan enabled her to communicate first with Nahuatl speakers and translate their words into Mayan for Aguilar, who could then speak them in Spanish to Cortés. But once Marina learned enough Spanish, Cortés was able to cut out the middleman. In any case, Aguilar's knowledge of Yucatec Mayan became less useful to Cortés as the Spaniards marched westward away from the Mayan-speaking coastal regions and toward the Nahuatl-speaking Valley of Mexico. The Indians—both the friendly and the hostile—whom the Spaniards encountered "came to think of [Marina] as Cortés's voice; indeed, they assimilated the two persons to such an extent that they would refer to Don Hernán as 'Malinche,' " or master of Marina.[21] As the Spaniards descended upon Tenochtitlán, the Aztec capital, Marina became both the go-between for all crucial communications with the Indians as well as Cortés's mistress. In 1522, she gave birth to a son, Martín, whom Cortés legitimized in 1529 through a bull issued by Pope Clement VII. Also through the efforts of his father, Martín was later made a Knight of the Order of Santiago, one of the most prestigious military orders of Spain.

The Aztecs and their Nahuatl-speaking tributaries referred to Doña Marina reverentially as Malintzin, there being no distinction between r and l in Nahuatl. The -*tzin* was an honorific, like *doña* in Spanish. Oddly enough, "La Malinche" is the name by which contemporary Mexicans remember her. For three centuries, both Spanish and indigenous sources portrayed Doña Marina as a powerful woman who was afforded great respect. The sixteenth-century mestizo historian Diego Muñoz Camargo, who was a child when Marina died, described her as being as beautiful as a goddess. But in the nineteenth century, after Mexico gained its independence from Spain, new depictions "condemned her role in the Conquest" of the Aztecs and gave rise to the peculiarly Mexican concept of *malinchismo*, a term used to describe the "rejection and betrayal of one's own."[22] But though her people spoke Nahuatl, Marina was not Aztec. Nor at the time of the conquest did indigenous people even have a word for a large-group category such as Indians. "Self-definition and differentiation between indigenous groups was primarily in terms of the *altepetl*, [a] type of local kingdom."[23] As historian Frances Karttunen explained, as a slave being traded from place to place, Doña Marina "saw her best hope of survival in Cortés and served him unwaveringly."[24]

It is somehow fitting then that Marina became instrumental in Cortés's strategy of leveraging indigenous resentment of imperial Tenochtitlán. In the early sixteenth century, central Mexico was "not a homogenous state, but a conglomerate of populations, defeated by the Aztecs who [occupied] the top of the pyramid."[25] Cortés skillfully appealed to those groups whom the Aztecs had subjugated as the lesser of two evils, "as a liberator, so to speak, who [would permit] them to throw off the yoke of a tyranny especially detestable because so close at hand."[26]

When the Spaniards reached Cempoala, the main city of the Totonac Indians, located in the present-day state of Veracruz, they were welcomed enthusiastically. According to Bernal Díaz, "they gave us food and brought us some baskets of plums, which were very plentiful at that season, also some of their maize-cakes."[27] The Totonac chief, a very obese man whom Díaz simply called the "fat Cacique," unburdened himself to Cortés and complained bitterly of "the great Montezuma and his governors, saying that the [Aztec] prince had recently brought him into subjection, had taken away all his golden jewelry, and so grievously oppressed him and his people that they could do nothing except obey him."[28] The Aztecs had confiscated their arms and enslaved some of their people. Of the many indignities they suffered few were more humiliating than the tax-collectors' practice of raping their most handsome women.

The Aztecs, who called themselves the Mexica, the origin of the word "Mexico," maintained several garrisons near the Veracruz coast. Sometimes the Totonacs sent their tribute—often the cotton clothing that was popular on that coast—to the local garrisons, which then delivered it to Tenochtitlán. At other times, Totonac porters carried the goods directly to the Mexican capital. The annual burden of their tribute payments made the Totonacs predisposed to welcome the Spaniards. In fact, they were among the Aztecs' most resentful subjects. After explorer Juan de Grijalva visited their stretch of coastline the previous year, the Totonacs were sorry to see him go. They gave Grijalva a girl "so finely dressed that, had she been in brocade, she could not have looked better."[29]

To cement their people's relationship with the Spaniards, the Cempoalan caciques presented Cortés with eight girls of high rank. According to Bernal Díaz, they "were dressed in the rich shirts that they wear, and finely adorned as is their custom. Each one of them had a gold collar round her neck and golden earrings in her ears, and with them came other girls to be their maids."[30] As the fat chief presented the girls, he said to Cortés, " 'Tecle' (which in their language means lord) 'these seven women are for your captains, and this one, who is my niece, is for you.' "[31] He explained that now that they were allies, "they would like to have us for brothers and to give us their daughters to bear us children."[32]

Though Cortés accepted the girls "with a gracious smile," he took advantage of the moment to preach the Christian gospel and condemn the Cempoalans' faith.[33] He told the caciques that before he "could accept the ladies and become their brothers, they would have to abandon their idols which they mistakenly believed in and worshipped, and sacrifice no more souls to them; and that when he saw those cursed things thrown down and the sacrifices at an end, our bonds of brotherhood would be very much firmer."[34] The Spaniards were particularly revolted by the Indians' practice of offering human sacrifices to their gods. Each day of the Spaniards' visit, the Cempoalans sacrificed "three, four, or five Indians, whose hearts were offered to those idols and whose blood was plastered on the walls."[35]

Cortés promised the caciques new provinces to control if they became Christians. When they balked at destroying their gods themselves, insisting that the very act would lead to their demise, Cortés was infuriated. The Indians wept and prayed when fifty Spanish soldiers later smashed the stone images. According to Hugh Thomas, the Totonacs were "astonished at the Castilian insistence. They were accustomed to seeing the gods of the defeated being destroyed. But victors, as they thought that they were themselves, never made such a concession."[36] The Spaniards then had the temple whitewashed and a cross and picture of the Virgin placed within it.

Before they departed Cempoala, the Spaniards celebrated a mass at which the caciques and others were present. The eight girls that were presented to the Spaniards were baptized and given Christian names. "The fat Cacique's niece, who was very ugly, received the name Doña Catalina and was led up to Cortés, who received her with a show of pleasure."[37] The daughter of a nobleman named Cuesco was given the name Doña Francisca. According to Díaz, "she was very beautiful, for an Indian, and Cortés gave her to Alonso Hernández Puertocarrero," who was evidently pleased.[38]

Two months later, peace was achieved in the same manner with Tlaxcala, an independent Indian nation that had resisted Aztec military incursions for many years. Despite their enmity for the Aztecs, the Tlaxcalans were also suspicious of the Spaniards and were determined to halt their forward march. Amassing a large number of warriors, they attempted to envelop Cortés's men, only to be repelled and routed. It was in Tlaxcala that the Spaniards' remarkable military prowess against a much larger Indian force was first demonstrated.

When Cortés finally entered Tlaxcala on September 18, 1519, he was warmly received. His soldiers were lodged in beautiful houses near the main temple. They, along with their Totonac and other indigenous allies, were well fed and cared for. Gracious in defeat, the Tlaxcalan chiefs "presented Cortés with more than three hundred beautiful women, good-looking and well-attired," who had been slaves destined to be sacrificed to the gods.[39] According to historian Diego Muñoz Camargo, after seeing "how well off [the slave girls] were among the Spaniards, the same caciques and princes gave their own daughters" to the Spaniards.[40] They hoped that they would become pregnant so that "there would remain among them offspring of men so brave and feared."[41] The Tlaxcalan chief, Xicotencatl, presented his daughter Tecuelhuatzin to Cortés, saying, " 'She is unmarried and a virgin. Take her for yourself'—he put the girl's hand in his—'and give the others to your captains.' "[42] But after she was baptized, Cortés gave Tecuelhuatzin, christened Doña Luisa, to his friend Pedro de Alvarado, reassuring her father that "he must be glad, since she would receive good treatment."[43] Just as the Spaniards gave the converted daughters of Indian noblemen the honorific of doña, the Tlaxcalans also accorded them great respect. Doña Luisa was showered with presents, and considered as powerful as a ruler. She and Alvarado would have two children, a son, Pedro, and a daughter, Leonor, who would one day marry a Spanish nobleman with whom she had several sons.

The beautiful daughter of another cacique, Maxixcatzin, was christened Doña Elvira, and given to Captain Juan Velázquez de León. Captains Gonzalo de Sandoval, Cristóbal de Olid, and Alonso de Avila were also given women. "From then on, all the senior commanders seem to have had indigenous girls attached to them. . . . Within a few weeks, many ordinary soldiers seem to have found girls too."[44]

By then, Cortés was in regular contact with the emissaries of Montezuma, the Aztec emperor. When word got back to Tenochtitlán that the Tlaxcalans were "giving their daughters to Malinche," Montezuma knew that "this alliance could do [the Aztecs] no good."[45] According to anthropologist Pedro Carrasco, "the donation of women as a way of establishing and maintaining political relations was customary in ancient Mexico."[46] Muñoz Camargo explains that among the Indians, "the rulers took absolutely whichever woman they wanted, and they were given to them as men of power."[47] But clearly sexual relations between the Spaniards and the Indians were not all governed by diplomatic protocol. As historian Asunción Lavrin observed, "From voluntary offer to open demand was only a short distance," and "The degree of abuse of such sexual contacts will remain unmeasurable."[48] In his chronicles of the conquest, Bernal Díaz repeatedly makes mention of soldiers looking for "spoil, especially of good looking Indian women."[49] On one occasion, according to Díaz, Spaniards formed "groups of fifteen or twenty and went pillaging the villages, forcing the women and taking cloth and chickens as if they were in the Moorish country to rob what they found."[50] For the priests on the expedition, the incidents of sexual assaults were deeply disturbing. As they attempted to preach the Christian Gospel, "they seemed unable or unwilling to control the behavior of male Spaniards for some time."[51]

In other words, while some women were "given" to the Spaniards, others were taken by force. Still, as their march progressed—and ultimately triumphed—other indigenous women "joined the conquerors by choice."[52] "The process of conquest resulted in a meeting of the sexes that broke—temporarily—the established rules of personal conduct in both Spanish and indigenous societies."[53] The women who accompanied the Spaniards "cooked for their men, nursed their wounds, carried their belongings, and shared their beds."[54] According to historian R. C. Padden, "However strenuous the fighting was at times, love-making was just as intense, certainly more frequent, and of infinitely greater consequence."[55]

From their first contact in the New World, Spaniards responded to the Indians with either "attraction or repugnance."[56] In general, however, they had "an agreeable impression" of their physical appearance.[57] Columbus described the first Indians he saw as "well put-together, with beautiful bodies and faces."[58] In 1519, a servant on Cortés's expedition wrote a letter home in which he mentioned the beautiful women he saw in Yucatán. Particularly if their people had surrendered to the Spaniards and agreed to become vassals of the king of Spain, "association with the conquistadores offered many advantages" to Indian women.[59]

The Tlaxcalans not only gave Cortés women but also thousands of warriors to accompany the Spaniards on their descent into Tenochtitlán. They played a crucial role in the next great battle, which took place in Cholula, the most populous indigenous center the Spaniards had yet seen. Cholula was only sixty miles from Tenochtitlán and was an ally of the Aztecs, who were plotting to trap the Spaniards. When Cortés arrived, the Cholulan caciques were reluctant to greet him.

But once they did make their appearance they pledged their friendship to the Spaniards and offered tribute. This peaceful accord did not last long. Doña Marina got wind of a plot to ambush Cortés's contingent. Thirty thousand Aztec warriors had assembled just outside the city.

Outraged by their deceit, Cortés signaled for the Spaniards' Tlaxcalan and Cempoalan allies to join the Spaniards in a horrible massacre at Cholula. Approximately six thousand Cholulans were killed in a five-hour battle and the ancient city was sacked. Days later, even as Cortés gave his now routine sermon to the Indians on the evils of pagan religion, Tlaxcalan warriors returned home with prisoners in tow, destined to be sacrificed to the gods. After the massacre, local Indians began calling the Spaniards *populucas,* or barbarians.[60]

Upon hearing of the slaughter at Cholula, Montezuma "began to suffer a crisis of confidence that found expression in his fateful decision to welcome the Spaniards into Tenochtitlán."[61] Hoping to assuage Cortés's anger, Montezuma sent messengers bearing "ten plates of gold, fifteen hundred cloaks of cotton, and a good deal of food."[62] Through his emissaries, the Aztec emperor apologized for the unsuccessful ambush and blamed it on rogue subordinates. He also pledged to provide anything Cortés desired if he would turn around and not proceed to Tenochtitlán. When Cortés replied that he could not turn back because he had promised his own king a description of the city, Montezuma invited him to an audience. Cortés's five hundred men and thousands of Tlaxcalan warriors were allowed to march peacefully into the Aztec capital.

As they descended into the Valley of Mexico, Cortés's men were a striking spectacle for the local Indians. According to one Nahuatl source, "they came in battle array, as conquerors, and the dust rose in whirlwinds. Their spears glinted in the sun, and their pennons fluttered like bats. They made a loud clamor as they marched, for their coats of mail and their weapons clashed and rattled. Some of them were dressed in glistening iron from head to foot; they terrified everyone who saw them."[63] Awaiting the arrival of the Spanish in Tenochtitlán, Montezuma was terrified. In the meantime, the Spaniards were being approached on their march by local Indians who complained of the emperor's tax collectors robbing them of all their possessions and violating their wives and daughters. At Ame-cameca, local dignitaries gave Cortés food, gold, and forty slave girls, who, according to one of the Spanish priests, were "well dressed and well painted."[64]

As the Spaniards approached the system of lakes that surrounded Tenochtitlán, they were "visibly impressed by the ordered landscape with its grid plan of towns and temple pyramids, and the regular pattern of raised fields bordered by lines of willows."[65] The Aztec capital was an island at the center of five shallow interconnected lakes. Three long causeways—twenty-five to thirty-five feet wide and with removable bridges—joined the city to the mainland. The first sight of the Aztec metropolis reminded Bernal Díaz of "an enchanted vision from the tale of Amadis. Indeed, some of our soldiers asked whether it was not all a dream. . . . It was all so wonderful that I do not know how to describe this first glimpse of things never heard of, seen or dreamed of before."[66] In his letter to the king of Spain, Cortés knew his words could not do justice to the wonders of Tenochtitlán. "I cannot describe one hundredth part of all the things which could be mentioned, but, as best I can, I will describe some of those I have seen which, although badly described, will, I well know, be so remarkable as not to be believed, for we who saw them with our own eyes could not grasp them with our understanding."[67]

With 250,000 inhabitants, Tenochtitlán was one of the largest cities in the world.[68] In the early sixteenth century, only four cities in Europe—Naples, Venice, Milan, and Paris—had populations larger than 100,000. Founded in 1325, it was less than two centuries old when the Spaniards arrived. Once a nomadic tribe, the Aztecs had arrived in the Valley of Mexico in the middle of the thirteenth century. In 1454, they began their quest for empire. Through warfare and intimidation, by the end of that century they dominated much of Mesoamerica.

By the early sixteenth century, however, the Aztec empire had reached its limits. For all the advances their people had made in a matter of a few centuries, Aztec society was beset by a foreboding of catastrophe. One of the bases of the Aztec religion held that time on earth was divided into five eras. "The first of these, known as '4-Tiger,' had been destroyed by wild animals; the second, '4-Wind,' by wind; the third, '4-Rain,' by fire; and the fourth, '4-Water,' by floods. The last, the fifth age, that of the [Aztecs], known as '4-Motion,' would, according to myth, one day culminate in a catastrophe brought on by terrifying earthquakes."[69] Astrology played a central role in Aztec society. "Unfavorable signs could paralyze rulers, delay battles, and perhaps even become self-fulfilling prophecies."[70]

The Aztecs, according to Juan Bautista Pomar, a sixteenth-century Spanish historian, "had many idols, and so many that almost for each thing there was one."[71] As their empire expanded, the Aztecs incorporated the principal gods of conquered nations into their pantheon. In fact, the very act of conquest was understood as the capturing of an enemy's principal deity. As for the Aztecs, their primary deity remained Huitzilopochtli, the god of the sun and of war. To ensure that the sun rose every day, the Aztecs nourished him with the blood of human sacrifices so that each night he could successfully battle the moon.

Given the Spaniards' "godlike technological capabilities (cannons, harquebusiers, sailing ships, horses, metal armor)," it seems certain that the Aztecs initially considered them of supernatural origin.[72] That may explain Montezuma's reluctance to engage them militarily. But by many accounts, Montezuma was also a fatalist and a "tragic figure" who "lived in the shadow of historical inevitability."[73] His efforts to employ diplomacy and magic to keep the Spaniards from the capital had failed. When Cortés and his men reached the gateway to Tenochtitlán, Montezuma was there to welcome them. He invited them to stay in the palace that had belonged to his father. It is possible that the emperor wanted the Spaniards inside the city in order to entrap them later. But if that was Montezuma's plan, he did not betray it publicly. After a welcoming ceremony, he told Cortés, "Malinche, you and your brothers are in your own house. Rest awhile."[74]

Not long after Cortés's arrival in Tenochtitlán, the Aztecs attacked the Spaniards' allies, the Totonacs, on the Gulf coast. "Whether in reaction or as a pretext," Cortés seized Montezuma, and for the next six months ruled his empire through him.[75] Before his capture, the Aztec emperor had offered Cortés some jewels and one of his daughters as "a delicious fruit."[76] He also wished to give several noblemen's daughters to Cortés's men. Cortés responded in the same way he had in earlier such instances, that he could not accept women as consorts unless they were baptized.

Even while imprisoned, Montezuma "took pains to see that his visitors were plied with attractive women."[77] He provided three hundred women to act as servants to his jailers. Cortés enjoyed the sexual favors of Montezuma's daughter, Doña Ana, and of his niece, Doña Elvira. Bernal Díaz himself asked Orteguilla, the Spaniard who acted as Montezuma's warden, to beg the emperor "kindly to give me a very pretty Indian girl. When Montezuma received this message, he sent for me and said: 'Bernal Díaz del Castillo, they say that you are short of clothes and gold. But today I will tell them to give you a fine girl. Treat her well, for she is the daughter of an important man, and they will give you gold and cloaks as well.' "[78]

Not all Aztec nobles were as compliant as Montezuma. To the contrary, there was growing resentment among them over the emperor's obsequious posture toward the Spaniards. In the spring of 1520, while Cortés was absent from the city, he left Pedro de Alvarado in charge in Tenochtitlán. For some unknown reason, Alvarado instigated a massacre of thousands of Aztec nobles who had gathered in the courtyard of the Templo Mayor for a religious celebration. In response, Aztec commoners rose in revolt, killed seven Spaniards, and laid siege to their quarters. When Cortés returned, either the Spaniards or the insurgent Aztecs killed Montezuma. At that point, the Spaniards had little choice but to retreat from the city. They did so at night while under attack from all sides. When he reached Tlaxcala, Cortés had lost more than half his men and one thousand Tlaxcalan soldiers.

After *la noche triste,* the sad night, as the Spaniards called their retreat from Tenochtitlán, Cortés and his men employed ever more brutal tactics against their indigenous enemies. After a period of rest and recuperation, the Spaniards marched on the Aztec dependency of Tepeaca. There, in a "departure from previous practice," after the battle, Cortés "enslaved the wives and children" of the thousands of men the Spaniards killed.[79] The women were then branded on their foreheads or cheeks to signify that they were slaves and sold. But those whom the Spaniards found most attractive usually wound up being taken by the soldiers and used as servants. According to

Bernardino de Sahagún, the sixteenth-century Franciscan missionary and archaeologist, the Spaniards enjoyed "beautiful young [Indian] women . . . pretty women, those who were light brown."[80] In order to avoid the Spaniards' gaze, many such women "smeared their faces with clay, wrapped their hips with old and torn serapes, wore ratty blouses over their bosoms and dressed in plain old rags."[81]

After Cortés demanded that taxes be levied on the value of plundered treasure and female slaves, competition among the soldiers over the prettiest women intensified. For accounting purposes, all soldiers were required to bring forward their loot as well as the women they were "sheltering." According to Bernal Díaz, they found "that not only [was the tax] taken, but all the best-looking women disappeared. There was not a pretty one left."[82] In response to his soldiers' complaints, Cortés promised that all women would thenceforth be sold at auction with the best-looking fetching the highest prices. Still, soldiers devised ways to keep their captains from stealing the women they had claimed for themselves. "We hid them and took them to be branded, and explained that they had fled," wrote Bernal Díaz, "and many stayed in our rooms, and we said that they were domestics who had come in peace."[83] The Indian women, however, developed their own strategies to protect themselves as best they could. They learned which Spaniards treated women well and which did not. If a particularly abusive soldier bid on them at auction, some women chose to escape and were never seen again.

Before launching a new offensive on Tenochtitlán, Cortés sought to strengthen his old alliances with indigenous groups as well as create new ones. He sent a delegation to speak with the Purépecha Indians in a region near the Pacific coast in what is now the present-day state of Michoacán. While their leader refused the Spaniards' offer for them to join the battle against the Aztecs, he did honor their request for girls from noble families. The Spaniards slept with the women on their way back to the Valley of Mexico. The Purépecha men who accompanied the Spaniards on their trip thereafter referred to them as "tarascue" or "sons-in-law" in the Purépecha language.[84] The Spaniards thus began to refer to the Purépecha as "Tarascos," a term by which they have largely been known ever since.

Several months after the *noche triste*, the Spaniards were aided in their military strategy by a silent but deadly ally. The smallpox virus, which the Spaniards had brought to the New World in 1518, made its way to the Valley of Mexico and reached Tenochtitlán in October 1520. Tens of thousands of Indians—both friends and foes of the Spaniards—perished in its wake, and "a sense of gloom which the [Aztecs] described as the loss of their soul" took hold.[85] Even Montezuma's successor, Cuitláhuac, contracted the disease. When he died, the Aztec nobility selected Montezuma's young nephew, Cuauhtémoc, as their last emperor.

In order to bring Tenochtitlán to its knees, the Spaniards ultimately employed a strategy that was rare in Mesoamerica. They sought to starve it into submission by cutting off access and supplies to the island city. Waging a war of attrition, each day Cortés sent soldiers to attack the city in several places. After three months, the siege left Tenochtitlán in the grip of famine. The Spaniards, in the meantime, were eating well in their camp outside the city. They had long been accustomed to eating indigenous foods, like tortillas and the fruit of the nopal cactus. Even during the siege, they continued to spend each night with their indigenous mistresses.

Cortés initially had no plans to destroy Tenochtitlán. Indeed, he had hoped to present it like a jewel to the king of Spain. But the fierce resistance of the Aztecs and their refusal to surrender left the Spanish captain with no alternative but to destroy the city. As historian Ramón Eduardo Ruiz observed, "to occupy [the] city, Cortés had to ravage it. No temple, palace, or idol survived the Spanish assault."[86] When the Spaniards finally pushed into the city from the south, the Aztecs retreated north toward Tlatelolco, the site of their great marketplace. By the time Cuauhtémoc was captured there on August 13, 1521, the city reeked of death. Still, Cortés either allowed or could not prevent his indigenous allies—who supplied more than two hundred men for every Spaniard—from continuing to kill and loot for four more days.[87] Once the fighting stopped, Cortés ordered the bodies cleared away and the aqueduct repaired. He mapped out where the separate Indian and Spanish quarters of the new city were to be built. For the conquerors, the only remaining loot to be found was women, many of whom were now widowed and "only too glad to go with the victors, and so assure themselves at least of the chance of food."[88]

Cortés hoped to administer New Spain in the same fashion as had the Aztec emperors. He intended to rule—and collect tribute—through local leaders. But the Aztecs' imperial organization had been crushed and humiliated. Shortly after the conquest, Cuauhtémoc and his surviving lieutenants complained to Cortés that the Spaniards had "carried off the daughters and wives of chieftains, and begged him as a favour that they should be sent back."[89] Cortés allowed a few of the former emperor's men to search the Spanish camps for Aztec women. But he insisted that the women themselves would decide whether to stay or go. According to Bernal Díaz, only three women returned home with Cuauhtémoc's men. "There were many women who did not wish to go with their fathers or mothers or husbands, but preferred to remain with the soldiers with whom they were living. Some hid themselves, others said they did not wish to return to idolatry, and yet others were already pregnant."[90]

After the conquest, just as before, most interracial sexual unions were characterized by concubinage rather than marriage. But the number of legal marriages between Spanish men and Indian women in the early colonial period was not insignificant. In a census taken of the eighty-one male Spanish residents of Puebla in 1534, sixty-five were married, and "20 had married Indian women, a proportion of 30.7 percent."[91] Later arrivals were more likely to have married Indian women than were the conquistadors. Indeed, 36.1 percent of Spanish males in Puebla who arrived in New Spain after the conquest had married Indian women.[92] According to anthropologist Pedro Carrasco: "This difference might be related to the fact that the conquerors had been in New Spain longer and had more time to bring their wives from Spain, but it is also probable that their higher status gave them an advantage in competing for Spanish wives in the first decade or two after the conquest, when there were few Spanish women in the colony."[93] In fact, in 1521, there were only seven Spanish women in New Spain.[94] Between 1520 and 1540, less than 6 percent of Spanish migrants to Mexico were women.[95]

Since the early sixteenth century, the Spanish Crown had grappled with the issue of interracial marriage, and its policy often wavered in conformity with theological trends. In 1503, the governor of Hispaniola, Nicolás de Ovando, received instructions from Spain to arrange marriages between some Spaniards and Indians. According to the governor's instructions, he was to try to ensure that "some Christian men marry some Indian women and that some Christian women marry some male Indians so that they will communicate with and teach one another in matters of Our Holy Catholic Faith."[96] At least for that moment, the Spanish government saw limited inter-marriage as a means to an end, the end being the conversion of the Indians to the Catholic faith and their assimilation into European civilization. In July of 1511, King Ferdinand instructed the new governor of Hispaniola, Diego Colón, to eliminate brothels in the Indies and encourage—but not compel—Spaniards to legitimize their unions with Indian women.

This is not to say that the Crown embraced the notion of wide-scale interracial marriage. In 1512, the government sent white female slaves to the Indies to discourage Spaniards from coupling with the Indians, who, according to the royal decree, were "people who are far from possessing reason."[97] Two years later, however, in 1514, the Crown issued a decree legally permitting marriage between Spaniards and Indians. The decree stated, "It is our will that male and female Indians have . . . complete freedom to contract marriage with whomever they wish . . . . And we command that no order of ours . . . or [any orders] that may have been made on our behalf prevent marriage between male and female Indians and male and female Spaniards and that everyone have complete freedom to marry whomever they wish."[98] The logic behind the decree was essentially religious in nature. According to historian José Pérez de Barradas, "if converted Indians were as human as whites, equal to the Spaniards in the divine and human realms, as the theologians had decided, there was no reason whatsoever that would justify forbidding mixed marriages."[99]

But the Spanish Church and Crown also understood that there were material and political benefits to promoting limited intermar-riage. In 1516, Cardinal Francisco Jiménez de Cisneros of Toledo instructed that Spaniards in the Indies should be encouraged to marry the daughters of Indian caciques when they were "the successors of their fathers in the absence of sons . . . because in that way all the caciques would soon be Spaniards."[100] According to historian Magnus Mörner, there were "quite a number of intermarriages of this category."[101]

After the conquest of Mexico, some conquistadors married Indian princesses and daughters of chiefs. Indeed, "The conquerors understood the fact that the indigenous nobility 'endowed' their daughters in a manner similar to the [Spanish] practice, a fast method to acquire property and status."[102] Spaniards often acquired land and the service of local Indians through such marriages. After the conquest, "Indian women of high rank seem to have had no difficulty finding a Spanish husband."[103] In a small act of reparation, Cortés provided generous dowries for four of Montezuma's daughters, thereby allowing them to marry high-ranking Spaniards if they so wished. Doña Isabel, daughter of Montezuma and widow of Cuauhtémoc, married three Spaniards in succession, Alonso de Grado, Pedro Gallego de Andrada, and Juan Cano. The later two marriages produced at least seven children. Spaniard Sebastián de Moscoso married a prominent Indian woman who bore him two daughters and a son. Doña Ana, the daughter of the ruler of Texcoco, married conquistador Juan de Cuéllar. Pedro Moreno de Nájera married a noble Indian woman named Leonor and had four sons and a daughter. Melchor de Villacorta wed Isabel, of a noble Tlaxcalan family, and had two daughters. Doña Marina, Cortés's former translator and mistress, married Juan Jaramillo, with whom she had a daughter, María. Although it was rare, some Spanish women married into high-ranking Indian families. Several members of the Aztec nobility married Spanish women, including the son and grandson of Montezuma. Spaniard Don Antonio Cortés married a woman cacique from Tacuba, and three members of the Purépecha ruling family in Michoacán married women from Spain.

It was not uncommon for Spanish men who had legitimate children with Indian women to also father illegitimate offspring. A certain Juan Ortiz de Zúñiga had four legitimate and three illegitimate offspring. Gonzalo Hernández de Mosquera had five and eight, while Serván Bejarano had eight and two. In addition to his son Martín, whom he legitimated, Hernán Cortés had two daughters with two other Indian noblewomen who had been given him by caciques. He had also fathered a daughter with an Indian woman in Cuba. "Almost all the *conquistadores* had illegitimate mestizo children."[104] Alonso Mateos, Antonio Anguiano, García del Pilar, and Hernando de Lorita each had a daughter with Indian women. Alonso Guisado had a son and a daughter. Francisco Granados had many children, and Bernal Díaz del Castillo had a mestizo son. But the Spaniard who seems to have had the most children with Indian women was not a conqueror but a Spanish sailor by the name of Alvaro. He fathered thirty mestizo offspring in three years before he was killed by Indians.

Both civil and religious authorities had grappled with the thorny problems of concubinage and casual unions since the establishment of the first Spanish colony in the Americas. During the conquest phase, civil authorities "were often satisfied with having the Indian women baptized prior to coition."[105] But once Spanish society began to stabilize, the authorities attempted new strategies. When Nicolás de Ovando arrived in Hispaniola in 1501, he found that the three hundred Spaniards on the island "were living in great freedom; they had taken the most important and beautiful women as mistresses."[106] Ovando thus ordered the men to either separate or to marry their mistresses within a given period of time. Despite the fact that many Spaniards considered the order too harsh, they nonetheless complied. This instance, however, was an anomaly. Spanish authorities generally had little success controlling the sexual conduct of Spanish men. In 1529, a bishop in the Antilles complained that since his parishioners were living in sin with their Indian servants, "nothing can be found out about it."[107] The fact that many illegitimate mestizo children were born in rural haciendas far outside of Spanish towns and away from government authority made efforts to discourage concubinage all the more difficult. According to one official source in 1533, in Hispaniola, "there are a great many mestizos here, sons of Spaniards and Indian women who are usually born in [country houses] and uninhabited places."[108] This was also true in post-conquest Mexico. But while widespread concubinage troubled the Church, it infuriated many Indian men. Indeed, they complained of it bitterly. According to historian C. E. Marshall, in 1546 it was one of the primary causes of a bloody Indian rebellion in Yucatán. "So incensed were the natives that they set out to kill all the Spanish settlers and all Indian women who had served them in any capacity."[109]

By 1524, Cortés had largely divided up the Indian population of central Mexico among "his companions-in-arms and to a few

[Aztecs] who had become Christians."[110] The Spanish Crown had developed the *encomienda* system in the Caribbean as a way to reward the conquerors for their service. In essence, the individual *encomendero* was to take on the responsibility of providing for the general welfare and the Christianizing of Indian villages. In return, the Indians would provide the *encomendero* with both tribute and free labor. (Cortés, for example, received an *encomienda* of twenty-two villages in which as many as 115,000 Indians lived.) The Crown had "hoped that by this system the Indians would be more easily acculturated, better controlled and protected. What happened in practice was quite another matter, as the system, subjected to every imaginable abuse, kept the Indians in a state of serfdom and led to all sorts of horrors."[111] In 1529, the first bishop of New Spain, Juan de Zumárraga, complained to King Charles I that many *encomenderos* used the *encomienda* to procure female concubines. "Many of those who have Indians," he wrote, "have taken from the chiefs of their villages their daughters, sisters, nieces, and wives under the pretext of taking them to their homes as servants but in reality for concubines."[112] Partly to curb such abuses, in 1539 the Crown decreed that all married *encomenderos* were to send for their wives and those who were unmarried were given three years to wed or risk losing their *encomienda*. Many married their Indian mistresses.

Needless to say, the conquistadors were hardly the ideal men to preside wisely over the establishment of a brand-new society. Indeed, they comprised an unlikely aristocracy as "Many were coarse in speech [and] unrefined in manner."[113] But the era of their authority over New Spain was a short one. Not long after the conquest, a more educated and patrician group of men were sent from Spain to administer the new colony. The Crown and the Church sought both to limit the power of the conquistadors and to impose greater administrative and social order. In order to foster the development of stable colonial societies, Spanish authorities sought to restore the sanctity of marriage among the Spaniards and to impose the practice of monogamous marriage on Indians, many of whom practiced polygamy. The Crown prohibited Spaniards from pressing women into household service, while the Church called for harsher penalties for Spaniards who cohabited with Indian women without benefit of clergy. Despite

these efforts, however, New Spain remained a "nominally monogamous society, with wide liberties countenanced for males."[114] For
their part, many Indians "were only too eager to enter the Spanish
households to escape the payment of tribute and personal services
which were exacted of them in their tribal villages. Thus there grew
up in the vicinity of many Spanish towns colonies of native squatters
who had deserted their tribal surroundings to sell their services as
domestics and day laborers to the Spanish residents."[115] Juan de
Solórzano, the early-seventeenth-century authority on Spanish America, observed that "many Indian women desert their Indian husbands
and neglect the children that they have by them, seeing them subject
to tribute-payments and personal services, and desire, love, and spoil
the children that they have out of wedlock by Spaniards . . . because
they are free and exempt from all burdens."[116]

Given the fact that mestizo children were commonly the issue of
casual sexual liaisons, the process of determining paternity was sometimes difficult, if not impossible. Diego de Ocaña, an early Spanish
settler, testified to the confusion that arose concerning the parentage
of a child living within his own household:

> I say that I once had relations with the said Antonica, my servant,
> who bore a child Alosico. But she was ill-watched for she also had
> relations with an Indian of my household. However, judging by the
> color of the child, everyone declares that he seems to be the son of a
> Christian. It seems so to me, for it may be that he is my son; and since
> in case of doubt it is better to acknowledge him than to ignore him, I
> command my sons to bring him up, have him indoctrinated, and so
> do something good for him, for I believe that he is a son of mine, and
> not of an Indian.[117]

Initially, mestizos did not "form part of any third community or
element distinguishable from Indian society and Spanish society.
Mixed bloods though they were, they lived either as 'Spaniards' or
else as 'Indians.' Those mestizos born within wedlock, or born without of aristocratic mothers, or who were adopted for some other reason by their fathers, were absorbed into the first generation" of
criollos, the term used to denote Spaniards born in the New World.[118]

Furthermore, a significant number of first-generation mestizos, both legitimate and not, "were raised as Spanish gentlemen and ladies. The Crown approved of this process, for it was thought expedient that the tiny Spanish presence in Mexico should be thus strengthened."[119] But a considerably larger number of mestizos were born to casual unions between Spanish men and Indian women. These children were generally raised as Indians, "learned no Spanish, knew nothing of their fathers, and tended to become a barely distinguishable part of the Indian community."[120] By the mid-sixteenth-century, many Indian caciques were in fact biological mestizos, presumably the offspring of noble women.

It was also true that the mixed offspring born of either casual unions or of the sexual abuse of poor Indian women were sometimes relegated to marginal status or rejected within Indian communities. It was this group, rejected by both Spaniards and Indians, that first came to be recognized as mestizos. In other words, "when the term 'mestizo' began to appear in the late 1530s, it referred to marginal individuals—persons of Spanish-Indian descent who were not full members of either group."[121] Indeed, in the early colonial period, the word "mestizo" was synonymous with bastard.

As early as 1523, a royal decree ordered Spaniards to send their mestizo sons to Spain, "probably reflecting a hope to assimilate them."[122] Ten years later, on October 3, 1533, the king issued an order stating that he had been "informed that throughout the land there is a great number of children that Spaniards have had with Indian women, who wander lost among the Indians."[123] He ordered the colonial authorities to gather those mestizo children living in indigenous communities. If it could be ascertained that any of their Spanish fathers were men of means, then they should be ordered to provide for the children. Those whose fathers were not of means or could not be identified were to be taught a trade and given a Spanish education. For this purpose, Spanish authorities founded El Colegio de San Juan de Letrán, a school for mestizo boys, as well as a convent for girls.

However, this patriarchal concern for mestizos was short-lived. In 1568, Phillip II, who had succeeded his father, Charles I, as king of Spain, expressed his concern over the colonial government's inability to control the growing mestizo population. "It has been reported to me," read a royal order, "that there are already large numbers of mestizos and mulattoes in those provinces and that they increase every day and are inclined to evil . . . and because they are the sons of Indian women, as soon as they commit a crime they dress up as Indians and hide out with their mothers' relatives, and they can't be found."[124] One viceroy of New Spain told the king of his profound fear that "mestizos, mulattoes, and free blacks" would stage a rebellion and "bring after them a large part of the Indians."[125] By the time the first generation of mestizos was reaching adulthood in the 1540s, Spanish authorities began imposing restrictions on their social mobility. For instance, illegitimate mestizos were barred from holding public office. "In one sense this ruling was no different from the bar that applied in the case of Spaniards, for Spaniards born out of wedlock were not eligible for office either, but whereas this bar applied only to a minority of Spaniards, in the case of mestizos it applied to the great majority."[126] The Church, on the other hand, was divided on the issue of ordaining mestizos into the priesthood. While the secular clergy—diocesan priests—were generally open to mestizos, the mendicant orders were not. The guilds also had competing policies regarding mixed blood workers. Some, "like the cotton dealers, glovemakers, milliners, and porcelain-makers, allowed [them] to become craftsmen; others, like the pressers, manglers, and calenderers, restricted mestizos to journeymen status."[127]

The Jesuits developed their own rationale with respect to mestizos. They refused them entry into the order, not because they held them in contempt, but because they viewed them as a special group in need of their attention. In their eyes, "mestizos were not so much 'sons of Spaniards' as a new and as yet unformed race that stood in particular need of moral and spiritual guidance. Like the [blacks] and mulattoes, the mestizos were, in the Jesuit view, neophytes of the Church, a precious but delicate spiritual acquisition."[128]

As mestizos became increasingly recognized as a distinct group— neither Spanish nor Indian—their reputation among the Spaniards deteriorated. "The epithet 'sons of Spaniards' [was] used progressively less while the association with [blacks] in the Spaniard's eyes [became] closer."[129] New Spain had been receiving shipments of

African slaves since the earliest days of the colony, and the Spaniards had regarded them with particular disdain. When it became clear that certain Indian groups in the coastal lowlands could not satisfy the labor demands of Spanish colonists, African slaves were imported in large numbers. Furthermore, in Mexico City, which was built on the ruins of Tenochtitlán, it was a sign of status for wealthy Spaniards to have African valets in their service. Between 1521 and 1594, approximately 36,500 slaves arrived in Mexico.[130] An estimated 200,000 African slaves were sent to New Spain throughout the colonial period.[131]

Another reason African slaves were imported to New Spain was that the Crown and Church wished to "shift the burden of enforced labor from the backs of the natives to the stronger backs of the African blacks."[132] While theologians may have wrung their hands over the true nature of the Indian, they generally did not concern themselves with the treatment of Africans. Even Bartolomé de Las Casas, the great defender of the Indians, had suggested in 1517 that each Spaniard be permitted to bring twelve African slaves to the New World as a way to relieve Indian laborers. With the exception of the urban valets who achieved a status higher than that of Indians, black slaves were generally burdened with the most arduous and distasteful tasks. Spanish authorities discouraged blacks from mixing with other groups, at one point even threatening them with castration if they had sexual relations with women of another race. But in 1527, a royal decree urged colonial authorities to encourage slaves to adopt the custom of monogamous marriage and marry female slaves in the hope that "with marriage and their love for wives and children and orderly married life they will become more calm and much sin and trouble will be avoided."[133] Yet, since the ratio of black women to men was never more than one to four, the policy had no effect.

Despite the efforts of colonial authorities, "black men generally took Indian women as mates. In some cases [they] kidnapped and raped the native women, but in most instances the Indian women entered such unions willingly."[134] In 1574, Viceroy Martín Enríquez wrote Phillip II that "the Indian women are very weak people and are easily led astray by the blacks whom they prefer in marriage to the Indian men."[135] African slaves also had practical reasons for fathering children with Indian women. Under Spanish law, the off-spring of a male slave and a free woman was born legally free. The rapid increase in the number of black-Indian children troubled colonial authorities. Not only did these children dilute the slave population, but in the eyes of Spanish officials, they posed a threat to the stability of the colony. Already fearful of slave revolts, the Spaniards concluded that a free mixed population would ally itself with slaves against them. In 1573, Viceroy Enríquez asked Phillip II to lobby Pope Gregory XIII to make black-Indian intermarriage illegal or at the very least decree that the children of such unions would remain slaves. The king declined the suggestion.

Despite their fear of black men, many Spanish men found black and *mulata* women attractive and even came to prefer them over Indian women. In general, "Spanish attitudes towards blacks reflected the tension between antipathy and attraction. As slaves, the blacks occupied a social space inferior to the plebeian Indians, but since as a group they were familiar to Spanish ways, they were at the same time more intimate with the Spaniards and more of a threat."[136] It took only one generation for *zambos*—people of mixed black-Indian ancestry—and mulattoes—those of white-black mixture—to out-number Africans in New Spain. By the 1570s, people of black ancestry still outnumbered mestizos. They made up the largest and most visible sector of *castas,* the generic term Spaniards used to refer to racially mixed people. As historian J. I. Israel observed, the mestizo population "grew up slowly around the fringe of [Spanish society] and in the shadow of the black" population.[137] While in theory mestizos were considered *gente de razón*, rational people with the equivalent intellect of whites, in practice they were increasingly associated with blacks and other *gente vil* (base folk). As their numbers increased, "Spaniards tended to lump mestizos, *mulatos,* and free blacks as undesirables."[138] As a result, the barriers between Spaniards and mestizos became more rigid, and marriage between Spaniards and Indians became increasingly rare.

The Spaniards had established colonial Mexican society on the premise that it would consist of two separate "republics," *la república de los españoles* and *la república de los indios*. Immediately after the conquest, Cortés had marked out thirteen square blocks in central

Mexico City where the Spaniards were to live. The area surrounding the Spanish city was reserved for Indian inhabitants. Conscious that they were a small ruling minority in an Indian land, the Spaniards viewed residential segregation as a form of self-defense. The Church also perceived segregation and isolation of the Indians to be conducive to their efforts to evangelize the population. Colonial policy was therefore designed to maintain the integrity and stability of each ethnic realm. By 1550, both civil and religious authorities had "delineated the relationship of (only) Spanish and Indian societies to the monarch, [and] regulated their internal structures."[139] African slaves also had their defined legal position in society. But manumitted slaves and "all new peoples recognized as of mixed parentage . . . had no place in the dominant ideology."[140] Because they clearly did not belong in either "republic," the *castas* were perceived as a threat to the stability of the society. They "had no preassigned place. They were not Spanish . . . nor could they claim the legitimacy of the land's original inhabitants. In short [they] were an anomaly."[141]

Because mestizos did not fit into the official racial system, Spaniards attempted to ignore their very existence. Some contemporary observers neglected to record the presence of mestizos in colonial society. For example, after Antonio Vásquez de Espinosa, a Spanish priest, visited Mexico City in 1612, he did not even mention the existence of mestizos in his writings. In 1654, a Church official in the capital noted that population statistics for mestizos and other *castas* were "unknown because of their confused ranks."[142] Thus, although they were the fastest growing segment of seventeenth-century New Spain, the mestizo, in the words of J. I. Israel, received "so little mention that one almost forgets his existence. By comparison with the Indian, Negro, or Spaniard, he is almost nothing; where he does appear, it is usually only as a tag on the end of the much bandied phrase 'Negroes, mulattoes, and mestizos.' Thus it may be said that the problem of the seventeenth-century mestizo is, in the first place, the problem of explaining his obscurity."[143]

This obscurity is partly explained by the fact that while mestizos became a recognizable third racial category, they did not evolve into a separate social class. As the term "mestizo" took on a negative connotation, biological mestizos who were members of the Spanish and

Indian elites dissociated themselves from the new mestizos, those who had no standing in either *república*. Having no firmly ascribed place in the social order, mestizos tended to fit in where they could. They were "present in every social category and group in the colony."[144] Given their biracial origins, some mestizos became mediators between Spaniards and Indians. In 1578, five of the six interpreters employed by the colonial government were mestizos. Their very heterogeneity afforded them a wide variety of experiences. Some found their niche in long-distance trade. "There was no guise which he did not assume; he could be a 'Creole,' 'Indian,' cacique, friar, secular priest, 'mestizo,' even a 'mulatto,' and it is difficult or impossible to say that it was more usual or typical for him to be one rather than another."[145]

Still, for the most part, the mestizo "could make only limited use of the heterogenous cultural heritage left him by his varied ancestors."[146] Their dual disinheritance forged a unique mentality in the group that would become the majority population in urban New Spain in the seventeenth century. Historian Charles Gibson labeled the colonial mestizo a "pragmatic opportunist."[147] According to anthropologist Eric Wolf, the mestizo's "chances of survival lay neither in accumulating cultural furniture nor in cleaving to cultural norms, but in an ability to change, to adapt, to improvise. The ever shifting nature of his social condition forced him to move with guile and speed through the hidden passageways of society, not to commit himself to any one position or to any one spot."[148] Unlike Spaniards or Indians, whose group identities conferred upon them specific legal rights and responsibilities, mestizo identity was legally and socially ambiguous. Thus, mestizos learned to "change [their] behavior as other men assume or doff a mask."[149] As a result, they did not develop a strong corporate identity. "For the mestizo, power is not an attribute of groups. The group exists to back the individual; the individual does not exist for the group."[150]

Just as the Spanish view of mestizos shifted over the centuries, it often varied from place to place. While their reputation suffered in cities where they were associated with blacks, on the frontier their white ancestry was emphasized. In 1621, a scholar in the province of Nueva Galicia, which encompassed the present-day states of Jalisco, Nayarit, and southern Sinaloa, described mestizos as "talented, energetic, and honorable, owing to their Spanish blood."[151] Although some Spaniards may have feared a mestizo-black alliance, others were certain that mestizos would remain loyal to the Spaniards. In a letter dated January 9, 1574, Viceroy Enríquez confessed to Phillip II that he was worried about the growth of the mulatto population but not that of the mestizos. "Although there are many among them who lead base lives and have base ways . . . [they] will always follow the faction of the Spaniards, and form a part of those they most respect."[152]

One of the Spaniards' greatest concerns about mestizos and *castas* in general was the allegedly poor example they set for the Indians. While Spanish authorities acknowledged the integral role the Indians played in the colonial economy, they generally considered mestizos little more than vagabonds. One official sixteenth-century document described them as "lazy persons . . . who do not have a manual trade, nor property from which they can sustain themselves."[153] Vagabondage was already a widespread problem in the colony. Even in the late sixteenth century, the economy of New Spain was still not large enough to sustain the growing settler population. Furthermore, many Spaniards came to the New World with visions of never having to work hard again. In their minds, hard labor was the province of Indians and black slaves.

While mestizos were not the only vagabonds, their role "within this vagrant element gradually expanded, to the point at which the terms vagrant and mestizo often became synonymous."[154] They were blamed for teaching the Indians "their bad customs and idleness and other errors and vices besides."[155] In 1565, a colonial judge complained that the number of vagabonds was "as numerous as the grasses and were increasing by leaps and bounds."[156] That same year, the conqueror's mestizo son, Martín Cortés, wrote Phillip II, "The viceroy himself told me that every morning in Mexico there arise eight hundred men who have nowhere to eat. . . . In addition to the great number of Spaniards, there are so many Mestizos and Mulattoes that they cover the land and these persons are naturally born with evil tendencies and they do the greatest harm to the natives."[157] At one point, Viceroy Luis de Velasco recommended shipping unruly mestizos and mulattoes off to Spain. In 1559, the conquest and settlement of Florida was approved in part to help relieve the problem of mestizo vagabondage.

This growing class of vagabonds gave impetus to a renewed policy of strict segregation between the Indian and the Spanish *repúblicas*. As early as 1550, Viceroy Enríquez expelled several "harmful mestizos" from Indian villages. In November 1578, a royal decree categorically forbade mestizos, mulattoes, and blacks from living among the Indians. Three years later, another decree added Spaniards to the list. For the remainder of the colonial period, the Spanish authorities and the Spanish colonial elite would attempt to impose a rigid racial system on a diverse population that had been mixing since the very first days of the conquest.

Two

The Rise and Fall of the Spanish Colonial Racial System

Mexican poet Octavio Paz described the cult of the Virgen de Guadalupe as "The most complex and original creation" of colonial New Spain.[1] The Brown Virgin, as she came to be known, became an object of popular veneration within a decade of the conquest. In 1533, a small shrine to her was erected on a hillside in Tepeyac, four miles north of Mexico City. It was built on the place where a poor Indian convert was said to have witnessed her miraculous apparition. Before the conquest, Tepeyac had been the site of the temple of Tonantzin, the Aztec mother of gods.

In recognition of the growing devotion to the Virgin, particularly on the part of the Indians, Archbishop Alonso de Montúfar had a basilica constructed on the site in 1556. In 1622, a new sanctuary was built and relocated to the bottom of the hill. By that time, Guadalupe was renowned for her miraculous healing powers and altars in her name had been erected all over the Valley of Mexico. In 1648 and 1649, the oldest known written accounts of the story of the Virgin of Guadalupe were published. The second and more authoritative version was written in Nahuatl by the chaplain of the Guadalupe shrine, Luis Laso de la Vega, who recorded the Indian stories that had been circulating around New Spain. The essence of the story was as follows:

Very early on a Saturday in early December 1531, a young Aztec named Juan Diego was walking past the hill at Tepeyac. A recent convert to Christianity, Juan Diego was on his way to church in Tlatelolco. As the first light of dawn broke onto the hill, he heard the sound of birds singing. They sang with such exquisite beauty that he was moved to stop and listen. "Where am I?" he asked himself. "Am I dreaming?"[2] He wondered if perhaps he had entered the earthly paradise that his ancestors had spoken of. The singing stopped. In the silence that followed, Juan Diego heard the voice of a young woman, tenderly summoning him to the top of the hill. She called him by name, "Juanito, Juan Dieguito."³

There on the hilltop, Juan Diego saw an apparition of the Virgin Mary. Speaking to him in his native language, she instructed him to go to the bishop of Mexico and inform him of her wish that a church be built in that place. Juan Diego complied, proceeding to the bishop's palace in Mexico City. After a long wait, Juan was ushered into an audience with Juan de Zumárraga, the first bishop of Mexico. The audience did not go well. The bishop appeared not to believe the story and instructed Juan to come back another day. Disappointed, Juan returned to the Virgin to inform her of his failure. He suggested to her as well that she send a more credible messenger than himself, a humble Indian, to meet with the bishop. She replied by telling him to return to the bishop's palace the very next day.

On his second visit to the episcopal palace, Juan Diego responded to a lengthy series of questions. He described precisely what he had seen and what the Virgin Mary had requested of him. Still skeptical, the bishop asked Juan for a sign from heaven to prove the truth of his story.

On Monday, Juan did not return to Tepeyac because his uncle, Juan Bernardino, was very sick. Later that day, the uncle asked Juan to find a priest so that he could confess before he died. Before dawn on the following morning, Juan set out for Tlatelolco in search of a priest, but since his mission was an urgent one he took a different route than usual to avoid seeing the Virgin. When she appeared to him on the road, he tried to explain to her the reasons for his evasion. She famously replied, "Know, rest very much assured, my youngest child, let nothing whatever frighten you or worry you. Do not be concerned. Do not fear the illness or any illness or affliction. Am I, your mother, not here?"⁴

Juan asked the Virgin for a sign to take to Bishop Zumárraga. She told him to climb to the top of the hill. There, in the middle of winter and in a place where they had not been known to grow, he found beautiful and fragrant flowers of every kind. At her direction, Juan cut and gathered them all in his cloak, which was made of coarse fiber and called, in Nahuatl, a *tilma*. She told him to open his *tilma* only in the presence of Bishop Zumárraga.

It was still dark when Juan reached the bishop's residence. The guards taunted him and kept him waiting for hours. When the bishop finally received him, Juan recounted what the Virgin had told him; that she wanted a church built at Tepeyac. When he opened his cloak and the flowers fell to the floor, a painted image of the Virgin was left imprinted on the *tilma*. The bishop fell to his knees and apologized for his unbelief. He untied the cloak from Juan Diego's neck and placed it in his private chapel. On the following day, Zumárraga followed Juan to Tepeyac and began making plans for the shrine. When Juan arrived home, he found that the Virgin had cured his uncle. This, the faithful believe, was the first of many miracles worked through the intercession of the Virgen de Guadalupe.

The origins of the holy image, which is preserved and still venerated in the Basílica de Guadalupe in Mexico City, are contested. So is the very existence of Juan Diego, who was canonized in 2002 by Pope John Paul II. What is certain is that the cult of Guadalupe swept Mexico in the colonial period. In the first few decades, mostly Indians visited Tepeyac to pay their respects and present offerings of food and drink, according to the Aztec custom. By the seventeenth and eighteenth centuries, her feast day had become "the greatest Indian religious event in all Mexico."[5] The conquest had been a cataclysmic event for Mexico's Indians. The "deep uprooting" that it caused "gave rise to intense religious movements that sought to give an indigenous meaning to the gods, to the saints, and to the conquerors' ceremonies. . . . Instead of rejecting the Christian religion and cult, these movements sought to make these values truly theirs by converting them into indigenous divinities, saints, and rites."[6] According to Mexican historian and anthropologist Enrique Florescano, Guadalupe became a "protective divinity of the uprooted universe of the Indians, the first divinity of the Christian religious pantheon that the indigenous made their own."[7] Octavio Paz wrote simply that "the Indians, who had seen the massacre of their priests and the destruction of their idols . . . took refuge in [the Virgin's] lap."[8]

The Indians' Virgin was not the first Guadalupe. The Spaniards had brought another Virgen de Guadalupe from the Monastery of Guadalupe in Extremadura, the region in Spain from which many conquistadors had hailed. The Spanish Guadalupe was believed to have revealed herself to a humble shepherd. The statue of her likeness, which appeared to be Byzantine in origin, was notable for its dark color. Indeed, she was known as a "black virgin." As late as 1575, the image of Guadalupe at the shrine at Tepeyac still resembled that of the Spanish Virgin. But sometime after that date, her likeness changed to its current form. The Indians appropriated her image and through a process that is shrouded by myth and legend, the Mexican Guadalupe became brown-skinned.

The Virgin Mary's apparition to a humble Indian in Mexico was consistent with the European Christian tradition. This pattern signified "that she, through the building of her shrine, offer[ed] protection to her devotees, to those like the humble witness chosen to experience the miracle."[9] In other words, the implication of Juan Diego's participation in the miracle was that "poor Indians [were] those who [would] be the first to enjoy the protection of the Virgin."[10] Other aspects of her story tie Guadalupe to the Indians. In addition to her brown skin, the Virgin also used flowers as a sign, which in Aztec tradition symbolized all that was pure and beautiful.

Spanish priests were not unaware of the syncretic possibilities of a Marian cult arising in the very place where the Aztecs had worshipped a feminine deity. The Franciscans, who believed that the conversion of the Indians to Christianity required a total break with polytheism, were fervently opposed to the cult of Guadalupe. Around 1570, Franciscan missionary and archaeologist Bernardino de Sahagún condemned the veneration of Guadalupe as idolatrous. At Tepeyac, he wrote, the Aztecs "made many sacrifices to honor this goddess and came to her from distant lands from more than twenty leagues, from all the regions of Mexico and they brought many offerings; men and women and young men and young women came to these feasts; there was a great gathering of people on those days and they all said let us go to the feast of Tonantzin."[11] But even after the new church of Our Lady of Guadalupe had been built, Sahagún continued,

the Indians also call her Tonantzin, on the pretext that the preachers call Our Lady, the Mother of God, 'Tonantzin'. . . . This is an abuse which should be stopped. . . . To me this looks very much like a satanic invention to palliate idolatry by playing on the ambiguity of this name Tonantzin. The Indians today, as in the old days, come

from afar to visit this Tonantzin, and to me the cult seems very sus-
pect, for there are everywhere numerous churches consecrated to
Our Lady, but they do not go there, preferring to come from afar to
this Tonantzin, as in the past.[12]

The cult of Guadalupe was indeed a product of the fusion of the
pre-Hispanic devotion to Tonantzin and the Christian veneration
of the Virgin Mary. But not all Catholic priests opposed her emergence as a popular religious figure. In the mid-sixteenth century, the
Dominican archbishop Montúfar not only sanctioned but promoted
the cult. By the end of the century, Spaniards and criollos began to
visit the shrine on Sundays. In 1648, one year before the publication
of Luis Laso de la Vega's Nahuatl account of the apparitions of the
Virgen de Guadalupe, another priest, Miguel Sánchez, published a
similar tract in Spanish, which further popularized her among the
criollos. Sánchez was one of a group of criollo scholars, theologians,
and priests who were eager to ascribe roots and identity to Mexican-
born Spaniards. Thus they exalted the apparition of Guadalupe as the
central event in the colony's history. For them, the Virgin Mary's
appearance increased New Spain's prestige, and helped criollos to
forge an identity distinct from that of Spain. Like other criollos
throughout the Americas, "those in Mexico experienced an identity
crisis between their Spanish ancestry and their loyalty to the land
where they had been born."[13] As a way to ease this tension, Mexican
criollos began to identify more strongly with their place of birth. In
other words, for the criollos, embracing the Brown Virgin was a conscious act of putting down roots in the New World.

In 1660, a new, grand avenue was built linking central Mexico
City with the shrine at Tepeyac. In 1695, construction began on a
majestic new basilica, designed to accommodate the thousands of pil-
grims who arrived daily from around New Spain. In 1737, during a
devastating outbreak of plague, Guadalupe was made the patron of
Mexico City. Nine years later, she was proclaimed the patron of all
New Spain. According to Mexican American theologian Virgilio Elizondo, "The synthesis of the religious iconography of the Spanish
with that of the indigenous Mexican peoples into a single, coherent
symbol-image ushered in a new, shared experience."[14] By the end of

the colonial period, the worship of Guadalupe "made [criollos], mestizos, and Indians a single people united by the same charismatic faith."[15] Thus Guadalupe became a symbol of an emerging mestizo nation.

Indians were not merely passive recipients of European ways. The culture of Nahuatl speakers "had to have structures and values close enough to the new Spanish elements to make them viable in the indigenous context. When this was the case, there was often no need for imposition or teaching."[16] Spanish missionaries, who began to systematically proselytize in 1524, sought to employ religious terms already familiar to the Indians. Despite their insistence on "totally eradicating aspects of the native religion that clashed head-on with Catholicism . . . [the Franciscans, in particular] were willing to be lenient and permit many identifications where similar rituals, ceremonials, and theological practices were found in both religions."[17] But the aspect of pre-Hispanic religion most beneficial to the missionaries was the tradition of accepting the gods of the conquering power. This practice made the Indians predisposed to convert to the Christian God. What they often could not understand, however, was the friars' insistence that the Christian God demanded to be worshipped to the exclusion of all others. By the late sixteenth century, it had become clear to the friars that the conversion of many Indians was incomplete, if not superficial. Many Indian communities continued to practice ancient religious rites in secret. "Because of the natives' ability to assimilate external religious concepts, a parallel religious system developed in many native communities. They worshipped their old gods as well as the new Christian deity and saints."[18] Contemporary scholars use the term "nepantlism" to describe the state in which many Indians must have found themselves, "in which a person remains suspended in the middle between a lost or disfigured past and a present that has not been assimilated or understood."[19] Although in 1539 the Church forbade the beating or imprisonment of Indians as punishment for deviating from Christian doctrine, the prohibition was clearly not always observed. In 1570, it was still common for Indian apostates to be punished with a "half dozen strokes on the outside of their clothing."[20] As historian Woodrow Borah noted, the Christianization of the Indians was ultimately achieved over time through "a mixture of syncretism and relentless persecution."[21]

According to French historian Robert Ricard, there is little doubt that the missionaries "loved their Indians; but they loved them as children, or as some parents love their children, never resigning themselves to seeing them grow up."[22] The Indians were not considered *gente de razón,* people of reason. Like children, they were in need of protection. Back in Spain, it was clergymen like Bartolomé de Las Casas, Archbishop García de Loaisa, and Dominican theologian Francisco de Vitoria who were primarily responsible for the promulgation of the New Laws of 1542, which "called for, among other things, the freedom of natives who had been unjustly enslaved and the easing of labor requirements."[23]

But as Ricard's observation suggests, the Church's paternalism also proved harmful to the Indians. In the mid-sixteenth century, the mendicants fervently endorsed a new policy to congregate the Indians in villages in the hopes that it would make the project of evangelization more efficient. Rural Indians had generally lived in huts scattered in fields rather than in compact communities. With only eight hundred friars in 1559, the missionaries had a difficult time reaching all of the indigenous population.[24] But from 1550 to 1605, colonial authorities undertook a massive program to relocate Indians into newly organized Spanish-style towns in which the church and government buildings were built around a central plaza. Existing Indian townships were sometimes relocated from, say, the top of a hill to the lowlands.

The friars hoped that the new policy of congregation would allow them to better protect the Indians "not only from violence and abuse but also from influences harmful to their morals and faith."[25] Franciscan friar and historian Gerónimo de Mendieta argued that it was the duty of both the Crown and Church to limit contact between Indians and non-Indians as much as possible. If they did not, he argued, they risked ruining Indian society and undermining the accomplishments of the missionaries. Placed under mendicant control, the new villages were declared off-limits to Spaniards, mestizos, and blacks. Spanish ranches were removed from Indian lands, and non-Indian travelers were prohibited from staying in indigenous villages for more than two days. Similarly, in Spanish towns and cities, Indians were to remain confined within their separate barrios, and workplaces and hospitals were to be segregated. For the most part however, the new segregation policy was aimed at excluding non-Indian vagrants and vagabonds from residing in Indian settlements. In other words, "the discrimination was not directed against the Indians but rather against the non-Indians."[26]

While the policy of congregation must have angered many Indians, the general concept of segregation appears to have had the support of many indigenous leaders. In 1574, a group of Indians filed a complaint with the king about the abuses they were suffering from Spaniards, *castas,* and blacks. They argued that it was "intolerable that natives be settled with [non-Indians] as a matter of course, because by reason of their being together many sins are committed and many illegitimate children are born. There is corruption of good mores and of propriety and even of the Christian religion. Therefore, we implore that it please His Majesty to ensure that Spaniards always be settled among themselves and the Indians among themselves."[27]

Ironically, congregation and the building of new settlements further endangered the Indians by weakening their resistance to the epidemics that repeatedly swept New Spain. According to historian George Kubler, "to urbanize the Indian population was to dislocate and destroy the patterns of indigenous culture. Such cultural extirpation, in turn, brought about the biological decrease of the Indian race."[28] While Kubler may have overstated the connection, it seems clear that the "dislocation of Indian life" did serve to lower the Indians' "vitality and will to survive."[29] The Indians were forced to leave the places "where for centuries they had been protected by their gods, where their common divinities were and their ancestors rested."[30] In many cases, they were obligated to live with other ethnic groups who practiced different customs and spoke other languages. This "change signified the uprooting, the brutal removal of a group of traditions that had accumulated for a long time, and the violent imposition of a new way of life."[31]

It was in the late sixteenth century, when Spanish authorities were most energetically promoting the congregation policy, that "authorities and clergy became increasingly aware of the terrible depopulation that had taken place since the conquest."[32] Before the conquest, central Mexico, roughly the size of France, may have had a population as high as 25 million.[33] But during the sixteenth century, pestilence was almost constant in New Spain. The navigational advances of the Renaissance had "unified the disease pools of Europe, Africa, and Asia and unwittingly import[ed] all into America."[34] Without the antibodies to combat Old World viruses, the Indians were defenseless. There had been three epidemics of smallpox between 1520 and 1545. Typhoid fever hit in 1545, 1576, 1735, and "twenty-nine times thereafter during the period of Spanish rule."[35] An epidemic of measles struck in 1595. "The most virulent epidemic, that of 1545–1548, reduced the native population to a little more than 6 million. A generation later the great [plague] of 1576–1579 diminished the Indian population to about 2½ million. By 1600, a mere 1½ million natives survived. The low point was reached between 1620 and 1630, when about 1 million Indians lived in Mexico."[36] The effect of the pestilence of the sixteenth century in Mesoamerica was greater than that of the Black Plague in Europe. All told, "the demographic disaster that took place [throughout the Americas] after 1492 is probably without counterpart in the history of mankind."[37]

Understandably, by the mid-sixteenth century, New Spain had been plunged into "depression and despondency."[38] The Indians became increasingly apathetic. "Systematic abortion and infanticide, as well as mass suicides, were reported in several areas."[39] Many Indians simply lost the will to live. According to one late-sixteenth-century chronicler, when the Indians "fall ill they have the most perverse habit of refusing to take food or even look at it, and not their son or wife nor anyone else would ask them to eat, and so they die like brutes."[40] The friars also shared in the general despondency. "In despair, they strove to comprehend how the Almighty could have struck the Indians down in their millions at the very moment that they had glimpsed the light and embraced His holy doctrine."[41] The population decline further fueled their desire to protect and isolate the Indians. Thus, the policies of congregation and segregation continued.

Despite their population loss, Indian villages remained obligated to perform work for and pay tribute to their Spanish overlords. Hence, in a cruel twist, until tax rolls were updated, the survivors were often obligated to shoulder an ever increasing burden of labor. As it was, the Indians spent roughly a quarter of the year working for the Spaniards, but during the remaining three-fourths they were free to work their own fields. Because indigenous cities were hit hardest by the recurring plagues, the demographic disaster of the sixteenth century made the Indian population more rural than it had been in pre-Hispanic times. For example, once home to roughly 110,000 people, Texcoco was reduced to eight thousand souls by 1644. By 1669, Cholula was only one-fifteenth of its preconquest size.[42]

Overall, depopulation heightened the colony's labor shortage. In order to avoid the increasing "burdens of tribute and draft labor, many [Indians] left their pueblos to live in [Spanish] towns and cities or to work on . . . estates where [they] became day laborers, skilled workers and artisans."[43] By 1640, the Spanish city of Puebla had seventeen thousand Indians, "mostly Mixtecs, Zapotecs, Tlaxcalans, and Cholulans; Valladolid [present-day Morelia] had approximately 3,000 Tarascans living within its borders; Querétaro was settled by some 10,000 Aztecs, Tarascans, Otomíes, and Chichimecas; Zacatecas and Celaya had several thousand natives of mixed origin, many of them part of the large floating population attracted to the prosperous new cities."[44]

The friars considered the Indians who left their villages for the *república de los españoles* to be lost souls beyond redemption. Franciscan historian Juan de Torquemada wrote that these Indians were "among the basest people of the world."[45] Both *encomenderos* and Indian caciques attempted to stem the outflow from Indian villages. "For them the drift . . . meant a serious loss of people to help meet tribute and labor quotas."[46] In the late sixteenth and early seventeenth centuries, caciques were able to secure court rulings ordering villagers who accepted wage employment to continue to shoulder their portion of the town's collective burden to provide labor and pay tribute. In the early seventeenth century, Viceroy Marqués de Cerralvo ordered Spanish officers to Mexico City to help the caciques of Texcoco hunt down "fugitives working in Spanish workshops, residences, and other establishments and take them back to their home town. Some of these Texcocans . . . had abandoned womenfolk, children, and plots of land in expectation of better things under the

Spaniards."[47] But over time, authorities were unable to stop the seepage. From its inception, the segregation policy conflicted with the labor needs of the emerging colonial economy. Despite the friars' best efforts, Indian centers never became self-sufficient communities isolated from the Spanish cities.

The decline of the Indian population opened up large tracts of land for Spanish use. The colonial economy, once dependent on community-based Indian labor and tribute, now revolved around Spanish haciendas (plantations) and *obrajes* (textile workshops). In 1630, colonial authorities abolished the collective Indian labor system for agriculture—but not for public works or mining—and "Spaniards who wanted temporary labor had to make individual arrangements (as many had already been doing)" with Indian laborers.[48] What this meant was that many Indian laborers no longer had to go through their caciques when signing on to work for Spaniards. They were now allowed to be "hired on directly, in a face-to-face situation, with a Spanish employer or his representative for the amount of time and under the conditions agreed upon."[49] The advent of wage labor spelled the "destruction of town or tribal control over a part of the Indian population. The laborers removed from the continuing centers of Indian culture were settled in centers of Spanish influence, where they would tend to adopt Spanish as their language, intermarry with other tribes or with mixed bloods, and become absorbed in the emerging hybrid Mexican culture. Debt peonage, ironically, helped forge the Mexican nation."[50]

Still, the notion of the two *repúblicas* persisted. Despite the advent of wage labor, Indians were expected to continue residing in their own villages. Nonetheless, by the late seventeenth century, *la traza*, central Mexico City, had become a magnet for Indians in skilled trades. There they found themselves surrounded by Spaniards and *castas*, who in the segregation between the Spanish and Indian republics, were assigned to the former. In this new environment, the Indians felt pressure "to adopt the clothing, bearing, and speech of their fellow tenants and workers. Some discarded their Indian identity altogether."[51] According to one contemporary observer, "Many of them take to wearing stockings and shoes, and some trousers, and they cut their hair shorter, and the women put on petticoats; and becoming *mestizos,* they go to church at the Cathedral."[52] In 1692, Fray Joseph de la Barrera disapprovingly described the same process: "When an Indian takes to wearing mestizo clothes . . . he becomes a *mestizo,* and in a short time will be a Spaniard, rid of having to pay tribute, and an enemy of God, of the Church, and of the king."[53]

In the late seventeenth century, authorities briefly forced the *traza* Indians back to their assigned barrios. But many of their Spanish employers helped them undermine the segregation laws, often hiding them whenever the authorities came to demand that runaway Indians return to their villages. In some instances, they even beat the collectors. According to historian R. Douglas Cope, "the city's parish priests also felt quite bitter over what they viewed as an unnatural alliance—almost a conspiracy—between Spaniards and Indians."[54] Father Antonio Guridí of the Santiago Tlatelolco parish described the situation thus: "I was a minister for many years outside this city of Mexico [i.e., outside the *traza*], and any Indians who were missing from the parishes that I served I found in this city . . . in various houses both of Indians and Spaniards; some fault, sir, lies with the Indians, some with the *gobernadores,* but most of the blame belongs to the Spanish householders of this city, who help and defend [the Indians] in their residences just to earn money from the rental of a *jacal* [adobe shack] or *aposento* [ground floor apartment], or because of the service they get from them."[55] Many Spanish employers developed personal ties with their Indian employees. Indeed, many became godparents *(compadres)* to their employees' children, thereby creating bonds of extended kinship. One priest from the Mexico City parish of San Pablo complained that whenever he went to take away Indians from Spanish houses, "two or three Spanish godparents" would argue with him. "If they do not get their way, [the Indians] flee and are hidden in their houses."[56]

Whether in cities, mining camps, or haciendas, detribalized Indians, whom the Spaniards called *ladinos,* were culturally distinct from the Indians who remained in their villages. Indeed, they "constituted a separate social grouping, different not only in economic and religious life but in speech, conduct, and dress."[57] According to historian J. I. Israel, *ladinos* exhibited "the traits of natives who went the whole way in discarding traditional Indian habits, completing a process which, for the bulk of the Indian population after the Conquest, had not gone beyond a certain point. The Indians of the 'Indian' republic had been stripped of their ancient religion and their warlike and polygamous customs, but had been moulded into a way of life that remained unmistakably Indian. . . . The ladino Indian, however, marked a real break with tradition and with the Indian community."[58] From a physical standpoint, *ladinos* and mestizos were often indistinguishable, given that the latter "possess[ed] a considerable amount of Indian genetic admixture."[59] By the seventeenth century, however, such terms had already taken on a cultural rather than a biological meaning. "Instead of depending upon physical appearance, Indian racial identity flow[ed] from the fact that one [lived] in an Indian community, [spoke] an Indian language, [spoke] Spanish with an Indian accent, [wore] Indian-style clothing or participate[d] in Indian-type fiestas."[60] In the practical sense, when observers described Indians as becoming mestizos it meant they no longer had to pay tribute to the Spaniards. But it also meant that these Indians were shedding their indigenous identity and assimilating into an emerging hybrid culture. By the late seventeenth century, a new mestizo colonial culture was being formed in and near the Spanish centers. By the middle of the eighteenth century, it would become the dominant culture in much of the rest of the country.

The decimation of the Indian population also brought surviving residents of the *república de los indios* into greater contact with non-Indians. "The impact of a few thousand Spaniards among millions of Indians was inevitably heightened as the numbers of [Indians] fell to half, then a quarter, then less than that. The relatively fixed amount of contact a given number of Spaniards could provide would be a larger proportion of the total experience of a reduced number of Indians and hence would represent 'more' contact."[61] Indigenous population decline "greatly fortified the impact of immigration and racial mixing so that recovery among the Indians, when it began [around 1630], always lagged behind the creation of a Europeanized population."[62] At the very least, wrote historian Magnus Mörner, "the advance of mestizaje . . . would have been much less conspicuous if the Indian masses had remained as numerous" as they had been at the time of the conquest.[63]

Increased interracial contact also had a significant influence on Spanish culture in central New Spain.

> Their enterprises were permeated by [indigenous] labor mechanisms, they made increasing use of essentially indigenous markets for everyday items of all kinds, they gradually adopted significant elements of indigenous diet and material culture, and their language too was affected. It was affected, in fact, in much the same way as Nahuatl was affected by Spanish. Known early loans into Spanish are a mirror image of those in the other direction, emphasizing markedly different plants and animals, artifacts, and role definitions. Later, the Spaniards began to borrow verbs, such as *pepenar,* "to glean, pick over," and *sacamolear,* "to clear land for cultivation."[64]

In addition to the considerable presence of indigenous loan words, the clearest sign of Nahuatl influence on the Spanish spoken in Mexico is the pervasive use of the diminutive.[65] The Aztecs' well-known courteousness also became part of the new hybrid culture. (In seventeenth-century Spain, the phrase "as polite as a Mexican Indian" was a common expression.)[66] Spaniards and *castas* adopted what Bernardino de Sahagún described as the Aztecs' "polished, polite, and curious mode of speech, with such preamble, tactfulness, and rhetorical devices, untaught and natural . . . as though it had been created by a lifetime in court."[67]

Because of the obvious Indian influence on Spanish colonial culture, Spaniards from the Iberian Peninsula tended to view the criollos as not fully white. Indeed, just as many Indians became mestizos by virtue of their social status and cultural accoutrements, a growing number of upwardly mobile mestizos "joined the ranks of American Spaniards, causing a perceptible 'darkening' of the criollo strata."[68] But even as many Spaniards and criollos helped facilitate—or were even products of—racial mixing in New Spain, they were also threatened by it. "Throughout the colonial period, Spanish civil and ecclesiastical authorities emphasized racial differences as a way of exerting their control over the population."[69] As it became abundantly clear that boundaries between New Spain's two republics were porous, authorities groped for a new system by which to make sense of—and control—the colony's diversifying population. From its inception, the Spanish had "justified their domination of Mexico . . . on the basis of lineage."[70] New Spain's three-tiered division of labor had been drawn along racial lines: "Spanish merchants and property owners, Indian laborers, black slaves and domestic servants."[71] But the colony's high level of miscegenation challenged not only the labor system but also the Spaniards' very claim to authority. "What was to prevent the descendants of Indians or even blacks from infiltrating into the Spanish group? Peninsular Spaniards already looked down on the [criollos], partly because many of the latter had some Indian ancestry. Naturally, elite [criollos] wished to avoid (or avoid recognizing) any further 'taint.' They therefore needed a method of social categorization that would reinforce their sense of exclusivity."[72]

Widespread miscegenation "led those at the top of society . . . to cling to the concept of racial purity in order to maintain their . . . position of power and authority in society."[73] To this end, in the seventeenth century, the Spanish and criollo colonial elite developed the *sistema de castas* (caste system). The *casta* system "was a hierarchical ordering of racial groups according to their proportion of Spanish blood. At its most extreme, this model distinguished more than forty racial categories, though few of these had any practical significance. The standard seventeenth-century format (there were, of course, regional variations) contained five to seven groups, ranked as follows, Spaniard, *castizo, morisco, mestizo,* mulatto, Indian, and black. (*Castizos* were the product of Spanish-*mestizo* unions, *moriscos* the children of mulatto and Spanish parents.)"[74]

One list of *castas* from eighteenth-century New Spain looked like this:

Spaniard and Indian beget mestizo
Mestizo and Spanish woman beget castizo
Castizo woman and Spaniard beget Spaniard
Spanish woman and Negro beget mulatto
Spaniard and mulatto woman beget morisco
Morisco woman and Spaniard beget albino
Spaniard and albino woman beget torna atrás
Indian and torna atrás woman beget lobo

Lobo and Indian woman beget zambaigo
Zambaigo and Indian woman beget cambujo
Cambujo and mulatto woman beget albarazado
Albarazado and mulatto woman beget barcino
Barcino and mulatto woman beget coyote
Coyote woman and Indian beget chamiso
Chamiso woman and mestizo beget coyote mestizo
Coyote mestizo and mulatto woman beget ahí te estás[75]

The idea underlying the *sistema* was the concept of *limpieza de sangre* (cleanliness of blood), which had been used in Spain to force the upper class to prove their ancestors had not been Muslims or Jews. In the New World, however, *limpieza de sangre* referred principally to race. In addition to assigning a name and rank to varying types of mixtures, the *sistema* also offered "the possibility of improving one's blood through the right pattern of mixing," by discouraging the mixing of blacks and Indians.[76] According to this scheme, if a European married an Indian, his mestizo offspring would belong to a lower caste than himself. However, a mestizo family could theoretically regain whiteness by marrying Europeans in later generations. The offspring of a mestizo and a Spaniard would be a *castizo;* the child of a *castizo* and a Spaniard would revert to a Spaniard. On the other hand, a mestizo could lower his family's status by marrying a non-European. Again, according to the *sistema de castas,* if a mestiza married an Indian man, her child would be demoted in the social scale and might be labeled as a *salta atrás*—or a jump backward.

In the eighteenth century, a popular pictorial genre known as *casta* painting emerged in New Spain. Most sets consisted of sixteen panels with each image portraying a man and a woman of different race with one or two of their progeny. Images were accompanied by inscriptions identifying the racial mixes depicted. The paintings were as much pedagogical—they cautioned viewers on the social consequences of forging interracial unions—as they were fantasy. They "promoted an image of the colony that served to counteract the elite's fear of social rupture and their loss of power."[77]

By the mid-seventeenth century, priests began employing the *casta* system's more common racial designations in their marriage records.

By the early eighteenth century, they began specifying infants' race in baptismal books. Yet while the colonial elite were committed to imposing a strict racial hierarchy, neither the Crown nor the Church ever fully institutionalized the system. For instance, while "social practice favored marriage between social and ethnic equals," the Church insisted on protecting "freedom of choice in legitimate marriages."[78] In fact, "Both the ecclesiastical protection and the defense of marriage for love set Hispanic society apart from other European societies in the sixteenth and seventeenth centuries."[79] Without legal restrictions on marriage, the *sistema de castas* was stripped of the most effective method of maintaining ethnic boundaries. Consequently, the *sistema* would remain more social convention than legal reality. Furthermore, "to function effectively, the sistema required a careful and systematic distribution of rights, privileges, and obligations, so that racial divisions would be clearly demarcated. Colonial legislation was far too inconsistent for this purpose. Some laws distinguished between *casta* groups, but others lumped all mixed-bloods together."[80] In other words, the burden of imposing the elite's new racial ideology belonged to the elites themselves.

After the immediate post-conquest period, the white elite generally avoided intermarriage. Even interracial cohabitation among the elite declined after the sixteenth century. As the new colony matured, high-ranking or upwardly mobile Spanish men generally reverted to Iberian social conventions. "They sought to reassert the concept of a clear *linaje* (lineage) by marrying peninsular women, who would preserve cleanliness of blood and legitimacy. Indeed, purity of blood was fundamental to those seeking to become members of the judiciary and the royal bureaucracy and those who aspired to ecclesiastical positions."[81] In other words, "Marital alliances with the 'impure' castas offered [criollos] few advantages. Indeed, insofar as they lowered the family's prestige, such marriages could be very damaging."[82] While this did not mean that members of the elite ceased engaging in sexual affairs with non-Spanish women, it did translate into a preference for light-skinned Spanish women as brides. Interracial mixing continued to occur largely outside of marriage.

This was also true among the lower classes. Not because they shared the elite's prejudices, but because for the first two centuries of the colonial period, they largely eschewed the institution of marriage in general. Despite the Church's campaign to regularize sexual relations in New Spain, illegitimacy rates were extraordinarily high into the seventeenth century—as much as "two-thirds of the births among *castas,* and one-third among [criollos and Spaniards]."[83] In mid-century Guadalajara, 58 percent of all children were born to unmarried couples.[84] For the first two centuries of colonial rule, illegitimacy was largely associated with *castas.*

Nor did *castas* buy into the racial logic that undergirded the *sistema de castas.* Indeed, they generally disdained the pretensions and regulations of polite society. "In particular, race had a different significance for the Spanish elite than for the [lower classes]. The urban poor rejected the elite's notion of a racial hierarchy; instead, as in other areas of culture, the plebeians demonstrated their creativity by redefining 'race' in a way that made sense to them and served their purposes."[85] The average person not only knew little about his racial ancestry, but in everyday life "depended on the assistance, friendship, and goodwill of men and women from a variety of racial groups."[86] According to historian Dennis Nodin Valdés, by the end of the eighteenth century, "There was indeed a great deal of confusion about race in Mexico City. . . . When individuals were required to describe themselves or others in court, their testimony was often inconsistent and contradictory."[87] During the course of a single trial, one person could be labeled with as many as four racial categories. Valdés concluded that in the absence of "clearly defined standards," racial categorization, particularly in the late colonial period, was "subject to human whim."[88] In 1770, Juan Antonio de Areche, an attorney for the Crown, explained the hopelessness of the *casta* system to the viceroy: "The liberty with which the plebs have been allowed to choose the class they prefer, insofar as their color permits, has stained the class of natives as well as that of Spaniards. They very often join the one or the other as it suits them or as they need to."[89]

Still, both civic and Church authorities attempted to record racial labels in the administration of the colony. The Spanish and criollo elite "stressed skin color as a guide to racial status among commoners."[90] But physical appearance was "not a flawless, objective standard."[91] The high level—and many combinations—of racial mixing in New Spain had given rise to a great variety of phenotypic traits. When "Miguel de la Cruz was imprisoned for a debt of thirty pesos in 1707, his creditor identified him as a castizo. Miguel had earlier described himself as a mestizo; and a prison official . . . referred to him as a Spaniard."[92] When describing someone's racial status to authorities, witnesses frequently drew on cultural, in addition to physical, traits. "Several criteria for racial identification existed, some of which could overrule appearance."[93] When Don Francisco Cano Moctezuma was arrested for fraud and witchcraft, his first accuser, María de Rodilla, said that he appeared to be an "*indio amestizado,* that is, an Indian with Hispanic physical and cultural traits."[94] The second witness, Felipe Salazar, also concluded that Cano Moctezuma was mestizo by virtue of his style of dress and the way he spoke. The court, however, based its decision on an entirely different criterion. They determined that Cano Moctezuma was an Indian because of his name. As a result, his case was tried in the court system whose jurisdiction was limited to Indians.

If skin color was an imperfect measure of race, clothing wasn't much better. "The Crown attempted to regulate dress by statute so that Spaniards, castas, and Indians could be easily distinguished."[95] In the 1690s, Gemelli Careri, a visitor from Italy, wrote that "Mestizo, mulatto and black women, who are very numerous in Mexico City, are not allowed to wear veils or to dress according to Spanish fashions. On the other hand, they scorn the Indian dress. They adopt an extravagant garb, wearing a thing like a petticoat, across their shoulders, or on their head, which makes them look like so many devils."[96] These laws, however, were impossible to enforce effectively.

Even close friends could not be expected to know a *casta*'s racial status. "Juana de Mesa, in denouncing a former lover to the [court], described him as a 'castizo or mestizo'; the accused man, Nicolás de Paniagua, succeeded in convincing the [judges] that he was really a Spaniard."[97] Twenty-five-year-old confectioner Juan Cadena referred to himself as a *castizo* in a case his former lover lodged against him. The lover labeled him a mestizo. "Some witnesses sided with one or the other while others said that he was mulatto or a pardo," which was a euphemism for mulatto.[98] Given all the confusion surrounding racial identity, some people weren't sure what to label themselves.

According to court documents, José Leandro Petiño, a twenty-year-old engraver from Tlatelolco, called himself a *castizo* when he first petitioned the court and then a mestizo when he testified later. Further complicating matters, the judge called Petiño "in appearance mestizo, or Indiado (probably of Indian and mestizo parents) or alobado (having black and Indian ancestry)."[99]

In addition to employing race, Spanish authorities had also pointed to high rates of illegitimacy among the *castas* to justify discrimination against them. But by the end of the seventeenth century, the incidence of illegitimacy among the elite began to rise. "Toward 1700, however, the features of the young illegitimate child were less marked, even growing lighter. The observer looking at a [criollo] might now wonder: legitimate or illegitimate?"[100] At the same time, the Church was achieving greater success in imposing the institution of marriage on lower-class *castas*. Their rates of illegitimacy declined dramatically, and a growing number of *castas* were born of legitimately married couples. "What had always been true of Spanish women—relatively high marriage rates and relatively low levels of illegitimacy—began to be true for casta women as well. The process tended to break down the perceived differences of behavior among the races."[101]

As early as the beginning of the seventeenth century—as Indian population loss reached its peak—both public and private Spanish employers were forced to hire *castas* to fulfill their labor needs. As *castas* became integral parts of the colonial economy, it became increasingly difficult to inhibit their social mobility in the way the *sistema de castas* had intended. While a small *casta* elite had existed as early as the late sixteenth century, the economic expansion of the first half of the eighteenth century allowed for unprecedented upward mobility. "The existence of such upwardly mobile castas weakened the association between race and class."[102] It also created racial tensions as socially ambitious *castas* sought to intermarry with the established Spanish elite.

While lower-class *castas* could shrug off the absurdity of the *sistema de castas*, the upwardly mobile "felt the full impact of Spanish racial ideology and were thus particularly jealous of their *buena fama y reputación* [good name and reputation]."[103] Having reached the higher levels of society, they sought the extra prestige and privileges of being considered Spanish. Whereas lighter-skinned mestizos or mulattoes with European features could pass for Spanish, those of darker skin found it more difficult to find acceptance in the upper caste. Some sought to marry spouses with lighter skin so that their children would be considered Spanish. Others bought their way into whiteness. By the eighteenth century, "The number of claimants to white status increased to such proportions that . . . the Crown established a legal procedure to accomplish it. In return for a sum of money, the king granted his American subjects a certificate of whiteness, a *Cédula de Gracias al Sacar.*"[104] As *castas* continued to acquire "the trappings of superior social standing" and intermarried into established families, they devalued "the traditional distinctions of Spanish social status. Not only was the social complexion of colonial Mexico irrevocably altered, but the traditional accoutrements of Spanish social prestige suffered wholesale devaluation."[105] Spanish status was no longer the sine qua non of high social status. Wealth began to replace race as the primary determinant of social position.

After 1720, interracial marriage began to increase in New Spain and would continue to rise for most of the eighteenth century. Many members of the elite saw it as yet another sign of the erosion of their status and lodged what historian Patricia Seed labeled "a full-scale attack on racially mixed marriages."[106] "The preceding two hundred years of interracial activity in New Spain had failed to provoke similar reaction because the unions had been, for the most part, nonmarital, and therefore not a challenge to the fundamental social distinctions of race."[107] As a result, the eighteenth century saw a sharp rise in prenuptial disputes lodged by family members protesting the mixed marriages of relatives. In 1744, the brothers of Don Jacinto Rodríguez de Zuaznavar, a councilman from Querétaro, protested his marriage to his *mulata* concubine, Ana Ocio de Taloya, on the grounds that the union would wind up "tarnishing his illustrious blood with such a hideous stigma, [leading to] ignominy for his house and a fall from honor."[108] Don Jacinto replied that the "scandals . . . and all [they alleged] exist only in the heads of men with law degrees."[109]

In 1776, the Crown imposed new measures designed to curb

"unequal" marriages in the Iberian Peninsula. Two years later, the law was extended to the colonies, where "the issue at stake was racial as well as class-based. The Crown sought to end 300 years of miscegenation. . . . The [new law] was an ex post facto attempt to codify marriage and curb the social porosity of the racial and class make up of the colonies."[110] The legislation now required that all white minors receive permission to marry from their parents or guardians. According to historian Asunción Lavrin, "The law aimed at giving parents veto power over marriage when they deemed that suitors were of mixed ancestry or too lowly in the social scale."[111] The law specifically targeted marriage between whites and any person with African ancestry as well as those between Indians and blacks. To circumvent the Church and its insistence on upholding marital free will, the legislation dictated that all cases arising from the new law be heard in civil rather than ecclesiastical courts.

The new law, however, came much too late to deter the ongoing process of *mestizaje* in New Spain. Indeed, as social status became determined more by money than by race, more parental objections were filed on the basis of class than on racial inequality. By the end of the eighteenth century, "The distinction between descendants of Indians and descendants of slaves, however clear in theory, had become hopelessly muddled in the real world of New Spain."[112] Even the Audiencia, the highest court in the Americas, "refused to define race on the basis of physical appearance or biological heritage, but defined it rather on the basis of social standing. One who was wealthy, whatever his physical appearance, was 'Spanish'; 'race' was only useful as an index of social status if it was not tied to great wealth or influence. If physical appearance was at odds with social status, social status took priority."[113]

Rendered absurd by rampant mixture and social mobility, the *sistema de castas* was abolished. By the end of the colonial period, the dual processes of Hispanicization and miscegenation had undermined two successive Spanish racial systems. After independence in the early nineteenth century, "The gradual physical and cultural homogenization" of Mexico gained greater momentum.[114] A century later, Mexico began to think of itself as a mestizo nation.

Three

The Spaniards Venture North

Spain began searching for an *otro México*—"another Mexico"—as soon as its soldiers had completed the conquest of the old one. Once firmly established in Tenochtitlán, conquistadors began fanning out from the Valley of Mexico to the far reaches of the south, west, and north. The rich rewards of Mexican and Peruvian gold fueled their hopes that more treasure would be found, particularly in the north whose vast terrain elicited legends of cities of gold. But other than the great lodes of silver they discovered in what is now the north-central Mexican state of Zacatecas, the northern frontier never yielded another Tenochtitlán.

By the mid-sixteenth century, it had already become painfully clear that the glory days of conquest were over. In the northern frontier, the rugged terrain, the forbidding climate, and the absence of a large and sophisticated Indian labor force compelled the Spaniards to reconsider their imperial strategy. Over time, the Crown realized that the nomadic hunting Indians of the north, whom the Aztecs contemptuously called Chichimeca—"sons of dogs"—could be more effectively pacified by priests than by soldiers. Thus the mission emerged as the primary means of asserting Spanish control. In 1573, the Franciscans were asked to lead the exploration and pacification of the northern frontier.

Near the end of the sixteenth century, the Spaniards developed yet another approach to pacification. They began sending colonies of Christianized Indians—particularly Tlaxcalans from the Valley of Mexico—to demonstrate to the Indians of the north the advantages of adopting the Catholic faith and Hispanic civilization. In 1591, four hundred Tlaxcalan families that were granted special privileges not usually enjoyed by Indian commoners were resettled in the north. Spanish frontiersmen also brought with them significant numbers of

Tarascans, Otomís, and, later, Opatas. These Indians served their expeditions as scouts, soldiers, strategists, and translators.

Once they had a toehold in the north, the Spaniards utilized newly Christianized local tribes such as the Yaquis, Seris, Tarahumaras, and Mayos as porters and guides in their travels to the far north. Over time, these allied Indians lost their separate ethnic identities by forging intimate unions—licit and illicit—with both Spaniards and the Indians they encountered on their trek northward.

Each northern tribe the Spaniards encountered had its own way of reacting to the intruders. Some resisted fiercely, while others adapted. The Opata Indians, in what is today the Mexican state of Sonora, began intermingling and intermarrying with Spanish settlers almost immediately. But generally the Spaniards were more likely to mix with *genízaros,* Indian slaves or ransomed captives they received from nomadic tribes.

In the mid-1560s, the Spaniards began to move north from Zacatecas in search of more silver. They established their presence in present-day Durango, and later in southern Chihuahua, where, on a tributary to the Conchos River, they founded Santa Bárbara, near what is today the city of Parral. In 1581, Fray Agustín Rodríguez along with two fellow Franciscans and an escort of nine soldiers and sixteen Indians departed Santa Bárbara and followed the Conchos northward. When they met what would later be called the Rio Grande, they followed it north for several hundred miles into the land of the Pueblo Indians, the name the Spaniards gave to a diverse group of farming peoples who lived in towns—*pueblos* in Spanish. The Pueblos' sedentary and culturally sophisticated societies were a welcome discovery for men weary of battling nomadic Indians. Two years later, King Phillip II of Spain authorized the viceroy of New Spain to select a man to spearhead the settlement of what the friars had christened San Felipe de Nuevo México. In 1595 the viceroy commissioned Don Juan de Oñate, an aristocrat from Zacatecas, to lead the settlement expedition. Incidentally, Oñate's wife was a dramatic example of the fusion of the conquistador and the conquered. She was the great-granddaughter of Montezuma and the granddaughter of Hernán Cortés.

After a lengthy delay, the Oñate expedition left Santa Bárbara on

January 26, 1598. Included in his train were "one hundred and thirty soldier-settlers . . . a band of Franciscans under Father [Alonso] Martínez, a large retinue of negro and Indian slaves, seven thousand head of stock, and eighty-three wagons and carts for transporting the women and children and the baggage."[1] Unlike those who were to follow, most of the first settlers were white Spaniards, the majority of whom were Iberian-born. At the end of April 1598, on the banks of the Rio Grande, not far from where El Paso would be founded almost one hundred years later, Oñate formally took possession of New Mexico. In the name of the king of Spain, he declared Spanish control over the Indians and the lands they inhabited, "from the leaves of the trees in the forests to the stones and sands of the river."[2] After the celebration of a solemn High Mass, a few of the settlers performed a play written by one of Oñate's officers that featured local Indians submitting joyfully to the Gospel of Jesus Christ. History, of course, was not destined to play out so harmoniously.

Three months later, the Spaniards established their first New Mexico settlement in San Juan de los Caballeros (north of present-day Santa Fe). From the outset, Indian resistance and food shortages made the colonists anxious. By the summer of 1598, more than a third of Oñate's soldiers were plotting a mutiny, and, with the arrival of winter, they began to prey on the Indians, stealing food and clothing and, despite a new decree outlawing all forms of violence against the Indians, raping and killing. To make matters worse the expeditions sent out from New Mexico failed to find any treasure that would bolster the settlers' hopes. Frustrated, the viceroy of New Spain ultimately concluded that New Mexico offered "nothing but naked people, false bits of coral, and four pebbles."[3]

Had it not been for the missionaries, who refused to abandon their new converts, Spain would have pulled out of New Mexico. In 1610, the territory's new governor, Pedro de Peralta, moved the original settlers to the newly founded town of Santa Fe. For seventy years, the Spaniards maintained only one civil settlement and scattered missions. Some Spaniards lived on farms and ranches along the Rio Grande from Taos to what is now Albuquerque. By 1630, when Santa Fe had a population of only 250, more than two dozen padres were running twenty-five missions with fifty thousand Indians as their wards. Each mission had a school and workshop where converts learned European ways. Three missions were built among the Queres Indians of New Mexico. According to one seventeenth-century priest the Queres were "very dexterous in reading, writing, and playing on all kinds of instruments and are skilled in all the crafts, thanks to the great industry of the friars who converted them."[4]

But the demands the Spaniards made of the Indians—from forced labor and tribute to the harsh regimen of daily mission life—led to growing discontent among the indigenous population. In 1680, the Pueblos united temporarily with the Apaches and Navajo to launch the Pueblo Revolt, which left more than four hundred Spaniards dead, and all the missions and settlements destroyed. Thoroughly routed, 2,500 Spaniards escaped, and New Mexico—which viceregal bureaucrats dubbed "the miserable kingdom"—would not be fully reconquered until the waning years of the seventeenth century. In the eighteenth century, however, the province achieved a humble and self-sufficient stability far removed from the interior of New Spain. With an economy based largely on farming and stock raising, New Mexico became an important buffer against the Plains Indians to the north and the restless French to the east.

Because so few migrants made their way into New Mexico, by 1680 almost 90 percent of the Hispanic population was native-born. Likewise, in the eighteenth century, New Mexico's population growth was driven almost entirely by births. As historian Ramón A. Gutiérrez wrote, "In such a closed and isolated population pool, few Spaniards, whatever their pretense, could have demonstrated racially pure ancestry, and most had undoubtedly become mestizos."[5] Only thirteen of the soldiers who arrived with Oñate in 1598 had brought their wives. As a result, the remaining bachelors "turned to Indian women, to black slaves, and to Apache captives for concubines, mistresses, and occasionally for legal brides."[6] Shortly after arriving in 1598, a certain Juan de la Cruz, nicknamed "El Catalán," married Beatriz de los Angeles, "a Mexican Indian fluent in Spanish and Hispanicized."[7] In colonial New Mexico, *mestizaje* was the rule rather than the exception. In 1631, Fray Estevan de Perea described the colonists as a bunch of "mestizos, mulattos, and zambohijos," the last term referring to the offspring of zambos, who were themselves the children of Indians and blacks.[8] Those *castas* whose lineages were so mixed that they were difficult to parse were simply said to be *de color quebrado*—"of mixed color." While the Pueblo Revolt of 1680 was primarily an indigenous uprising, the Spanish governor of New Mexico, Antonio de Otermín, claimed that some *castas* had also taken part in the rebellion.

By the mid-eighteenth century, sexual relationships between male settlers and female Pueblo Indians were common. Most such unions took the form of concubinage, and the children of these relationships were often rejected by the tribes. If the child was rejected by both the Spaniards and the Indians, they became *hijos de la iglesia,* or children of the Church, which baptized and placed them in Christian homes. But the mixed children of legitimate unions between Pueblos and Spaniards usually lived among the settlers and were accepted as Hispanics. Sometimes, Hispanic households adopted *genízaro* servants into their extended families. Over time, they blended into Hispanic society.

Most *genízaros* in domestic servitude, however, were extremely vulnerable to the darker side of Spanish-Indian sexual relations: rape. Although Indian slavery had been banned in 1542, it persisted in the more remote parts of Spanish America. While many Indian slaves were captured on the battlefield, others were captives purchased from the Comanches and the Apaches. In 1761, Fray Pedro Serrano wrote that "when these barbarians bring a certain number of Indian women to sell, among them many young maidens and girls . . . before delivering them to the Christians who buy them, if they are ten years old or over, they deflower and corrupt them in the sight of innumerable assemblies of barbarians and Catholics."[9]

Pueblo Indian women working in Spanish towns were also vulnerable to sexual abuse. In 1707, the leaders of fourteen *pueblos* lodged a complaint with the viceroy about the many rapes their women had suffered. "When Indian women enter Santa Fe to mill wheat and spin wool they return to their pueblos deflowered and crying over their dishonor or pregnant," Fray Serrano observed.[10] The padres in New Mexico were also reputed to have had more sexual interaction with the local Indian woman than did their brethren in other frontier provinces. Taking advantage of the custom of Pueblo women to offer "their love and bodies in return for gifts and benefits," many, perhaps most, friars had concubines. In 1671, one Franciscan fretted over the fact that "All the pueblos are full of friars' children."[11]

These abuses notwithstanding, Indians enjoyed greater acceptance in New Mexico's Spanish society than they did in central Mexico. By the end of the eighteenth century, "Pueblo Indians, Comanches, Apaches, Navajos, Utes," and *genízaros* "lived in Spanish communities and were readily accepted into the general society. They even married Spaniards and castes and practiced some of the same occupations as those of the settlers."[12] The few blacks in colonial New Mexico also became so thoroughly blended into the gene pool of the Indian and Spanish population that by the start of the nineteenth century they were no longer an identifiable group.

The traditional strategy of contracting socially beneficial marriages in order to move up the social ladder was difficult to maintain on the far northern frontier. So was the elite's practice of selecting spouses in order to maintain racial purity. In short, there were not enough light-skinned Spaniards in New Mexico to perpetuate a "pure" white elite. As a result, racial purity was not as essential to upward mobility in New Mexico as it was in the interior of Mexico. The collection of racial data also proved to be more relaxed on the frontier. Ambitious mestizos, Hispanicized Indians, and mulattoes could "upgrade" their racial status. A nonwhite individual could advance to the next class simply by adopting Spanish ways or by marrying a spouse who claimed greater amounts of Spanish blood. And social mobility was more attainable for mestizos in New Mexico than it was in the Mexican interior. "If a mestizo made a good soldier, he was a welcome member of the community," noted historian Frances V. Scholes. "Many of them attained high military rank, and some became *alcaldes mayores* or members of the cabildo of Santa Fé."[13] Census takers did not scrutinize citizens' racial backgrounds and tended to take respondents at their word. As David J. Weber has written, "inevitably, the frontier population became 'whiter' as Indians and mulattos declared themselves *mestizos*, and *mestizos* described themselves as *españoles*."[14] Nonetheless, the term "Spaniard" did not become fully inclusive and some forms of institutionalized discrimination did persist. For example, the Spanish government continued to insist that the provincial ruling elite be either criollo or *peninsular,* white Spaniards of either American or European birth.

Racial mixture, the demands of frontier life, and the distance from Mexico City all converged to transform Hispanic culture in the far north. Like all frontiers, New Mexico was a place where settlers could more easily elude the strictures of conventional society. And colonists took full advantage of their freedom. "Just as the light of the sun is less powerful at a distance and there is danger of darkness and shadow," a Spanish clergyman wrote of New Mexico, "so, at a distance, from your Majesty and your councils and the pontifical power, one finds provinces as remote as these exposed to great errors and misunderstandings."[15] Life was also shorter on the frontier. A hostile environment, a limited diet, and epidemic diseases took a heavy toll. As a result, Spanish culture and society in New Mexico were not mere replications of what they were in Seville or even Mexico City.

Over time, the Spanish soldiers who had been granted isolated parcels of land near Indian villages developed peaceful relations with their neighbors. Intermarriage often forged ties of kinship and fostered cultural borrowing—of foods, crafts, and methods of agriculture. Spanish culture spread even faster than did the migrants themselves. The settlers introduced plants and animals that changed the local ecology. Their horses, pigs, and cattle, all originally from Spain, forever altered Indian cultures. But in the towns, where Spanish civilization was clearly dominant, Indian foods, languages, and styles of dress also influenced Spanish culture. The Spanish culture and people in New Mexico were so mixed—both culturally and biologically—that religious and civil authorities in Mexico City considered them inferior if not inauthentic. By 1790, estimates historian Antonio Ríos-Bustamante, "anywhere from 70 to 80 percent of the population of Albuquerque were *mestizo* in fact, if not in convention."[16] Describing mid-eighteenth-century Sonora, the territory to the southeast of New Mexico, the German Jesuit Ignaz Pfefferkorn commented that "besides the governor . . . the officers of the Spanish garrisons, and a few merchants . . . there is hardly a true Spaniard" in the area.[17]

New Mexico was the first permanent Spanish settlement on the far northern frontier, and it was to remain the most populous throughout the colonial period. From there, the Spaniards made *entradas,* incursions, into Texas, where the Franciscans led the way, and into Arizona, where the Jesuits founded the first missions. In 1716, after the Spanish determined that the French were encroaching too far to the west, they founded their first settlement in northeast Texas near the Neches River. To protect that first colony from Indian attacks, the Spanish founded a second settlement halfway between northeast Texas and the province of Coahuila, which lay just south of the Rio Grande. Although both civilian and religious authorities wanted to colonize the settlement that was to become San Antonio, Texas, with white Spaniards, most of those willing to risk life and limb for a chance at free land were *castas.* Father Antonio de San Buenaventura de Olivares, the cantankerous Franciscan who founded San Antonio's first mission, San Antonio de Valero—later known as the Alamo—feared that these nonwhite colonists would not remain loyal to Spain. Because they were biologically and culturally mixed, he believed them to be poor exemplars of Spanish culture. After San Antonio was established, Olivares asked the governor of Coahuila, Martín de Alarcón, who was in charge of the civilian settlement, to recruit more *peninsulares*—Iberian-born Spaniards—to colonize the area. On June 22, 1718, Olivares wrote the viceroy, the Marqués de Valero, to request his assistance in convincing Alarcón to send higher-quality citizens. He complained bitterly about the opportunistic treatment the racially mixed settlers meted out to the Indians:

> Such people are bad people, unfit to settle among gentiles, because their customs are depraved, and worse than those of the gentiles themselves. It is they who sow discontent and unrest among them and come to control the Indians to such an extent, that by means of insignificant gifts they make them do what they please. When it is to their interest, they help the Indians in their thefts and evil doings, and they attend their dances and *mitotes* [religious ceremonies] just to get deer and buffalo skins from them. . . . It is with this sort of people, Your Excellency, that he wishes to settle the new site on the San Antonio [River] and the Province of Tejas.[18]

Although Olivares did not get the Spaniards he requested, he was sent more Tlaxcalans, whom he considered good Christian role models for the Indians of the far north. But missionary work was much more problematic among the nomadic and warlike tribes of Texas than among the Pueblos of New Mexico. As a consequence, there was less *mestizaje* between the Hispanic settlers and the local Indians. Nonetheless, having come from the "staging areas in northern Mexico where racial mixing had been prevalent," most settlers to Texas were already mestizos.[19] Indeed, the first Hispanic Texans were often the offspring of unions between Spaniards and Christianized Indians from northern settlements in Coahuila, Nuevo León, and Nuevo Santander. Anthropologist Martha Menchaca argues that discrimination against the *castas* in the more settled parts of New Spain "generated the conditions for their movement toward the northern frontier, where the racial order was relaxed and people of color had the opportunity to own land and enter most occupations."[20] Blacks and mulattoes from northern New Spain—as well as from Louisiana—came to Texas to try their luck. In Texas, it was possible to "earn" one's way out of a lower racial caste through the performance of heroic acts on behalf of the state. Mixed blood soldiers could rise to the rank of officer and even receive the prestigious title of *don,* an achievement less possible in the more established areas of New Spain. In the eighteenth-century, Antonio Gil Y'Barbo, a highly respected mulatto, rose to the rank of lieutenant governor and captain of the colonists in northeast Texas.

As it did in New Mexico, the Spanish caste system broke down rapidly in Texas. Census enumerators allowed people to change their racial categories. Skilled mestizos and *afromestizos,* who worked as carpenters, blacksmiths, and cobblers, often chose to reclassify themselves racially. "Antonio Salazar of Zacatecas, the master mason who directed work on the mission of San José at San Antonio, appears in four different documents between 1789 and 1794 with three different ethnic identities—Indian, mestizo, and Spaniard."[21] In 1779, sculptor Pedro Huízar was listed as a mulatto in the census. But after amassing some money, he was labeled Spanish in 1793. In colonial Texas, socioeconomic mobility trumped racial exclusivity. In 1731, the Crown sent fifty-five white Spaniards from the Canary Islands to San Antonio, where they were to govern the nonwhite population. But though they tried valiantly to preserve their racial purity, over time the Isleños were also subsumed by the mestizo melting pot.

For most of the colonial period, settlers in Texas and Pimería Alta—later to be known as Arizona—lived in fear of the local Indians. Relatively few migrants from central New Spain could be induced to settle there. The colonial population reached four thousand at the turn of the nineteenth century. Most people who moved to the region settled in Nuevo Santander, south of the Rio Grande. Arizona's hot climate made it an even less desirable destination. Its population was the smallest of New Spain's northwest territories, growing only through the conversion of the indigenous population. In time, many of the settlers were Hispanicized Indians. But while the missionaries did manage to convert many Indians, the Navajos and most Apaches continued to resist the Spanish, making Arizona one of the most hostile frontiers in the Spanish empire.

Alta California was the last territory Spain colonized on the far northern frontier. King Charles III decided to colonize the region after Russia began establishing settlements along the Pacific coast. The founding expedition was to have consisted of five distinct phases— three voyages by sea and two land expeditions. The first objective was to occupy Monterey and San Diego, sites of the territory's two most valuable natural harbors. But Spain's failure to establish successful colonies in Baja California made its goal of taking Alta California all the more difficult to accomplish. Starting in 1697, the Jesuits had built a chain of seventeen missions in Baja California, but no adjoining towns were developed. The Jesuits wanted it that way. They preferred to perform their labor of conversion in isolation without the added burden of dealing with the seductions and depredations of Spanish laymen. But after Charles III expelled the Jesuits from the Americas in 1767—he feared their resistance to his secular reforms—even Baja California's missions fell into disrepair.

Nonetheless, José de Gálvez, New Spain's inspector general and the man Charles III had commissioned to occupy Alta California, insisted on pushing northward from Baja California. To lead the expedition to Monterey, he selected Captain Gaspar de Portolá, the governor of Baja California, Fray Junípero Serra, a Franciscan who had been sent to manage the missions that the Jesuits were forced to abandon, and Captain Fernando Rivera y Moncada, the commander of the presidio, or military fort, at Loreto. The plan was to have three ships depart Baja California headed north to San Diego, followed by two land parties. Once the expeditions were reunited in San Diego, Portolá would continue on land to Monterey Bay. But the journey to Alta California was a torturous one. One ship was lost, and scores of men on the other two had either fallen ill or died. While the expedition led by Rivera y Moncada suffered relatively few casualties, the company headed by Portolá and Serra shrank drastically from fifty-nine to twenty-seven members. When the expeditions met in San Diego, only 150 survivors remained to colonize the territory, many of them Christianized Indians from Baja California. Still, in July of 1769, Father Serra established San Diego de Alcalá, the first in a chain of missions in Alta California. That same month, Portolá departed for Monterey Bay, where a presidio was founded eleven months later.

Initially, the diverse tribes of California's coastal Indians greeted the newcomers amiably. But the Spaniards soon wore out their welcome by blatantly disregarding Indian customs and property rights, and abusing their women. Having traveled a large distance without Hispanic women, many soldiers resorted to assaulting local women. "It is as though a plague of immorality had broken out," Father Serra wrote.[22] As David Weber has observed, either the "sexual violence toward Indian women" . . . [was] "more excessive than on earlier frontiers or [it was] better documented."[23] At the very least, Spanish authorities took these crimes seriously. In 1785, Governor Pedro de Fages issued an order: "Observing that the officers and men of these presidios are comporting and behaving themselves in the missions with a vicious license which is very prejudicial because of the scandalous disorders which they incite among the [Indian] and Christian women, I command you, in order to prevent the continuation of such abuses that you circulate a prohibitory edict imposing severe penalties upon those who commit them."[24] In a practice reminiscent of what occurred during the conquest of Mexico, some Indian men offered tribal women to the Spaniards in order to better their own circumstances. In 1780, Father Serra complained about an Indian leader at the San Gabriel Mission who "was supplying women to as many soldiers as asked for them."[25]

Father Serra also began promoting intermarriage as a means to discourage attacks against Indian women. According to historian Antonia I. Castañeda, Serra viewed the practice as "a way to establish Catholic family life" and "to foster alliances between the soldiers and the Indians."[26] He saw to it that soldiers who married "daughters of the land" received farm animals, a horse, and land to cultivate. The first such marriages in Alta California took place at the Mission San Carlos Borromeo near Monterey in 1773. Three Rumsien Indian women, baptized as Margarita Domínguez, María Serafina, and María de Gracia, took three Catalan soldiers as husbands. Later that year, three more mixed couples were married at Mission San Antonio de Padua near Monterey and three at San Luis Obispo. From 1773 to 1778, 37 percent of marriages in Monterey were between Hispanic men—be they Spanish, mestizo, black, or other *casta*—and Indian women.[27] But colonial officials did not consider the number of mestizos that issued from such intermarriages sufficient to settle Alta California. Beginning in 1774, Fernando Rivera y Moncada and Juan Bautista de Anza made three expeditions to Guadalajara and the northern provinces of Sonora and Sinaloa to recruit and bring back settlers to Alta California. The first expedition, which arrived at San Diego on September 26, 1774, was made up mostly of women and children. These were the first non-Indian Hispanic females to reach Alta California. As historian Charles E. Chapman wrote, "though their whiteness of skin was undoubtedly tinged with Indian red, they were suitable wives for a limited number of soldiery and by their children were able to contribute yet more to the permanence of the colony."[28]

The truth of the matter was that there were very few Spaniards of "pure" European lineage available to populate Alta California. As a result, by 1794, the majority of Spanish-speaking persons in the Californias—Alta and Baja—were officially categorized as mixed bloods.[29] The majority of the colonists that de Anza had recruited in Sinaloa in 1775 were poor mestizos seeking an opportunity to improve their lot. In 1777, only one-third of the men and one-fourth of the women who founded San Francisco and San José identified themselves as white Spaniards.[30]

Less than half of the third recruiting expedition, which was organized in Sonora and Sinaloa by Rivera y Moncada, reached Alta California. Rivera and 131 other settlers, priests, and soldiers were massacred by Yuma Indians as they made their way across the inhospitable Sonora desert. Fortunately, the expedition had been split into two divisions that took separate routes. The majority of the families who went on to found the *pueblo* of Los Angeles and the *presidio* at Santa Barbara had some African ancestry. Of the original forty-six settlers of Los Angeles, twenty-six were either African or part-African.[31] Antonio Mesa, a thirty-six-year-old "negro" from Los Alamos, his *mulata* wife, Ana Gertrudes López, twenty-seven, and their two children were among the first Angelenos. But heavy intermarriage among the earliest Angelenos quickly absorbed those of African ancestry until blacks soon disappeared as an identifiable group. Of the eleven first couples, "seven involved some degree of intermarriage and hybridization, while two involved persons already of hybrid ancestry."[32] Only two marriages—between Indian men and women—did not involve racial mixture.

Having been contracted to work early on by Los Angeles's settlers, the local Indians had close contact with the newcomers. Pedro de Fages, the governor of Alta California, even warned of the "pernicious familiarity that is had in the pueblo with the gentile Indians."[33] The Indian settlement adjacent to the *pueblo* of Los Angeles was made up of individuals from a variety of tribes from near and far. These were people who wished to reap the material benefits of living near the Spanish settlement without having to shoulder the burdens of life in nearby San Gabriel Mission. These Indians could earn "handkerchiefs, food, cast-off clothing, knives and other tools, and *avalorios,* the strings of beads" that they valued as currency.[34] Many absorbed Hispanic culture through their proximity to the settlers and ranchers. In 1795 Father Vicente de Santa María noted that "the whole pagandom . . . is fond of the Pueblo of Los Angeles. . . . Here we see nothing but pagans passing, clad in shoes, with sombreros and blankets, and serving as muleteers to the settlers and rancheros." For their part, the Spaniards benefited greatly from the Indians' cooperation. "If it were not for the [Indians] there would be neither pueblo nor rancho," Father Vicente added.[35]

In some cases, the cultural borrowing was mutual. San Gabriel Mission priests Luis Gil y Taboada and José María Zalvidea noted that the Indians "who deal more with the people of the other classes, especially with the settlers of the town, speak Spanish, though these settlers commonly speak the Indian idiom also, and even better and more fluently than their own language, which is the Spanish."[36] Some marriages created even closer ties between the Hispanic and Indian populations. The first such marriage in Los Angeles occurred three years after the *pueblo*'s founding. Carlos Rosas married María Dolores, an Indian woman from Yabit, the neighboring Indian village. A few months later, Carlos's brother Máximo married María Antonia. Both women were baptized so that they could marry the Rosas brothers. Twelve years later, another Rosas brother, Marcelino, married María Vejar, a neophyte from the San Gabriel Mission.[37]

Marriages also occurred at nearby *presidios*. Four Hispanic soldiers married Indian women at San Juan Capistrano between 1778 and 1781. At San Buenaventura in present-day Ventura County, Bartolomé Miguel Ortega married María Rosa. The couple later bought a ranch near Malibu called Las Virgenes. It was much less common for Hispanic women to marry Indian men. Yet it sometimes happened. At San Buenaventura, as many Hispanic women married Indians as did men. In 1820, Manuela Quijada wed Policarpo; years later Teresa Verdugo married Antonio de la Cruz.[38] Still, intermarriage became much less common after the Crown reversed its policy of providing land incentives to settlers in the early 1790s. In Monterey, no Indian-Spanish intermarriages were recorded after 1798. Paradoxically, however, with the passage of time, the local Indians became increasingly acculturated to the dominant Hispanic culture. As historian Douglas Monroy has noted, "at the same time as Indians . . . and Hispanics were polarizing, they were also amalgamating."[39]

California was home to perhaps the largest concentration of Indians anywhere in what is now the continental United States. By and large, they did not offer strong resistance to the Spaniards. By the turn of the nineteenth century, the missionaries had converted more than fifty thousand neophytes to Christianity. The mostly heavily Christianized Indians were the Chumash, who lived in what is today Ventura and San Luis Obispo counties. By 1803, 85 percent of the Chumash had relocated to the missions, where they learned the Gospel but were reduced to virtual servitude by the Spaniards.[40] But as occurred elsewhere in the Spanish empire, European diseases took a deadlier toll on the indigenous population than did forced labor. Along the coast, the Indian population declined from about sixty thousand in 1769 to about 35,000 in 1800.[41]

In the meantime, California's Hispanic population, which enjoyed a low infant mortality rate, grew from 990 in 1790 to 1,800 in 1800. By the end of the Spanish period in 1821, the Hispanic population had reached 3,200.[42] But census data on the racial backgrounds of settlers was not anywhere as straightforward. As in other territories on the northwestern frontier, settlers routinely reclassified themselves racially. Historian Jack D. Forbes compiled a list of settlers of Los Angeles who changed their race between 1781 and 1790. "The changes in racial classification were all away from Indian or mulatto and towards *Español*, i.e., everyone acquired some fictitious Caucasian ancestry and shed Negro backgrounds—becoming, in effect, lighter as they moved up the social scale."[43] A person who claimed three-quarters Indian and one-quarter Spanish background was classified as a *coyote*.

NAME	RACE IN 1781	RACE IN 1790
Pablo Rodríguez	Indian	Coyote
Manuel Camero	Mulatto	Mestizo
José Moreno	Mulatto	Mestizo
María Guadalupe Pérez	Mulatto	Coyote
Basilio Rosas	Indian	Coyote
José Vanegas	Indian	Mestizo
José Navarro	Mestizo	Español
María Rufina Navarro	Mulatto	Mestizo (or Indian)

Yet, despite the racial mixture and the fluid nature of racial categories, whiteness was still a privileged status in frontier society. While nonwhite ancestry may not have been an insurmountable barrier to upward mobility, California's racially mixed elites still adhered to the pretense of whiteness. This pretense would help some integrate more easily into the wave of Anglo-Americans that was on the verge of changing California society. New England patrician Richard Henry Dana, who visited California in 1835–1836, described the very few Californios, the state's native-born Hispanics, who were of "pure Spanish blood" and whose complexions were "as fair as those of

English-women." Given that Spanish civil and religious authorities still discriminated in favor of whites when appointing top administrators, it makes sense that these few "pure" whites were described as being "mostly in official stations, or, who, on the expiration of their offices, have settled here upon property, which they have acquired."[44]

By the dawn of the nineteenth century, however, the Spanish caste system that favored whites, especially those born on the Iberian Peninsula, was coming under increasing strain in New Spain. In 1809, a year after Napoleon Bonaparte kidnapped the Spanish king, the Cortes, the Spanish parliament, assumed the reins of government and made Spain a constitutional monarchy. To head off any colonial rebellions, over the next few years the Cortes passed legislation designed to better integrate Indians and mestizos into Spanish society and its economy. By the first decade of the nineteenth century, nonwhites made up four-fifths of New Spain's population of a little more than six million. The lion's share of nonwhites constituted the lower classes. While their status had improved over the years in central Mexico, there was growing discontent with a caste system that allocated varying levels of power, privilege, and position on the basis of race and place of birth. In 1811, the Cortes opened craft guilds to nonwhites, thereby increasing their chances of achieving upward mobility. Before that time, only *peninsulares* and criollos could become master craftsmen. A year later, legislators passed the Law of Cádiz, which declared that Indians, mestizos, criollos, and *peninsulares* were all equal under the law.[45]

Because racial restrictions were already more relaxed on the far northern frontier, the new laws did not have a profound economic effect. But they did allow nonwhites to improve their lot politically and socially. More significantly, nonwhites were now eligible for high-level civil and religious posts. However, when King Fernando VII was returned to the Spanish throne in 1814, the reform movement was brought to a halt. By that time, however, the colony's War of Independence against Spain was already well underway. In 1810, the colonial order, which had endured for three centuries, exploded in a revolution that would last more than a decade and result in an independent Mexican republic.

Mexicanidad—Mexicanness—of course, preceded the existence of independent Mexico. With independence, Mexico's nascent nationality was transformed into a nation. Long before independence was achieved in 1821, the criollos had developed a creole patriotism whose themes would later become part and parcel of Mexican nationalism. Weary of being treated as second-class elites by *peninsulares,* criollos had begun to embrace a New World identity, ceasing to view themselves as merely transplanted Spaniards in America. The Spaniards often viewed criollos, most of whom had never set foot in Spain, as congenitally tainted by their American origins. Consequently, the descendants of the original conquerors—as well as the children of later Spanish immigrants—began to forge "a distinctively Mexican consciousness based in large measure upon a repudiation of their Spanish origins."[46] Perhaps ironically, the emergent criollo nationalism denigrated the conquest and exalted the Aztec past. They resented the Spaniards whom they derisively called *gachupines* and were devoted to the Virgen de Guadalupe, the quintessential symbol of New Spain's mestizo culture. Around two a.m. on September 16, 1810, Miguel Hidalgo y Costilla, the criollo priest who started the War of Independence, launched his campaign under a banner of the Virgin, shouting "Death to the *gachupines!*"

For the people of the far northern frontier, the Mexican period was a brief interlude between the Spanish and American periods. It would only last fifteen years in Texas, and only a dozen more in California, Arizona, and New Mexico. The Constitution of 1824 made Mexico a federal republic and made citizens out of subjects. The Estados Unidos Mexicanos were organized into nineteen states and four territories. While California and New Mexico remained territories, Texas became part of the state of Coahuila y Tejas, and Arizona was the northern edge of the state of Sonora. The Constitution, which was modeled in part after that of the United States, also promoted more regional autonomy and, in the spirit of the Law of Cádiz, proclaimed that all races and classes, with the exception of slaves, were equal under the law.

By independence, most provincial censuses had long since ceased collecting racial data. By the beginning of the nineteenth century, the Catholic Church, whose priests conducted such surveys, discouraged the practice on the grounds that the data was used for discriminatory purposes and that rampant *mestizaje* had rendered most categories obsolete. Instead, priests began to record cultural categories. Whites, mestizos, and detribalized Indians who spoke Spanish and practiced Hispanic traditions were recorded within the broad category of *gente de razón,* or people of reason. A person who spoke an indigenous language and practiced pre-Columbian ways was classified as an Indian. In New Mexico, according to historian Ramón Gutiérrez, "Beginning in 1800 the proportion of racial status labels declined both in absolute terms and in relation to civic status, nationality, and 'no mentions.' . . . The intermediate hues of race, so important between 1760 and 1799, had begun to disappear from the records."[47]

Even more important to the people of the northern frontier were the immigration policies of the new republic. In 1824 the Mexican Congress passed the Colonization Law, which "guaranteed land, security, and exemption from taxes for four years to foreign settlers."[48] Mexican officials had been pressing for a more liberal immigration policy since the final days of Spanish rule. In January 1821, Moses Austin became the first Anglo American to be granted permission to settle in Texas. After Moses's death, his son Stephen petitioned authorities of the newly independent Mexico to become an empresario, whereby he would be granted land in exchange for settling three hundred families. Each family would be granted around three thousand acres along the Brazos River. The only requirements were that they obey Mexican law, learn to speak Spanish, and convert to Catholicism.

Some Mexican officials did question the wisdom of colonizing the far north with settlers from an adjoining—and expanding—nation. But by the time the Mexican Congress passed the Colonization Law, Austin's colony was such a success that roughly three thousand Anglo Americans had migrated to Texas and were squatting illegally on Mexican land. Lacking the military capacity to expel them, Mexico chose to placate the migrants and secure their loyalty by granting them land. The new immigration law also allowed individual states to devise their own policies toward migrants. In 1825, the Congress of Coahuila y Tejas agreed to grant Anglo settlers additional land if they married Mexican women. Legislators hoped that such marriages would facilitate Anglo assimilation into Mexican culture. A similar federal law was passed in 1823 that stated: "All foreigners who come to establish themselves in the Empire, and those who, following a profession or industry, in three years, have sufficient capital to support themselves with decency and are married, shall be considered naturalized; those who, under the foregoing conditions, marry Mexican women, acquire a special right to have their letters of citizenship given them."[49]

Without knowing it, the Anglo newcomers were paving the way for the eventual American conquest of the region. For their part, many frontier Mexicans were convinced that Anglo Americans were a positive addition to the borderlands. They foresaw great advantage in forging stronger ties to the United States and viewed Anglo migrants not only as go-betweens who would improve relations between Mexico and the United States, but as welcome representatives of a burgeoning economic system.

By the time officials in Mexico City became alarmed at the number of Americans in Texas it was too late. By 1830, Anglo Americans outnumbered Mexicans 25,000 to four thousand. Even then, Tejano (Texas Mexican) elites, aware that Anglo settlers had invigorated the economy, argued against new laws designed to curb American migration. Seven of San Antonio's wealthiest residents, including José Antonio de la Garza, Angel Navarro, and Juan Angel Seguín, signed a petition testifying to the contributions Anglo Americans had made to the state. "The industrious, honest North American settlers have made great improvements in the past seven or eight years," the petition proclaimed. "They have raised cotton and cane and erected gins and sawmills. Their industry has made them comfortable and independent, while the Mexican settlements, depending on the pay of the soldiers among them for money, have lagged far behind."[50] Similarly, in 1830, José Francisco Ruiz, a prominent citizen of San Antonio who had been dispatched to establish a military post to prevent further Anglo migration, wrote to his friend Stephen Austin, "I cannot help seeing advantages which, to my way of thinking, would result if we admitted honest, hard-working people, regardless of what country they come from . . . even hell itself."[51]

These commercial ties had cultural implications. By the early nineteenth century, contacts with the Americans changed the way Texas

Mexicans spoke their native Spanish. As American influence grew, the English language insinuated itself into the Spanish spoken in Texas. In 1828 José María Sánchez, a sublieutenant in the Mexican artillery corps sent to Texas as a member of a federal investigative team, was appalled at the state of Mexican culture on the northern frontier. "Accustomed to the continued trade with the North Americans," he noted in his diary, "[Tejanos] have adopted their customs and habits, and one may say truly that they are not Mexicans except by birth, for they even speak Spanish with marked incorrectness."[52]

In West Texas, where early Anglo settlers mixed into a predominantly Mexican society, ethnic relations were relatively good. Before the Texas Revolution against Mexico broke out in 1836, many wealthy Mexicans in San Antonio admired American political ideals. They welcomed American newcomers into their homes. In 1831, Kentucky-born Jim Bowie married Ursula Veramendi, the daughter of Juan Martín de Veramendi, governor of the province of Texas and vice governor of the state of Coahuila y Tejas. From 1837, one year after Texas gained its independence, until 1860, "at least one daughter from almost every [wealthy] family in San Antonio married an Anglo."[53] In 1828, a visiting Swiss scientist observed that the blending of aspects of American culture into San Antonio society made San Antonians "a little different from the Mexicans of the interior."[54] At least one prominent Mexican diplomat, Juan Nepomuceno Almante, who later became Mexican minister to Washington, believed that the state of Coahuila y Tejas should be officially bilingual and that all laws and state business should be translated into English.

But racial blending was decidedly not the norm in the areas of Texas in which Anglo settlers predominated. The majority of Americans were isolated in Anglo-majority colonies in eastern and central Texas. Not only did they vastly outnumber Mexicans there, but the Mexican government exercised little control over the colonists. In 1828, Mexican General Manuel Mier y Terán became alarmed at the antagonism that existed between the Mexicans and Americans in Nacogdoches. In East Texas, Anglos did not feel compelled to assimilate into Mexican culture. Many viewed themselves as superior to the Mexicans. They sent their children to English schools or to secondary schools up north. Even as Tejanos became increasingly dependent on American trade, it was unclear how much naturalized American settlers valued their newly gained Mexican citizenship. In 1825, Mexico's minister to Washington told colleagues in Mexico City that American journalists wrote openly that "the colonists in Texas will not be Mexicans more than in name."[55]

While Texas was their main destination in Mexico, growing numbers of Anglo Americans also began to migrate to New Mexico and California. Whereas most Anglos in Texas were colonists, the earliest Americans to New Mexico tended to be trappers and traders. The opening of the Santa Fe Trail had strengthened commercial ties between the United States and New Mexico. In 1821, William Becknell, "the Father of the Santa Fe Trail," led a trading party into northern Mexico. Once in Santa Fe, New Mexican governor Facundo Melgares invited the Missourians to his office, where he expressed interest in promoting greater trade with Americans. Ultimately, it was the profitability of Becknell's visit that encouraged more Americans to head south, where Taos became their base of operations. Since the Americans exported cloth and various manufactured goods, the Mexicans sold them wool, gold, rugs, and mules. As trade boomed, more Americans began to settle in New Mexico and mix with the Mexican population. Kit Carson, one of the most successful early traders, married his third wife, María Josefa Jaramillo, at Guadalupe Church in Taos. They had seven children. Like Carson, who converted to Catholicism, many of the early Anglo settlers integrated into New Mexican society, which was many times larger and more sophisticated than either Texas or California. By 1841, fifteen of the twenty-two Americans in Taos had either married or lived with local Mexican women.[56]

This high rate of intermarriage has led historian Rebecca McDowell Craver to conclude that New Mexicans, "both rich and poor, male and female, readily accepted many of the new arrivals as settlers in their midst. The initial contact between Mexicans and non-Hispanic foreigners in New Mexico seems to have been not a clash of cultures but a cooperative fusion."[57] The Mexican partners represented a cross section of New Mexican society. While some couples simply cohabited, others married after having children. Kentuckian Simon Turley, also known as Francisco Toles, lived with María Rosita Vigil y Romero, who bore him seven children. In 1839, New Orleans journalist Matt Field attended a wedding in Santa Fe between an American man, who had arrived in the territory five years before, and "a dark-eyed Mexican brunette of about twenty."[58] "Just as this ceremony concluded, three merry little children came bouncing into the room, the oldest a girl, and the other two dark haired and dark eyed boys, bearing a strong resemblance to the bride. They flew to our American friend, the bridegroom . . . the children were his own."[59]

For many U.S.-born men, marriage to a Mexican woman helped them acquire Mexican citizenship and thereby legitimate their trading or trapping businesses. Some men who married into prominent families gained access to land, but most newcomers wed women of modest means. All tended to blend into Mexican society, and some even became respected local politicians. Antoine and Charles Robidoux moved from Missouri to New Mexico, lived with Mexican women, and eventually ran for political office. Both were elected president of the Santa Fe city council. In 1844, Mariano Martínez, the governor of New Mexico, appointed Irishman John Scolly (Juan Escolle), the husband of Juana López, to a committee in charge of planning that year's Mexican Independence Day celebration.

For women, the legacy of white privilege in Spanish and colonial society may have created a preference for fair-skinned men. The tradition of the upwardly mobile to whiten their identities may have encouraged New Mexican women to seek "whiter" babies with American men. Some New Mexican families benefited socially from the marriage of their daughters to *norteamericanos*. Through marriage, the families broadened their contacts with the prosperous nation to the northeast. By the 1830s, some of the most prominent New Mexican merchant families, the Chávezes, Pereas, and Pinos, were having their sons educated in St. Louis or New York. But in addition to the practical value of such marriages, love and physical attraction must also have played a key role. During the Mexican period, more than 70 percent of Anglo-Mexican couples in New Mexico had children, producing "at least two hundred and seventy-three children."[60] Like their Spanish-speaking children, the American fathers lived in adobe houses, and ate *tortillas, pozole,* and *frijoles.* During the Mexican period, most children of mixed couples were raised as Hispanics and, with few exceptions, married Mexicans themselves. But after the arrival of American conquering forces in 1846 more daughters of mixed unions began to marry Anglo men. Undoubtedly, their marital choices reflected the shifting social and political winds.

Anglo-Mexican intermarriage was also common in California, particularly among the elites. While California officials initially distrusted its first overland visitors—Governor José María Echeandía had trapper Jedediah Smith jailed—Californios generally welcomed the Americans and other foreigners who began to trickle into the territory in the 1820s. Over the next two decades, California received more settlers than did New Mexico in the same period. But the numbers were never large. Nonetheless, their business acumen and connections gave the recent arrivals disproportionate influence in their new home. In the 1820s and 1830s, most foreigners not only did not establish separate colonies but they assimilated into Hispanic culture. In 1841, naturalized Mexican citizen and future U.S. congressman John Bidwell noted that California's foreign settlers were "scattered throughout the whole Spanish population, and most of them have Spanish wives . . . they live in every respect like the Spaniards."[61] In fact, most Californio elites—like the Picos, Carrillos, and de la Guerras—had Anglo in-laws. Among them were Abel Stearns, a leading trader from Massachusetts, who became a naturalized Mexican citizen and married Arcadia Bandini, the daughter of Southern California rancher Juan Bandini. Bandini family ties helped make Stearns the largest landowner in the region.

Though many early Americans writers did not reciprocate the feeling, Californios generally admired America and Americans. Even after it had become clear that the settlers were a threat to Mexican sovereignty, many Californio observers gave the industrious Americans their due. In the 1840s, after the type and tenor of Anglo migration had changed, Pío Pico, the last Mexican governor of Alta California, wrote: "We find ourselves threatened by hordes of Yankee immigrants who have already begun to flock into our country and whose progress we cannot arrest. . . . Whatever that astonishing people will next undertake I cannot say, but on whatever enterprise they embark they will be sure to be successful."[62] When Mexico City

finally attempted to curb foreign immigration, Californians continued to receive Americans warmly. Territorial officials were reluctant
to order overland immigrants back over the mountains. In a letter to
a friend, California military commander José Castro wrote of the
conflict between his sense of "duty" and "the sentiment of hospitality
which characterizes the Mexican people."[63] But at least some of the
Californios' hospitality was motivated by self-interest. In 1840, Santa
Barbaran Pablo de la Guerra told a friend that foreigners were
"about to overrun us, of which I am very glad, for the country needs
immigration in order to make progress."[64] Even those who eventually became wary of American immigration, like General Mariano
Guadalupe Vallejo, admired the Americans and had close ties to the
newcomers. Not only did three of his sisters marry Americans, but all
but one of his children married foreigners. Years later, Vallejo would
write, "The arrival of so many people from the outside world was
highly satisfying to us [Northern Californians] who were . . . gratified
to see numerous parties of industrious individuals come and settle
among us permanently. Although they were not possessed of wealth,
due to their goodly share of enlightenment, they could give a powerful stimulus to our agriculture which, unfortunately, was still in a
state of inactivity."[65]

Like other prominent Californios, Vallejo learned English in order
to better engage his American contacts. Though early newcomers did
learn Spanish, English increasingly became the language of commerce. Just as migrants adopted many Hispanic ways, they in turn
introduced their own cultural attributes and values to California society and culture. Juan Bautista Alvarado, governor of California from
1836 to 1842, recalled that the "foreigners gradually modified our
customs."[66] Early Anglo immigrants had so successfully insinuated
themselves into local society that the provincial delegate to the Mexican Congress noted that Californios treated them "as brothers"
whose "ties of marriage and property" made their bond all the
stronger.[67] Successive Mexican governors granted Americans large
amounts of land. Mexican officials remained receptive to American
settlers until the end of Mexican rule. But as the Mexican period wore
on, growing numbers of foreign migrants settled in isolated colonies
and failed to integrate into Californio society. Many resented being

governed by people to whom they felt superior. The 1836 Texas Revolution against Mexico certainly made Mexicans more wary of the Americans' intentions in California, and it may have also made the newcomers less solicitous to the concerns of their hosts. In 1846, there were over seven thousand Hispanics, 1,300 mostly U.S.-born immigrants, and 64,000 Christian Indians in California.[68] Four short years later, the state's non-Indian population had reached 92,000. By 1852, the state had 250,000 people, and Mexicans were a small and increasingly displaced minority. The Anglo American frontier had expanded from coast to coast and its standard-bearers showed little interest in assimilating the people who had inhabited these lands before them.

Four

Mexicans and the Limits of Slavery

An estimated 200,000 Africans, most of them slaves, arrived in New Spain during the colonial period.[1] But by the time New Spain became independent Mexico in 1821, blacks had almost disappeared into a mixed race society. In 1822, an Anglo American visitor saw so few blacks in Mexico City that he thought they had become "nearly extinct."[2] Like other groups, Africans mixed into the melting pot that was the New World. With a ratio of African women to men at less than one in four, black slaves usually took Indian women as mates. Because Spanish law dictated that mixed black-Indian children born of indigenous women were born legally free, within one generation Afro-Indian—as well as mulatto—offspring made up the largest portion of the population of African descent. By the end of the colonial era, very few black slaves remained. In part because it threatened virtually no vested interests, by the early nineteenth century abolitionism was a popular cause in Mexico.

Slavery was a major point of contention between Anglo settlers and the Mexican government. While Mexico's attempts to curb the Peculiar Institution in Texas were mostly halfhearted, they nonetheless succeeded in inhibiting its development. Anglo American settlers, many of them Southern slaveholders who brought their slaves with them, were anxious about the uncertain future of slavery under Mexican rule. In the fall of 1829, President Vicente Guerrero issued a decree emancipating slaves throughout Mexico. Less than three months later, however, he issued a second order exempting Texas from the general emancipation. While many Mexican officials were sincerely opposed to slavery, they were also convinced that it was necessary for Texas's development.

While the immediate actual causes of the Texas rebellion were Mexico's instability and the resistance of American settlers to a more centralized Mexican government, tensions over slavery were never far from the surface. As historian Eugene Barker noted, slavery in Mexican Texas persisted "like a dull organic ache."[3] In 1827, the Congress of the state of Coahuila y Tejas issued an order demanding that "no one shall be born a slave in the state, and after six months the introduction of slaves under any pretext shall not be permitted."[4] But American settlers quickly found a way to circumvent these new restrictions. Before leaving the United States, owners appeared with their slaves before a notary public and drafted legal documents proving that each slave had chosen to follow his master to Texas. The slave was then legally free, but he now owed his value plus the cost of moving to his master, a debt he could only pay through servitude. In other words, despite Mexico's crude attempts to inhibit slavery, American-owned slaves were as firmly in servitude in Mexican Texas as they had been in the United States.

Still, free blacks and runaway slaves from the United States sometimes made their way to Mexican Texas, where they "found themselves in a society where they enjoyed juridical equality as well as considerable tolerance of racial differences."[5] The racial prejudice that did exist on the New Spain frontier was much tamer than that which they encountered in the United States. In 1833, a former slave working as a blacksmith in San Antonio claimed that "Mexicans pay him the same respect as to other laboring people, there being no difference made here on account of color."[6] While frontier Mexicans were not oblivious to race and tended to favor lighter-skinned individuals, "skin color alone was not a major obstacle to social advancement."[7]

Because racial categories in Mexico's northern frontier were more fluid than they were in the United States, the upwardly mobile could achieve a degree of "whiteness" distancing themselves from their Indian or black ancestry. Furthermore, Mexicans defined people by culture and class in addition to race. While Anglo Americans viewed black or Indian as purely racial—and as such inflexible—classifications, Mexicans understood them as cultural categories as well. An Indian was not simply someone with Indian blood, but he was also an individual who behaved, dressed, and spoke "like an Indian." A mid-nineteenth-century American visitor to the Southwest commented that while nomadic Indians hostile to Mexican settlements were considered *indios* by the Mexicans, those assimilated natives who spoke Spanish and lived largely according to Hispanic custom were considered Mexicans.[8] When race is considered a question of culture, it is a more fluid and even changeable category.

For three centuries Spain had sought to maintain a separation between the races in Mexico by imposing a hierarchical racial order. Whites, blacks, mestizos, and Indians were assigned different levels of access to property, power, and prestige. But through the centuries, racial mixing eroded both the categories and the strict racial order that relied on them. Legal racial categories came to have little value as they described fewer and fewer people of flesh and blood. As categorization became more illogical and hence more difficult to enforce, race became secondary to class as a means of social stratification. The system of racial hierarchy had broken down even more rapidly on the northern frontier. For one, there were very few Spaniards of "pure" European lineage available to settle the north, so most pioneers were mestizos, Hispanicized Indians, or blacks. As on other frontiers, the absence of a large pool of native workers also tended to democratize the northwest by making it imperative for pioneers to work with their hands. Located as they were so far from the seat of government, the northern outposts were also largely out of reach of the government's methods of social control. The rigid racial hierarchy was further weakened by Mexican independence and the liberal philosophical underpinnings of the movement for sovereignty.

While the Texas Revolution may not have been an explicit struggle over slavery, both sides recognized that its outcome would inevitably determine the future of the institution. In 1836, orator and Texas revolutionary leader William H. Wharton indicated that Anglo American leaders understood the implications that the Texas independence movement had for slavery. The Mexicans, he wrote, were threatening Anglo Texans with a "sickly philanthropy worthy of the abolitionists of these United States."[9] Likewise, in February of that year, General Antonio López de Santa Anna wrote the Mexican minister of war and marine stating that "There is a considerable number of slaves in Texas . . . who have been introduced by their masters under cover of certain questionable contracts, but who according to our laws should be free. Shall we permit those wretches to moan in chains any longer in a country whose kind laws protect the liberty of man without distinction of caste or color?"[10]

After Sam Houston's troops routed General Santa Anna's overconfident Mexican army at San Jacinto in April 1836, slavery was secured in the Lone Star State for one more generation. But even in the Texas Republic, Mexicans and Mexico continued to be viewed as threats to slavery. In October of 1854 the *Texas State Gazette* accused local Mexicans of lowering themselves to the level of slaves and of stirring up insubordination among black bondsmen. Three years later, noted American landscape architect, travel writer, and abolitionist Frederick Law Olmsted described how Anglo Texans complained of Mexicans tampering with slaves and fraternizing with blacks. "They helped them in all their bad habits, married them, stole a living from them, and ran them off every day to Mexico," he wrote.[11] "They are regarded by slaveholders with great contempt and suspicion, for their intimacy with slaves, and their competition with plantation labor."[12] Some Anglos feared that Texas Mexicans would forge a triple alliance against them with slaves and Indians.

As soon as Texas gained its independence, slaves began escaping to Mexico by the thousands. In 1837, William B. DeWees from Colorado County in south-central Texas wrote that several of his neighbors' slaves had made a dash for the Rio Grande and freedom. Local Indians then prevented the owners from capturing the escapees. In 1839, a United States appraiser general from New Orleans commented that the possibility for escape that Mexico afforded led Anglo Texans to prefer Mexicans over black slaves as servants. "The frequent escape of slaves from the American side of the Rio Grande into Mexico, and the folly of any attempt to capture them—although you might meet your own property in Matamoros—has been one of the excitants of bad feeling between the citizens of Mexico and [Anglo Americans] on the frontier."[13]

After the United States took control of Texas in 1845, state representatives urged the federal government to negotiate a treaty that would facilitate the extradition of fugitive slaves from Mexico. Mexico was not interested in such an arrangement. In fact, it had an interest in encouraging slaves to flee south across the Rio Grande.

Officials figured that fugitive slaves were not only useful in protecting the border against American intrusions, but they weakened the slave system, thereby reducing the chances of further U.S. territorial aggression. In 1859, the *San Antonio Herald* opined that Texans were justified in crossing the international frontier to retrieve fugitive slaves. "We have often wondered," wrote the editor, "why some bold and enterprizing men in our state do not club together and go into Mexico and bring away the large number of fine likely runaways known to be not far over the line, forming a pretty respectable African colony."[14]

While Mexico provided a refuge for fugitive slaves, Texas Mexicans sometimes helped slaves escape. In the 1840s and 1850s, some Tejanos risked fines and imprisonment by sabotaging the chattel system, rescuing slaves from bondage, and transporting them to the open frontier between central Texas and the Rio Grande. In 1845, at the Texas constitutional convention, a delegate complained that "peons of the west have come in and enticed our Negroes away."[15]

Still, there were other Tejanos who had no qualms about slavery. Some even counted themselves among the slaveholders. Santos Benavides, the Laredo native who later became the highest-ranking Mexican American in the Southern Confederacy, was known for having restored many runaway bondsmen to their owners. In November of 1860, Benavides crossed into Nuevo Laredo, Mexico, to retrieve a fugitive slave. According to one contemporary Anglo Laredoan, Benavides had been "foremost in confronting danger in support of the laws and institutions of Texas."[16]

Nonetheless, to many Anglos, the actions of an unknowable number of Mexican abolitionists cast a shadow of suspicion on all Mexicans. After a planned slave insurrection was thwarted in Colorado County in September 1856, investigators discovered that one of the plotters was a Mexican named Frank. Consequently, and despite the fact that there was no evidence against them, all Mexicans in the county were suspected of playing a role in the conspiracy. Investigators concluded that the insurrection had been scheduled for the middle of the night on September 6, when Mexicans were to help the slaves to escape. Before fleeing, the slaves had purportedly planned to slaughter the white population, sparing only the young women, who would be taken captive. After word of the plot got out, all local

Mexicans were arrested and given five days to leave the county. A resolution was then passed "forever forbidding any Mexicans from coming within the limits of the county."[17]

Other counties also summarily expelled Mexicans for fear that they would tamper with slaves. In 1856, Mexicans were ejected from Matagorda County after being accused of stealing horses and the "likeliest negro girls for wives" and carrying them off to Mexico.[18] Two years earlier, residents of Austin attempted to curtail the movement of transient Mexican laborers. Claiming that they made slaves "discontented and insubordinate," a citizens meeting ordered all transients to leave the city within ten days or be expelled by force.[19] By the last days of October 1854, the few remaining Mexicans in Austin were those who had been vouched for by Anglos of social standing. The following year, some Mexican families returned only to be turned away again. One visitor described the situation thus: "wherever slavery in Texas has been carried in a wholesale way, into the neighborhood of Mexicans, it has been found necessary to treat them as outlaws."[20]

The town of Seguin in Guadalupe County drafted a resolution prohibiting Mexican "peons" from entering the area and forbidding anyone from associating with slaves without the permission of their masters. In case the new laws were not obeyed, the *Texas State Gazette* editorialized, residents of Guadalupe County could solve any abuses by their own hands. In October 1854, representatives from eight counties—Travis, Gonzales, De Witt, Lavaca, Hays, Caldwell, Guadalupe, and Fayette—convened in Gonzales to discuss what they considered to be the Mexican threat to slavery. The delegates sought stronger laws and asked the state's federal representatives to urge Mexico to instruct its nationals not to tamper with slaves. They also concluded that counties should form vigilance committees and encourage all citizens to make a diligent effort to prohibit Mexicans from communicating with blacks.

In truth, Texas Mexicans never posed a significant threat to the institution of slavery. But the combination of the large numbers of Tejanos and the presence of an adamantly abolitionist Mexico on the state's southern border did effectively limit the expansion of slavery in the region west of the San Antonio River. Proposals to stem the loss of slaves varied from stationing rangers along the Rio Grande to establishing a fund to pay for rewards for the return of slaves, dead or alive. The *Texas Almanac of 1857* also claimed that the nearness of Mexico was "making this kind of property [slaves] a very uncertain one."[21] Likewise, in 1852, the *San Antonio Ledger* observed that Mexico "has long been regarded by the Texas slave as his El Dorado for accumulation, his utopia for political rights, and his Paradise for happiness."[22] The editor boasted that despite slavery, the United States was preferable to the grinding poverty and debt peonage of Mexico. Thousands of slaves apparently begged to differ. Among them were Tom and Esau, who once belonged to Sam Houston, the revolutionary hero who became the first regularly elected president of the Texas Republic. The two black men, who had been Houston's barbers, sought shelter in Matamoros, just over the border from Brownsville. Their former owner's reaction to their escape was remarkably accommodating. Houston said he believed the two runaways "were smart, intelligent fellows . . . [who] would help to civilize and refine Mexico, as their associations in Texas had been remarkably good."[23] He did not lift a finger to retrieve the runaways.

An American general who was briefly imprisoned in Mexico later caught sight of Tom and Esau outside Matamoros. The former slaves had indeed become gentlemen south of the border. They were seen riding in the company of a Mexican military officer, General Pedro Ampudia, who was celebrating a recent victory. The imprisoned American officer later recorded his encounter with one of the men: "Tom treated us with marked respect and attention, spoke of his prospects in that country, his intended nuptials, invited us to the wedding, and said that General Ampudia was to stand godfather on the occasion."[24] For Tom at least, there was no comparing the quality of life north and south of the Rio Grande.

But the road to freedom in Mexico also took its toll. Many runaways were killed or starved to death on their trek southward. Others wound up in misery after squandering their meager belongings in a short, joyous burst of spending on wine, women, and song. After all, they had no prior experience taking care of themselves. But those who learned Spanish quickly and worked hard could live well in Mexico. The wages may have been low, but they were theirs to keep. Newcomers also inevitably heard stories about the Mexicans of

African descent who had gained wealth and prestige in Mexican society. Such stories also made their way northward. In Texas bars of the mid-nineteenth century, Anglo men liked to joke that "a nigger in Mexico is just as good as a white man."[25]

The presence of a neighboring Hispanic challenge to slavery was not new to Anglo America. Beginning in the early eighteenth century, the Spanish government began granting freedom to fugitive slaves from the Carolinas and Georgia who fled to Florida. In exchange for their support against the British and their conversion to Catholicism, the runaways were allowed to choose their own leaders, to own property, and to bear arms. In 1783, when more than one hundred slaves had settled in St. Augustine, Spanish officials established the fort and town of Gracia Real de Santa Teresa de Mosé, which was the first legally sanctioned free black community in what is now the United States. These new, free black Spaniards played a critical role in protecting the colony against British attack.

The first known African runaways arrived in St. Augustine as early as 1687. In that year, eight men, two women, and a nursing child made their way to Spanish Florida. Escaping sometimes with the assistance of Indian allies, slaves sought to take advantage of the conflict among England, Spain, and Native Americans. The Seminole blacks, African slaves whose association with Seminole Indians played an important role in creating their unique identity, became experts in borderland diplomacy in both the Southeast and the Southwest. From the early nineteenth century to the first quarter of the twentieth, the black Seminoles fought for Spain and Britain against the United States; they fought for Mexico against Indians and Texans; and finally for the United States against frontier bandits and Indians. In 1850, a group of black Seminoles immigrated to Mexico in search of freedom. Eager to welcome new settlers, Mexican authorities granted their petition for land. In fact, Mexican officials had recommended that fugitive American slaves be settled on the frontier in order to defend the border from Anglo American incursions. Indian raids had also ravaged several Mexican border towns and prohibited further settlement of the area. In exchange for their help in defending the region, the black Seminoles were granted Mexican citizenship along with seventy thousand acres in the state of Coahuila.

Not only did Mexico and Mexicans present a challenge to slavery, but the acquisition of a vast portion of Mexican territory—first Texas and then, after the conclusion of the Mexican-American War in 1848, the remainder of the Southwest—pushed the United States down the road to civil war and the end of slavery. In 1845, the annexation of Texas revealed sharp political divisions in the United States. New Englanders feared that expansion would dilute their standing in national politics, while abolitionists feared it would extend slavery. For those reasons, pro-slavery Southerners generally supported annexation.

At the same time, many Northern and Southern proponents of annexation argued that Texas could provide a solution to America's worsening racial troubles. Beneath the nation's optimism was a brooding disquietude over the future of slavery. With a growing number of Northern states prohibiting slavery and with others establishing programs for the gradual emancipation of slaves, by the mid-nineteenth century the number of free blacks had risen dramatically. Slave owners were increasingly concerned that the growing presence of free blacks—from 59,000 in 1790 to 319,000 in 1830—encouraged indocility if not defiance among their bondsmen.[26] If slavery was justified on the grounds that blacks were innately inferior, then free black artisans surviving, if not prospering, outside of bondage threatened to subvert the very foundations of the institution.

First proposed as early as 1714, the idea of sending free blacks to Africa gained new currency in the early nineteenth century. In 1817, the American Colonization Society was founded with the express purpose of establishing black American colonies in Africa. Within fifteen years, more than a dozen state legislatures had given their official approval to the society's plans. There was widespread support for the organization, but due to the exorbitant cost of transporting people across the Atlantic, fewer than fifteen thousand American blacks ever migrated to Africa. Furthermore, while initially open to the idea of leaving the United States, black leaders increasingly opposed the idea of colonization.

The failure of the colonization movement and the rise of radical abolitionism made politicians eager to seek new solutions to the nation's racial quandary. Though many Northern Democrats opposed slavery, they also feared that the potential emancipation of more than three million slaves would flood the North with blacks. Thus they supported annexation in the hope that it would facilitate the migration of free blacks to Mexico. Southern expansionists were fond of promoting this fantasy. In his widely distributed *Letter on the Annexation of Texas,* Robert J. Walker, President James K. Polk's secretary of the treasury, argued that blacks slipping into Texas could find their way to a warmer climate and a more congenial racial environment. He warned that without annexation, the eventual emancipation of slaves would encourage millions of blacks to move northward to compete with whites for jobs. Likewise, Democratic congressman John Tibbatts of Kentucky professed his belief that annexation would cause the black population to "gradually recede from the North, which is uncongenial to their natures."[27] The congressman envisioned a massive southward migration that would culminate in blacks becoming "blended with the mixed population of Mexico."[28] The free states would then "be clear of a degraded and wretched population with which they are now infested, crowding their hospitals and jails, and with which their larger cities will be overrun."[29] Tibbatts also hoped that European immigrants would eventually replace blacks both below and above the Mason-Dixon line.

This concept of a racial dumping ground was not new. The United States had been pushing unwanted Indians into the far-western frontier for many years. But by the mid-1840s, Southerners were all too aware that slavery was being hemmed in by the Indian territory on the southwestern frontier. The annexation of Texas held out the prospect whereby white Americans could cut the Gordian knot and free themselves from having to continue their problematic coexistence with blacks.

Of course the annexation of Texas was only a prelude to a much larger acquisition of land. In the fall of 1845, Polk had sent an emissary to Mexico with instructions to offer $5 million for New Mexico or $20 million if California were included in the deal. The following May, after Mexico refused to receive his representative, Polk decided to take the Mexican northwest by force and declared war. In September, General Winfield Scott marched triumphantly into Mexico City.

The Mexican-American War was particularly popular in the

Southern and Western states. But some prominent Americans were convinced that this act of territorial expansion would tear the nation apart. South Carolina's favorite son, Senator John C. Calhoun, feared that territorial expansion would both centralize government and shift the balance of power in the Senate against the South. He compared Mexico to "the forbidden fruit. The penalty of eating it would be to subject our institutions to political death."[30] For altogether different reasons, New England writer and abolitionist Ralph Waldo Emerson expressed similar concerns for the fate of the nation. He entered these prophetic words in his journal: "The United States will conquer Mexico, but it will be as the man swallows arsenic, which brings him down in turn. Mexico will poison us."[31]

For twenty-six years, the Missouri Compromise helped maintain a tenuous truce in the political struggle over slavery. In 1820, Congress had established that line to demarcate where slavery would and would not be permitted in the territory acquired in the Louisiana Purchase. It allowed the nation to avoid facing its core contradiction. But the conquest and annexation of northern Mexico—the enormous swath of land that included Texas, New Mexico, Arizona, California, Nevada, Utah, and portions of Colorado, Oklahoma, and Wyoming—forced Americans to ask themselves whether they wished to live in a free or a slave nation. President Polk oversaw the acquisition of more territory than any chief executive in the country's history. During his one term in office, the size of the United States increased by two-thirds. The Mexican-American War alone resulted in the addition of a million and a quarter square miles of new territory, almost half of it south of the old Missouri Compromise line of 36° 30'.

Before the outbreak of war with Mexico, President Polk tried to obtain funds that could be used to acquire territory from Mexico as part of peace negotiations. Not wishing to admit publicly that the acquisition of land was the true aim of the war, the president sought approval for the money from a secret executive session of the Senate, where it could be approved and sent to the House of Representatives without public discussion. But politics forced Polk to show his hand and at midday on August 8, 1846, he sent a message to the House requesting an appropriation of $2 million with which to pay Mexico "a fair equivalent" for "cession of territory" upon conclusion of the war.[32]

On a sultry Saturday night near the end of the congressional session, House debate on the appropriations request opened with New York Whig Hugh White condemning the Polk administration's crude expansionism and suggesting that the extension of slavery was the underlying motive for the war. Three other gentlemen spoke—one against the bill, two in favor—before David Wilmot, an obscure freshman Democrat from Pennsylvania, crossed party lines and forever tied the fate of Mexico's northwest to the future of slavery in the United States.

Wilmot was not against expansion. He had even agreed that in the case of the annexation of Texas, where slavery already existed, human bondage could continue lawfully. But he was deeply opposed to allowing slavery in any newly acquired free territory. "God forbid that we should be the means of planting this institution upon it," he said.[33] It was in this spirit that the novice congressman offered an amendment to the appropriation bill that would be remembered as the Wilmot Proviso. The amendment provided "That as an express and fundamental condition to the acquisition of any territory from the Republic of Mexico . . . neither slavery nor involuntary servitude shall ever exist in any part of said territory, except for crime, whereof the party shall first be duly convicted."[34]

Within hours, the House approved the proviso by a margin of 80 to 64, with all but three nays coming from the slave states. Alarmed and eager to quash the newly amended appropriations bill, Southerners moved to table the issue. The roll call of the vote was an ominous portent of the future. It divided the House not along party—Whigs versus Democrats—but regional lines—Southerners versus Northerners. Ninety-one Northerners and three Southerners voted against tabling the issue, while seventy-four Southerners and four Northerners voted to do so.[35]

Once passed by the whole House—again along regional lines—the amended appropriations bill then expired in the Senate as the session adjourned. But Wilmot's small amendment had already shaken the political landscape. Barely a week after Congress adjourned, the *Boston Whig* editorialized, "As if by magic, [the Wilmot Proviso] brought to a head the great question which is about to divide the American people."[36] Indeed, the failed proviso both consolidated anti-slavery forces and provoked a fierce defensive reaction in the South. "The acquisition of Texas and the Mexican provinces . . . has aroused the free people of the free States, so that one pulse beats from Maine to Oregon," proclaimed Congressman Orin Fowler of Massachusetts.[37] For their part, Southerners, who provided the bulk of soldiers sent to conquer Mexican territory, were offended by any proposal that would deny them the fruits of war. "When the war-worn soldier returns to his home," a resident of Alabama asked, "is he to be told he cannot carry his property to the country won by his blood?"[38] Still, the significance of the proviso was not apparent to a furious President Polk. In his journal he called it "a mischievous and foolish amendment." Nor did he believe that Wilmot's actions had been caused by anything other than factional intrigue. "What connection slavery had with making peace with Mexico it is difficult to conceive," he wrote. As historian Bernard DeVoto observed, Polk's "blindness was his country's evasion, and evasion was now going to end. Slavery was out of the closet, and it was going to stay out."[39] The issue, which heretofore had been diffused and legislated at the state level, now became national as Congress considered whether new territory would be free or slave. National politicians who had been content to have state legislatures decide the matter locally could no longer skirt the broader issue. As Representative James Wilson of New Hampshire declared, "Where slavery exists within the States, and recognized by the Constitution of the United States, the northern people claim no right to interfere. . . . But gentlemen need not ask me for my vote to extend the institution of slavery one single inch beyond the present boundaries."[40] Whether he knew it or not, David Wilmot had ushered in a new era in which the issue of slavery would dominate national politics.

The fate of the newly acquired Mexican territories would not be settled until Congress cobbled together the clumsy Compromise of 1850. Under its provisions, California entered the Union as a free state while New Mexico and Utah were organized as territorial governments, which would decide for themselves whether slavery would be allowed. To appease pro-slavery interests, the compromise also strengthened the Fugitive Slave Act, which gave the federal government greater power to enforce the return of runaway slaves to the South. Washington rejoiced on the passing of the compromise. President Millard Fillmore called the deal "a final settlement" to the nation's sectional rift.[41] He was wrong. The schism that territorial expansion had wrought between North and South would only intensify.

But the debate inspired by the Mexican-American War was not only about territory and slavery. It was also about the character of the Mexicans themselves. By the fall of 1847, the rapid success of U.S. troops made the president and a small but enthusiastic group of Democrats hungry for more territory. Proponents of the "All Mexico" movement saw the successful taking of Mexico's northern provinces as a mere precursor to the conquest of the entire country. But with the exception of a few hard-liners willing to take land at all costs, most expansionists still weighed the presumed value of the territory to be acquired against the price of incorporating the land's inhabitants.

While the acquisition of California, Texas, New Mexico, and the rest of the Southwest would lead to the addition of roughly 100,000 Spanish speakers into the United States, the conquest of all of Mexico would have brought no fewer than eight million foreigners into the burgeoning American empire.[42] Even before the start of the Mexican War, there was great concern over the prospect of so many Mexicans inhabiting American territory. The debate wound up reinforcing Anglo American racial identity. Whig senator Jabez W. Huntington from Connecticut was moved to declare that the U.S. Constitution was "not for people of every color, and language, and habits." William Wick, Democratic congressman from Indiana, flat-out stated that he did "not want any mixed races in our Union, nor men of any color except white, unless they be slaves. Certainly not as voters or legislators."[43] Indeed, the acquisition of all of Mexico would have added more than one hundred representatives and twenty senators to Congress. Not surprisingly, however, proponents of Manifest Destiny, the triumphalist notion that Providence favored U.S. expansion across the continent, had not taken into consideration the practical details of governing the new territory.

Many expansionists simply assumed that the fast-growing Anglo

American population would overwhelm all inhabitants of any new territories. Others saw the Anglo American displacement of Native Americans as a model for the conquest of Mexico. Some suggested that Mexico's nonwhite people be isolated in reservations to make room for American settlers. New York senator Daniel S. Dickinson testified that most Mexicans were members of "the fated aboriginal races . . . destined, by laws above human agency, to give way to a stronger race from this continent or another."[44] Similarly, James Gordon Bennett, the publisher of the influential *New York Herald* and fervent advocate of Manifest Destiny, predicted that as Americans poured into a conquered Mexico, its "imbecile" inhabitants were "as sure to melt away at the approach of Anglo-Saxon energy and enterprise as snow before the southern sun." The fate of the Mexicans, he said, would be "similar to that of the Indians of this country—the race, before a century rolls over us, will become extinct."[45]

Other less genocidal plans envisioned a colonial military occupation of the conquered territory and the cultural and commercial "Saxonization" of Mexico. There was little or no support, however, for the idea of incorporating Mexicans as U.S. citizens with the same rights of all other citizens. There were a few members of Congress, however, who believed that education could prepare Mexicans for U.S. citizenship. But most doubted the Mexicans' capacity for democratic government. "How should we govern the mongrel race which inhabits [Mexico]?" asked James Buchanan, President Polk's secretary of state. "Could we admit them to seats in our Senate and House of Representatives? Are they capable of Self Government as States of this Confederacy?"[46] Several years later, Senator John Clayton of Delaware expressed his fear that the incorporation of Mexicans as American citizens would threaten white privilege. "Yes! Aztecs, Creoles, Half-breeds, Quadroons, Samboes, and I know not what else— 'ring-streaked and speckled'—all will come in, and, instead of our governing them, they, by their votes, will govern us."[47]

Fearful that the United States would move deeper into Mexico, Andrew Jackson Donelson, the former U.S. chargé d'affaires in Texas and nephew of President Andrew Jackson, warned President Polk in early 1848 that "We can no more amalgamate with her people than with negroes."[48] Such widespread repugnance at the prospect of integrating more Mexican mestizos into the United States is what ultimately killed the All Mexico movement. "We do not want the people of Mexico, either as citizens or subjects," declared Senator Lewis Cass of Michigan. "All we want is a portion of territory, which they nominally hold, generally uninhabited, or, where inhabited at all, sparsely so, and with a population, which would soon recede, or identify itself with ours."[49] The *Augusta Daily Chronicle and Sentinel*, a Whig newspaper, also condemned the further expansion because "It would likely prove to be a sickening mixture, consisting of such a conglomeration of Negroes and Rancheros, Mestizoes and Indians, with but a few Castilians."[50] Given the vehement opposition to conquering all of Mexico, the Treaty of Guadalupe Hidalgo, which brought an official end to the war in 1848 and drew the United States–Mexico boundary at the Rio Grande, was the only viable political option. It secured the biggest possible portion of Mexican land with the fewest Mexicans inhabiting it.

In an 1846 editorial, James Gordon Bennett reminded readers that unlike Mexicans whose "imbecility" was caused by the "amalgamation of races," racial purity was the source of white American superiority. Contending that "the idea of amalgamation has been always abhorrent to the Anglo-Saxon race on this continent," Bennett lauded Americans for keeping "aloof from the inferior races" as they pioneered westward.[51] In a famous speech before the Senate on January 4, 1848, South Carolina senator John C. Calhoun reasserted the primacy of whites in America. "We have never dreamt of incorporating into our Union any but the Caucasian race—the free white race," he declared. "To incorporate Mexico, would be the very first instance of the kind. . . . Ours, sir, is the Government of a white race."[52] Still, the esteemed senator felt obliged to concede that some Mexicans had "Castilian blood in their veins—the old Gothic, quite equal to the Anglo-Saxon in many respects—in some respects superior."[53] He, like many other Anglo Americans, still insisted on parsing the mixed Mexican lineage into manageable categories. As he saw it, Mexico had "a population of about only one million of [white] blood, and two or three millions of mixed blood, better informed, all the rest pure Indians."[54] The downfall of Spanish America, he claimed, was its inability to separate the races properly. "The greatest misfortunes of Spanish America are to be traced to the fatal error of placing these colored races on an equality with the white race," he roared. "That error destroyed the social arrangement which formed the basis of society."[55]

Even after the Treaty of Guadalupe Hidalgo was signed, some politicians continued to fulminate against the idea of granting civil rights to the Mexicans who remained in the territory. Senator James D. Westcott of Florida was outraged that the United States was "compelled to receive not merely the white citizens of California and New Mexico, but the peons, Negroes, and Indians of all sorts, the wild tribe of Camanches, the bug-and-lizard-eating 'Diggers,' and other half-monkey savages in those countries, as equal citizens of the United States."[56] Significantly, the debate over Mexico and Mexicans also inspired Americans to envision themselves clearly and emphatically as an Anglo-Saxon race destined to dominate the world. Not until the mid-1840s did the term "Anglo-Saxon" begin to be commonly used as a racial term. While the pioneers' confrontation with the Western wilderness may have forged the American character—as Frederick Jackson Turner contended—it was their contentious encounters with Mexicans that gave shape to their racial identity as Anglo-Saxons. It was during the conflict with Mexico that the centuries-old belief in the superiority of Anglo-Saxon political institutions morphed into a faith in the innate superiority of the Saxon-Teutonic branch of the white race. Defining themselves in contradistinction to the mongrel Mexicans, a growing number of white Americans began to view territorial expansion in purely racial terms. The racial justifications that white Americans had used to subjugate blacks and Indians now became more articulated and assertive during the push westward into Mexican territory.

From the beginning, Americans viewed the Texas Revolution of 1836 as a racial clash rather than a struggle by aggrieved colonists against a tyrannical ruler. Senator Thomas Hart Benton of Missouri claimed that the revolution in Texas had "illustrated the anglo-Saxon character, and given it new titles to the respect and admiration of the world. It shows that liberty, justice, valour—moral, physical, and intellectual power—discriminate that race wherever it goes."[57] As America's first imperialist war, the Mexican-American War established the standard rationale and logic for future conflicts around the world. The Mexican War made it clear that U.S. expansion into heavily populated areas thereafter would be achieved either by way of economic penetration or colonial mandate. Americans were eager to exert economic control over other areas of the world, but they were not willing to absorb nonwhites into their body politic. As historian Reginald Horsman wrote, "A search for personal and national wealth was put in terms of world progress under the leadership of a supreme race."[58]

As a Whig congressman from Massachusetts put it, the Polk administration had not sought "peace with Mexico, but a piece of Mexico."[59] Yet even as their nation expanded, Americans recoiled in horror at the thought of absorbing an alien population. Mexico and Mexicans represented the outer boundaries of Anglo American racial thinking. Much as slavery did, conquest put America's ideals to the test, thereby fortifying its racial identity. The annexation and conquest of the Mexican northwest led to the admission, so to speak, of the first large group of Mexicans into the United States. With the abolition of slavery in 1865, Mexico lost its allure for American blacks and never did serve as an escape valve for the racial pressure that beset a nervous white America. But Mexico did provide an example of an alternative racial order that Anglo American expansionists felt obliged to condemn. Attacking that racial order served also to help them define themselves and their own racial ideology. Meanwhile, the largely mixed Mexican population that the United States acquired along with the territory would continue to defy the American racial system. Too powerless and too few in number to present a serious challenge to Anglo racial logic, Mexican Americans would nonetheless never fit neatly into a hierarchical racial order based on purity.

Five

The Anglos Move West

The Mexican-American War of 1846–1848 had been provoked, in part, by the tensions sparked by the Texas Declaration of Independence. Mexico had refused to recognize the fledgling Texas Republic and threatened to retake the runaway province by force. A dispute over the location of the southern boundary of Texas had also made for constant skirmishes on the borderlands between the Texas Republic and Mexico. When the United States annexed Texas in 1845, Mexico severed diplomatic relations, and the boundary dispute intensified. The U.S. claimed that Texas territory extended as far south as the Rio Grande, while Mexico insisted that the frontier was the Nueces River 150 miles further north. Eager to fulfill his expansionist campaign promises, newly elected President Polk used the border dispute as a proximate cause to justify taking the disputed Mexican territory. The reality was that Mexico was presuming to stand in the way of America's Manifest Destiny to expand its territory from coast to coast. It was a vain presumption.

In January 1846, Polk dispatched troops under the command of General Zachary Taylor to the disputed territory between the Rio Grande and the Nueces, a move that provoked a confrontation with Mexican forces. Four months later, in a pronouncement "remarkable for its distortion and provocative to the absurd," Polk declared war on Mexico and announced that the enemy had invaded American territory and shed American blood on U.S. soil.[1] The ensuing war, fought largely south of the Rio Grande, on territory indisputably Mexican, took a heavy toll on both countries. The United States suffered 13,780 dead and thousands more badly wounded. The cost in dollars was upwards of $100 million.[2] Though no precise figures exist, the Mexicans suffered considerably greater losses, in lives, money, territory, and national dignity. Forced to forfeit its claim to Texas,

Mexico also surrendered its entire northwest territory. In total, it was forced to give up 947,570 square miles of land, almost half its national territory. Yet despite its great expanse, less than 1 percent of the Mexican population had lived there.[3] Those who did, however, became the first Mexican Americans.

The U.S. did not wait for the war to end to take control of the Southwest. In June of 1846, General Stephen W. Kearny was dispatched to Santa Fe to occupy New Mexico. It is not clear whether New Mexican governor Manuel Armijo was bribed or whether he was simply overwhelmed by the prospect of fighting the Americans, but he abandoned his province and headed south, thereby allowing it to be taken without a shot being fired in its defense. In August of 1846, after General Kearny had promised New Mexicans U.S. citizenship and a prosperous future, Acting Governor Juan Bautista Vigil y Alarid responded by explaining the New Mexicans' ambivalent reaction to American occupation:

> Do not find it strange if there has been no manifestation of joy and enthusiasm in seeing this city occupied by your military forces. To us the power of the Mexican Republic is dead. No matter what her condition, she was our mother. What child will not shed abundant tears at the tomb of his parents? . . . Today we belong to a great and wonderful nation, its flag, with its stars and stripes, covers the horizon of New Mexico, and its brilliant light shall grow like good seed well cultivated.[4]

As in Texas a decade earlier, Mexicans who inhabited their country's northwestern frontier were not happy with their government's insistence on centralizing political power and often found their self-interest at odds with federal policies. Centuries of isolation from the authorities in Mexico City had not encouraged the development of a strong nationalist sentiment on the frontier. According to one historian, "a century of internal turmoil and civil war followed Mexican independence so that there was neither a consistent government nor a consistent ideology that could command an overriding loyalty."[5]

In 1836, the year of the Texas Revolution, the California legislature declared their province "independent of Mexico until the federal system adopted in 1824 shall be reestablished."[6] In 1846, after experiencing four rebellions in ten years, the Mexican republic granted California semiautonomous status. But conflicting regional interests led to growing political discontent in the province. Although the governor in Los Angeles wielded administrative power, California's economic center was centered on Monterey Bay. Northern and Southern Californians didn't see eye-to-eye.

In Arizona, Apache attacks were so ferocious that "the impoverished Mexican aristocracy of Tucson welcomed the American annexation."[7] Indeed, even after the American conquest, "Apaches brought about a feeling of comradeship between the resident Mexican population and the incoming Anglos."[8] In New Mexico, chronic political instability caused some Mexicans to look with favor at the prospect of an American takeover. There had been a series of insurrections in the territory in the years leading up to the Mexican-American War. A governor was murdered, his successor was executed, and civic life was in disarray.

In California, no less a figure than the prominent merchant General Mariano Guadalupe Vallejo concluded that his state's interests would be best served if the province were to become part of the United States. After the occupation, other prominent Mexicans acknowledged the futility of resisting American rule and recognized the potential benefits of cooperating with the new rulers. "The conquest of California did not bother Californians, least of all the women," wrote Angustias de la Guerra Ord, the daughter of a prominent Santa Barbara family and wife of an Anglo-American doctor. "It must be confessed that California was on the road to the most complete ruin."[9] While her account is undoubtedly exaggerated, de la Guerra Ord's testimony is nonetheless indicative of the willingness of some elites to cooperate with the Americans. In his *History of California,* which was published twenty years after the American occupation, former Alta California governor Juan Bautista Alvarado gave a more nuanced account of the Spanish-speaking Californians' response to the U.S. invasion. While many Californios could see the advantages of allying themselves with the Americans, they were troubled by the idea of abandoning Mexico in a time of war:

Even though we knew that nothing short of a Divine miracle would enable us to force the [Americans out] . . . not even for this reason would we desist from making a supreme effort to show the world that although we had strong motives for complaint against Mexico, which had for so many years been the bane of our existence and had robbed us unmercifully, we, ever generous, were not willing to take advantage of an occasion when the Mexican Republic was engaged in a foreign war to settle our family differences; nor were my fellow citizens and I who had read the papers and knew the constitution of the United States, unaware that Alta California stood to gain a great deal by the change in flag, for it was well-known that the enterprising spirit of the North Americans . . . would know how to make their influence felt on California soil and make towns grow where there had been only rocks before. Although we knew all of the advantages which would accrue to us from the new alliance which [U.S. Navy Commodore John Drake Sloat] was proposing, we preferred the life of privation, uncertainty and snares which we expected to continue until the mother country had come out defeated or victorious in the unequal contest to which she had rashly provoked her powerful neighbor. Our resistance was not motivated by the hatred we had for the North Americans, or their government or institutions, but was dictated by a conscience which aspired to fulfilling as far as possible our duties as Mexican citizens. As was to be supposed, our efforts were without effect. Victory chose to rest in the enemy camp, and a majority of those of us who were taken prisoners had to bow our proud heads before the might of the North American government and its valiant marines.[10]

Although the initial phase of occupation was largely peaceful, armed resistance to U.S. forces eventually emerged. In New Mexico, for example, after witnessing American soldiers bully their country-men, more Hispanos, the local term referring to descendants of Span-ish settlers, began to voice their resentment of U.S. control. In early 1847, New Mexican insurgents staged the Taos Rebellion and assas-sinated the newly appointed Anglo governor. For a brief time rebels resisted the U.S. troops that had been ordered to the northern part of the state to quash them.

In California, the harsh rule of the U.S.-installed mayor of Los Angeles briefly united the Californios. Angelenos cheered on guerrilla fighters who managed to achieve one significant victory against American forces. But internecine tensions were never far from the surface. "Despite the fact that the great majority of *pobladores* supported armed resistance, there were significant defections and divisions among the Californio leadership."[11] The Californios' lack of unity contributed to their defeat.

According to historian Robert J. Rosenbaum, Mexicans responded to the American conquest "with four basic tactics: withdrawal, accommodation, assimilation, and resistance."[12] But withdrawal was the "preferred tactic of the majority," and social fragmentation and the absence of a strong Mexican nationalism limited the scope and efficacy of any efforts at resistance.[13] In the same way that isolation from Mexico City had not nurtured a strong sense of Spanish or Mexican nationalism, physical distance allowed Southwestern Mexicans, particularly those in Texas and New Mexico, to live their lives relatively unaffected by the shift in imperial power. Historians Richard Griswold del Castillo and Arnoldo de León concluded that "most Mexican Americans probably compromised with [American] society, wishing to live peaceful and practical lives as ethnic Mexicans."[14] Furthermore, a traditional rural economy bred loyalties to "family, locality, or class," and not to province or nation.[15]

Nowhere were Anglo-Mexican relations worse than in Texas. In the course of dispossessing Mexicans of their lands, Anglo Americans were often extremely brutal to Tejanos. The Texas Rangers, a paramilitary law enforcement group, were infamously anti-Mexican, and Anglo justice was not in the least bit blind. In 1878, the American consul in Matamoros observed that "when an aggression is made upon a Mexican it is not minded [by the Texas civil authorities]. For instance, when it is known that a Mexican has been hung or killed in the neighborhood of Brownsville, or along the frontier, there is seldom any fuss made about it; while on the contrary, if a white man happens to be despoiled in any way, there is generally a great fuss made about it by those not of Mexican origin. . . . It has always appeared to me that people of Mexican origin regarded themselves as not protected equally with those of Anglo-Saxon origin."[16] One estimate places the number of Mexican Americans killed by extralegal violence in the Southwest between 1850 and 1930 as being "greater than the number of lynchings of black Americans during that same period."[17] Consequently, interethnic violence was endemic to the Texas border region.

Most armed Mexican resistance to U.S. control occurred in Texas's Rio Grande Valley. It came in the form of both individual and collective outbursts. The South Texas border region produced figures like Gregorio Cortez, who became a folk hero after he shot a Texas Ranger in self-defense and then avoided capture; revolutionary Catarino Garza, who hoped to initiate a popular uprising; and the bandit Juan Cortina, the Red Robber of the Rio Grande. Born into a landowning ranching family, Cortina became enraged at the manner in which Mexicans were losing their land to conniving Anglo American newcomers. On July 13, 1859, after witnessing an Anglo marshal pistol-whip a Mexican prisoner in Brownsville, Cortina shot and killed the lawman. In retaliation, the town's Anglo citizens "initiated a reign of terror against 'greasers.' "[18] In September, Cortina and a band of his men raided the city, initiating a "long period of virtual warfare between Anglos and Mexicans."[19] Members of the local Mexican American establishment, who had managed to maintain possession of their property and make peace with the American rulers, were caught in a kind of no-man's-land. Some tacitly approved the uprising, while others worked to suppress the rebellion. A group of ranchers led by Santos Benavides, the grandson of Tomás Sánchez, the founder of Laredo, actively supported Anglo authorities.

California had its own bandits, men like Joaquín Murieta and Tiburcio Vásquez, but armed resistance there and in New Mexico was not nearly as intense as it was in Texas. Mexican Americans in New Mexico had the advantage of outnumbering Anglos, and many continued to live in self-supporting communities. As a result, there was more organized collective resistance in New Mexico than in other states. The most famous band of New Mexican insurgents was a group of masked riders who called themselves Las Gorras Blancas (The White Masks). Seeking to protect the rights of the native inhabitants, in 1889, they began destroying railroad ties, cutting fences and telegraph lines, and torching ranches. A year later, they formed a political party that enjoyed early success. Ultimately, however, it came under attack by less confrontational elements of New Mexico's Hispanic population.

In the end, "the separate, local nature of revolts kept them from having anything more than a delaying effect" on the ongoing Anglo conquest.[20] Furthermore, they were never large enough to pose a real threat to U.S. forces. Historian Robert Rosenbaum has argued that unity is the central ingredient of ethnic self-preservation, which requires "transcend[ing] class and regional differences, particularly those that affect perceptions of the threat from and the attractions of the Anglo world."[21] In the final analysis, Mexicans were not united and a sufficient number of them, particularly among the upper classes, were attracted to the Anglo world and therefore not disposed to engage in long-term resistance to the United States.

In the nineteenth century, members of the Hispanic elite "worked closely with Anglo-Americans as the Southwest underwent the transition from Mexican to American sovereignty."[22] The three primary reasons for their alliance with the Anglos were "disillusionment with Mexico, sincere idealism, and the retention of economic and political power."[23] Exasperated by Mexico's troubled political and economic climate, some of the earliest upper-class Mexican Americans admired America's vitality and its political institutions. Men like Arizonan Estevan Ochoa took great pride in their American citizenship. In 1862, when Confederate troops occupied his native Tucson, Ochoa chose to battle the Apaches alone rather than ally himself with those he considered traitors. In 1875, Ochoa was elected mayor of Tucson. Others like Santa Barbaran Pablo de la Guerra, who fought against the U.S. occupation and was no great admirer of the Americans, chose to work within the new system and was the most effective of the eight Mexican representatives to the California Constitutional Convention of 1849. He later ran successfully for political office, including mayor of Santa Barbara. His leadership in his native town helped other Californio ranchers maintain local political influence for a few more years.

In New Mexico, many landowning families maintained their privileged status by adapting quickly to Anglo political institutions. The Armijos, the Chávezes, the Ortizes, the Pinos, and the Oteros retained their influence by cooperating with the Americans. Donaciano Vigil, the cousin of Juan Bautista Vigil, the acting governor when General Kearny's forces arrived in Santa Fe, was instrumental in helping the Americans consolidate their power. When insurgents rebelled against the Americans in January 1847, assassinating the first American governor, Vigil sent out a circular urging New Mexicans to remain loyal to the United States. Dismissing the rebels as shameless ruffians, he exhorted New Mexicans to "keep yourselves quiet and engaged in your private affairs." Acknowledging the increasing contacts between New Mexicans and Americans, he asked "whether [New Mexico] has to belong to the government of the United States or return to its native Mexico, is it not a gross absurdity to foment rancorous feelings toward people with whom we are either to compose one family, or to continue our commercial relations?"[24] The rebels, who were largely poor Hispanics and Pueblo Indians, wound up killing several Anglo and Hispanic supporters of the American regime. The threat of wider violence obliged Hispanic elites to take sides and help the Americans put down the rebellion. But, as historian Manuel G. Gonzales cautions, the cooperation of the upper classes should not be mistaken for loyalty to the United States. For them, the 1847 Taos Rebellion could lead only to anarchy. "Indeed, given the choice between the two, both of them pernicious alternatives, the oligarchy preferred foreign occupation. Patriotism was less powerful than property."[25] In the long run, most New Mexicans came to acknowledge and accept the inevitability of an American future. In late 1847, Donaciano Vigil was appointed territorial governor.

But even as Mexican elites resigned themselves to cooperating with the Americans, some of the earliest U.S. allies became disillusioned by the harsh reality of American rule. After the Texas Revolution, the anger many Anglos felt toward the Mexican army was vented on local Tejanos, including those who had supported the rebellion. All Mexicans became subject to suspicion of complicity in General Santa Anna's atrocities. Even San Antonio mayor Juan N. Seguín, who backed the revolution, was forced to take refuge in Mexico in part because Anglos were turning his city into "the receptacle of the scum of society" and treating Mexicans "worse than brutes."[26] In California, Mariano Vallejo, who had favored the American acquisition of his native state, was dismayed by the dismal treatment Californios received at the hands of the Americans. That the conqueror "seeks his own good fortune, not ours . . . [is] very natural in individuals," he wrote, "but I denounce it on the part of a government that promised to respect our rights and to treat us as its own sons."[27]

In signing the Treaty of Guadalupe Hidalgo, the United States had undertaken to grant to the Mexican inhabitants of the Southwest who remained within the territory "all the rights of citizens of the United States." Article VIII of the treaty proclaimed that "property of every kind, now belonging to Mexicans . . . shall be inviolably respected."[28] But the imposition of American law onto the existent framework of Spanish and Mexican land law produced much confusion. In California, Mexican American landowners had the burden of proving to the government that their titles were legitimate. If they could not, their land became part of the public domain. Ranchers, many of whom spoke little English and most of whom knew even less about the American legal system, were forced to rely on Anglo lawyers to protect their property rights. Mexican landowners did in fact successfully prove three-quarters of their land claims. To pay the attorneys' fees, however, they ended up deeding over large portions of their properties to their erstwhile defenders. These lawyers also perpetrated a considerable amount of fraud on their unsuspecting clients. By the late 1850s, Californios in the northern half of the state had lost most of their economic clout.

The marginalization of Mexicans proceeded at varying rates of speed in different regions, depending largely on the size of the Anglo population and its ratio to that of the Hispanics. In Texas, the process of subjugation had been completed by the beginning of the Mexican-American War. While treatment of Mexicans was not uniform, they were generally understood to be at best second-class citizens. In California, the discovery of gold at Sutter's Mill a little over a week before the signing of the Treaty of Guadalupe Hidalgo lured hundreds of thousands of Americans and other foreigners to the state. An estimated 100,000 prospectors arrived in the province in 1849 alone. By 1850, Spanish-speaking Californians made up only 11 percent of the state's population.[29] Twenty years later, they were down to 4 percent.[30] In Southern California, where Anglo migration remained relatively slow until the completion of the transcontinental railroad in the 1880s, Mexicans managed to hold on to their economic and political power longer than in the north.

The Gold Rush brought to California thousands upon thousands of rough-hewn adventurers who harbored little sympathy for the native inhabitants. That attitude dashed any hope of a peaceful melding of Mexican and American cultures. Faced with what historian Leonard Pitt has called a "flood tide of gringo hostility,"[31] California Mexicans did not respond in unison. Nor did the eight—out of forty-eight—Mexican delegates to California's Constitutional Convention of 1849 vote as a reliable bloc. In thirty-five significant roll calls, they broke rank seventeen times. The most prominent exception was when they voted unanimously to reject an Anglo delegate's proposal to limit the franchise to white males only.

Even before the American takeover, Mexican California had become starkly divided by class. The egalitarian nature of early California society had been eroded by the Mexican government's decision to dismantle the Indian mission system in 1834. While the millions of acres of fertile land were to have been divided among Indian neophytes and the government, they ultimately wound up in the hands of two hundred or so Californio families. Not only were the Indians more impoverished than before the end of the mission system, but a *rancho* aristocracy had been formed. Anglo Americans were very much aware of these class distinctions. According to sociologist Tomás Almaguer, the Anglos' "ambivalence toward the social integration of all Mexicans was clearly the product of the way class lines internally stratified this population both before and after U.S. annexation of California."[32] While segments of the Mexican upper class could be assimilated into Anglo American society, the Mexican working class was generally viewed as unassimilable. Pioneering California historian Hubert Howe Bancroft referred to them as "the baser stock of Hispano-Californians . . . [the] greasers."[33] Although most of the *ranchero* elite were of mestizo origin, the incoming Anglos sometimes "credited" them with being of "pure" Spanish descent. This practice dovetailed neatly with the traditional Mexican upper-class practice of "whitening" themselves. Mexican laborers, on the other hand, were generally treated as nonwhites.

In theory, the U.S. had promised to protect the rights of all Mexicans when it ratified the Treaty of Guadalupe Hidalgo. In practice, however, Mexicans enjoyed varying degrees of legal rights based on their perceived racial background. Given that Mexicans, even those from the same family, come in many shades, there could be no uniformity in the implementation of laws based on skin color. In general, the darker a person's skin color and the lower a person's status the more vulnerable were that individual's rights. When they married Mexicans, Anglo Americans preferred partners with lighter skins. But as in Mexico, money could "whiten" people with darker complexions. A dark-skinned landowner was not treated the same as a poor man with essentially the same color. Once in charge, Anglos attempted to establish a hierarchy of races. People of obvious African heritage and Indians had fewer rights under the new regime than they did under Mexican rule. The first anti-miscegenation laws in the Southwest were passed not long after the American occupation. Although Mexican Americans were generally not affected by this type of legislation because the federal government classified them as white, they were nonetheless sensitive to the prejudice that inspired it. While Texas and Arizona passed anti-miscegenation laws early on, New Mexico, with its large number of Mexican American legislators, refused to approve a similar measure.[34] In general, however, the U.S. had nullified Mexico's liberal racial laws and reimposed a hierarchical racial order more akin to that of colonial New Spain.

The arrival of new migrants from Mexico further stratified the Mexican population. Between 1848 and 1852, the Gold Rush lured an estimated 25,000 miners from Sonora and other northern Mexican states to California.[35] By 1850, Mexican immigrants, whom the native-born Californians sometimes contemptuously called *cholos,* made up the majority of the state's Hispanic population. These Mexican miners, in addition to others from South America, were a source of great consternation to some Anglo Americans who resented the sight of foreigners extracting gold from their soil. Resentment against Hispanics of foreign nationality also negatively affected Mexican Americans. As occurred in Texas, Anglo newcomers to California often made no distinction between citizens and noncitizens. To them, a Mexican was a Mexican. By 1849, it was common for Mexicans in the mining camps to be robbed, beaten, and even lynched. That fall, the Mexican minister in Washington, Luis de la Rosa, filed a formal protest with the U.S. secretary of state condemning the "violent enmity and persecution" of Mexicans in California.[36]

The anti-Mexican atmosphere in the Northern California mining camps drove migrants southward. By 1860, Mexican immigrants made up 40 percent of Santa Barbara's Spanish-speaking population.[37] Newcomers generally integrated into existing Hispanic society, but tensions between the native- and foreign-born grew steadily. Anglo migration had begun to radically change not only the city's demographics but its economy. Capitalism was beginning to supplant the pastoral economy. The Gold Rush briefly fostered a cattle boom that benefited Californio ranchers. But a severe Southern California drought that lasted from 1862 to 1864 dealt a fatal blow to the local cattle industry, which accelerated the dispossession of Mexican landowners. By 1870 many *rancheros* were reduced to farming on rented lands, and Anglo Americans controlled Santa Barbara's economic life. Hispanics were increasingly displaced within the new economy. They were also losing control of other local institutions, including government. Almost overnight, it seemed, the rapid migration of Anglos had transformed Mexicans into minorities.

According to historian Albert Camarillo, "The loss of land, the decline of the pastoral economy, and the continuation of racial antagonism, together with the onset of political powerlessness," led to a process of "barriorization" in Santa Barbara in which Mexicans became "residentially and socially segregated."[38] A similar process occurred in Los Angeles. In their growing isolation many Mexicans began to nurture a more robust ethnic consciousness. Their victimization in the form of lynchings, murders, and robberies made "many Mexican Americans aware of their new status as a separate ethnic group."[39] In the 1850s, the open hostility between Anglos and Mexicans in Los Angeles took on the aspect of a race war. But even in those dire circumstances, the local Hispanic population did not find common cause against the enemy. After Deputy Constable William W. Jenkins shot and killed Antonio Ruiz when the latter resisted eviction from his home, hundreds of Mexicans formed a posse to arrest Jenkins. Fearful of an insurrection, a group of former Texas Rangers rode into town to fight the Mexicans. But Hispanics themselves were divided on how to deal with Ruiz. While friends of the dead man, predominantly from the lower classes, wanted to avenge his death, more established Californios were willing to negotiate a peaceful resolution. Similarly, Hispanics were divided in their attitudes toward

Juan Flores, a bandit whose gang was terrorizing Southern California and occupied the mission at San Juan Capistrano. While many poorer Mexicans—largely immigrants—were sympathetic to Flores and helped him avoid arrest, several native-born Californios helped vigilantes capture the outlaw. Tomás Sánchez, a prominent Californio who aided the vigilantes, was later elected Los Angeles County sheriff for his role in the Flores affair. After the Flores gang had robbed and killed Americans, Californios, a Frenchman, and a Jew, *El Clamor Público,* a Spanish-language paper that championed the rights of the Spanish speaking, denounced the bandits for being "without principles, without religion and without piety." In January of 1857, its editor, Francisco Ramírez, urged his readers to recognize that "our society is linked with indissoluble bonds to that of the Americans," and to "lay aside all animosity" toward them, forget past wrongs, and show that they were "loyal citizens and good patriots."[40] Seeking to put an end to the racial hostilities now widespread in the region, Ramírez asked his readers to take a good look around them. "Race war," he wrote, "the idea is ridiculous—if only rational men calmly look around them in Los Angeles and see how our society is composed."[41] Several months later, a correspondent for the same paper lamented that native-born and foreign-born Hispanics were nearly as alienated from one another as Anglos and Hispanics. "It is very sad to see the asperity and antipathy that reigns among Mexicans in California—they have no union—they have no fraternity—everywhere is hatred and this is principally observed among the majority of *hijos del país* [native sons] who behave with more animosity towards the Mexicans who were not born in California than towards the Indians."[42]

By the end of the 1860s, Anglo American businessmen were establishing a commercial society with a booming real estate market in Southern California. As Mexican Americans found themselves left out of the new economy, the "barrio swelled, unemployment remained high, and the overall quality of life stagnated at best."[43] Still, Mexican Americans continued to be tolerant of intermarriage with both Anglos and Indians. The U.S. government's plan to clear hundreds of thousands of acres of land to make room for Anglo settlers drastically reduced the Indian population from 310,000 in 1850 to fifty thousand in 1855.[44] Consequently, after the American occupation, many indigenous survivors married mestizos and otherwise assimilated into the Hispanic minority.

After a decline in the tumultuous 1850s, marriages between Mexicans and Anglos increased after the depression of the 1860s when "one marriage in three was mixed."[45] But unlike intermarriage in the Mexican era, the Anglo partner felt increasingly less obliged to assimilate into Hispanic culture. And whereas newly arrived Anglos once benefited socially from marrying into well-established Californio families, their declining economic status may have made Mexican Americans even more receptive to marriage with Anglos. Indeed, by the mid-1890s, "almost every Californio family had daughters and occasionally sons who had married Americans."[46]

Most Anglo-Mexican intermarriages involved Anglo men and Californio women. Ranching families like the Bandinis, Domínguezes, Picos, Sepúlvedas, and Yorbas all had daughters who married Anglos. The children of these mixed marriages were generally accepted in Anglo society and were assimilated. According to historian Leonard Pitt, for a few brief years, before marrying Mexicans became déclassé, Los Angeles was home to a "remarkably cosmopolitan [business] class: an alliance of Californians, Mexicans, and South Americans; of Yankees, Britons, Frenchmen, and Germans; of mestizos and whites; of merchants, gentry, and lawyers; of Protestants, Catholics, and a sprinkling of Jews."[47] Ultimately, intermarriage "made the Yankee conquest smoother than it might otherwise have been."[48]

There were also instances in which Californio men married Anglo women. The son of Juan Sepúlveda, who owned Rancho Los Palos Verdes near Los Angeles, married an American woman, as did Mariano Vallejo's son, Platón, who met his wife while attending medical school in Syracuse, New York. More famously, Romualdo Pacheco, who had been elected lieutenant governor in 1871 and served as governor of California for a year after the previous chief executive took a seat in the U.S. Senate, also married an Anglo woman. In the way that earlier Anglos had become, in Leonard Pitt's words, "Mexicanized gringos," using the disparaging term Mexicans sometimes called Anglos, Pacheco symbolizes the emergence of the gringoized Mexican.[49] Though born in California, Pacheco had spent his childhood in Hawaii and by the age of twelve no longer spoke Spanish. His widowed mother had remarried an Anglo man. The symbolism of Pacheco's cultural profile and his ability to appeal to both Anglos and the small Mexican American electorate helped make him attractive to the Republican Party. He went on to serve two terms in the U.S. Congress.

As the Anglo population grew and Mexicans became even more of a minority—no more than 1 or 2 percent of Californians by 1900—racial prejudice became a greater obstacle to intermarriage.[50] In response to their growing social isolation, some Mexican Americans fled to Mexico. But most did not. Fearing competition, merchants south of the border opposed the immigration of Mexican Americans to Mexico. In the old country, Mexican Americans and their Anglicized version of Spanish were considered culturally alien. Elite Mexican nationals grumbled that gringoized Mexicans would debase their culture. In an editorial, the Mexico City newspaper *La Integridad* expressed the fear that Mexican American migrants would "corrupt the language . . . and ultimately result in converting us into strangers in our own country."[51]

In Los Angeles, their deepening isolation led to the formation of Mexican American social and political associations. Between 1850 and 1900, at least fifteen mostly politically oriented community groups were founded.[52] Yet, as historian Richard Griswold del Castillo concluded, "The very nature of Mexican-American society . . . tended to diffuse ethnicity as a force for political unity."[53] The most well-established Mexican Americans, those most capable of exercising political leadership, often opted out of the ethnic community to assimilate into Anglo-American society. Furthermore, the ethnic openness that had characterized their experience as a majority population persisted even as Mexicans became minorities. "Despite the violence and discrimination they endured, Mexican Americans held their society remarkably open to Anglo participation."[54] For example, in Los Angeles, James Hayes was elected to the founding board of La Sociedad Hispano-Americana in 1875, and John Kays was elected secretary. A. R. Roth was treasurer of La Junta Patriótica Mexicana while C. M. Forester was vice president of El Club Filarmónico Mexicano. Corte Colón, an exclusive Hispanic club, counted Ryan and L. Seamons as members.

The more established Californios were generally eager to participate in American civic life, in part as a means to bridge the gap between the Hispanic minority and American government. In 1872, Ygnacio Sepúlveda gave a speech in English at a July 4th event. "We are the recipients of infinite gifts," he declared, "we the recipients of the fruits of the labors of our great patriots, in the midst of a universal prosperity, we unite today to pay tribute to their valor; to renew our adherence to the principles they proclaimed and to demonstrate by our happiness our infinite gratitude."[55] But Sepúlveda's observation notwithstanding, when the Civil War broke out Mexican Americans were as divided on the conflict as the rest of the nation. Nearly ten thousand Mexican Americans fought for either the Union or the Confederacy.[56] Though Texas and California supplied their share of soldiers, nearly half the Mexicans who played a role in the Civil War came from New Mexico.

Neither Texas nor New Mexico experienced the postwar demographic avalanche that California did. In New Mexico, their numerical superiority helped Hispanics maintain economic, political, and cultural power longer than they did in California or Texas. Even after the American conquest, Anglos who settled in northern New Mexico still married into Hispanic families of all classes, learned Spanish, and formed business partnerships with the locals. In 1870 and 1880, "the overwhelming majority of married Anglo men residing in the territory were married to Hispanic women."[57] Unlike pre-conquest marriages, however, Anglo spouses were not simply "assimilated into Hispanic society," but rather became "agents of social change."[58] In the 1870s and 1880s, it was Anglos married to Mexican American women who led the territorial campaign to provide public education. For their part, those Mexican American wives helped Hispanic society to adjust to the growing Anglo presence. Many soldiers who arrived during the Civil War married local women and settled in New Mexico. Lieutenant Albert J. Fountain, who was stationed at Fort Fillmore, married sixteen-year-old Mariana Pérez. Lieutenant John E. Oliphant of New York took Helena Martínez as his bride, while Private Patrick Higgins married a fourteen-year-old girl in a Catholic ceremony.[59] The last two surnames testify to the fact that the most common cross-cultural relationship in Santa Fe was between working-class Mexican American women and Irish-born men. While most inter-marriages involved Hispanic women and non-Hispanic men, there were some exceptions, including two prominent statewide politicians, Miguel Antonio Otero and J. Francisco Chávez, both of whom married Anglo women.

As a territory, New Mexico's leadership was divided between Mexican Americans and Anglos. While top officials such as the governor, secretary, and federal judges were all appointed in Washington and were therefore mostly Anglos, Mexican Americans continued to make their presence felt in the territory's electoral politics. New Mexico's delegate in Congress, the only territory-wide elective office, was held by Hispanics for thirty-seven of the territory's sixty-one years. From 1857 until statehood in 1912, Hispanics made up from 25 percent to 100 percent of the territorial Council and from 42 percent to 95 percent of the territorial House. A Mexican American was elected Council president twenty times and House speaker fourteen times.[60] The size of the Mexican American electorate ensured that Hispanics would not be excluded from the political process.

But much to the dismay of Spanish-language newspapers, native New Mexicans never "attain[ed] sufficient political unity . . . to dominate New Mexico's government."[61] In fact, because Mexican Americans found "niches in the patronage systems of both parties," there was little hope of putting together a unified Hispanic vote or leadership class.[62] Nor could political influence ultimately protect Mexican American landowners from the avarice of Anglo lawyers. As occurred in California, New Mexicans were required to have the titles to their lands verified by the U.S. government. "Naturally the lawyers of Santa Fe extracted their fees," historian Howard Lamar wrote, "for clearing titles. Being paid in land, they themselves gradually acquired ownership of the largest land grants and became, as it were, their own clients. Eventually over 80 percent of the Spanish grants went to American lawyers and settlers."[63]

The building of the railroads in the Southwest in the 1880s and the arrival of more Anglos also contributed to alter the balance of cultural power. Although life in the northern villages remained largely unchanged, urban Mexican Americans were increasingly obliged to accommodate the growing presence of Anglo Americans. In 1897, a man who symbolized an ethnically and culturally mixed New Mexico ascended to the governor's office. Thirty-seven-year-old Miguel Antonio Otero became the first and only Mexican American ever appointed the territory's chief executive. Born in St. Louis, Missouri, to a Mexican father and an Anglo mother, Otero was, according to historian Howard Lamar, "the representative of a new generation of Spanish-Americans who felt equally at home in both cultures."[64] Widely popular, particularly among Mexican Americans, the bilingual Otero served as governor from 1897 to 1906. In 1898, Governor Otero, who was a friend of President William McKinley's, offered New Mexico's support in the Spanish-American War. "New Mexico will furnish, as she did during [the Civil War], more men in proportion to her population, than any [other] state or territory in the Union," he told a group of journalists. "A large majority of her soldiers are Spanish-speaking and are as loyal to this country as any New England troops; they will rally round the stars and stripes."[65] Indeed, both Mexican Americans and Anglo Americans responded so enthusiastically to the call for volunteers that the New Mexican companies were oversubscribed. New Mexico's Spanish-speaking soldiers played an important role in Cuba as members of Theodore Roosevelt's Rough Riders.

For native New Mexicans, Americanization did not entail denying their ethnicity or their traditional culture and language. More than any other Mexican American population in the Southwest, New Mexicans, even those who lived in the more isolated villages, could pick which aspects of American life they chose to adopt. Hispanic New Mexicans had, in the words of historian Sarah Deutsch, "a long history of such cultural borrowing on the Spanish frontier," and in the late nineteenth century "they 'improved' their homes with iron beds, steel ranges, glazed windows, sewing machines, and oilcloth tablecloths."[66] The lure of American consumer goods reached well below the international frontier. In 1879, an Arizona journalist reported that a labor shortage in the Mexican state of Sonora was caused by the workers' desire to head north to earn enough money to buy "shoes, Levis, and flannel shirts."[67] After the 1880s, all of the Southwest—and northern Mexico as well—became increasingly

Americanized, and Mexican Americans did not hesitate to adopt new "consumer products, foods, fashions, and recreational forms."[68] One Anglo observer described migrants coming "north with no money and little clothing, sandals (hurraches) [sic] instead of shoes, wide sombreros, and blankets wrapped around them instead of coats. They are returning with rolls of money, often several hundred dollars, with good suitcases in their hands and most of them are dressed in the dearly-loved blue suits."[69]

Hoping to survive in the new economy, many native New Mexicans enthusiastically "sought to acquire Anglo skills."[70] But as the nineteenth-century came to a close and more Anglos arrived in the Southwest, congregated among themselves, and nurtured the anti-Mexican prejudices they brought with them, intermarriage and biculturalism became less acceptable among Anglos. Indeed, much of Anglo America at large found the idea of a Mexican American oxymoronic. In 1889, the *Chicago Tribune* called New Mexico's population "not American, but 'Greaser,' persons ignorant of our laws, manners, customs, languages, and institutions."[71] When New Mexico convened a constitutional convention in 1910, thirty-five of its one hundred delegates were Mexican Americans. These representatives successfully safeguarded the use of the Spanish language within the political system, and the first state legislature made both Spanish and English the official languages of state business. But by then biculturalism was already under attack. A 1904 editorial in *El Independiente,* a Spanish-language newspaper in Las Vegas, New Mexico, suggested that the Hispanic effort to adopt what was new without disregarding tradition was already being threatened. "It has become fashionable here in New Mexico to treat with a kind of reproach and contempt not only those who speak Spanish, but the language itself," the editor wrote. While acknowledging the advantages of learning "the national language," the editor saw no reason for native New Mexicans to "belittle and despise their own tongue."[72] Furthermore, he argued, the maintenance of Spanish would in no way preclude the learning of the language of the new order.

Like the New Mexicans, Tejanos were not culturally static and negotiated cultural and political change as best they could. After the Texas Revolution, the Anglo-Mexican political alliance that had allowed Lorenzo de Zavala to become the first vice president of the Texas Republic began to crumble and the names of the Tejanos who fought alongside Sam Houston and Jim Bowie were forgotten. The Mexicans who suffered most from Anglo depredations were those who lived in closest proximity to Anglo American settlements. But even those who lived in majority-Mexican areas along the Rio Grande were not safe from Anglo hostility. According to one memoirist, in postwar Laredo some Americans "began a movement to clean out the Mexicans. They would rant at public meetings and declare that this was an American country and the Mexicans ought to be run out."[73]

Still, American control was not maintained through force alone. Even after the Texas Revolution, nearly every wealthy Mexican American family in San Antonio had a daughter who had married an Anglo.[74] Just as before the revolution many Anglos married Tejanas to better integrate themselves into local society, after independence Texas Mexicans were keenly aware of the advantages of having an Anglo American in-law. Several of the most prominent families had more than one such relative. Many mixed marriages united wealthy landed Mexican families and politically powerful Anglos. In addition to easier access to property, politically ambitious Anglo spouses could reap the rewards of their connection to a Hispanic family. Though the number of Mexican politicians in San Antonio declined after 1840, Anglo candidates with Mexican in-laws "consistently won election to city office during the 1840s and 1850s."[75]

By 1840, non-Mexicans dominated San Antonio's economic and political life. In 1856, Mexican Americans made up only 38 percent of the city population. As a consequence, there was strong incentive for the children of upper-class mixed marriages to identify more strongly with the ethnic group of their fathers. As adults, most children of mixed marriages married non-Mexicans and assimilated into Anglo society. But intermarriage was not the sine qua non of Americanization for the Tejano upper classes. In San Antonio, wealthy Tejanos generally lived in the same neighborhoods as Anglo Americans. Some Texas Mexicans sent their children to American schools in the East. But depending on the demographics of where the couple lived, intermarriage did not necessarily lead to full Anglicization. In

Laredo, where Mexicans retained majority status, Anglo husbands and their Mexican wives still tended to maintain culturally Hispanic households. Families such as the Blocks, Deckers, Marxes, and Monroes spoke Spanish at home. The town's Mexican-American majority and the presence of a Hispanic elite allowed for greater ethnic and cultural mixture than in places with Anglo majorities. According to one contemporary, "There were neither racial nor social distinctions between Americans and Mexicans, we were just one family. This was due to the fact that so many of us of that generation had a Mexican mother and an American or European father."[76]

Still, most Texas Mexicans did not have such intimate contact with Anglos and often found themselves living in the shadows of discriminatory barriers. As occurred in other Southwestern states, all Mexican Americans were not treated alike in Texas. "Landed Mexicans," according to sociologist David Montejano, "represented the complicating factor in the Mexican-Anglo relations of the frontier period. Even during the worst times of Mexican banditry, the permanent Mexican residents who were landowners were seen as 'good citizens' while the large 'floating' population temporarily employed on ranches were seen as sympathizers of the raiders."[77] Color-conscious Anglos sometimes went to great lengths to refer to well-off Mexicans as Spaniards, highlighting their white European heritage and overlooking their Indian heritage. In 1890, L. E. Daniell, who wrote *Successful Men in Texas*, described José María Rodríguez as "five feet nine inches in height, complexion dark, but not a drop of Indian blood in his veins."[78] As a result, many Mexicans engaged in the practice of passing themselves off as "Spanish" rather than "Mexican." Particularly along the border, upwardly mobile Mexican Americans sometimes felt compelled to distance themselves from Mexico and their mestizo heritage. Their hope was that by emphasizing the white European aspect of their heritage they could better protect themselves from discrimination.

But while many Hispanic elites tried to distance themselves from the masses, others did not. For some, elite interethnic cooperation was a way to protect the less powerful. Tucson's Estevan Ochoa, who believed firmly that Anglos and Mexicans could live together harmoniously, donated land and supervised the building of the town's first public school. Similarly, Mariano Samaniego, another *tucsonense* who strongly supported public education, acted as go-between for Mexican Americans and Anglos. He served on the first Board of Regents of the University of Arizona. Whether their intentions were benevolent or not, the cooperation of members of the Hispanic elite with Anglo authorities did in fact often protect the masses from further mistreatment. After the Texas Revolution, a " 'peace structure'—an accommodative arrangement between the leaders of the victors and those of the defeated," actually contained racial antagonism in heavily Mexican areas of the state.[79] It allowed Anglos to establish authority over the Mexicans "without the constant use of force."[80]

In the same way that the emergence of large numbers of free blacks undermined the racial justification for slavery in the early nineteenth century, the presence of "acceptable" Mexicans—whether by virtue of their class, education, skin color, or history—also complicated racist arguments that Mexicans were an inferior "race." Although interviewed in the early twentieth century, the comments of one large landowner in South Texas are applicable also to the late nineteenth century: "On the border they mix. . . . On the border you do business with the Mexicans and they were a great social class there once. You can't be quite so rough with them."[81] A contemporary Anglo professional from Nueces County echoed these sentiments. "The Mexican is an inferior. But in Laredo there are many influential Mexican citizens and they can't be treated like a *pelado* (lowlife). The treatment given to Mexicans depends partly on the individual Mexican, who may be of high class, and partly on numbers; in Laredo there are so many you have to give them social recognition. In Corpus Christi there are no prominent Mexican families. . . . There is absolutely no social recognition in San Antonio."[82]

Members of the Hispanic establishment derived their power from their presumed ability to exercise authority over the masses. But as more Anglos arrived in Texas in the 1880s, they were better able to establish local control through sheer force of numbers. Consequently, the "peace structure" was abandoned, and the local Hispanic upper classes declined in social significance. Anglos set about building a more racially exclusive society. In Texas, the era of Jim Crow was dawning, and Mexican Americans were destined to feel its noxious effects. Throughout the Southwest, Anglo Americans became much less willing to mingle with Mexican Americans. Even in Arizona, whose small population had enjoyed good Anglo-Mexican relations, Geronimo's capture in 1886 and the pacification of the Apaches had lessened the need for Anglos to get along with Mexican Americans. Soon newcomers from the East numerically overwhelmed the Mexican population. The one exception was New Mexico, where Hispanics maintained majority status until around World War II.

In the meantime, after two generations of living as Americans, Mexicans were adapting to life in the United States. In Los Angeles, "the Mexican American population of the city now resembled their Anglo neighbors more than their Mexican cousins."[83] Working men wore denim jeans while the remaining wealthy Californios built Victorian-style homes. "Children with names like Gutiérrez and Coronel understood their Spanish-speaking grandparents and parents, but usually answered them in English which both understood."[84] In Texas, proximity to Mexico helped keep tradition and language alive. But Tejanos mixed them with newly acquired cultural attributes. Through contact with Anglo employers, merchants, and institutions such as schools and churches, many learned to speak English, though not always fluently. American themes were celebrated in Mexican *corridos* (folk ballads), and American holidays, like Independence Day and George Washington's Birthday, were "observed as part of a group consciousness."[85] According to sociologist Kenneth Stewart and historian Arnoldo de León, Tejanos "did not strive to maintain archaic traditions; they were resilient in adapting to circumstances as changes unfolded."[86] The completion of rail service from the interior of the United States to El Paso, San Antonio, and Laredo in the 1880s led to a more intense phase of Americanization. Many traditional Mexican ways were replaced, including styles in architecture and clothing. After the arrival of the railroad, Laredo saw the construction of buildings with "modern American design."[87] By 1900, many Mexican Americans had begun to follow American baseball. In El Paso, they organized local teams, the most popular of which was the Internationals. The all-Hispanic team played against Anglo-American ball clubs. In 1917, the Internationals boasted the best pitcher in the league, José "Curly" Villareal. By the close of the nineteenth century, there were Mexican Americans living at varying levels of civic and cultural acculturation. Those who were most established north of the border had learned to negotiate the tension between their national and ethnic identities. In 1897, a group of Mexican Americans in El Paso refused to support the annual Mexican Independence Day celebration, the largest Hispanic cultural event in the city, with the explanation that it had no significance for them. The local Spanish-language paper promptly chastised them. "To these 'Agringados' (Americanized Mexicans) who negate that they are Mexicans because they were born in the United States, we ask: what blood runs through their veins? Do they think that they are members of the Anglo-Saxon race who only happen to have dark skins because they were born on the border! What nonsense! (¡Qué barbaridad!)."[88]

Six

Caught Between North and South

By the turn of the twentieth century, the increase in migration both from the East and the South had undermined the tenuous ethnic arrangement that Mexicans and Anglos had negotiated in the nineteenth century. Before mass Anglo migration, a more fluid understanding of race prevailed in many areas of the Southwest, one that reflected the Hispanic-Catholic view of race. A person's "race" was determined by cultural behaviors and class status as much as it was by phenotypic traits. The in-between categories and the exceptions to the rule were gradually erased by a more rigid understanding of race. Prior to the turn of the century, a three-tiered system of racial classification was common in many Southwestern towns. Poor Mexicans occupied the bottom of the scale, while Anglo Americans perched at the top. In the middle were the more affluent Mexicans, those whom Anglos sometimes referred to, out of courtesy, as Spanish. Those were the Mexicans who blurred the racial boundaries and who could make a claim to whiteness.

But the new Anglo migrants, many of whom came from the American South, did not countenance such exceptions. More often than not, they sought to transform the three-part racial classification system into a binary one. A century earlier, under French rule, Louisiana also had had a ternary racial system, consisting of whites, blacks, and free people of color, who were racially mixed. As Anglo-Americans gradually solidified their legal and cultural control, the system was pared down to two categories. Indeed, by 1892, Homer Plessy, who was seventh-eighths white, was arrested for sitting in a railroad car reserved for whites. Plessy became the plaintiff in the landmark U.S. Supreme Court decision *Plessy v. Ferguson,* which enshrined the concept of "separate but equal" in the law. The imposition of a binary racial system necessitated the downgrading of the more socially acceptable, in-between racial category as well as the reassertion of the primacy of racial purity.

In the Southwest, the result was that Mexicans, no matter how light-skinned, now faced greater obstacles to the achievement of white status. In the nineteenth century, while Mexicans may not have been considered fully white, neither were they deemed fully non-white. Long used to their own racial traditions, Mexicans now found that their upward social mobility was being constricted on the grounds of race. In the South, the absence of black blood was the primary determinate of whiteness. In 1848 New Mexican Santiago Tafolla was considered white by default in Georgia where he worked as an overseer on a slave plantation.[1] But in the Southwest, whiteness—indeed Americanness—was more often defined in contradistinction to Mexicans.

Not long after the Treaty of Guadalupe Hidalgo was ratified, the U.S. Congress reneged on its promise to protect the political rights of the Mexicans and granted to the legislatures of the ceded territories and states the power to determine the citizenship status of the new population. Thus, each state would decide which Mexicans, if any, would receive U.S. citizenship and the political and legal rights that status conferred.

The California constitution, drafted in 1849, granted the right to vote only to white Mexicans, while Indians, mestizos, and those of black ancestry were disenfranchised. An early draft of section one of the constitution stated "Every white male citizen of the United States, of the age of 21 years . . . shall be entitled to vote."[2] It was quickly suggested that the section be amended to read "Every white male citizen of the United States and every male citizen of Mexico, who shall have elected to become a citizen of the United States, under (Article VIII of) the Treaty of Peace."[3] The delegate from Monterey, however, having no desire to confer the franchise on nonwhites, objected to the addition and proposed an amendment to insert the word " 'white' before male citizen of Mexico."[4]

The eight Mexicans present at the convention all voted against the amendment. It seemed absurd to them to approve the measure in a delegation that included men like Los Angeles representative Manuel Domínguez, a dark-skinned man of clearly mestizo origins. Though

Domínguez himself was one of the signers of the new constitution, it was not clear whether Mexicans of similar skin tone would be permitted to vote. Nor was it clear what "white" really meant. Even the Monterey delegate who introduced the "white Mexican" amendment was ambivalent about the meaning of the term. He said that "he had no objection to color, except in so far as it indicated the inferior races of mankind."[5] He was willing to extend the franchise to deserving Mexicans, but not to "the African and Indian races."[6] Another delegate, W. S. Sherwood of Sacramento, declared that he had no desire to "debar the Spanish" from voting. Even though they might be "darker than the Anglo-Saxon race," he said he considered them "white men."[7]

Californio delegate Pablo de la Guerra also preferred to define the term "white" in a way that would be most advantageous to Mexicans. "Many citizens of California have received from nature a very dark skin; nevertheless, there are among them men who have heretofore been allowed to vote, and not only that, but to fill the highest public offices. It would be very unjust to deprive them of the privilege of citizens merely because nature had not made them white. But if, by the word 'white' it was intended to exclude the African race, then it was correct and satisfactory."[8] Some Anglo delegates, like W. M. Gwin, reluctantly agreed. Gwin, who had earlier voted to disenfranchise "pure uncivilized Indians," thought that "the descendants of Indians should not be excluded from the franchise."[9] Likewise, Kimball Dimmick of San Jose declared that "the mixed race, descended from the Indians and Spanish," should be permitted "to enjoy the right of suffrage as liberally as any American citizen."[10] Indeed, he observed that even "some of the most honorable and distinguished families in Virginia are descended from the Indian race."[11]

Their equivocal racial status and the murky definition of "whiteness" made Mexicans highly vulnerable to violations of their rights. Essentially, each political jurisdiction had the legal authority to determine whether an individual was white or not. Not surprisingly, this often depended literally on the color of his skin. In 1857, Manuel Domínguez, then a member of the Los Angeles County Board of Supervisors, was called to testify in a San Francisco courtroom when an objection was made to his taking the witness stand. The basis for the objection was that Domínguez was ineligible to testify because he was an Indian. The judge agreed and dismissed the witness. In 1870, Pablo de la Guerra, another signer of the state constitution as well as a judge, state senator, and prominent citizen of Santa Barbara, was prosecuted by the state for unlawfully assuming the rights of a white citizen. Although de la Guerra was in all probability a man of predominately Spanish ancestry, his lineage, like that of so many New World Hispanics, was unclear. In a hearing in the California Supreme Court, state attorneys claimed that de la Guerra was not a citizen because he was more Indian than white. They further argued that the Treaty of Guadalupe Hidalgo did not require California to grant citizenship to all Mexicans. De la Guerra's defense was that he was white. He testified that he "was born at Santa Barbara in 1819, and has ever since resided at that place and is admitted to have been a White male citizen of Mexico."[12] The Supreme Court ultimately agreed. But even as it allowed de la Guerra to retain his white status, it reaffirmed the state's authority to strip nonwhite Mexicans of their rights. The legal system had decided that the state of California was under no obligation to grant equal rights to all Mexicans.

The process of "racializing" the Mexican American population—dividing a heterogenous population and granting its subgroups varying degrees of status and privilege—also occurred in Texas.[13] In 1836, the Constitution of the Republic of Texas granted citizenship to Mexicans who were not Indian or black. That remained the law even after the United States annexed the state in 1845. Similarly, Arizona's territorial constitution granted full rights of citizenship only to white males and white Mexican males. Only in the territory of New Mexico, where the majority of constitutional delegates were Mexican, was the Treaty of Guadalupe Hidalgo accepted as binding and dispositive of the matter. Its first territorial assembly granted full political rights to free whites and all citizens of Mexico who had become citizens of the United States by virtue of the treaty.

Anglo notions of racial separation had reached Texas with the first American settlers. But by the close of the nineteenth century, segregation was becoming institutionalized. While the exclusion of blacks had been clearly defined by tradition and Jim Crow laws, the segregation of Mexicans was generally extended informally and extralegally.

According to historian F. Arturo Rosales: "To Americans it became clear that the Jim Crow laws employed for blacks could be applied to the new foreigners. Even though new codes did not avowedly target Mexicans, laws regarding vagrancy, weapon control, alcohol and drug use, and smuggling were partially designed to control Mexican immigrant behavior. In addition, education policy, private-sector housing, and labor segmentation combined with the judicial web to keep Mexicans powerless and easier to control."[14]

Anglo newcomers arriving on the railroad soon outnumbered Texas natives. Unfamiliar with Mexicans, many of the incoming migrants treated them all—even those who had been Americans for several generations—as undesirable foreigners. Unlike the Anglo old-timers, the newcomers did not bother to distinguish between elites and peons. While the established Anglos were known to mistreat Mexicans, race relations were generally characterized by "paternalism and patronage. The new settlers, on the other hand, did not understand Mexicans and frequently subjected them to indignities and discriminations that the older Anglo-Americans would never think of doing."[15] While Mexicans were clearly second-class citizens and did not benefit from an evenhanded system of justice in the late nineteenth century, there had nonetheless been an understanding that "Mexicans in areas acquired by the United States had a right to remain, and upper-class Mexicans in the Southwest were acceptable for socializing and for marriage."[16] More importantly, however, incoming Anglo Americans were replacing the old cattle ranching economy with one based on commercial farming. With few exceptions, by 1920 the new economy had reduced Texas Mexicans to a class of landless laborers.

In South Texas, the remaining Tejano landholders either sold out to Anglo speculators or were otherwise obliged to make way for the newcomers. As in mid-nineteenth-century California, the displacement of the landed Tejano class in Texas also involved coercion and fraud. Texas Mexican elites scorned this "American invasion." According to Jovita González, a contemporary folklorist and historian, for the Tejano elites, "It was a blow to see these new arrivals ruthlessly appropriate all that had been theirs, even the desert plains. They saw all political power slipping from their hands; they saw themselves segregated into their own quarters."[17] The disappearance of an intermediating elite class led many Anglos to view the social order as now being composed of a simple binary: Anglos versus Mexicans. While Mexicans had once been perceived as diverse, they were now more likely to be viewed as a monolithic, subordinate class. This infuriated established Texas Mexicans. "The friendly feeling which had slowly developed between the old American and Mexican families," wrote González, "has been replaced by a feeling of hate, distrust and jealousy on the part of the Mexicans."[18] As one prominent Tejano told González,

> We Texas Mexicans of the border . . . although we hold on to our traditions and are proud of our race, are loyal to the United States . . . in spite of the treatment we receive from some of the new Americans. Before their arrival, there were no racial or social distinctions between us. Their children married ours, ours married theirs, and both were glad and proud of the fact. But with the coming of the pushing Americans from the North and Middle West we felt the change. They made us feel for the first time that we were Mexicans and that they considered themselves our superiors.[19]

In the meantime, Anglo newcomers established their own clubs, saloons, churches, and fraternal organizations. Recently arrived Anglo women, in particular, helped redefine mixed marriages between Anglo men and Mexican women as disreputable and hence to be avoided. Perhaps more importantly, interethnic contact as equals, a necessary precondition for mixed marriages, diminished. Tolerance toward intermarriage persisted longer in places where Mexicans remained part of the upper classes. But by 1908, a federal investigator noted that while intermarriage still sometimes occurred, it had become "a subject for apology."[20] Consequently, intermarriage rates across the Southwest declined precipitously and did not rise again until after 1945. Particularly in Texas and Arizona, by the early years of the twentieth century, only a few Hispanic families remained "socially accepted by Anglos as Spaniards or 'a better class' of Mexicans, but the number was declining. In a remarkable process of unlearning, many Anglos were primitivizing Mexicans as classless, a pure type, just 'Mexican.' . . . To Anglos 'Mexican' had come to *mean* poor, ignorant, degraded."[21] Mexican also meant foreign.

Mass immigration from Mexico in the early 1900s furthered the impression that all Mexicans were foreigners. Anglo hostility toward Mexican immigrants affected all ethnic Mexicans. Meantime, Mexican Americans were acutely aware that the influx of newcomers had served to marginalize them further and make it more difficult for them to be acknowledged as Americans. In the 1920s, a prominent Mexican American in Nueces County, Texas, complained, "We are handicapped by the steady flow of immigration of the laboring peon class. The native-born don't get a chance."[22]

Indeed, throughout the twentieth century, the Mexican American experience would be characterized by a mixture of conflict and cooperation between the native- and foreign-born, between Mexican and Anglo American cultures, between the English and Spanish languages, between past and future, between immigrant parents and their acculturated children. At any given historical moment, Mexicans in the United States lived at varying distances, physical and psychological, from the immigrant experience and at different levels of acculturation.

In the early 1900s, it was not uncommon for Mexican Americans to distance themselves from Mexican immigrants. In Santa Barbara, California, the influx and growing visibility of migrants rekindled anti-Mexican prejudice among Anglos. Thus, the native-born often sought to "disassociate themselves from the newcomers, in order to avoid the possibility of being stigmatized as foreign-born Mexicans."[23] Though they both occupied the lower stratum of society, the two groups of Hispanics remained socially separate. While it did occur, intermarriage between native- and foreign-born Mexicans was more uncommon than not. Just as Mexican Americans would sometimes refer to newcomers as *cholos,* for their part, immigrants called Mexican Americans *pochos,* an insult meaning "watered-down Mexican." According to one native-born Mexican American with Mexican-born parents, "you had two classes of [Spanish-speaking] people. The old time people . . . didn't want anything to do with [foreign-born] Mexicans. Mexicans never wanted anything to do with the 'pochos.' "[24] In 1916, a Mexican immigrant recounted her first impression of Mexican Americans. They "were a very stand-offish people. They were very proud, those that lived here. They were angered at those who came from Mexico . . . We didn't like each other . . . and many difficulties began between us. Because those from here used to treat us as the gringos did—as 'dirty Mexicans.' "25

There were, of course, genuine social distinctions between Mexican Americans and their foreign-born cousins. For one thing, U.S.-born Mexicans could speak English, while recent immigrants tended to speak only Spanish. But over time acculturation made the newcomers more like the longtime Americans and the distinctions between the two began to blur. Recent immigrants and Mexican Americans would learn from each other's cultural experiences. Still, as long as there were new arrivals, culture clashes persisted.

Of course, the first Mexican Americans were not immigrants at all. In 1850, two years after the signing of the Treaty of Guadalupe Hidalgo, between 86,000 and 116,000 Mexicans resided in the Southwest—two-thirds to three-quarters of them in New Mexico.26 California had as few as nine thousand Spanish speakers in 1850 and Texas only five thousand more. Arizona had no more than 1,600 Mexicans residing there. The lack of adequate records and the back-and-forth nature of Mexican migration make it difficult to estimate how many people chose to settle north of the Rio Grande in the decades following the treaty. The keeping of such records was of such little consequence to government officials that no migration figures at all were kept between 1886 and 1893. Furthermore, in the late nineteenth century, the border was of little social or economic significance. "There were no guards . . . no checking of papers, and indeed no one had papers; [west of the Rio Grande] few residents knew exactly where the border was."27

The arrival of the railroads in the 1880s both from the east and the south facilitated the collision of two waves of migration—one Anglo, the other Mexican. While the Southern Pacific and the Santa Fe railroads reached El Paso in 1881, the Mexican Central line between Mexico City and El Paso was completed in March of 1884. *The Lone Star,* one of El Paso's earliest newspapers, welcomed the new connection to the Mexican capital, which it dubbed the "Paris of America," and encouraged local businessmen to increase their trade with

Mexico.[28] Four years later, the Mexican National Railroad Company connected Mexico City with Laredo, Texas. By 1890, nearly all of Mexico's main population and production centers were "connected to markets in all forty-eight contiguous U.S. states and territories."[29]

By linking the region's natural resources to the growing markets and industries in the eastern United States, the railroads fostered a period of prosperity in the Southwest. Concomitantly, the westward expansion of American capitalism required new infusions of labor. As in the East and Midwest, Southwestern industries—mining, ranching, farming, and transportation—looked to immigration to fill the growing need. Initially, a variety of European, Asian, and Mexican workers fit the bill. But by 1900, the Southwest was almost entirely dependent on Mexican labor.

Indeed, Mexican workers played an instrumental role in building the transportation network that was to transform life in the Southwest. In the final decades of the nineteenth century, the Southern Pacific and the Santa Fe railroads employed many Mexican laborers to lay tracks across the desert. (Incidentally, the lines were built on trails that Mexicans—and the Spaniards before them—had blazed throughout the Southwest.) After the main rail links were completed, more Mexicans were hired to maintain the lines. In 1894, the Southern Pacific opened an employment office in El Paso where its agents routinely crossed the border into Mexico to recruit workers. By 1909, a federal commission concluded that, in the previous several years, Mexicans had performed most of the railroad construction throughout the Southwest. Employment on the railroad made Mexicans geographically mobile. By 1912, large numbers of Mexicans could be found working in Missouri, Iowa, and Illinois.

The Chinese Exclusion Act of 1882 and the 1907 Gentleman's Agreement with Japan brought Asian immigration to a halt, thereby making Southwestern industries even more dependent on Mexican labor. In 1910, the Japanese were still the dominant group of laborers in the fields of California. But, unable now to recruit more Asian workers, farmers turned their attention to Mexico. In 1907, the trade publication *California Fruit Grower* concluded that Mexicans were "plentiful, generally peaceable, and are satisfied with very low social conditions."[30] Two years later, farmers brought more than one thousand Mexicans to compete with the Japanese in the state's sugar beet fields. Mexicans also gradually began to replace Japanese workers in the citrus fields. By 1919, seven thousand Mexican migrants toiled in California's citrus groves, comprising 30 percent of the workforce.[31]

Mexicans also worked in the burgeoning mining industry. After the pacification of the Apaches in the mid-1880s, coal, copper, and silver were discovered in New Mexico and Arizona. The southern sliver of Arizona, which the U.S. had acquired as part of the Gadsden Purchase in 1853, was particularly rich in precious metals. Fortunately for the mining companies, the Mexican state of Sonora, just south of the international border, had been a mining center since 1640, and Sonora laborers could be lured north by the promise of higher wages. By the mid-1920s, Mexicans made up 43 percent of Arizona's copper miners.[32] They were also heavily employed in a variety of unskilled jobs throughout the region. After 1900 when it had become clear that the expanding Southwestern economy would require a steady source of labor, enterprising businessmen set up shop as labor agents connecting American firms with Mexican workers. In 1909, a labor agent in Corpus Christi, Texas, advertised, "Plenty of labor: I secure Mexican laborers for all kinds of work at reasonable prices and in any number."[33] The largest such agencies dealt exclusively with railroad companies. Their agents "met penniless aliens at the border, provided them with provisions, and transported them to railroad lines in need of labor."[34] In 1907, one recruiter sent 6,474 Mexican workers to four railroad companies in one nine-month period. Within eight months in 1907–1908, six agencies "supplied 16,479 Mexican laborers to railroads, an average of 2,060 per month."[35] In 1909, Mexicans made up 17.1 percent of workers on nine Western railroads. By 1929, that figure had risen to 59.5 percent.[36]

At times, agencies recruited workers deep in the interior of Mexico and paid their passage to the border. An employee for one recruiting agency, the Holmes Supply Company, explained why he thought Mexican workers were in such great demand throughout the Southwest: "Mexican labor is good. It is the best common labor in California. It isn't rapid, either mentally or physically, but it is steady. The Mexicans will take a vacation from their work every once in a while. The Mexican father says, 'My son will take care of me (in my old age).' The Mexicans are peculiarly adapted to agriculture. They are good miners and the best track labor available."[37]

With clients desperate for workers, some recruiters resorted to the use of coercive methods to lure Mexican laborers to jobs in the United States. The infamous *enganchadores,* a term that refers to people who lure, or hook others, would follow the rail lines as far as the west-central Mexican states of Guanajuato, Jalisco, Michoacán, San Luis Potosí, and Zacatecas to recruit laborers. There they would tell stories of the high wages Mexicans could earn for a day's work. Typically, these recruiters would loan migrants the cost of the passage northward. The migrant would then have the loan, plus the interest, deducted from his wages. Once in the United States, they would invariably discover that their earnings were much less than they had been promised and the interest rate higher. For the time it took them to repay their debt, they were considered *enganchado*—hooked.

By 1910, nearly two-thirds of Mexican migrants had headed for Texas. From 1890 to 1910, the ethnic Mexican population of the Lone Star State more than doubled, and 45 percent were foreign-born.[38] Most Mexican migrants, no matter where they were ultimately headed, passed through the booming metropolis of El Paso, which by 1920 was half-Mexican.

The vast majority of early Mexican migrants were men hoping to go north temporarily to resolve their financial difficulties back home. Many, particularly farmworkers, worked seasonally and returned to Mexico for a spell before their next tour of duty in the U.S. Before 1917 there were few restrictions on Mexican immigration. Not only did the U.S. immigration authorities lack the personnel to enforce the regulations that did exist—fewer than sixteen mounted officials guarded the 1,900-mile-long frontier before the establishment of the Border Patrol in 1924—but the government was lax about enforcing the few restrictions that were on the books. In 1882, Congress passed the first general immigration law, which ordered officials to refuse admittance to, among others, persons likely to become a public charge. But the so-called LPC—likely to be a public charge—clause was rarely enforced on the Mexican border. According to historian Mark Reisler, "If employment agencies were demanding labor, Mexicans would be routinely admitted, and they would not have to prove that they possessed any funds."[39]

As word of job opportunities reached sending villages back in Mexico, women and children joined their husbands and fathers north of the border. "Ten years ago our Mexican migrants were chiefly men," one railroad official observed. "It was rare to see a woman among those who came through. . . . About 1900, men who had been in the United States and returned to Mexico began to bring back their families with them. . . . Most of the men who had families with them did not go back the following season, but some of the men without their families did, and some of them in turn came back the next year with their families to remain permanently. So the process goes on, with . . . a larger proportion of women and children among the immigrants each year, and a larger proportion remaining in this country."[40] By 1920, the Bureau of Labor estimated, half of all immigrants from Mexico were women and children. Still, while more stayed, others continued their familiar migration pattern—coming north for seasonal work and then returning to Mexico for a few months or years.

Yet many who wound up staying permanently in the U.S. never abandoned the hope of returning to Mexico. With their homeland in such close proximity, returning there always remained a distinct possibility. Nonetheless, Mexicans were not immune to the pain and alienation inherent in migration. They were still leaving their homes, bidding adiós to tearful loved ones, and making their way as strangers in a strange land where they were often exploited.

Because of lingering illusions of returning to Mexico, few immigrants sought to become American citizens. Of the tens of thousands of foreign-born Mexicans who lived in El Paso in 1920, fully 90 percent remained noncitizens.[41] This unwillingness to press for citizenship made immigrants all the more vulnerable to exploitation. As it was, Mexicans were routinely paid lower wages than other workers. In 1910, the California Immigration Commission found that Mexican railroad workers generally earned 25 percent less than their non-Mexican co-workers.[42] While they valued Mexicans' hard work, many employers nonetheless felt justified in exploiting them. Indeed, Mexicans had a reputation for being a pliable workforce. Both employers and government officials assumed that Mexicans were temporary sojourners and would therefore not aggressively demand better wages and working conditions. A 1909 federal commission concluded that "Mexican immigrants are providing a fairly acceptable supply of labor in a limited territory in which it is difficult to secure others, and their competitive ability is limited because of their more or less temporary residence and their personal qualities, so that their incoming does not involve the same detriment to labor conditions as is involved in the immigration of other races who also work at comparatively low wages. While the Mexicans are not easily assimilated, this is not of very great importance as long as most of them return to their native land after a short time."[43] The presumption both on the part of the employers and many migrants themselves that Mexicans were mere sojourners in the United States gave credence to the myth that America could avail itself of cheap labor without having to incorporate the laborers themselves into its national life. Employers expected Mexicans to provide much needed labor without causing too much "trouble." In 1911, the United States commissioner-general of immigration described why railroad companies preferred Mexican workers. Mexican labor, he said, "met an economic condition demanding laborers who could stand the heat and other discomforts of that particular section. The peon makes a satisfactory track hand, for the reasons that he is docile, ignorant, and nonclannish to an extent which makes it possible that one or more men shall quit or be discharged and others remain at work; moreover, he is willing to work for a low wage."[44]

But Mexicans in fact often did protest such exploitation by walking away from these jobs and seeking new employment. The commissioner-general's assessment notwithstanding, it was not uncommon for entire groups of pickers to abandon the fields if one of their *compadres* was mistreated by the foreman. Indeed, Mexican immigrants were uniquely distinguished by their highly transient lifestyles. Both farm and railroad work were seasonal occupations. Thus, workers often found jobs on the railroad, in the fields, and in mines all within the span of several months. In 1908, this tendency led Victor Clark, an investigator for the Bureau of Labor, to conclude that Mexican farm laborers "do not occupy a position analogous to that of the Negro in the South. They are not permanent, do not acquire land or establish themselves in little cabin homesteads, but remain nomadic and outside of American civilization."[45] By the 1920s most Mexican immigrants still led rural lives, but they were not entirely isolated from the rapidly Americanizing towns. A study conducted in central Texas in the late 1920s found that while no Mexican families owned radios and only a few had telephones, 45 percent owned automobiles.[46] The population was urbanizing rapidly. In fact, after 1930, a majority of Mexicans—both U.S.- and foreign-born—lived in urban communities.

In Los Angeles, which became one of three primary clearing centers for Mexican migrants between 1910 and 1930—along with El Paso and San Antonio—Mexican immigrants were more spatially mobile than both native- and foreign-born whites. A high proportion of Mexican workers routinely moved in and out of Los Angeles, either to work outside the city or to return to Mexico for a spell. Job discrimination and lack of opportunities for upward mobility also induced people to take to the road in search of greener pastures.[47]

But Mexican immigrants often tolerated inferior conditions both because they felt that they would one day return to Mexico and because jobs were scarce back in their homeland. The jobs that did exist in Mexico generally paid lower wages. In the last quarter of the nineteenth century, the living standards of Mexico's rural poor deteriorated. Land policies instituted by President Porfirio Díaz helped large landowners acquire acreage that had previously been communally held by villagers. By 1910, more than 95 percent of Mexican rural households were landless.[48] At the same time, improvements in public health led to a population explosion. Wages were depressed even further. In 1905, an agricultural worker in Jalisco could earn around 12.5 cents per day plus some maize. By comparison, a track worker in the Southwest who worked fewer hours could earn $1.25 daily. Likewise, at the peak of the season, a Mexican family could earn as much as $5 a day picking cotton in Texas.[49] In other words, as bad as things could sometimes be in the United States, they were likely to be worse in Mexico.

After several decades of migration, stories—good and bad—circulated all over Mexico about life in the United States. Like any other migrants, Mexicans had to balance the risks and the benefits of seeking work in the U.S. Conditions in some states were rumored to be better than in others. Northerners were said to treat Mexicans better than did Southerners. Generally, Mexicans who never migrated to the U.S. had a worse impression of Americans than those who had spent time north of the border. In the early 1930s, during the Depression, economist Paul S. Taylor interviewed migrants in the Jalisco village of Arandas. All things being equal, most would have preferred to live in Mexico. But most also said they would return to the United States, possibly for the remainder of their lives, if work were available there. The majority of migrants, even those who had faced mistreatment in the U.S., hoped to return, at least temporarily. "In the minds of the returned emigrants, the agreeable aspects of their experience in the United States far overshadowed the disagreeable." Even one man who had been kicked off a Texas farm without receiving his pay hoped to return one day. "I don't think I can ever get there anymore," he told Taylor wistfully, "maybe—maybe—maybe."[50]

The influx of immigrants in the early twentieth century complicated ethnic Mexican identity in the United States. Mexican Americans were, in effect, caught in the middle, pushed and pulled by social pressures from both Anglos and Mexican immigrants. According to historian David G. Gutiérrez, "They were torn between the strong cultural affinities they felt toward Mexico and Mexicans on one hand and their desire to be accepted—or, at the very least, to be allowed to function—as equal members of American society on the other."[51] Given the ongoing nature of the migration, Mexicans and Mexican Americans were constantly obliged to evaluate their feelings for one another. Recent arrivals continually brought reminders of their heritage and reinforced the importance of Mexican culture and language north of the border. At the same time, American culture, the English language, and the desire for economic stability had their own seductive power. "They sensed the contagion of American culture, which made the Mexicans themselves 'greedier and more selfish,'" wrote historian Linda Gordon. "On the other hand, they loved beer, Coca-Cola, blue jeans, higher wages, and opportunity. Both sexes sang this litany of love and hate."[52] Proximity to the homeland and ongoing migration may have made it easier for Mexicans in the United States to retain aspects of their traditional identity and culture, but the cultural riptides pulled in more than one direction.

It isn't that America embraced Mexicans or that it was eager to accept them as Americans. More often than not, acculturation to American lifestyle and customs occurred in segregated environments. Nor did cultural adaptation necessarily translate into civic assimilation, particularly in strictly segregated communities. "If acculturation promised relief, racism did not," wrote historian Richard A. García. "Mexicans became Americanized, but discrimination kept them, for the most part, Mexicans. The intellectual dilemma was clear: they were not quite Americans, but neither were they quite Mexicans."[53] The working-class children of immigrants often found themselves in a cultural no-man's-land. As sociologist Emory Bogardus wrote in 1929, "He is no longer satisfied with his parental culture; he feels himself a part of the United States and would like to be accepted as such. But because of his color and heritage he is . . . classified as a Mexican, an outsider, a foreigner. He grows discouraged and falls back upon native parentage for status, but at the same time continues to speak English and in other ways enters into the new culture about him."[54]

The Mexican Revolution, which began in 1910, had only intensified the conflicting social pressures on Mexican Americans. The revolution, which began as an attempt to overthrow President Porfirio Díaz and which continued intermittently into the 1920s, drove unprecedented numbers of Mexicans northward. In addition to the agricultural and unskilled laborers, this new wave of migrants included professionals and middle-class political refugees. Generally, migrants from the northern Mexican states of Tamaulipas, Nuevo León, and Coahuila went to Texas, while those from Guanajuato, Michoacán, Jalisco, and San Luis Potosí gravitated to California. Newcomers from Mexico's Central Plateau often bypassed the Southwest altogether, preferring to head for the American heartland. By 1930, approximately 29,000 Mexican immigrants resided in Illinois and eleven thousand in Kansas.

Increased migration and the fear that political radicalism would creep northward from the revolution inspired a wave of anti-Mexican sentiment that historian Ricardo Romo has called the "Brown Scare." The presence of radical Mexican political exiles in the United States alarmed American authorities. In fact, it was not uncommon for Mexican revolutionary factions to seek haven in the American Southwest.

El Paso became a base of operations for some. Some migrants, particularly exiled members of the professional classes, sought to support the insurrection through fund-raising. But gunrunning for the revolutionaries and illegal enlistments for the Mexican forces also occurred north of the border. In one instance, the U.S. Department of Justice arrested Mexican consular officials for enlisting Mexican migrants in Texas. Concerned about violations of neutrality laws, the U.S. government sent a slew of secret agents to El Paso. In 1914, federal authorities arrested two Mexican nationals attempting to transfer twelve thousand rounds of ammunition to the revolutionary leader Francisco Villa, just south of the border.

In 1913, after the *Los Angeles Times* editorial page warned of potential cross-border incursions by Mexican forces, the Los Angeles Police Department stepped up their surveillance of Mexican neighborhoods and began arresting suspected revolutionaries. The Anglo public's growing suspicion of Mexican insurgents caused a further deterioration of race relations. The growing international tensions between the United States and Mexico also put Mexican immigrants and Mexican Americans in uncomfortable positions. Revolution in a neighboring country that was also America's chief recipient of foreign investment made Washington nervous. In April of 1914, after Mexican authorities arrested American sailors entering Tampico Bay to protect American property and lives, President Woodrow Wilson ordered the occupation of Tampico and the bombardment of the city of Veracruz. Back in El Paso, soldiers at Fort Bliss "were ordered to sleep with boots and saddles at their sides" in the event that Mexican forces attempted to retaliate from across the border or ethnic Mexicans on the U.S. side tried to intervene on behalf of their motherland.[55] A day after the Veracruz invasion, El Paso mayor Charles Kelly proudly announced that there had been no trouble in Chihuahuita, El Paso's largest Mexican neighborhood. He countered the Anglo public's growing suspicion of Mexicans. "Of course nothing is more groundless, and I might say, more foolish than this," he insisted. "The American citizens of Spanish [Mexican] birth have every right here that the Americans have and we have every reason to believe they will meet the obligations resting on good citizens of supporting the government and preserving peace and quiet."[56] The subsequent arrest of Efreno M. Franco, the Mexican-born editor of the newspaper *El Libre,* did little to relieve Anglo suspicions. According to authorities, Franco had published an appeal to El Paso's Mexicans to revolt against the Americans and support Mexican strongman General Victoriano Huerta.

Prominent Mexican Americans, in the meantime, sought to defuse the situation and assure the Anglo American establishment of their loyalty to the United States. They also served as mediators between U.S. authorities and Mexican refugees and immigrants. The day after the invasion of Veracruz, El Paso politician Isaac "Ike" Alderete told a reporter that he had spent all day "circulating among the Mexican refugees in El Paso and urging them to remember that they are in a foreign country here for protection, which they have and are still enjoying." He reported that the Mexicans he spoke to understood the situation and had no plans to create any disturbances.

Six hundred Mexican Americans led by El Paso district clerk José A. Escajeda told Mayor Kelly that, if called upon, they would be willing to patrol Chihuahita to keep order. Several months before the Tampico Incident, Escajeda had organized a company of Mexican Americans prepared to surveil the Mexican district or serve with U.S. forces in case of an invasion of Mexico. "While we are called Mexicans," said Escajeda, "we are not. We are Americans; born and brought up under the Stars and Stripes and as loyal to it as any other American. Many people in this city have said that we would rise up and incite riots in this city if President Wilson was forced to land American troops or bluejackets on Mexican soil, but quite on the contrary we are ready to shoulder a rifle and march in the ranks with the American soldier who is of Anglo-Saxon or Celtic origin."[57] Mexican Americans in Phoenix organized a regiment, and in San Antonio fifty Mexican Americans sent a telegram to President Wilson pledging their services in the event of war with Mexico.

Despite the efforts of their native-born brethren, the migrants who were welcomed by employers for their supposed docility were now feared for their reputed revolutionary fervor. After the Tampico Incident, many border residents became convinced that further armed conflict between the United States and Mexico was inevitable. The impression that Mexicans north of the border were a fifth column in waiting was underscored by the presence of political operatives and radical Mexican exiles in the Southwest. In 1914, exiled Mexican anarchist Ricardo Flores Magón drew large crowds of supporters in Los Angeles. Some radical refugees saw the Mexican Revolution as an opportunity to bring about drastic social and political change in the Southwest. In 1915, authorities in Texas uncovered a mysterious document containing plans for a Mexican insurrection in the Southwest to wrest control of the territory from the United States. While the origins of the so-called Plan de San Diego—it was signed in the town of San Diego in Duval County, Texas—were unclear, it may well have been inspired by anarchists. An insurrectionist movement did emerge in northern Mexico and South Texas. From 1915 to 1917, small bands of men from both sides of the border engaged in the sabotaging of ranches, irrigation pumping plants, and rail lines in the lower Rio Grande Valley. While some historians believe the movement was homegrown, others claim there is evidence linking these raids to the followers of Mexican revolutionary general Venustiano Carranza, who sought official U.S. recognition after he seized power in 1914. The revolt itself did not last long in the face of repression by the Texas Rangers. In the hostile environment of South Texas, three hundred Mexicans and Mexican Americans were summarily executed.

By the summer of 1915, the Plan de San Diego had become national news. "Mexican anarchy," wrote the *Chicago Tribune*, "now thrusts its red hand across our border and with an insane insolence attempts to visit upon American citizens in their homes the destruction it has wreaked upon American persons and property abroad."[58] In the fall of 1915, the U.S government recognized Venustiano Carranza as president of Mexico, angering his adversary, northern revolutionary Francisco Villa, in the bargain. Villa avenged the affront by an attack on American citizens. On January 10, 1916, his men killed eighteen American employees of the American Smelting and Refining Company in Chihuahua state. El Paso Mexicans bore the brunt of American outrage over the incident. Three days after the massacre, American soldiers attacked two Mexicans in the downtown area and a number of racially charged barroom fights broke out. A group of twenty-five to fifty Anglos pummeled any Mexican they could find on the streets. According to a correspondent for the *New York Times,* "by 10 o'clock . . . knives frequently were used and all ambulances in El Paso were rushing through the streets, while physicians were hurried to all parts of the city."[59] To keep the mob at bay, El Paso police declared martial law and barricaded Chihuahita. Mayor Tom Lea feared the mob would massacre Mexicans. After visiting the city's largest barrio, the mayor reported that far from causing trouble, the neighborhood's Mexican residents had taken refuge in their homes. In the tense ensuing days, there were more calls for revenge. The *Herald,* an El Paso newspaper, urged its readers to remain calm and treat Mexicans decently:

There are tens of thousands of persons of Mexican descent in El Paso, who are our neighbors and many of whom have been our friends; they work for us and with us, they own property here, patronize the business institutions, and take part in the life of the city. The lives, acts, thoughts, and intentions of most of these people are orderly; they are citizens, or at least residents, of El Paso and entitled to the same guarantees as any other citizens or residents. They are in no sense hostile to the United States or to Americans, and they deplore the terrors and crimes of Mexicans in Mexico, as others do.[60]

Two months later, however, Villa struck again. This time, 485 of his men crossed the international border and raided Columbus, New Mexico, where they killed seventeen Americans and lost one hundred men of their own. The incident marked the first time the United States had been invaded by foreign forces since the War of 1812. A week later, President Wilson ordered Brigadier General John J. Pershing on a year-long "punitive expedition" of about 1,500 men into Mexico to pursue Villa. The Columbus attack inflamed racial tensions in El Paso. Mexicans were again attacked downtown. In one incident, a dark-complexioned man reportedly sought to protect himself from the mob by shouting, "I am not a Mexican. I'm a nigger, I'm a nigger."[61]

Following Villa's Columbus raid, President Wilson sent troops to El Paso and mobilized more than 100,000 national guardsmen along the border from Texas to California. By the end of summer in 1916,

65,000 U.S. troops were bivouacked in El Paso. Before long, four-fifths of the regular U.S. Army was either in Mexico or stationed along the border. The Mexican population in the U.S. was under close scrutiny. Suspected revolutionary sympathizers were arrested and deported. Spanish-language newspapers in El Paso were monitored and closed if they published any negative opinions regarding Pershing's expedition. Though they were hundreds of miles away from Villa's stronghold in Chihuahua, police in Los Angeles were also on alert for Villistas. The city was tense after the mayor announced that he had received an anonymous tip that local Villa sympathizers were planning to sabotage federal buildings and public works. The police department imposed restrictions on local Mexicans. "No liquor will be sold to Mexicans showing the least sign of intoxication. No guns can be sold to Mexicans, and all dealers who have used guns for window display have been ordered to take them from the windows and to show them to no Mexicans until the embargo is lifted."[62] Chief of Police Clarence E. Snively organized a special force to keep an eye on Mexicans and tripled patrols in the central Mexican neighborhood known as Sonoratown. The *Los Angeles Times* was convinced that at least 10 percent of L.A.'s Mexicans were "rabid sympathizers with the outlaw, Villa." The *Times* editorialized that "firebrands—and they are not few—must be watched and snuffed out; the preachers of insurrection must be sequestered and confined."[63]

This fear of Mexican radicals cast suspicion on all Mexicans, the majority of whom took no part in any such activities. Within a month of Villa's incursion, the Los Angeles County Board of Supervisors called for the deportation of those Mexicans likely to become public charges. They asked the federal government to take note of "the prevalence of disease, poverty, and immorality among these people" and, to no avail, they urged the "deportation of all undesirables of this class who have come here within the past three years."[64] Even when news of the war in Europe began to dominate the nation's front pages, Mexicans were still not off the hook. Stories about a German-Mexican connection had been circulating for several years before the United States entered World War I in April 1917. Indeed, there had been those who blamed Germany for the Plan de San Diego and Villa's raid on Columbus.

In fact, Germany, whose armies were stalemated in trench warfare on the European continent, did seek an alliance with Mexico. In January 1917, the British intercepted a telegram from German foreign secretary Arthur Zimmermann to his ambassador in Mexico authorizing a German-Mexican alliance in the event that the United States entered the war. In exchange for its support in a war against the U.S., Mexico was offered generous financial support and the possibility of regaining some of the territories it lost to the U.S. in the mid-nineteenth century. On March 1, President Wilson made the telegram public, sparking a wave of anti-German sentiment and further fueling suspicion of Mexicans and Mexico. On April 1, the *Los Angeles Times* proclaimed,

> If the people of Los Angeles knew what was happening on our border they would not sleep at night. Sedition, conspiracy, and plots are in the very air. Telegraph lines are tapped, spies come and go at will. German nationals hob-nob with Mexican bandits, Japanese agents, and renegades from this country. Code messages are relayed from place to place along the border, frequently passing through six or eight people from sender to receiver. Los Angeles is the headquarters for this vicious system, and it is there that the deals between German and Mexican representatives are frequently made.[65]

The climate of fear and distrust did not subside until well after Armistice Day.

Meantime, the German threat and the fear of foreign insurgents helped revive an immigration restriction bill in Congress that President Wilson had blocked only two years before. The Immigration Act of 1917 was the first in a series of restrictive statutes that would ultimately put an end to America's open-door immigration policy. By the time it passed over Wilson's veto, however, the war had already drastically reduced the number of transatlantic migrants. Nonetheless, restricting the future arrival of immigrants who were considered susceptible to divided national loyalties was considered by many to be a form of national defense. The statute was the first federal policy that restricted the entry of immigrants on the basis of a system of ranking. That system now favored immigrant groups that were thought to be easily assimilated into U.S. society. Under the new law, no workers were allowed from the "Asiatic Barred Zone," which included India, Indochina, Afghanistan, Arabia, and the East Indies. A literacy test for all newcomers over sixteen years of age was instituted in addition to an $8 head tax on each entry. While Mexicans were not the prime targets of the legislation, the last two measures were particularly burdensome for them. Indeed, in the first full year in which the law was in effect, "1,771 illiterate Mexicans withdrew their immigration applications and another 5,745 were turned away at the border for being 'unwilling or unable to pay the head tax.' "[66] Desperate to find work, many Mexicans began to cross the border illegally. An illicit trade in trafficking migrants across the Rio Grande was also born. According to one U.S. border inspector:

> Hundreds of aliens who arrive at the border hungry and penniless, were literally forced to cross the international line in search of food and work, it being their philosophy apparently that whatever happened their plight could be no worse and, luck with them, might be materially bettered. The drastic provisions of the present immigration act have led to the creation of a new and thriving industry, if by such a term it may be dignified, having for its object the illegal introduction into the United States of Mexican aliens on a wholesale scale by means of organized efforts.[67]

But the restrictions affecting the legal entry of Mexican laborers did not last long. Not only did the war create a labor shortage, it led to the expansion of agricultural production. In desperate need of workers, Southwestern growers protested the new immigration statute, and the federal government responded favorably to their pleas. The Labor Department relaxed the new rules on the nation's southern border and even got into the business of contracting foreign labor. On May 23, 1917, Secretary of Labor William B. Wilson ordered that the literacy test and head tax be waived for Mexican agricultural workers, who would henceforth be permitted to stay in the United States for a maximum of six months. Interested employers could submit an application to the Labor Department indicating "the number of workers desired, the length of time they were required, and the wages and housing conditions offered."[68] To ensure that migrants returned to Mexico after their work permit expired, the Labor Department withheld a portion of their monthly wages and deposited it in a bank account that could be accessed only after the worker returned to Mexico. In its first year, the program admitted 9,401 Mexican laborers.[69]

The new allowances for Mexican labor, however, did not satisfy Southwestern farmers. Nor were representatives of the railroad and mining companies pleased not to have been included in the deal. Citing continued labor shortages, they pressed the secretary of labor to drop all restrictions on Mexican migrants. Due in part to the heavy lobbying of U.S. Food Administrator Herbert Hoover, Secretary Wilson ultimately agreed to broaden the list of industries in which Mexicans could be allowed to work and extended their work period until the end of the war. In addition to eliminating the practice of withholding wages, the secretary also mandated that more immigration inspectors be sent to the border in order "to facilitate the entry of Mexicans."[70] Continued lobbying by Southwestern industries ensured that the program of temporary admissions was extended until well after the war had ended. By the time it was terminated in 1921, 72,862 Mexican workers had been admitted under the program.[71] No provisions were made to ensure that these laborers returned to Mexico. Nor did northward migration cease when the program expired. The recession of 1921–1922 saw a sharp drop in the number of migrants and triggered the first effort to repatriate unemployed migrants back to their homeland. But once the economy began to rebound in 1923, a large wave of migration would continue until the late 1920s at a rate not equaled again until the 1990s.

Because government statistics counted only legal entries, which constituted a small portion of the total number of migrants from Mexico, it is difficult to know precisely how many Mexicans came north in the 1920s. It is clear, however, that the temporary admissions program operative from 1917 to 1921 had served to encourage more migration as family and friends back in Mexico learned of the job opportunities up north. By March 1923, "as many as 1,000 Mexicans were arriving daily in Juárez with the intention of entering the United States."[72] After 1922, growers again began pressuring the federal government to relax restrictions against Mexican migrants.

The passage of the quota acts of 1921 and 1924, which effectively brought European immigration to an end, deepened U.S. dependence on Mexican labor. Though the American public may have been fed up with immigrants, the nation's booming economy still demanded more workers. By the mid-1920s, Midwestern industries began to compete against Southwestern farmers for Mexican migrants. Texas farmers took the threat so seriously that the state legislature passed the Emigrant Agent Act, which imposed a $1,000 fine on any labor recruiter who sought to lure workers out of their state.

While the new restrictive immigration laws did not impose quotas on migration from the Western Hemisphere, the 1924 quota act did mandate that all prospective migrants apply for a $10 visa at the closest American consular office. This, added to the $8 head tax, constituted a formidable obstacle for Mexican migrants, many of whom opted to cross the border without papers. In 1924, to stem the rising tide of undocumented migrants from Mexico and Europe, a 450-man Border Patrol was established to guard the nation's northern and southern frontiers. Consequently, the number of Mexicans deported for illegal entry spiked dramatically in the late 1920s, from 1,751 in 1925 to more than fifteen thousand in 1929.[73]

While the new force could clearly not halt this mass migration, it did make the act of crossing more harrowing. Ironically, the prohibitively expensive entry fee and the thought of having to recross illegally made many Mexicans reluctant to continue their circular migration. As a result, once their seasonal employment on the railroads or in the fields ended, more migrants gravitated to the cities of the Southwest where they settled permanently. Some, like Jesús Pérez, who entered illegally in 1923, sought to legalize their status once they could afford it. In 1928, after the Border Patrol intensified its activities around his hometown in Texas, Pérez became a legal immigrant. "I gathered my coins and I came, arriving exactly on September 1, 1928 to the immigration station on the other side," he said almost a half-century later. "Right away I took care of this business in seven days. On the 7th of September they gave me my passport to cross into the United States and until this day here I am, yes sir."[74]

The creation of the Border Patrol made the international boundary more rigid than it had ever been. The distinctions between Mexicans and Americans and legal and illegal immigrants hardened. At the same time, many Mexicans entered the country "through a variety of means that were not illegal but comprised irregular, unstable categories of lawful admissions, making it more difficult to distinguish between those who were lawfully in the country and those who were not."[75] The term "alien" was introduced to describe Mexicans in the Southwest, and the uncertain legal status of so many immigrants heightened the "otherness" of Mexicans in the United States. While migration had always required uprooting, immigrants now experienced a more definitive break with the past than ever before. Still, the border was not as intractable as some would have liked. Southwestern growers had the power to convince the Labor Department to ease up on enforcement during labor shortages. As historian George J. Sánchez noted, "Both American officials and entering aliens understood that it was the labor needs of the American Southwest that defined Mexican migration to the United States and not laws drawn up in Washington."[76]

Bad economic times spurred a nasty backlash against Mexican immigrants. This aggravated an already ungenerous attitude toward immigrants in general in the 1920s. In his 1916 book, *The Passing of the Great Race,* Madison Grant, the most famous American nativist of the era, pointed to Mexicans as an example of what an open-door immigration policy would produce. "The world has seen many such mixtures and the character of a mongrel race is only just beginning to be understood at its true value," he wrote.[77] While immigrants encountered many difficulties in the 1920s, Mexicans, by virtue of the tenuousness of their claim to whiteness, were, as a rule, treated worse than European newcomers. This hostile environment gave rise to a heightened sense of nationalism among Mexican migrants. But unlike American nationalism, which was essentially offensive in nature, Mexican nationalism was by and large defensive. As social historian Douglas Monroy has noted, Mexican nationalism was "formed in negative contexts. Whereas the Americans could celebrate great military victories over indigenous and foreign foes (including the Mexicans), Mexican nationalism emerged first from the wounds suffered at the hands of rebellious Anglo Texans, then from the loss of one-third of its land to the American army, then from defeat at the hands of the French in 1864, and then from the loss of so many of its most vital people through emigration to the country that had routed them so soundly in 1846."[78]

Feeling unwelcome in the United States, many Mexicans cherished idealized memories of the motherland and, like so many immigrants, clung together and sought to create *México de afuera* (Mexico abroad) in the United States. They founded businesses and associations geared to serve the immigrant community. Echoing the Mexican government's official line, Spanish-language newspapers in the United States often characterized assimilation into America as a kind of betrayal of Mother Mexico. Perhaps protesting too much, they argued that even while Mexicans adjusted to their new environment, they continued to be Mexicans through and through. In 1920, *El Heraldo de México,* a Los Angeles paper, insisted that immigrants "continue, in spite of that absorbing [American] civilization, feeling as Mexicans, with all of their defects and all of their virtues."[79] Rival paper *La Opinión* asserted that even though Mexicans came to the U.S. to improve their lot in life, "we must always respond to the requirement of continuing to feel fully Mexican, in love, in intent [and] in deeds."[80]

Among adult immigrants, speaking English was sometimes perceived as a sort of cultural capitulation. While they wanted their children to learn English, they "hoped that [they] could grow up bilingual and learn to appreciate both Mexican and American cultures."[81] Similarly, few Mexicans chose to naturalize in the 1920s. Asked by a teacher why they were so reluctant to become U.S. citizens one student replied: "Well, what good would it do us? The Americans wouldn't treat us any better if we did. They say we are black, they call us Indians, Greasers, Cholos, and getting naturalized wouldn't make us any different."[82] Another student traced the reluctance to Mexican pride. "Mexicanos are very patriotic. They love their own birthplace, their own land, better than anything else. A Mexican who becomes an American citizen is looked upon as a renegade, a traitor; and since Americans also look down upon him, he is like a 'man without a country.' "[83] One survey of Mexicans in Los

Angeles revealed that 55 percent of respondents felt it was their "duty to remain loyal to Mexico, while less than a third responded that they expected to live permanently in the United States."[84] The most famous Mexican immigrant in the U.S., the actress Dolores del Río, embodied the defiant nature of Mexican nationalism of the era. "Never will I become an American citizen. Never!" she declared in 1928.[85]

But sometimes retaining Mexican citizenship was more than just about nursing wounded cultural pride. Poor migrants in trouble often had nowhere to turn but to Mexican consular officials. Indeed, consuls played an important role in defending immigrants from abuses endured in the U.S. In 1929, sociologist Emory Bogardus wrote that "by remaining a citizen of Mexico and by calling on the Mexican consul for assistance, the Mexican can secure justice, whereas if he becomes an American citizen he feels helpless. He does not understand our courts and is not able to secure as adequate a hearing as if he remains a Mexican citizen."[86] Even some U.S.-born Mexican Americans went so far as to pretend to hold Mexican citizenship in order to receive legal assistance from the consulate. In 1923, an Italian national, who had been condemned to die in California's San Quentin prison, claimed Mexican citizenship to qualify for legal support from the Mexican consulate in San Francisco.

But neither the need for protection in troubled times nor sentimental nationalism kept immigrant families, particularly their U.S.-born children, from selectively adopting—and even appreciating—American ways. In 1929, after her divorce from her Mexican husband, the proudly nationalist Dolores del Río gushed to a Spanish-language newspaper about the virtues of American men. Though she thought they could learn something about romance from Latin Americans, del Río considered American husbands to be "tender, noble, and loyal." Indeed, because she felt their men were less bound by traditional mores, she insisted that the "most important contribution which the United States had made for the progress and the happiness of the world was the quality of its husbands."[87] Six months later, the Hollywood star wed MGM art director Cedric Gibbons.

At the turn of the twentieth century, the Mexican immigrant family remained essentially unchanged north of the border. In 1900 El

Paso, no mothers and few daughters were employed outside the home. But the longer families remained in the United States, the greater the likelihood that women joined the workforce. A 1928 survey of Mexicans in Los Angeles found that economic necessity had pushed the majority of Mexican women into jobs in industry.[88] Not surprisingly, the shift in employment patterns produced radical changes within the family culture. Women gradually began to expect and demand greater personal freedom. Many Mexican men resented—or were ashamed by the fact—that their wives desired to work outside the home. The most profound cultural effect, however, was on working daughters who quickly adopted many of the habits and modern fashions they encountered in the workplace. Furthermore, their ability to earn their own money made them feel less obligated to follow traditional family roles and customs. Caught between the more restrictive practices of Mexican family life and the more liberal mores of Anglo American society, these daughters' choices of clothing style and recreation often became a source of conflict within the family. Second-generation women sometimes took their newly acquired assertiveness into their own marriages. Upon getting married at nineteen, one young Los Angeles resident said that the "first thing I did was to bob my hair. My father would not permit it and I have wanted to do [it] for a long time. I will show my husband that he will not boss me the way my father has done all of us."[89]

The English language also worked its way into households. Its increasing use influenced the way Spanish was spoken north of the border. Anglicized Spanish words like *troque* (truck), *sitijol* (city hall), and *tochar* (touch) became common. Phrases such as *watchear un rato* (to watch a while), *parkear un carro* (park a car), or *flunkear una examinación* (flunk an exam) were uttered by young people without any trace of irony.[90] Knowledge of English and increased exposure to mainstream American culture had an impact on the children of immigrants. While young Mexican American women began to wear nylon stockings and use cosmetics, young men tried new recreational activities, like movies or American sports. The children of immigrants often took pleasure in introducing new activities, foods, and clothing styles to the family. They were generally the first to attend motion picture theaters, which became a favorite pastime among Mexican families in the United States. After 1910, many Mexican immigrants experienced the acculturating influence of silent movies. In El Paso, Mexicans attended the early theaters such as the Crawford, the Grand, the Little Wigwam, and the Bijou. Their attendance increased after World War I, when a local Mexican American politician opened seven theaters, including the Alcázar, the Eureka, and the Paris, which catered to Mexicans and Mexican Americans. While these movie theaters screened some films produced in Mexico, "for the most part Mexican audiences paid 6 or 11 cents admission, depending on where one sat, to see American movies featuring such stars as Charlie Chaplin, Mary Pickford, and Fatty Arbuckle."[91] These movies introduced audiences to Anglo American styles and mores.

In the 1920s, movies—in Spanish and in English—that featured leading Mexican actors were exceedingly popular with Latino audiences. Dolores del Río, Ramón Novarro, Donald Reed né Ernesto Guillén, Lupe Vélez, and Lupita Tovar were all the rage in the gossip columns of Spanish-language newspapers. In 1929, redheaded Lupe Vélez, "the Mexican Spitfire," who gained notoriety when she starred opposite Douglas Fairbanks in *The Gaucho,* was linked romantically with Gary Cooper. Dolores del Río starred in *Evangeline,* which was directed by Edwin Carewe and based on a poem by Henry Wadsworth Longfellow. Two years later, Lupita Tovar starred in *Santa,* the first talking picture produced in Mexico. Mexican audiences loved movies with or without Mexican actors. In a 1929 survey of thirty-seven young Latinas in a Los Angeles settlement house, six listed their favorite actress as Billie Dove, who was known as "the American Beauty," three preferred Greta Garbo and Dolores del Rio, and four favored Lupe Vélez, Clara Bow, and Mary Pickford. When asked to name the "best movie you ever saw," the most popular pick, with five votes, was *The Singing Fool,* a sentimental 1928 love story that featured Al Jolson.[92] A U.S. Labor Department study conducted in Los Angeles between 1934 and 1936 found that most of the money that Mexican families spent on recreation went to purchase movie tickets. In fact, 90 percent of families surveyed had spent money going to the movies, averaging $22 a year per family.[93]

By the late 1920s, several Mexican-owned businesses in Los Angeles had sponsored baseball clubs. The most prominent Mexican teams of the day were El Porvenir Grocery, Ortiz New Fords, and El Paso Shoe Store. In 1929, Fox's newest starlet, Lupita Tovar, introduced El Paso Shoe Store at their championship game against the Pacific Electric Trainmen on Cinco de Mayo. Mexican men were also great fans of boxing. In that era, ethnicity played a huge role in promoting boxing matches. Fighters' backgrounds were part of the backstory that engaged fans. During the 1920s, Bert Colima of Whittier, California, was the dominant middleweight fighter in California. When he fought at the Hollywood Boxing Stadium in 1924, the English-language press dubbed him "The Whittier Flash," while the Spanish-language newspapers preferred "el ídolo de Whittier." He was a particular draw with Latino fans. A few Mexicans, like Colima, made it big and even got rich fighting. At the 1924 Olympic Games in Paris, Joe Salas, a Mexican American, won the silver medal in boxing.[94]

Immigrant families also experienced subtle yet profound changes in their everyday home life. If their budgets permitted, mothers would add meat to the weekly diet, a commodity that was rare in Mexico. Newcomers showed little reluctance to trade their traditional Mexican clothing—from muslin trousers to *rebozos,* long narrow shawls—for contemporary American garb. Stores in El Paso did good business selling clothing to Mexicans who had just crossed the border. In the 1920s, Mexican women in Los Angeles commonly preferred cotton housedresses, while the men wore cotton shirts with overalls or pants.

Although socioeconomic mobility was extremely limited for Mexicans and Mexican Americans in that era, homeownership in Los Angeles became increasingly common during the 1920s. By 1930, 44.8 percent of residents of the Belvedere neighborhood in East Los Angeles owned their own homes.[95] This trend allowed some communities to gain a sense of permanence. While most Mexican immigrants refused to apply for U.S. citizenship, their children were usually born citizens. Americanization programs in schools did encourage American identity among the children of immigrants. But governments—north and south of the border—did not play as important a role in the shaping of identity as they supposed.

Over time, as Mexican families acclimated themselves to life in America, they ceased to be Mexicans living in the U.S. and assumed a new identity, that of Mexican Americans. Like countless others who have struggled to make their way in a new environment, Mexican families developed a local syncretic culture to help them negotiate the contretemps of everyday life. While most of their cultural practices and values had origins in Mexico, they were increasingly influenced by their experiences in the United States. While Mexican areas in the U.S. were not as isolated from each other as they had been in the nineteenth century, experiences still differed from place to place. Needless to say, cultural practice was determined in large part by the environment in which Mexicans found themselves. Mexican American culture in the borderlands was more traditional than it was in Los Angeles. Acculturation in Chicago, where Mexicans were only one of many ethnic and immigrant groups, bore little resemblance to that of Texas, where memories of the Alamo and the Mexican-American War persisted. To be Mexican in Bethlehem, Pennsylvania, where their numbers were few and anti-Mexican prejudice was slight, meant something very different than it did to farmworkers in Imperial County in Southern California.

The longer Mexican families resided in the United States the more they harbored expectations of being treated fairly. Mexican American veterans of World War I were among the first to demand their full civil rights. Noncitizen immigrants had been exempt from the military draft. Some fled to Mexico for fear that they'd be conscripted; thousands of others volunteered for the armed forces. But Mexican American men between the ages of eighteen and forty-five were required by law to register for the draft. Federal, state, and local authorities made great efforts to integrate the Mexican American public into both the civilian and the military aspects of the war effort. In fact, World War I was the first time that the American government had ever sought to promote the participation of Mexican Americans in national life. As home to some of the most long-established Mexican American communities in the Southwest, New Mexico was disproportionately affected by the war. Approximately ten thousand Hispanic New Mexicans, two-thirds of the state's contingent, served.[96] New Mexico also had the singular distinction of having more volunteers per capita than any other state. Sixty percent of them were Mexi-

can American.[97] Because so many rural communities were still culturally isolated, the military gave some soldiers their first contact not
only with the U.S. government but with Anglo Americans. Some soldiers returned home having experienced prejudice at the hands of
Anglo officers. Others felt that their service had been appreciated and
that their fellow American soldiers treated them as equals. In either
case, veterans returned to their villages with a greater desire for modern conveniences and a heightened sense of their rights as American
citizens.

In Texas, many Mexican Americans sought to prove their patriotism by contributing to the war effort. The town of Laredo, which had
been majority-Hispanic since 1755 and had a high percentage of
native-born Mexican Americans, exhibited more widespread patriotism than areas dominated by immigrants. There, as well as in San
Antonio and other towns, Mexican Americans actively raised funds
for the Red Cross. Employees at Texas Mexican Printing contributed
50 cents or a dollar each to the cause. Prominent Mexican Americans
started War Savings Stamp Clubs and encouraged other Mexican
Americans and Mexicans to participate. Indeed, many more acculturated Mexican Americans felt it their duty to urge the majority of
Mexicans who were less assimilated to find common cause with
American troops. One wealthy Laredoan, Luis R. Ortiz, bought
$30,000 worth of bonds, the maximum amount for an individual.
The local Spanish-language press also urged its readers to buy bonds
and stamps. While mostly urban Mexican Americans participated in
these efforts, the campaigns also reached into small, rural towns.
Wartime outreach by both the government and the more established
Mexican Americans connected even the most heavily immigrant *colo-
nias* (neighborhoods) to the larger society in a way that they had
never been. The predominately Mexican student body at Lincoln
Park School in El Paso donated nickels and dimes in order to raise
enough money to buy their school a new American flag. According to
historian Carole E. Christian, World War I "greatly accelerated
assimilation" of Texas Mexicans into the American mainstream as
"wider sectors of Texas's [Mexican] population were exposed to
assimilating influences than ever before."[98]

Mexican Americans also fought in the war, though it is difficult to
determine how many. Because the U.S. government did not officially

consider Mexicans as nonwhite, Mexican American recruits were not assigned to segregated units as were African Americans. Nor were Mexican American soldiers forced to perform manual labor duties, like most black recruits. The 360th Infantry Regiment of the 90th Division, which was formed in September 1917 at Camp Travis, Texas, and which fought in France and then occupied Germany, included several Mexicans and Mexican Americans as well as Americans from a variety of European backgrounds. The Hispanic soldiers "included uneducated unskilled laborers, railroad workers, small-scale ranchers, and a few economically well-situated or high school educated Mexican Americans. Some spoke only Spanish, others limited English, and some were bilingual. Some of these soldiers were from rural areas, others from small towns and cities. One noncommissioned officer, fluent in English and assimilated to Anglo culture, was the son of a Texas Ranger."[99]

Forty young men, both U.S.- and Mexican-born, from St. Ignatius parish in El Paso enlisted for service. Several served with distinction. Marcos B. Armijo, who was killed in combat, posthumously received the Distinguished Service Cross for saving an American nurse from drowning. Manuel J. Escajeda was awarded the Croix de Guerre by the French government. The parish's most decorated soldier was also one of the most decorated military men in Texas. Marcelino Sierra, who was born in Mexico, received not only the Distinguished Service Cross and the Croix de Guerre, but also the British Medal of Bravery, the Italian Cross of Merit, and two Purple Hearts. He was nominated for the Congressional Medal of Honor for single-handedly capturing twenty-four German soldiers.

Particularly in Texas, many men who served honorably in the military came home to discover that they were still not treated like Americans. According to one contemporary observer, "they found that they were not served drinks [at some soda fountains], and were told that 'no Mexicans were allowed.' They raised the question then, 'What are we, Mexicans or Americans?' "[100] Having served in the nation's armed forces, veterans felt entitled to assert the latter. They were less inclined to submit to the indignities of discrimination and segregation. "The world war taught us a lesson," said one veteran. "We had thought we were Mexicans. The war opened our eyes. . . . We have American ways and think like Americans. We have not been able to convince some people that there is a difference between us [and the Old Mexicans]. To the average American, we are just Mexicans."[101] After the world war, more Mexican Americans held out hope for the prospects of integration and acceptance in U.S. society.

By the end of the 1920s, an identifiable Mexican American middle class was asserting itself and demanding an end to discrimination. Their primary focus was on educational equality, the right to serve on juries, and the desegregation of public places. These Mexican Americans were described by one contemporary scholar as retaining "a keen respect for their Mexican background, but are acquiring even a keener respect for their status as American citizens. They deeply resent the discriminations which they have to bear, and some of them are fired with a desire to improve the status of their racial brothers who are less fortunate."[102] But others saw the less fortunate, particularly immigrants, as part of the problem. Resentful that Anglo Americans tended to lump all people of Mexican ancestry into one class, some middle-class Mexican Americans were eager to make distinctions. They did not seek to end discrimination against all Mexicans, irrespective of social qualifications. On the contrary, they "sought to educate their fellows to avoid giving offense, and pled for distinction on an individual rather than a race basis."[103] One light-skinned middle-class Mexican American appealed to laborers in Nueces County, Texas. "If you suffer humiliation, don't blame anyone but yourself; you have not been prepared. There is no such thing as [race] discrimination. For example, I go to American barber shops. If discrimination exists, it is their own fault. We tell them, 'Do you expect to be received at the Nueces hotel in overalls and sombreros? If you are prepared, and live all right, and are financially all right, you will get a room at the hotel.' "[104]

Mexican American activists generally saw their own interests as different from those of immigrants. In 1928, when Congress was hearing testimony on new proposals to restrict Mexican migration, not one ethnic organization attended to represent the interest of Mexican workers. As historian Mark Reisler wrote, "Unlike other immigrant groups, Mexicans had established no organizations to proclaim their worthiness as potential Americans and to defend the continued admission of their brethren before Congress."[105] In fact, it was not until 1930 that anyone of Mexican ancestry testified before Congress on the subject of Mexican migration. That year, three members of the League of United Latin American Citizens—LULAC—which had been founded a year earlier, appeared before a congressional committee that was considering a proposal to impose further quotas on Mexican migration. The three members' testimony was ambivalent at best. While the first two witnesses were not entirely hostile to further restrictions, the last speaker made arguments that were both pro and con. LULAC had been founded by middle-class Texas Mexicans and its membership was restricted to U.S. citizens out of the belief that only citizens could effectively demand the reforms the group desired. Hence, its point of view was not that of immigrant workers themselves. Dedicated to fighting discrimination, LULACers were also interesting in developing "within the members of our race the best, purest and most perfect type of a true and loyal citizen of the United States of America."[106] In other words, LULAC was equally interested in preparing Mexican Americans for integration as they were with combating prejudice. As a result, the league divided over the issue of whether Mexican immigration should be further restricted. While some objected to the racist arguments of restrictionists, other members openly favored new quotas on migrants. They feared that increased migration would serve to incite further prejudice among Anglos and thereby undermine the league's efforts. "We are working our heads off to educate one fellow to know right from wrong, but 100 uneducated Mexicans come in for every one we teach," said one LULAC member.[107]

LULAC sought to promote both ethnic pride and allegiance to the United States. At its first convention, LULAC delegates approved a code that read in part:

Respect your citizenship, conserve it; honor your country, maintain its traditions in the minds of your children, incorporate yourself in the culture and civilization;

Love the men of your race, take pride in your origins and keep it immaculate; respect your glorious past and help to vindicate your people;

Study the past of your people, or the country to which you owe your citizenship; learn to handle with purity the two most essential languages, English and Spanish.[108]

The emergence of a politically conscious middle class with a sense of entitlement and possessed of skills with which to defend their rights as Americans was a significant moment in Mexican American history. While membership in early civil rights organizations was limited to the more acculturated minority, their public efforts to curb discrimination gained them support among less assimilated sectors of the population. In other words, a pivotal segment of the Mexican American population with influence that outspanned its numbers was promoting and effectively accelerating the Americanization of Mexican Americans at large.

Seven

Becoming Mexican American

Between 1900 and 1930, more than one million Mexicans—perhaps as much as 10 percent of Mexico's population—came north to the United States and "transformed earlier nineteenth-century Mexican communities (with the exception of northern New Mexico) into predominately immigrant communities."[1] But after 1930, the Great Depression, the subsequent decline of immigration, and the anti-immigrant sentiment that attended the mass joblessness of the era transformed the internal demographics of Mexican America.

In late 1930, Secretary of Labor William Doak pledged to rid the nation of the roughly 400,000 illegal aliens he claimed were taking jobs from American citizens. Because the understaffed Border Patrol wasn't up to that formidable task, local governments hoping to reduce their relief rolls signed on to a broad effort to encourage Mexican immigrants to return to their homeland. On January 26, 1931, Secretary Doak and Colonel Arthur Woods, the national coordinator of the President's Emergency Committee for Employment, issued a press release announcing an impending campaign to rid Los Angeles of its illegal aliens. A month later, federal agents conducted a well-publicized midday raid on La Placita, the heart of Mexican Los Angeles. Four hundred people were detained and asked to produce proof of legal entry and residence. Similar raids were conducted in other cities. On Ash Wednesday in San Fernando, California, county sheriff's squad cars, sirens wailing, cruised Mexican neighborhoods blaring out orders to cooperate with authorities.

While that campaign resulted in the deportations of fewer than three hundred undocumented Mexicans, it nonetheless succeeded in creating a climate of fear and encouraged "Mexicans of varying legal status—including American-born citizens of Mexican descent—to contemplate leaving" the United States.[2] Indeed, that is precisely what local and federal officials had hoped for. They were aware that deportations required lengthy formal legal hearings and proof of illegal entry. And not all undocumented Mexicans had arrived in the country illegally. Furthermore, Mexican laborers had been granted several exemptions over the years, which made the legal status of many immigrants far from clear. Nor could the Immigration Bureau, a division of the U.S. Department of Labor, simply execute mass deportations of legal immigrants who had become public charges. The law allowed expulsion only of those immigrants who had become public charges within five years of their arrival due to causes originating before their arrival in the U.S. In other words, requesting aid after becoming unemployed during an economic depression did not constitute sufficient legal grounds for deportation. Only a small portion of those who were repatriated to Mexico in the 1930s left the country as a result of deportation proceedings.

Instead, local welfare agencies in several cities played on immigrants' fears and then offered to pay for their one-way tickets back to Mexico. Sometimes their approach was incontestably coercive. Some welfare workers pressured immigrants to return home convincing them that they had little choice in the matter. Naturalized citizens were not immune from the pressure. In Detroit, the Department of Public Welfare referred all Mexican relief applicants to its recently established Mexican Bureau, which chartered trains to the border. According to one account, caseworkers exerted "threats of deportation, stoppage of relief (wholly or in part, as, for example, in the matter of rent), or trampling on customary procedures."[3] In St. Paul, Minnesota, Mexicans stopped applying for aid for fear of being deported. In 1933, Los Angeles sociologist Emory Bogardus wrote:

Many Mexican immigrants are returning to Mexico under a sense of pressure. They fear that all welfare aid will be withdrawn if they do not accept the offer to help them out of the country. In fact, some of them report that they are told by relief officials that if they do not accept the offer to take them to the Border no further welfare aid will be given them and that their record will be closed with the notation, 'Failed to cooperate.' Rumor becomes exaggerated as it passes from mouth to mouth. It takes only an insinuation from a welfare official in the United States to create widespread fear among Mexican immigrants.[4]

Los Angeles County's repatriation program was the most ambitious effort in the country. The county began its program a mere fifteen months into the Depression and continued it for four years. "Between 1931 and 1934 the Los Angeles Department of Charities launched 15 special trainloads averaging 1,000 Mexicans each."[5] County officials calculated that they could save considerable amounts of money by repatriating foreign-born Mexicans, who accounted for 9 percent to 11 percent of the county's welfare cases during the Depression.[6] Purchased wholesale, tickets to Mexico City cost only $14.70 a head. Including food and transportation, the cost of repatriating the average family was $71.14. In other words, the direct cost of repatriating a trainload of one thousand Mexicans came to $77,249.29. Had that same number of individuals stayed in Los Angeles and received "such charitable assistance as they would have been entitled to," the county would have expended a total of $424,933.70.[7] A single trainload of repatriates could save the county a total of $347,468.41. Yet beneath the cold language of cost analysis lay a deeper assumption about the disposability of Mexican labor. Both the U.S. government and growing segments of the business community now took for granted the fact that Mexican laborers could be imported during the good times and banished when times turned bad.

Though the Mexican consul in Los Angeles, Rafael de la Colina, had protested the Immigration Bureau's tactic of intimidating Mexicans with threats of deportation, he was more than willing to assist the county in its voluntary repatriation efforts. While he may have indeed been moved by the plight of destitute immigrants in Los Angeles, Consul de la Colina was also abiding by official Mexico's "desire to see immigrants return to Mexico, particularly after they had acquired experience in the American labor force."[8] The departure of so many migrants from the country had been a source of deep embarrassment to Mexico, particularly since the rhetoric of its revolution had promised to bring a new, more equitable regime to their homeland. There was also some concern that outmigration depleted Mexico's human capital. In May 1927, a headline in a Spanish-language news-paper read "10,000 More Mexicans Emigrate in 2 Months." The article went on to explain that "the problem of the depopulation of our vast territories is frightful. . . . One could predict that the time will arrive when Mexico is so depopulated that, for the few that remain, no other recourse will remain but to ask for annexation to [the United States]." A few days later, the same newspaper declared that emigrants represented "a good part [of Mexico's] creative and progressive capacity."[9]

In the winter of 1930–1931, the Mexican consulate in Los Angeles arranged reduced train fare to El Paso for immigrants who wished to return to Mexico. The headline on one flyer distributed by the consulate read "México llama a sus hijos," "Mexico calls out to her children."[10] In Detroit, where the Mexican consul worked side by side with welfare officials, a group of repatriates was given a celebratory send-off attended by renowned Mexican artist Diego Rivera and his then lesser-known wife, Frida Kahlo. The Mexican federal government also adopted policies that helped defray the costs of repatriation. For one thing, they allowed repatriates to import their possessions—including such things as household appliances, machinery, and animals—duty-free. The Mexican government also provided free transportation from the border to the interior. "As congestion in the border towns increased, the government increased the number of trains and passenger cars to relieve the pressure on towns like Ciudad Juárez and Nogales."[11] At the end of 1931, "the peak year of repatriation," the American consul in Ciudad Juárez reported that 35,000 repatriates had gone through the city in the previous twelve months.[12]

Not all repatriations were coerced. Nor were all repatriates destitute or on relief. Some chose to leave as soon as they saw economic conditions worsen and the racial climate deteriorate. Most of the early repatriates came from Texas, but Los Angeles saw the departure of a significant number of people as early as the winter of 1929–1930. Many in that first group "returned with automobiles and furniture accumulated by hard years of work and saving in the United States."[13] In general, however, single male migrants with shallow roots in the United States were the first to head back home. Conversely, Mexicans with the deepest roots in the north, property own-ers, and those with the longest tenure in the U.S. were the most likely to stay. In other words, those most acculturated to American life were the most likely to remain behind.

The vast majority of repatriated Mexicans returned to the villages of their birth. A mere 15 percent retuned to large cities.[14] Those with the least experience in the U.S. adapted the quickest. Women and older children in a family often had the most difficult time adjusting to their new surroundings. "Here it is harder," said one *repatriada*. "Cooking is more difficult. There we had gas ranges, but not here, and we used flour while here it is *maíz*."[15] One woman whose family returned to Mexico when she was a child recalled being treated as an outsider because she was an American. "Yes, we were a novelty, because, I guess, we spoke mostly English. We used to go to the store and we used to refer to the money as pennies, not *centavos*. So you know, the people used to laugh at us."[16] Villages with large numbers of repatriates often experienced conflict. The *repatriados* were some-times referred to as gringos, " 'Yankified' innovators, Masons or pagans, destroyers of the old customs, freakish, [or] intruders."[17] Not surprisingly, by the mid-1930s, a growing number of repatriates sought to return to the U.S.

Most scholars estimate that 400,000 Mexicans returned to Mexico in the early 1930s. An estimated 60 percent were American-born chil-dren and therefore U.S. citizens.[18] While the largest share of repatri-ates came from Los Angeles, the Midwest was disproportionately affected. Although only 3.6 percent of Mexican nationals in the United States lived in the Midwestern states of Indiana, Michigan, and Illinois, those three states accounted for more than 10 percent of *repatriados*.[19] By the mid-1930s, Chicago had lost 30 percent of its Mexican population and Los Angeles slightly more.[20] In Texas, an estimated 250,000 Mexicans headed south in the 1930s.[21] Between 1930 and 1940, the number of Mexican-born persons in the United States declined from 639,000 to a little over 377,000.[22] Immigration had also slowed dramatically. "Whereas during the 1920s the annual flow of legal immigrants had averaged around 46,000, throughout the 1930s it never exceeded 2,700."[23]

The repatriations left many Mexicans who remained in the U.S.

feeling vulnerable. According to historian George J. Sánchez, "The majority who stayed in Los Angeles became ambivalent Americans, full of contradictory feelings about their place in American society."[24] Fearing they'd be targeted for repatriation, some families avoided visiting doctors, applying for relief, or even venturing into downtown areas. Blamed for both taking jobs away from native-born Americans and burdening the relief rolls, many Mexicans faced growing hostility from Anglos. Incidents of harassment and discrimination were common, particularly in Texas. Mexicans and Mexican Americans would carry the anxiety of the era well into the first years of World War II.

On December 11, 1935, Timoteo Andrade, a native of Jalisco, Mexico, stood before Judge John Knight of the First Federal Circuit Court in Buffalo, New York, eager to become a citizen of the United States. Much to Andrade's surprise and disappointment, however, Judge Knight disapproved the petition for naturalization on the grounds that the petitioner was a "Mexican Indian" and, as such, ineligible for citizenship pursuant to Section 359, Title 8, of the U.S. Code. According to that statute, only persons of the white and black races were permitted to become naturalized citizens. Although the country's first immigration laws, as early as 1790, restricted citizenship to "free white persons," eighty years later their scope was extended to include people of African ancestry. Being neither white nor black, Andrade did not qualify for citizenship.

In point of fact, Andrade, who had entered the United States at El Paso, Texas, thirty years before, was a test case in a campaign to curtail Mexican immigration. The California Joint Immigration Committee, an organization that had been founded to put a halt to Japanese entering the U.S., was now focusing its efforts on immigrants from Mexico. Under the direction of its chairman V. S. McClatchy, a member of the family that published the *Sacramento Bee*, the committee now sought to develop a legal precedent that would require Congress to stop Mexican immigration. Attempting to capitalize on a provision in the 1924 National Origins Act that barred the entry of persons who were ineligible for citizenship, the committee wanted Mexicans to be classified as Indians, thus rendering them ineligible to enter the United States. Although Native Americans had been collectively granted U.S. citizenship in 1924, the privilege of naturalization was not extended to indigenous peoples born elsewhere in the Western Hemisphere until 1940, years after Andrade filed his petition.

The law that governed cases like Andrade's and that decided his fate had an absorbing, if not bizarre, history. The passage of the 1921 Immigration Act and the 1924 National Origins Act had effectively brought European immigration to a near halt. Fearful that undesirable immigrants would begin to degrade the nation's Anglo-Saxon heritage, nativists had lobbied for quotas that would preserve its then existing ethnic balance. To that end the law was changed to favor the admission of migrants from western and northern Europe over the more swarthy people from that continent's eastern and southern reaches. But though the new laws would protect the country from the threat of a darkening of the national complexion, they, perhaps ironically, made no mention of immigrants from the Americas. Unaffected by the new quotas and exclusionary provisions, migration from Mexico into the U.S. continued unabated. Before 1924, Mexican immigration had been numerically overshadowed by the huge waves of newcomers from Europe and had gone largely unnoticed by nativists. But with the drastic decline in European immigration, Mexicans suddenly became a larger share of new arrivals. Whereas in the first decade of the century Mexicans made up only 0.6 percent of all legal immigrants, by 1924 they comprised 12.4 percent, an increase that ensured that they would no longer enter the United States unnoticed.[25]

Nativists were shocked when they realized that Mexicans had not been included in the exclusionary acts of 1921 and 1924. In 1925, Robert Foerster, a Princeton economist and author of a study commissioned by the U.S. Department of Labor detailing the racial implications of Latin American immigration, insisted that because Mexicans were not "racially better stocks" than Europeans, "there would appear to be no valid justification for permitting" their continued entry into the United States.[26] Madison Grant, the well-known nativist who had heavily influenced the debate over immigration, was outraged at the omission of Mexicans from the quotas. "From the racial point of view," he wrote in 1925, "it is not logical to limit the number of Europeans while we throw the country open without limitation to Negroes, Indians, and half-breeds."[27]

To Grant, not only were Mexicans degraded half-breeds who threatened to dilute the purity of America's Anglo-Saxon blood, but their country of origin was an object lesson in the horrors of race mixing. "What the Melting Pot actually does in practice can be seen in Mexico," he wrote in The *Passing of the Great Race,* "where the absorption of the blood of the original Spanish conquerors by the native Indian population has produced the racial mixture which we call Mexican and which is now engaged in demonstrating its incapacity for government."[28] The nineteenth-century preoccupation with the mongrel Mexican had survived into the twentieth. Indeed, while anti-European nativism exhibited three strands, "anti-Catholicism, antiradicalism, and Anglo-Saxon racial nationalism," the case against Mexican immigration was overwhelmingly framed in terms of race.[29]

Texas congressman John C. Box, one of the era's most vociferous anti-Mexican activists, was particularly fearful that Mexicans would engender greater racial mixture in the United States. In 1930, he and Ohio representative Thomas A. Jenkins argued that because Mexicans were the product of mixing, they had a relaxed approach to interracial unions and were likely to intermingle with blacks and whites in America. According to the two congressmen, Mexican-style *mestizaje* would "make the blood of all three races flow back and forth between them in a distressing process of mongrelization."[30] "No other alien race entering America," Box testified before his colleagues on the House Immigration and Naturalization Committee, "provides an easier channel for the intermixture of blood than does the mongrel Mexican. . . . their presence and intermarriage with both white and black races . . . create the most insidious and general mixture of white, Indian, and negro blood strains ever produced in America."[31]

In 1930, Max Handman, a Texas economist and student of Mexican immigration, pondered the long-term racial impact of Mexican migration. America "has no social technique for handling partly colored races," he wrote. "We have a place for the Negro and a place for the white man: the Mexican is not a Negro, and the white man refuses him an equal status. What will result from this I am not prophet enough to foretell, but I know that it may mean trouble."[32]

Handman feared that the growing Mexican population would further inflame America's perennial racial conflict. "The negro-white situation is difficult enough," he wrote, "but it is simple."[33] Mexicans, on the other hand, only complicated matters. "In Texas where the negro is such an integral element of our population the usual Southern view prevails. The Mexican present shades of color ranging from that of the negro—although no negro features—to that of the white. The result is confusion."[34] Handman was primarily concerned that Mexicans would refuse to be subjected to the binary Southern perspective, which permitted the existence of only two racial strata, the white and the nonwhite.

The ambiguous racial status of Mexicans was a major source of befuddlement for nativists. From 1850 to 1920 the federal government routinely counted Mexicans as "whites" in the decennial census. But by the late 1920s, a campaign was launched to officially reclassify them as nonwhites. "American public opinion regarding Mexican immigration is confused, chiefly because of the confusion of races in Mexico," wrote California economist Glenn E. Hoover in the October 1929 edition of *Foreign Affairs*. "There is a tacit but universal understanding among government officials that the biological characteristics of the Mexican people shall be assumed to be what they are not in fact."[35] Like other restrictionists, Hoover was frustrated by the federal government's apparent complicity in what they felt was a major conspiracy. "The Immigration Bureau is not enforcing the law," he wrote.

There is no evidence that the immigration authorities on our southern border are rejecting full-blood Indians from Mexico or requiring those of mixed blood to prove that they are predominantely white. It seems, rather, that there is a tacit understanding among all the departments of the federal government that they will proceed on the false assumption that anyone born south of the Rio Grande is a white person. In spite of a mountain of anthropological evidence to the contrary, the Bureau of the Census lists all immigrants from Mexico among the foreign born whites, and this practice has extended to our state authorities.[36]

Nativists were successful in lobbying the Census Bureau to remove Mexicans from the category of white people. Arguing the need for more precise statistics with which to study the impact of Mexican immigration, Representative Albert Johnson of Washington state, the chairman of the House Immigration and Naturalization Committee, urged Secretary of Commerce Robert P. Lamont to direct the head of the census to classify Mexicans as a separate race. Thus, in the 1930 census, "persons of Mexican birth or parentage who were not definitely reported as white or Indian were designated Mexican" and tabulated with "other races," such as Chinese, Japanese, or Native American.[37] In an era in which many legal rights, including that of citizenship, were available only to whites, the decision by the Census Bureau was more than merely academic. It had potentially far-reaching consequences for Mexican American civil rights. Not surprisingly, nativists were overjoyed. "The significance of this racial classification of Mexicans in our next census is obvious," wrote restrictionist Remsen Crawford in February 1930. "A Mexican may be a white man of education and refinement and entirely desirable, but a Mexican with one-eighth Indian blood would be excludable under our existing laws as ineligible to citizenship, though this does not apply to native American Indians. This move on the part of the census officials indicates a full appreciation of the menace of Mexicanization and a desire on the part of the government to diagnose the case so that Congress may be able to prescribe the remedy."[38]

Although it availed them nothing, restrictionists also lobbied the Department of Labor, which oversaw the Immigration Bureau, and went so far as to accuse it of flouting the law. In 1929, California attorney general Ulysses S. Webb filed a brief with Congress arguing that because Mexicans were neither white nor black—and therefore not eligible for citizenship—their entry into the United States was unlawful. The Labor Department responded with contradictory arguments. The secretary of labor, James J. Davis, the first under President Herbert Hoover, declared that Mexicans were indeed "generally spoken of as belonging to the white stock . . . [if they] speak

Spanish, and our Government, in its relations with the Mexican people, has uniformly recognized them as belonging to the white race."[39] At the same time, however, a Labor Department attorney conceded that "Mexicans are principally of mixed Indian blood" and that "anthropologists, following their strict scientific classification of racial groups, might not class Mexicans with the white race."[40]

In late 1935, the nativists who sought to convert the rejection of Timoteo Andrade's petition for naturalization into a controlling legal precedent were seeking to overturn the holding of the 1897 Ricardo Rodríguez case, in which a United States District Court judge ruled that "native citizens of Mexico, whatever may be their status from the standpoint of an ethnologist, are eligible to American citizenship and may be individually naturalized."[41] The case involved a thirty-eight-year-old immigrant living in San Antonio whose citizenship application was rejected on the grounds that he was a Mexican Indian and therefore ineligible for naturalization.

Described by the court as having "copper-colored or red" skin with "dark eyes, straight black hair and high cheek bones," Rodríguez testified that he belonged neither to the "original Aztec race in Mexico" nor to the Spanish "race" of Europe. Instead, he claimed to be "a pure-blooded Mexican."[42] Rodríguez was targeted in an effort to create a legal precedent whereby all nonwhite Mexicans would be deemed ineligible for naturalization.

What the presiding district judge, T. S. Maxey, ultimately concluded, however, was that Rodríguez was eligible for citizenship based on international laws of territorial cession. Not only had Mexicans been incorporated into the U.S. through collective naturalization under the Treaty of Guadalupe Hidalgo, but the possibility of individual naturalization had been granted them by treaty between 1868 and 1882. Furthermore, Judge Maxey did not feel compelled to settle the question of Rodríguez's racial background. As one scholar pointed out, "although the effect of the decision was to treat the Mexican *as if* he were *white,* the decision itself did not rule Mexicans *to be white.*"[43]

Thirty-eight years later, the California Joint Immigration Committee wanted to remove Mexicans from this legal racial limbo to make easier targets of them. To do so, they had to first find a test case that would work its way up to the Supreme Court. V. S. McClatchy had to go clear across the country to find his willing accomplices. Buffalo Naturalization Examiner John L. Murff was a good candidate. Federal Judge John Knight, a state GOP stalwart, was ready to play along. In late 1935, McClatchy contacted Examiner Murff and Judge Knight and urged them "to rule against the naturalization of Mexicans of Indian blood."[44] Timoteo Andrade applied for naturalization not long afterward.

In one affidavit, Andrade had stated that he was a mestizo "of Indian and Spanish blood in equal proportions."[45] Examiner Murff therefore dismissed the petition on the grounds that Andrade was racially ineligible. Citing several racially restrictive High Court rulings, Knight then declared that the 1897 *Matter of Rodriguez* was "not consistent with the later decisions of the Supreme Court."[46]

McClatchy and the Joint Committee were ecstatic. They imagined that other judges throughout the country would follow the new ruling and that the federal government would be forced to curtail Mexican migration. Better yet, there might well be an appeal to the Supreme Court, where Mexicans would be legally defined as members of an excluded race. On December 30, the Joint Committee issued a press release proclaiming their victory. "The U.S. Federal Court at Buffalo, N.Y., John Knight, Judge, has declared Mexican Indians ineligible to American naturalization and therefore inadmissible as immigrants."[47]

But what McClatchy and the Joint Committee failed to appreciate was how the unique relationship between the United States and Mexico would drastically affect their efforts to exclude Mexican migrants. As soon as they heard of Judge Knight's decision, U.S. State Department officials worried about its potentially "deplorable effect on relations between the United States and Mexico."[48] Using Mexican government statistics, the State Department estimated that 30 percent of Mexicans were Indians and nearly 60 percent were mestizo. If Judge Knight's decision became U.S. policy, Mexican immigration would come to a standstill.

The Mexican government, for its part, took the Knight decision as an insult to the nation's dignity and responded rapidly. It instructed its consul general in New York to help Andrade and two other Mexican petitioners to appeal unfavorable rulings. The U.S. State Department assisted by preventing broad circulation of the news of the Knight holding and suppressed the publication of the decision in the *Federal Reporter.* The Labor Department then notified its field officers that the Knight ruling was not consistent with federal policy. Officials from both governments appealed to Judge Knight to delay putting his signature on the ruling.

Mexican ambassador Francisco Castillo Nájera then retained an influential Buffalo lawyer to help with the case. Not only was attorney Frederick T. Devlin familiar with immigration law, he was on friendly terms with Judge Knight, local immigration officials, as well as with the mayor of Buffalo. Devlin's first move was to petition Judge Knight to reconsider his decision. He was successful. At the rehearing, Devlin focused on Andrade's conflicting accounts of his racial heritage. In one affidavit, Andrade had stated that he was 50 percent Indian, on the other he estimated 75 percent. Andrade sought to clear up the confusion by explaining the post-revolutionary racial ideology that romanticized the Indian in Mexico. "In Mexico," he told the court, "even if we have full Spanish blood, we say we have Indian blood, because in Mexico we are all Mexicans."[49]

Devlin then asked Andrade if having Indian blood was something to be proud of in Mexico. Andrade responded: "We are proud that we are Mexicans and we don't like to be told that we have Spanish or French blood." Their exchange continued:

DEVLIN: Do you know whether it was a common practice for Spaniards, who had no Indian blood, to boast of having Indian blood in their veins?
ANDRADE: Yes.
. . . .
DEVLIN: Will you explain the circumstances under which you changed your statement concerning the percentage of Indian blood and the percentage of Spanish blood to fifty percent Indian?
ANDRADE: I was asked how much Indian blood I had in me. I said, 'Maybe I have seventy-five percent; maybe fifty."[50]

Upon further questioning, Andrade clarified his prior testimony by testifying that subsequent to his first hearing, he had asked his mother how much Indian blood he actually had. She replied that it was probably less than 2 percent. Devlin and the new immigration examiner who had been selected for the rehearing then questioned the mother, María Andrade. She swore that her parents and grandparents had all been white. And although she had never met Timoteo's paternal grandmother and grandfather, she had been informed that they were Spanish and French, respectively.

On redirect questioning of Andrade, Devlin asked whether Andrade's original answer regarding his Indian heritage could have been an effort to appease his fellow Mexicans who lived in Buffalo. "Is it possible that you may have had in mind what the effect would be upon the good will of [the] Mexican colony if you indicated that you did not have Indian blood in you?" he asked. "I might have," Andrade responded.[51]

Near the end of the hearing, the immigration examiner asked Mrs. Andrade why her son knew so little about his heritage, while she knew so much. "We never had any conversation about this," she said. "He worked and then when he came home, he went out and we had no time to talk about things like this."[52] Given the new testimony establishing that Andrade had "exaggerated" his indigenous heritage, the examiner recommended that Judge Knight approve the application for naturalization. The government withdrew its previous objections to his application, and Timoteo Andrade became a U.S. citizen on June 1, 1936.

But the struggle over Mexicans' racial identity and legal status was far from over. After all, Judge Knight had not in fact rescinded his opinion or changed his opinion of the applicable law. What he did was to allow Andrade, by his own testimony, to reclassify himself as a white person.

As citizens, Mexican Americans like Andrade had the right to vote, to testify in a court of law, to hold public office, and to own homestead land. But the de facto "white status" that Mexicans enjoyed related exclusively to the fundamental right to citizenship. It did not mean that Mexicans were to be regarded as whites socially nor did it accord them the full range of legal rights enjoyed by other citizens in all areas of the law.

In asserting their rights, Mexican Americans tended to argue that, as white people, they were unfairly excluded from rights to housing, schooling, and public facilities. Consequently, to diminish their official status as white people was to make them all the more vulnerable to infringements of their civil rights. As it was, despite their official status as whites, Mexican Americans encountered at every turn severe forms of discrimination and segregation, particularly in Texas. But unlike the case of African Americans, who faced legally sanctioned discrimination through enforcement of Jim Crow laws in the South, discrimination against Mexican Americans was based more on custom, tradition, and personal bias than on statutory authority.

This uneven social landscape and their ambiguous status within it made Mexican American elites jealous and protective of their legal white status. They sought to exploit their intermediary position between white and black and to secure social and political recognition of their de facto whiteness. By the 1930s, as Mexican Americans began to align themselves more fully with whites, the openness with which they had once treated blacks began to dissipate. They were learning to negotiate the Anglo American racial hierarchy to their advantage. A black cotton picker observed the change in attitudes in 1920. "The Negroes and Mexicans mix some if the Negroes can speak Spanish. They come to some of our dances and dance with our girls if we will let them. They used to, more than they do now. They won't let us dance with their girls, so now our boys won't let our girls dance with them."[53]

In 1929, an Anglo worker who was disdainful of Mexicans thought he detected a hint of opportunism about them. "They try to be white folks with the whites and niggers with the niggers, and aren't either one," he said.[54] Sometimes ethnic Mexicans were segregated along with blacks in movie theaters. But more often, whites treated the two groups quite differently. At times, the difference in treatment translated into three-way graded distinctions in service. According to one employee of a Texas drugstore soda fountain, "We serve Mexicans at the fountain but not at the tables. We have got to make a distinction between them and the white people. The Negroes we serve only cones."[55] In Seguin, Texas, a drugstore clerk claimed: "We let them drink at the soda fountain and if they want a table we have one set apart from the others for them. If a Negro comes, we will serve him a cone, but if he asks for a soda, we just tell him we haven't any bottled soda."[56] Sometimes, particularly in the bigger cities, Mexicans were allowed to sit at any table. In other places, they would be refused entrance altogether or the waitress would simply not take their order. Other establishments would make exceptions for certain Mexicans—like the local minister or the Mexican consul—while refusing to serve anyone else. Even in the same town, the practice of segregating Mexicans varied greatly.

Mexicans and Mexican Americans could be quite unsubtle and crass in their efforts to disassociate themselves from blacks. Without a hint of irony, a dark-skinned cotton picker from Nueces County, Texas, told a white researcher that "Negroes and Mexicans do not mix. It does not look right to see Mexicans and Negroes together. Their color is different. They are black and we are white. It is all right for Americans and Mexicans to mix. We are both of the white race."[57] Many Mexican Americans felt they had to distinguish themselves from blacks in order to safeguard the status and rights they had achieved. As Berkeley economist Paul Taylor noted, they adopted the racial attitudes of the local white community, "in so far as they [applied] to the black race beneath them."[58]

Some blacks were resentful that Mexicans were afforded a different status in the eyes of whites. There were others, however, who sought to marry Mexicans in order to "whiten" their children. "The Negro women think they are going up [socially] to marry Mexicans and may be classed as white," said one black South Texan in 1929. "There are plenty in the Mexican schools classed as white who have colored blood; you know a Negro knows a Negro. They have Mexican names."[59] While Mexicans were legally white, law enforcement didn't always regard them as such. Even though anti-miscegenation laws forbade black and white intermarriage, authorities rarely prosecuted Mexicans for marrying blacks.

Mexican Americans attempted to negotiate this middle ground of being not quite white enough to enjoy full civil rights but not black enough to suffer the worst indignities of Jim Crow. As historian Neil Foley has written, "Although Mexicans and Anglos lived in a segregated society that strongly discouraged social interaction, the line of separation was not as rigidly maintained between the two groups as it was between whites and blacks. In some towns, for example, Mexicans could attend Anglo schools if they were 'clean,' which often was a euphemism for 'white,' " or if they had sufficient social or economic standing.[60] In 1929, one white farmer in Nueces County declared that he "would not mind Jim Crowing the filthy Mexicans, but I would not Jim Crow a Mexican if he was educated and . . . nearer the white race."[61] Anglos were undecided whether Mexican inferiority was a consequence of biology or culture. While many thought Mexicans were unassimilable into American society, others thought they could elevate their status. "I don't think the Mexican race is biologically inferior," said a county official in South Texas. "We know the Negro is."[62]

Not surprisingly, many Texas Mexicans chose to emphasize their European rather than their Indian lineage. In 1929, the founders of LULAC chose to use the term "Latin" in their organization's name. "Latin," like "Spanish," highlighted the white side of their ancestry. In an era in which the term "Mexican" was often considered an insult, "Latin American" was deemed less offensive. LULAC's name also reflected its integrationist goals. The organization's newsletter explained that the term had been a compromise that reflected the peculiar status Mexican Americans held in the Southwest. The group chose a name that they felt would not offend Anglos and help convince them that Mexican Americans were also Americans.

In the 1930s, LULAC had many successes fighting the segregation of Mexican Americans in restaurants, swimming pools, hospitals, and other public facilities. They protested all attempts to segregate Mexican Americans as a nonwhite people. On October 1936, just four months after Timoteo Andrade was granted his U.S. citizenship, the city registrar and health officer of El Paso, Texas, announced that the city would begin classifying Mexicans as "colored" on birth and death certificates. Alex K. Powell, the registrar, explained that he was merely following the lead of the Census Bureau, which in 1930 had reclassified Mexicans from "white" to their own "Mexican" racial category. Furthermore, he explained, several other Texas cities—San Antonio, Dallas, Fort Worth, and Houston—had already established similar policies. Although Powell did not state his reasons publicly, his decision had been based on the desire to "clean up"

El Paso's embarrassing health statistics. City officials had been promoting their city as a health resort, and Mexicans, who made up more than half of the city's population, were undermining their publicity campaign. Northward migration spurred by the Mexican Revolution had turned El Paso into a big city by 1930 and many of its Mexicans lived in squalor with terrible public health conditions. By reclassifying Mexicans as nonwhite, the city would immediately improve the health statistics for whites, particularly the infant mortality rates.

The small but respectable number of lower-level Mexican American officials, ethnic advocates, and organizations did not take the decision lightly. They understood that the attempt to reclassify Mexicans as "colored," if successful, would subject them to de jure as well as de facto segregation. Consequently, they reacted with outrage at El Paso's decision to downgrade them racially. Members of the El Paso chapter of LULAC sued to enjoin the reclassification. Cleofas Calleros, a prominent El Pasoan and the head of the immigration office of the National Catholic Welfare Conference, called a citywide meeting at which Mexicans could plan a protest. "I will spend my last cent to fight such a proposal," Calleros declared. He insisted that "classifying Spanish-speaking persons as colored is a violation of Texas Law."[63]

El Paso's most respected Spanish-language daily, *El Continental,* called the classification of Mexicans with blacks an insult. At first, the paper's editorial page argued simply that a Mexican who is not a "pure Indian" is therefore a member of the "Caucasian race." A few weeks later, however, the paper changed tactics, contending that all Mexicans belonged "to the racial group of their mother country, Spain, and therefore to the Caucasian race."[64] In letters to the editors of both English- and Spanish-language papers, Mexican Americans expressed their displeasure with the decision. Evangelist Pablo Delgado wrote that under this new rule, the fair-skinned U.S. senator Dennis Chávez of New Mexico would be listed as black. Although he believed that all races were one in the eyes of God, Delgado did not believe Mexicans should be grouped with blacks. "The Negroes that are here are the offspring of Negroes brought for slavery to this country," he wrote.[65]

The 65th District Court agreed to hear the petition for an injunction. Activists distributed flyers urging "Ladies and Gentlemen" to "come and defend our Sacred rights."[66] At the hearing, El Paso's city health officer, Dr. T. J. McCamant, announced that the controversy was the result of a misunderstanding and that, in any case, the decision had been reversed. The case was dismissed. Emboldened by their success, Texas Mexicans fought on. This time, they were going to challenge the Census Bureau for its decision to recategorize Mexicans as belonging to the "Mexican" race.

LULAC's San Antonio council issued a resolution protesting "against the insult cast upon our race by the Census Bureau of the Department of Commerce." At the same time, they asked U.S. representative for San Antonio Maury Maverick to launch an investigation, "with a view of having persons of Mexican or Spanish extraction definitely and permanently classified as whites and not as a color."[67] It took only one day for Maverick to respond to the note and to inquire of the head of the Census Bureau whether Mexicans had indeed been denied their white status in the 1930 census. If this was the case, he observed, then the bureau had made a grave mistake. "In the State of Texas the Mexican people have been citizens for 100 years," he wrote in a follow-up letter. "They have gone to our Texas schools; they speak the English language like anyone else and are no different than, for instance, an Italian, a Roumanian, or a Hollander who settles in Oshkosh, Wisconsin, or in New York City."[68] Although he would prefer that Mexicans be classified as "white," the congressman also suggested that the Census Bureau could create a new category that would allow for statistical separation, such as "other White—Mexican." But he insisted that something had to be changed. "To classify these people here as 'colored,' " he wrote, "is to jumble them in as *Negroes*, which they are not and which naturally causes the most violent feelings."[69]

The Mexican American unit of the Veterans of Foreign Wars also joined the protest. So did New Mexico Senator Dennis Chávez, U.S. representative from El Paso R. E. Thomason, and the Mexican ambassador, Francisco Castillo Nájera. The Census Bureau bowed to the pressure and fixed the "error." On October 15, 1936, William Lane Austin, head of the Census Bureau, issued a memo stating:

The Classification by color or race must be as follows:
    a.-white
    b.-Negro
    c.-All other
The text and the tables (either by note at the head of the table or by footnote) must state definitely that the classification white included Mexicans. Mexicans are whites and must be classified as *white*.[70]

By 1935, Mexican communities throughout the United States had been thoroughly transformed. The repatriations—coupled with a high birth rate among Mexican immigrants—hastened the emergence of the second generation, which strengthened the trend toward Americanization. "Within the span of five years, what had been largely an immigrant community before the Depression became one dominated by the [second generation]."[71] (At the start of the decade, third-generation Mexican Americans made up less than one-fifth of the ethnic Mexican population.)[72] In the city of Los Angeles, the U.S.-born portion of the ethnic Mexican population rose from 45 percent to 65 percent between 1930 and 1940.[73] This had a profound effect on Mexican American culture, politics, and identity.

Mexico's influence in the barrios of the Southwest waned. No longer did Mexican communities in the United States think of themselves as *México de afuera*. As a result, "more Mexican Americans were experiencing acculturation or Americanization by the 1930s than ever before."[74] The focus of politics also shifted northward. Before 1930, the small Mexican American middle class in Texas had had to compete for influence with wealthy refugees from the Mexican Revolution and Mexican consuls. The refugee elite focused their attention primarily on events in Mexico and, as a rule, opposed the integration of ethnic Mexicans into American society. They opposed the founding of the League of United Latin American Citizens (LULAC) in 1929. They had hoped that *Mexicanos de afuera* would one day return to work for a united Mexico. In Los Angeles, influential Mexican refugees had been more concerned with the politics of the homeland than with creating a better future for Mexicans in the United States.

The increased demographic importance of U.S.-born Mexican Americans in the 1930s also hastened the emergence of a native-born leadership that was interested first and foremost in events occurring north of the Rio Grande. Having grown up in the United States, second-generation Mexican Americans "were increasingly more acculturated, bilingual, and, as a result, more politically functional. Formally educated to a greater extent than ever before, they became better socialized to their rights as U.S. citizens."[75] As is often the case with the children of immigrants, second-generation Mexican Americans tended to have higher expectations than did their parents. "Even the immigrants from Mexico who got involved in the politics of [the era] increasingly came from the ranks of those who had migrated as children with their parents, and who connected intellectually and experientially with the perspectives of the American-born."[76] As a result, the 1930s saw an upsurge in civil rights activism. Middle-class Mexican Americans launched a variety of initiatives to defend their civil rights and to end segregation and other discriminatory practices. Educational segregation was the form of discrimination that most angered both Mexicans and Mexican Americans. In 1930, a group of parents in Lemon Grove, California, filed the "nation's first successful legal challenge" to segregation.[77] Their suit forced their local school district to desegregate schools. In 1931, LULAC sued to end school segregation in Del Rio, Texas.

Second-generation Mexican Americans also began to combine the struggle for civil rights with that of workers' rights. More committed to life in the United States and less reluctant to participate in American political institutions, working-class members of the younger generation were interested primarily in achieving economic security. They joined labor unions in greater numbers during the 1930s. As historian Douglas Monroy has noted, assimilation to American ways was linked to a new "expression of assertiveness."[78] The combination of working-class unionization and middle-class political activity further integrated Mexican Americans into the fabric of American life. By the late 1930s, every Southwestern state had elected at least one Mexican American to their state legislature. New Mexico's Hispanos were significantly better represented in politics than Mexican Americans in surrounding states. (After World War I, in an attempt to disassociate themselves from Mexican immigrants, longtime Hispanic New Mexicans began to refer to themselves either as Spanish Americans or Hispanos.) In 1935, New Mexicans had elected Dennis Chávez to the U.S. Senate, where he would serve until 1962. Nor was Chávez the first Hispanic U.S. senator from New Mexico, which had become a state in 1912. In 1928–1929, Mexican-born Octaviano Larrazolo served six months in the U.S. Senate before taking ill. He had also served as governor of New Mexico from 1918 to 1919.

Though many Anglos continued to perceive Mexican Americans as a homogenous bloc, more astute observers began to notice the growing stratification within the Mexican population. Writing on South Texas in 1930, political scientist O. Douglas Weeks commented that "from county to county, one meets with a variety of aspect and condition. Strong contrasts exist even in a single county, and the Mexican element may be observed in all stages of development."[79] Most Mexicans, those in the countryside in particular, remained largely culturally and economically isolated from the mainstream. But a growing number of Mexican Americans in towns and cities were "anxious to secure their own rights as citizens."[80] Four years later, economist Paul Taylor noted that most Mexicans in Nueces County, Texas, were "content to remain Mexican, and [were] willing to endure discrimination in silence."[81] The "points of friction," he wrote, "do not haunt the daily lives of [most] Mexicans."[82] However, the nascent American-born middle class was deeply offended by, and therefore most willing to take a stand against, discrimination. The most acculturated Mexican Americans and those with the most contact with Anglos were in the vanguard of the struggle for civil rights. By the late 1930s, "acculturation, class stratification, and ideological differentiation" among generations had become more noticeable in San Antonio.[83] The number of Mexican American businesspeople was growing. They served as living proof that upward mobility was within the realm of possibility. Still, the combination of discrimination and the coming of the Great Depression limited possibilities for advancement in the 1930s. The Americanization of the second generation would occur mostly in a working-class context. As historian George J. Sánchez has argued, Mexican American acculturation occurred largely in the absence of upward mobility.

No matter the class background, the coming of age of the second generation created tensions within families. Adult children of immigrants had developed a distinct identity and different priorities from those of their parents. In 1939, a Los Angeles newspaper published a series of articles by second-generation young women that addressed intergenerational issues. One writer, Dora Ibáñez, a college graduate and music teacher in Los Angeles, acknowledged the obligation that the second generation often felt to respect their parents' worldview while developing their own. While addressing parents' concerns, she nonetheless encouraged them to give their blessing to their children's new identity. "What is happening with our children?" she asked. "Why do they reject our behavior? Why don't they respond harmoniously with our way of thinking? Don't they feel the warmth of our traditions and customs like we do? Many of you don't get answers to these questions and see that your son or daughter doesn't find satisfaction in themselves, nor in the home, nor in the community nor in their own people in general."[84] The second generation was in the process of creating a new identity and a new culture. By and large, they did not feel a need to summarily reject their parents' ways. They were comfortable adopting and melding elements of both Mexican and American cultures. As Douglas Monroy concluded, Mexican Americans in Los Angeles "neither passively received the messages of popular culture and schooling nor consciously assimilated the surrounding culture nor militantly protected their traditions. Rather, they drew on a storehouse, which included all of these means as each situation in the strange, threatening, attractive, and hostile environment appeared to require."[85] Even in the isolated Hispano villages of New Mexico, cultural borrowing continued apace. By the 1930s, "Many houses now had slanted metal, not flat adobe, roofs; many women wore high-heeled shoes and elaborate hats instead of shawls, danced modern dance steps, got permanents, and occasionally, in urban areas or villages with cars, went on dates while a mildly scandalized older generation looked on."[86]

The United States' entry into World War II in 1941 accelerated the Americanization of Mexican Americans. Responding to the nation's call, Mexican Americans signed up for military service in large numbers. Most were drafted, but many volunteered. Nationwide, an estimated 400,000 to 500,000 ethnic Mexicans—both native- and foreign-born—served in the U.S. armed forces during the war. In proportion to their percentage of the population, more Mexican Americans served in combat divisions than any other ethnic group.[87] Many served with distinction in both the Pacific and the Atlantic theaters. Seventeen Mexican American servicemen were awarded the Congressional Medal of Honor. Five of the fourteen Texans who won the medal in World War II were Mexican Americans.[88] "Proportionately, Mexican Americans achieved the distinction of gaining more decorations for bravery in the battlefield than any other [ethnic] group."[89] According to historian Manuel Gonzales, José M. López of Brownsville, Texas, killed more enemy soldiers than any other American during the war. On December 17, 1944, López, a machine gunner with K Company of the 23rd Regiment, 2nd Division, cut down more than one hundred Germans during a battle in the Krinkelt Wald in Belgium.

Though Mexican Americans were not segregated in the armed forces as a matter of policy, Company Z of the 141st Regiment of the 36th Division was made up almost entirely of Tejanos. It played an important role in the invasion of Sicily in 1943. Two of its members, Sergeant Manuel S. Gonzales of Fort Davis and Lieutenant Gabriel Navarette of El Paso, were awarded the Distinguished Service Cross. At Bataan in the Philippines, Mexican Americans made up one-quarter of the combat troops.[90] They were also well represented in the 1944 Allied invasion of the European mainland. Indeed, they made up a large percentage of three of the infantry divisions—the 3rd, 36th, and 45th—which suffered the heaviest losses. Overall, Mexican Americans died in battle at a rate out of proportion to their numbers. For example, while Mexicans accounted for roughly 10 percent of the population of Los Angeles, "they accounted for about twenty percent of the Angelenos killed in action."[91] *La Opinión,* the local Spanish-language newspaper, published the names of the dead under the title "*La Lista de Honor.*" On April 6, 1945, with heavy fighting in Europe and the Pacific, *La Lista* included forty-eight names of local Mexican Americans.[92] In February of that year, the paper published a photograph on the front page of Doña R. de Alviso, who lived on Maple Avenue in Los Angeles. She was pictured receiving the Bronze Star that had been posthumously awarded to her son, Jesús, who had died fighting in the Pacific. "On the home front the number of blue stars (signifying a son or husband in the military) and gold stars (signifying a battle death) multiplied in the windows of the homes of the Mexican colonies."[93]

The contribution of Mexican Americans to the war effort did not go unnoticed at the time. California congressman Jerry Voorhis commented that as he

read the casualty lists from my own state, I find anywhere from one-fourth to one-third of these names are names such as Gonzales or Sánchez, names indicating that the very lifeblood of our citizens of Latin-American descent in the uniform of the armed forces of the United States is being poured out to win victory in the war. We ought not to forget that. We ought to resolve that in the future every single one of these citizens shall have the fullest and freest opportunity which this country is capable of giving him, to advance to such positions of influence and eminence as their own personal capacities make possible.[94]

Director William A. Wellman's 1949 war movie *Battleground*, which portrayed a band of American soldiers under siege in the Battle of the Bulge, featured a Mexican American character played by Mexican-born actor Ricardo Montalbán. During the war many Mexican Americans saw their fellow co-ethnics being honored as Americans for the first time. In 1945, Private Cleto Rodríguez was given a hero's welcome when he returned to his native San Antonio. "City officials, khaki-clad buddies and mantilla-covered neighbors jammed the [city council] chamber to render official plaudits to the 22-year-old Congressional Medal of Honor winner and proclaim 'Cleto Rodríguez Day.'"[95] In his brief remarks, Rodríguez, who had fought in the Philippines, honored a friend who had fallen in battle. "I am indeed happy to have had the great privilege of serving our country in the global war, and I thank God for the victory achieved by our nation and its Allies. I wish to ask you to be good enough to join me in a moment of silent prayer to the memory of my buddy, Johnny Reece, and all my other comrades in arms who died for our country."[96]

As was the case in the First World War, World War II was often the first instance in which many Mexican American soldiers became familiar with other sectors of American society. "Some were forced to deal with Anglos for the first time, and the experience in interethnic relations was generally positive. Cooperating against the common enemy tended to break down mutual prejudices."[97] In a letter from Luxembourg, Private First Class Henry Castillo of San Antonio wrote that his "squad consisted of a German, a Frenchman, a Spaniard, a Mexican, an Italian, a Jew, and guys with names like Joe." He was deeply impressed with his crew, who helped capture a town on the Siegfried Line. "They were infantrymen. A mongrel crew. . . . But the squad had something to teach the world. . . . What man can do when teamed with others. . . . Too bad everyone can't belong to one small squad in one small battle. To learn how men of different breeds and creeds can live and work together when they must."[98]

It was in such squads where many Mexican Americans first experienced being treated as equals by Anglos. In 1946, California journalist Ignacio L. López observed that "every Southwest community has in it young men . . . who were able to act as complete Americans for three to four years. They know what it is to be released from the minority burden."[99] Although discrimination was not entirely absent, Mexican American servicemen did often find opportunities open to them in the military that had not been available in civilian life. "We learned new languages and trades and how other people lived, too," said one veteran. "So we came home with a lot of ideas and plans. . . . The war opened the doors for us."[100] Historian and veteran Raúl Morín described the respect that Mexican American soldiers had earned throughout the war from their fellow soldiers. "No longer were we chided and shunted [sic] by other GI's and Army officers. Where we had been held in contempt by others who disliked us because of our constant Spanish chatter or our lax in military discipline, we were now admired, respected, and approved by all those around us including most of our commanding officers."[101] In fact, more than a few soldiers were eager to prove their Americanness. According to Morín, "We felt that this was an opportunity to show the rest of the nation that we *too* were also ready, willing, and able to fight for our nation. It did not matter whether we were looked upon as Mexicans, Mexican-American, or belonging to a minority group; the war soon made us all *genuine* Americans."[102]

Never before had so many Mexican Americans felt such confidence and pride in their Americanness. Stateside, Mexican American civilians, like most Americans, supported the war effort in many small ways. They bought War Bonds and donated blood to the Red Cross, which, unlike the blood of African Americans, was accepted for "transfusions into all wounded soldiers."[103] In 1945, a LULAC newsletter heralded what its editors considered the positive assimilative effect of the war on Mexican Americans. "The primary or general objective of the League, to teach Americans of Latin American origin to be better and more loyal citizens has been accomplished by war."[104] At the same time, few believed that becoming patriotic Americans required the obliteration of ethnicity. In Los Angeles in December 1944, the float at the head of the parade honoring La Virgen de Guadalupe, the Patroness of Mexico, displayed the blend that was Mexican American identity. From the float flew the American and the Mexican flags, while the words "E Pluribus Unum" were written on the front.[105] As historians S. Dale McLemore and Ricardo Romo have noted, most Mexican Americans appeared "determined to find a middle way wherein American culture may be added to, rather than substituted for, their own heritage."[106] They had learned to distinguish between their singular patriotism to the United States and their increasingly mixed cultural identity as Mexican Americans.

Just as Mexican Americans were learning about the ways of Americans from different backgrounds, other Americans were learning about them. Raúl Morín describes receiving a Christmas care package from his wife and kids while stationed in Alsace-Lorraine. It included candies, cookies, and *chiles jalapeños*. "Needless to say, all the 'hot' stuff was quickly devoured by the G.I.'s who were possessed by that wolfish craving for hot seasoning—not only the Mexican Americans but many other G.I.'s who had picked up the taste during our long associations. There were also a few who out of curiosity ventured a taste only to tear away yelling bloody murder and crying for water!"[107]

In their 1949 book, *Democracy in Jonesville,* W. L. Warner and his co-authors explained how social barriers can disappear in times of war. "In wartime internal antagonisms are drained out of the group onto the common enemy. The local antagonisms which customarily divide and separate peoples are often suppressed. . . . The local ethnic groups, too frequently excluded from participation in community affairs, are given an honored place in the war effort, and the symbols of unity, rather than the separating differences, are stressed."[108] This was largely true for Mexican Americans. Consequently, World War II was a watershed in their history. The war widened their social and economic frontiers. According to writer Carey McWilliams, "In every phase of the war, including the defense plants and the training schools as well as the armed services, similar opportunities opened up for thousands of Mexican Americans: to learn new skills, to acquire new experiences, to come in contact with entirely new currents of thought and opinion."[109] But heightened Americanization also had its costs, and social equality had not yet been achieved. The rapid urbanization of Mexican Americans had weakened traditional family bonds, and not every member of the second generation had learned to balance the old and new cultures. A combination of cultural aliena-tion, the breakdown of the family, and discrimination helped create a Mexican American gang subculture whose members were called *pachucos,* or zoot-suiters.

In Los Angeles in 1942, a murder trial of a group of twenty-two *pachucos,* all but one of them Mexican American, captured the atten-tion of the local media. Testimony in the case was laced with racist characterizations about Mexicans' presumed biological predisposi-tion toward violence. After an unfair, racially charged trial in which seventeen of the youths were convicted—though the guilty verdicts were later reversed on appeal—of varying crimes, the press promoted a campaign to get tough on the "Mexican crime wave." Newspapers had already perfected the tactic of mistaking the most dysfunctional or marginal part of a minority group for the whole. They treated the *pachucos* as if they were representative of Mexican Americans at large. So did the police, who increased their patrols of Mexican neighborhoods. In 1943, the anti-Mexican propaganda culminated in the so-called Zoot Suit Riots in which U.S. sailors and marines on leave roamed downtown streets and attacked Mexican American youths, many of whom had nothing to do with the *pachucos.* The violence lasted a week and eventually spread to other cities in California and even the Midwest. The local police failed to intervene. Only after the Mexican government lodged a protest on behalf of some Mexican nationals caught up in the melees did President Franklin D. Roosevelt order the military to rein in its men. As champion of the Good Neighbor Policy, which promoted better relations between the United States and Latin America, Roosevelt may have felt that he had no other choice. These incidents served as a reminder that despite the wartime easing of ethnic barriers and their widespread support of the war, Mexican Americans were still not fully accepted as "genuine Americans." In the meantime, many Mexican American servicemen were coming home "more assertive, ready to take their place in a society which by any reckoning they had fought to preserve."[110] Tejanos in particular were rudely awakened by the discrimination they encountered upon their return. The father of one veteran said of his son, "After he came home and found that things hadn't changed, he felt that he would rather be just another sailor than the kind of human being the Anglos treated him like."[111]

One high-profile incident caught the attention of radio commentator and newspaper columnist Walter Winchell. Staff Sergeant Macario García, the third Mexican American to win the Medal of Honor in World War II, was refused service at the Oasis Café in Sugar Land, Texas. "The proprietor, Mrs. Donna Andrews, told him no Mexicans were served there. When he insisted on being served, there was a fight between García, aided by two sailors, and customers in the café."[112] Adding insult to injury, the police later arrested García for aggravated assault on Mrs. Andrews. Not long before, Medal of Honor recipient Sergeant José M. López was unceremoniously ejected from a restaurant in a small town in the Rio Grande Valley. In Phoenix, Arizona, city officials attempted to prohibit Mexican American servicemen from moving into federally funded veterans housing. But it was an emotional incident regarding the burial of a fallen soldier that energized and transformed a small Mexican American veterans group in Corpus Christi, Texas, into an influential civil rights organization.

In January of 1949, Dr. Héctor García, founder of the American G.I. Forum, a group established to ensure that Mexican American veterans received the government benefits due them, was asked to intervene in a matter involving the remains of Private Félix Longoria. Killed in combat four years earlier in the Philippines, Longoria's remains had only just been returned home. The trouble started when the owner of the funeral home in Three Rivers, Texas, a town halfway between San Antonio and Corpus Christi, informed Mrs. Longoria that her husband's body would be buried in the town's segregated "Mexican cemetery" and that the family could not use the funeral home's chapel for the service because "whites would not like it."[113]

García immediately contacted several legislators, among them newly elected U.S. senator Lyndon B. Johnson. In his telegram to Johnson, García characterized the incident as "a direct contradiction of those same principles for which this American soldier made the supreme sacrifice in giving his life for his country, and for the same people who now deny him the last funeral rites deserving of any American hero, regardless of his origin."[114] Johnson responded with a telegram offering to have Longoria buried at Arlington National Cemetery. The successful ending to the episode convinced García and his fellow veterans to broaden the mission of the G.I. Forum to include the fight to end discrimination against all Mexican Americans. In the 1940s and 1950s, the G.I. Forum filed a series of class action suits aimed at segregation, educational inequality, and other discriminatory practices. By the 1950s, the G.I. Forum had joined LULAC in the ranks of the most influential Mexican American organizations. Like LULAC, the G.I. Forum was an integrationist organization that emphasized patriotism. Postwar Mexican American politics by and large followed the trajectory that had been set in the late 1920s and 1930s. Armed with higher expectations, a sense of entitlement, and the skills with which to make a difference, World War II veterans had reenergized the movement for Mexican American civil rights.

This activism, coupled with industrialization and the increased urbanization of the Mexican American population, brought about improvements in Texas's cities. (Rural areas, however, would continue to be burdened with institutionalized discrimination for at least another decade.) By the 1950s, "Mexican Americans succeeded in eliminating some of the more openly racist practices against them."[115] By 1960, the school segregation that did persist was "closely analogous to the segregation of Negro children in northern cities, i.e., it often does occur in fact, but it is far from absolute and usually is the result of housing and of prejudice, not of law."[116] In the postwar years, the standard of living of Mexican American urbanites began to improve. The G.I. Bill played a significant role in facilitating the upward mobility of many Mexican Americans. In the 1940s and 1950s, their presence in colleges and universities increased significantly. Veterans Administration home mortgage loans contributed to the rise in Mexican American homeownership in the postwar years. A small but growing number was able to move out of the barrio. "Expanding cities offered modern amenities, wider employment prospects, and better schooling opportunities. Mexican Americans confronted greater acculturating influences, and some experienced upward mobility and developed cultural tastes that differentiated them from those left in the lower stratum."[117]

For decades, many Tejanos chose to leave Texas for better prospects in Southern California. As bad as they sometimes got, race relations in Los Angeles were rarely as severe as they were in the Lone Star State. In the postwar years, Southern California saw a growing number of Mexican Americans moving to mixed suburban areas. Restrictive covenants, designed to limit the geographic mobility of minorities, were outlawed in California in 1948. By 1960, the once largely white, working-class Los Angeles suburbs of Hawthorne, Huntington Park, Inglewood, Lynwood, South Gate, and Bell were home to more than nine thousand Mexican Americans.[118] More than 47,000 Mexican Americans resided in the largely middle-class suburbs of Alhambra, Arcadia, Baldwin Park, Burbank, Carson, Culver City, Downey, Glendale, Manhattan Beach, Norwalk, Paramount, Redondo Beach, Torrance, and West Covina.[119] One 1952 study of a Southern California suburb found that 45 percent of whites interviewed would tolerate a Mexican American living next door. By contrast, only 23 percent said they would live next door to an African American. According to historian Josh Sides, "This relative tolerance of Mexican Americans translated into a much more timid campaign of exclusion against them than the campaign waged against blacks."[120]

Increased upward mobility and greater contact on an equal plane led to more Mexican-Anglo intermarriage. Some soldiers "married into Anglo-American families from other parts of the country," where anti-Mexican prejudice was not as high as in their home states.[121] Indeed, "It was not until [the war] that rates of exogamy began to rise."[122] By 1963, 25 percent of married Mexican Americans in Los Angeles County had wed non-Mexicans.[123] Of all the Southwestern states, California had the highest rate of Mexican American intermarriage while Texas had the lowest. In the 1950s, the Mexican American population became more integrated into American society. By 1960, almost 55 percent of the ethnic Mexican population was native-born of native-born parents; in other words they were at least third-generation Americans.[124] The cultural distance between a Mexican immigrant and a third-generation Mexican American had widened through the years. This was evident in intermarriage patterns in Los Angeles in the early 1960s. In 1963, a third-generation Mexican American man or woman was more likely to marry an Anglo than they were a first- or second generation Mexican American.[125]

The postwar upswing in intermarriage produced a landmark court decision that struck a blow against anti-miscegenation laws in the United States. Although these laws did not apply to Mexican Americans because they were legally white, it was a Mexican American woman who filed the lawsuit that led to the striking down of California's anti-miscegenation statute. Indeed, the California Supreme Court's 1948 decision in *Pérez v. Sharp* "became one of the main cases used to strike down antimiscegenation laws at the national level."[126] The case involved Andrea Pérez, who was denied a license to marry Sylvester Davis, an African American. Under California law, no marriage license could be issued to a couple that consisted of a white and black person. Pérez's lawyers argued that the offending statute infringed on their client's freedom of religion. They contended that since both Pérez and Davis were Roman Catholics, and the Church did not forbid such marriages, they were both entitled to receive the sacrament of matrimony. Agreeing that the prohibition violated Pérez's constitutional right to freedom of religion, the court handed down a ruling that "set the precedent allowing marriage to be included as part of the rights guaranteed under the Fourteenth Amendment."[127]

But just as World War II had expanded the frontiers of the Mexican American experience and identity, it also created the conditions for a new migration that would bring Mexico closer than it had been since before the Depression. While Mexican labor had been recruited in the 1920s, then pushed out in the 1930s, in the 1940s the U.S. government established a program to import contract laborers. The mobilization of American industry for the war effort and the contemporaneous loss of manpower to the armed services created a labor shortage, particularly in agriculture. Between 1939 and 1943, the U.S. had lost 2.8 million agricultural workers.[128] Growers turned to the federal government for help. In the summer of 1942, the Roosevelt administration negotiated an agreement with Mexico, whereby the latter would provide braceros—from the Spanish word *brazo,* or "arm"—to help ease the labor shortage for the duration of the war. Mexican officials were amenable to the program in part because they saw it as their nation's contribution to the war effort. In May of that year, Mexico had declared war on the Axis powers. But since it had no "intentions of sending large contingents to the fighting fronts, it felt obliged to assist in every way possible the country that was bearing the brunt of the war."[129] Mexico also benefited in other ways. Not only did migrants send money back home in the form of remittances, but they often picked up new farming techniques that could later benefit their home communities. Nonetheless, the Mexican government was concerned about the treatment of the workers. They pushed the U.S. government for "guarantees concerning hours, conditions, housing, health care, sanitation facilities, transportation, a minimum wage of thirty cents per hour, and [paid] repatriation."[130] For the first five years of the program, the Mexican government refused to send braceros to Texas due to its reputation for widespread discrimination against Mexicans. On September 29, 1942, federal authorities delivered the first five hundred workers to farms outside Stockton, California.

As historian Neil Foley wrote, "For the next seventeen years the government functioned as a national labor contractor for southwestern growers at taxpayers' expense."[131] From 1942 to 1945, 168,000 braceros were recruited to the United States.[132] While the program was initially established as a temporary wartime measure, Congress later extended it annually through the late 1940s. In 1949, the government issued around 100,000 bracero visas.[133] By 1951, that number had doubled. That year, Congress bowed to pressure from growers and enacted a law that made the Bracero Program permanent.[134] By 1953, braceros made up 87 percent of cotton pickers and 74 percent of the cowboys in Texas.[135] By the late 1950s, 150,000 to 200,000 braceros labored in California's Central Valley.[136] By the time the program was discontinued in 1964, roughly five million workers had been employed in twenty-six states.

Still, farmers were never satisfied with the number of laborers they were allotted, and "during the late 1940s agricultural growers increasingly took matters into their own hands by recruiting undocumented workers."[137] Indeed, the Bracero Program was in part responsible for spurring a rise in illegal immigration. First, it "significantly widened the road to the United States."[138] Many of the risks that had formerly been involved in undertaking the trip north had been removed, thus encouraging a broader cross section of Mexicans to consider going to the United States. News of available jobs reached Mexican villages, and because there were more applicants than visas, many opted to cross without papers. In the spring of 1955, residents of Aguacaliente de Garate, a *pueblo* in the state of Sinaloa, learned that agricultural workers could earn up to 50 cents an hour in Texas, far more than the prevailing wage of 65 cents a day at home. Some read about it in the newspaper, while others heard announcements on the radio. The town's mayor distributed a sheet to those interested in signing up.[139]

Over time, braceros established relationships with employers and "realized that there would be work waiting for anyone who showed up, with no questions asked."[140] Many growers actually preferred undocumented workers to braceros, and that preference would grow along with their need for labor. Not only did illegal immigrants have few rights under the law, but they could be hired without any concern on the employer's part about contracts, health benefits, and the minimum wage. Meantime, throughout the 1940s, the Immigration and Naturalization Service practiced a policy of selective enforcement. In 1948, one year before Mexico lifted its bracero ban on Texas, an INS district director in El Paso told his staff, "We do not have the personnel and means to prevent all these farmers from using illegal labor; therefore, unless and until Texas farmers are given the privilege of legally importing farm laborers from Mexico, their farms should not be indiscriminately raided."[141] The INS sometimes went so far as to normalize the legal status of undocumented workers simply in order to accommodate growers. In October 1948, agents allowed seven thousand migrants to cross the border in El Paso, where they were arrested and then paroled to employers.

The onset of the Korean War in 1950 resulted in a new labor shortage that stimulated an increased supply of undocumented workers. In 1950, an unprecedented high of 469,000 illegal immigrants were apprehended at the border.[142] Meantime, an unknown number of braceros skipped their contracts and became undocumented. Some looked for better-paying agricultural work; others headed for the cities. The longer they stayed the more they gravitated toward non-agricultural labor. Those who remained in the U.S. tended to integrate themselves into established Mexican American barrios. According to a 1951 study, "the wetback [a usually derogatory term for an illegal immigrant] naturally establishes contacts with those most like himself. He does his shopping in the 'Mexican' section of town . . . he rents a shack on the back of one of the lots owned and inhabited by a Spanish-speaking family; he turns to Spanish-speaking truckers for employment; when he has money he patronizes cantinas and pool halls in the 'Mexican' area; he attends social affairs and *bailes* [dances] with the Spanish-speaking people; he may go out with or even marry the daughter of Spanish-speaking citizens."[143] Many learned that "they could become legalized if they established families in the United States and some waited the requisite seven years to apply for a suspension of deportation and adjustment of their status to permanent resident."[144] At the same time, the number of legal migrants from Mexico increased exponentially in the postwar years, particularly in the 1950s. It was not uncommon for immigrant families to have members with varying levels of legal status in the United States.

But even as the agriculture industry sought more laborers—both legal and illegal—a growing number of Americans demanded that immigration be halted. Many Mexican Americans were among those concerned about burgeoning immigration from Mexico. When news of the Bracero Program was first reported in 1942, several Mexican American organizations were quick to express their concerns. LULAC firmly opposed both illegal immigration and the Bracero Program. So did the G.I. Forum. Both organizations had worked hard to promote the image of Mexican Americans as being akin to the nation's many European-origin ethnic groups. The growing presence of unassimilated newcomers complicated their task. Critics of illegal immigration associated undocumented immigrants with "misery, disease, crime, and many other evils."[145] Many Americans believed that because they were by definition illegal, these aliens were prone to engage in criminal behavior. Mexican American civil rights advocates were well aware that such characterizations often influenced the public's opinion of Mexican Americans at large. They feared that the rising number of migrants would lead to an increase in acts of discrimination against all people of Mexican heritage. In 1951, former LULAC director and prominent Mexican American historian George I. Sánchez declared, "No careful distinctions are made between illegal aliens and local citizens of Mexican descent. They are lumped together as 'Mexicans' and the characteristics that are observed among the wetbacks are by extension assigned to the local people."[146] Sánchez feared that new immigration would retard Mexican Americans' process of integration into American society. He told the *New York Times* that "from a cultural standpoint, the influx of a million or more wetbacks a year transforms the Spanish-speaking people of the Southwest from an ethnic group which might be assimilated with reasonable facility into what I call a culturally indigestible peninsula of Mexico. The 'wet' migration . . . has set the whole assimilation process back at least twenty years."[147]

Mexican American civil rights and labor advocates were concerned as well that the new migrants were taking jobs from and lowering wages for Mexican American workers. Representative Henry B. González, the first Mexican American ever elected to the House of Representatives from Texas, complained that braceros were "used to bring the misery of a people in one country to further depress the misery of a people in another country."[148] In a letter to President Dwight D. Eisenhower, one Mexican American from Texas wondered why the government enforced more protective labor regulations for braceros than it did for American citizens. "One glaring inequality which people cannot understand is why the United States will guarantee to an *alien* a specified wage and deny the same to its own citizens. Doesn't charity begin at home?"[149] In her 1959 study on the barrio of San Jose, California, anthropologist Margaret Clark noted that the "general feeling among resident Mexican Americans is that the importation of *braceros* . . . increases job competition and keeps farm wages pitifully low."[150] The National Agricultural Workers' Union (NAWU), which represented thousands of Mexicans and Mexican Americans, complained that braceros not only exerted downward pressure on wages, but they undermined labor organizing and further eroded working conditions. At one point, pioneering Mexican American scholar and NAWU organizer Ernesto Galarza worried that tension between Mexican Americans and migrants—both legal and illegal—could create a "brew of . . . racial strife."[151] Some Mexican Americans considered braceros the equivalent of scabs, and there were occasional fights over jobs or women. One bracero recalled that "the ones who treat us bad are the . . . Mexicans that are born [in the United States]. They felt resentment against us. They feel uncomfortable with us. . . . They try to take advantage of us. . . . They laugh [at] us."[152]

At the same time there existed a certain ethnic affinity between Mexican Americans and Mexican migrants. The fact that many Anglos made no distinctions between the two groups fostered sympathetic concern among many Mexican Americans for their foreign-born co-ethnics, legal and illegal. One foreign-born Californian expressed the conflicting emotions that some native-born and naturalized Mexican Americans felt. "I still don't know if I'm for or against the braceros. I guess that's because I first came to this country as a bracero myself in 1944, and know something about their problems. But I also know that when the braceros come in, the wages stay very low; that's pretty bad for people who have to earn their whole year's income just during the harvest season."[153] A native-born Mexican American activist concurred:

Naturally, we feel sorry for the *braceros*. We do what we can to see that they are exploited as little as possible up here. After all, our own parents were in pretty much the same position as the *braceros* a generation ago. . . . But look at what the program is doing to us. We're trying to climb our way up the social ladder. . . . It's a hard enough fight, at best. The *braceros* come along, and hang on to the tail of our shirts. We can't brush them off, because that wouldn't be human. But their weight is dragging us down.[154]

Mainstream Mexican American organizations were careful not to lay the blame for undocumented immigration on the migrants themselves. The G.I. Forum criticized both the federal government and the growers for their complicity in illegal immigration. LULAC blamed "Mexico for being unable to correct its unemployment crisis" and "U.S. agribusiness for knowingly hiring" illegal immigrants.[155] It criticized the Immigration and Naturalization Service for "allowing an avalanche of illegal Mexican labor" to lower wages.[156] In testimony before a House committee in 1955, Ernesto Galarza accused the U.S. government of rescuing Mexico from its own mismanagement and doing so at the expense of the American worker. While he sympathized with and understood that the "so-called wetback is a product of the political and social conditions of Mexico," he nonetheless came down on the side of native-born and naturalized workers.[157] LULAC also called for the deportation of illegals. In 1948, the organization sent telegrams to President Harry S. Truman calling illegal immigration "a direct danger to our own citizens."[158] For its part, the G.I. Forum supported the expansion of the Border Patrol.

In 1952, Cold War fears pushed the McCarran-Walter Act through Congress despite President Truman's veto. Most Mexican American activists supported its provisions. The omnibus bill both liberalized immigration—by finally removing racial barriers to American citizenship—and at the same time tightened controls over the screening and entrance of immigrants. The new law "decreed that any [unnaturalized] alien who had entered the United States since 1924 was subject to summary deportation from the United States—regardless of his or her character, length of stay in the United States, employment record, or familial relationship to bona fide American citizens."[159] Public exasperation over the issue of illegal immigration—coupled with the fear of communist infiltration—also led the INS to begin stepping up its enforcement in the early 1950s, even raiding farms in search of illegal workers. In February 1950, the Border Patrol increased its monthly apprehensions by 30 percent in Texas.[160] Four years later, the INS launched the well-publicized Operation Wetback, a massive roundup of illegal immigrants in the Southwest.

Conducted by a retired general as if it were a military campaign, Operation Wetback mobilized approximately 750 law enforcement agents, three hundred vehicles, and seven airplanes. Over a period of two years, the operation netted more than one million illegal immigrants.[161] While Texas and California were the regions most affected, the operation also extended to cities as far from the border as Spokane and St. Louis. During the raids, the INS, which apprehended an average of two thousand people a day in California, routinely violated the constitutional rights of both illegal and legal residents. Not only were many U.S.-born children deported along with their parents, but American-born adults were sometimes stopped and required to produce proof of citizenship. Longtime immigrants were deported alongside recent arrivals. Indiscriminate INS sweeps of Mexican American neighborhoods created plenty of confusion and fear. According to historian David Gutiérrez, "INS dragnets not only were affecting putative illegal aliens but were also devastating Mexican American families, disrupting businesses in Mexican neighborhoods, and fanning interethnic animosities throughout the border region."[162]

At the same, however, the INS more than doubled the number of braceros that could be imported each year. From 1955 to 1960, the annual quota of guest workers fluctuated between 400,000 and 450,000.[163] The irony of the situation was not lost on many contemporary observers. In 1955, Ernesto Galarza duly noted that "while one agency of the United States government rounded up the illegal aliens and deported them to Mexico . . . [an]other government agency was busily engaged in recruiting workers in Mexico to return them to U.S. farms."[164] In fact, the emergence of immigration as a hot button political issue made many Mexican American activists and an emerging cadre of intellectuals reassess their views of the relationship between Mexican Americans and immigrants—both legal and illegal. Even the leading Mexican American civil rights organizations, whose membership had long been restricted to American citizens and whose goals were to achieve the full rights of American citizenship, began to discern the links between the rights of citizens and those of immigrants. By the late 1940s, most Mexican American political activists believed that the ethnic Mexican population had stabilized and would eventually join the American mainstream. In the words of historian Mario T. García, "They genuflected—like most other Americans—to the concept of the 'melting pot.' "[165] Yet, particularly after 1950, the issue of immigration could not be ignored. Simply declaring their opposition to further immigration no longer sufficed as a strategy. In 1954, Albert Armendáriz, the national president of LULAC, argued that Mexican Americans had to come to terms with ongoing immigration from Mexico. He contended that the Mexican American experience was distinct from that of other ethnic Americans. Not only did newcomers continually reinforce the culture of the old country, he said, but "the constant influx of immigrants (*braceros* and wetbacks too) . . . make[s] the process of integration a perpetual one."[166] After witnessing the effects of summary deportations on Mexican American neighborhoods, LULAC declared its opposition to the McCarran-Walter Act on the ground that it was "oppressive and unjust and creating great hardships to thousands of families in the deportation of aliens who entered the country illegally but have established residence."[167] In the 1950s, the percentage of immigrants to the United States who came from Mexico doubled.[168] By the end of the decade, many activists were realizing that Mexican Americans were "constantly compelled to assess and define their own sense of social and cultural identity vis-à-vis the recent arrivals."[169]

But just as many Mexican American activists were exploring their connection to immigrants, the anti-Mexican sentiment that had been exacerbated by Operation Wetback prompted greater numbers of newly middle-class Mexican Americans to downplay their ethnicity. As more avenues for upward mobility opened, many Mexican Americans felt it necessary to disassociate themselves from anything Mexican in order to avoid the sting of lingering prejudice. By 1960, over half of ethnic Mexicans in the United States were at least third generation Americans, and thus highly acculturated.[170] In other words, they—particularly those with lighter skin—were more capable of obscuring their "differentness" when among Anglos. Not that this strategy was entirely new. For decades, unknown numbers of upwardly mobile Mexican Americans passed themselves off as Spanish in order to receive better treatment from Anglos. Terms like "Latin" or "Latin American" were frequently substituted for "Mexican." The largest Mexican American organizations—League of United Latin American Citizens, the American G.I. Forum, and later the Political Association of Spanish-Speaking Organizations—studiously avoided using the term Mexican in their names. But in the late 1950s and early 1960s, the paradoxical combination of increased mobility and strong anti-Mexican sentiment encouraged greater numbers of Mexican Americans, particularly the most accomplished, to go one step further and completely deny their ethnic background.

By the 1960s, one-quarter of Mexican Americans in California were in business, held white-collar jobs, or were in the professions. The same portion could be found in low-skilled work—farm, factory, or domestic. The other half could be considered working to lower middle class.[171] Nearly 80 percent of Mexican Americans in the Southwest lived in cities.[172] While economic, geographic, and social distinctions made it difficult to speak of a single Mexican American culture, the working-class Mexican American subculture was best regarded "as a variant of the United States working class subculture, but influenced to a lesser or stronger degree by traditional Mexican folk culture."[173] According to one contemporary sociologist, they should be understood as "partially Mexicanized Americans rather than as partially Americanized Mexicans. No one who has carefully observed the way of life of rural and of urban lower-class people in Mexico . . . would make the mistake of considering them the reverse."[174] One 1970 survey of Mexican Americans in San Bernardino, California, revealed that 30.2 percent of children spoke "mostly English" to their first generation parents, 81.6 percent to second-generation parents, and 93.8 percent to third-generation parents.[175]

Mexican Americans had made impressive social and economic gains in the postwar years. But while the most blatant aspects of discrimination had largely been overcome, other, more subtle, forms endured. Nor had the gains they made put them on a par with the Anglo population. While the median income of "Spanish-surnamed" families in the Southwest did rise by more than 70 percent in the 1950s, that was still only 65 percent of the median income of Anglo families.[176] And while the high school completion rate increased almost 75 percent in the same period, the education gap between Mexican Americans and Anglos had not changed dramatically.[177] In the early 1960s, greater attention began to be paid to those who had not benefited from the postwar boom.

Eight

The Chicano Movement

By the late 1950s, Mexican American activists had begun to emulate, "consciously or unconsciously," many of the strategies of the black civil rights movement.[1] Black leaders could boast of a collective solidarity that Mexican American activists could not. They had learned how to wrest concessions from members of the Anglo establishment by using aggressive tactics—such as demonstrations and boycotts— and by accusing Anglo America of racism. Beginning with the Montgomery, Alabama, bus boycott of 1955, the movement for black civil rights had also found a charismatic national spokesman in the person of Dr. Martin Luther King, Jr. The crusade King led against segregation would have lasting effects on how all Americans viewed issues of fairness and race. "Though they were not as discriminated against or segregated as blacks," wrote historian John R. Chávez, "Mexican Americans realized that they had in no way become the equals of Anglos."[2]

While mainstream Mexican American organizations had long insisted that they represented an ethnic group like those of European origin, in the 1960s they were seduced by the benefits of boasting a distinct racial identity. In addition to employing "the rhetoric of racism," activists became more assertive.[3] In mid-decade, as the federal government's War on Poverty began instituting "compensatory programs for blacks, Mexican Americans demanded similar opportunities from the federal government."[4] After the Los Angeles Watts riot of 1965, a coalition of Mexican American organizations sent a letter to President Lyndon Johnson calling for aid for Mexican Americans as well. In spite of the fact that Mexican Americans had not rioted, the activists insisted that the Johnson administration not overlook them when they handed out federal funds. While remaining ideologically integrationist, the League of United Latin American

Citizens began accepting federal funding for job retraining centers and housing that had been earmarked for Mexican Americans. In March 1966, fifty mainstream activists walked out of a meeting with the Equal Employment Opportunity Commission, a federal watchdog group, demanding that the commission place Mexican Americans on its board and punish corporations for failing to hire qualified co-ethnics. In 1967, LULAC endorsed President Johnson's decision to create a special Inter-Agency Committee on Mexican-American Affairs. They also called for the formation of a similar department within the United States Commission on Civil Rights. As historian Mario García noted, among Mexican American activists, "A separate identity from other Americans in conjunction with separate programs now came to be seen as legitimate."[5]

This "minoritization" of Mexican Americans was further intensified by the advent of a new generation of activists who were as interested in asserting cultural pride as they were in achieving equal rights and opportunity. By the mid-1960s, the black civil rights movement had spawned a concomitant campaign to promote black racial and cultural pride. The emergence of black nationalism subsequently inspired an "outbreak" of what sociologist Stephen Steinberg called "ethnic fever."[6] "One after another, the nation's racial and ethnic minorities sought to rediscover their waning ethnicity and to reaffirm their ties to the cultural past."[7] Nonwhite groups were heavily influenced by the trend, but so were "white ethnics," the majority of whom were at least three generations removed from the immigrant experience. Indeed, by 1970, the foreign-born population of the United States was the lowest it had been in the nation's history. Fewer than 5 percent of Americans were immigrants.[8]

Like many Americans of the time, Mexican Americans became increasingly involved in progressive political activism throughout the Southwest. By the mid-1960s, United Farm Worker leader César Chávez had gained national attention for his fight for better wages and improved working conditions. In 1967, militant New Mexico activist Reies López Tijerina led an armed raid on the courthouse in Tierra Amarilla. His cause: to help a handful of northern New Mexicans recover land grants they had lost over the years to Anglo landowners or to the federal government. That year in Texas, radical student leader and doctor's son José Angel Gutiérrez helped found MAYO, the Mexican American Youth Organization, which was dedicated to fostering "an obsession with cultural pride" and militancy "against the gringo."[9]

In 1969, Rodolfo "Corky" Gonzales, a Denver-born boxer and insurance agent turned poet and political activist, gave this groundswell of activism a name and a mythology. That year his social service organization, Crusade for Justice, sponsored a Youth Liberation Conference to which 1,500 young activists from throughout the Southwest were invited. It was there that he christened the young Mexican Americans in the movement "Chicanos." Having been variously described as Mexicans, Mexican Americans, Spanish-Speaking Americans, the Spanish-surnamed, or Hispanos, activists could now rally around one unifying term and call themselves and their families Chicanos. While the origins of the term are unclear, "Chicano" had long been used as "a slang or perjorative in-group reference to lower class persons of Mexican descent."[10] It was a term that would have made most of the parents of these young activists cringe. But that was partly the point. "Chicano" was a defiant term that identified those who adopted it as sympathetic to the downtrodden. It suggested as well that, unlike the middle-class Mexican American activists of the 1930s, 1940s, and 1950s, this new generation of advocates had no interest in further integrating themselves into mainstream American life.

Delegates at the 1969 Youth Liberation Conference adopted a cultural manifesto clearly influenced by Corky Gonzales. Inspired by an Aztec legend, the Plan Espiritual de Aztlán, Spiritual Plan of Aztlán, was a call for ethnic unity and nationalism. Six centuries before, went the legend, the Aztecs of Mexico arrived at Tenochtitlán, modern Mexico City, after leaving Aztlán, their homeland in the north. The Plan Espiritual maintained that the mythical homeland was, in fact, the contemporary American Southwest and that Chicanos were spiritually "reclaiming the land of their birth." As its title suggests, the Spiritual Plan was more a cultural than a political statement. Gonzales argued that economic and political change could not occur without the creation of a new cultural consciousness. "We have to be able to identify with our past, and understand our past, in order that we can dedicate ourselves to the future, dedicate ourselves to change," he said.[11] But the Chicano Movement, as it came to be known, was anything but a celebration of historical and cultural continuity. On the contrary, it represented a fundamental break with the Mexican American past, particularly with the Mexican American identity that had been emerging since the late 1920s and 1930s.

The emerging Chicano Movement was in large part driven by an identity crisis. The sentiment that inspired many young politically conscious Mexican Americans was similar to that which had moved so many young whites and blacks to action in the 1960s: alienation. They sought to combat their alienation, in part, with a renewed search for cultural rootedness. For decades, Mexican American advocates had struggled for integration into the nation's economic, political, and social mainstream. But just as the aspirations of the previous generation had been kindled by the social climate created by World War II, this new so-called Chicano Generation was part of a broader movement of alienated young people who sought "to affirm their right to a separate identity within the framework of a pluralist nation."[12]

In 1971, a Mexican American literary critic credited the Chicano Movement for creating a cultural renaissance. But the flowering of Chicano art and writing and the subsequent establishment of a myriad cultural groups and publications represented less a renaissance than an original invention. While Chicano Generation artists and intellectuals did encourage Mexican Americans to learn more about the history, art, and literature of Mexico, they more often ended up inventing a romanticized cultural legacy and history that suited their personal psychic and ideological needs. As historian F. Arturo Rosales has written, "Not being conversant or interested in the folksy Mexicanness of older generations, myth-making ensued on a large scale."[13] In fact, as they attempted to forge a new identity, many young people "revolted against their parents . . . admonishing them for failing to teach them Spanish and for not preserving the Mexican culture."[14] In other words, the process of becoming Chicano was less about preserving a heritage than creating one. In his 1971 book, *Chicano Manifesto,* journalist Armando B. Rendón described the process of becoming Chicano as "find[ing] out something about one's self which has lain dormant, subverted, and nearly destroyed."[15] He went on to describe his "ancestry" as having "become a shadow, fainter and fainter about me. I felt no particular allegiance to it, drew no inspiration from it, and elected generally to let it fade away."[16] But after he reclaimed his lost identity, Rendón "no longer face[d] a dilemma of identity or direction."[17] Now, he felt part of a "unique people" who represented "a prophecy of a new day and a new world."[18]

Just as previous generations of Mexican American activists had stressed the European side of their heritage to emphasize their whiteness, Chicanos began to pay homage to their pre-Columbian roots because to do so dovetailed with their goal of distinguishing themselves as separate from white America. Chicano Generation activists had adopted the New Left's politics of "oppositional identity" and joined them in decrying "the dominant ideology." Many young activists had also begun to identify and call attention to the interests they shared with African American and other minorities. Others concluded that "Mexican Americans have for too long been cheated by tacitly agreeing to be Caucasian in name only. They say they would rather be proud of their Indian blood than uncertain about their Caucasian status."[19] In the same way that many young African Americans clung to romanticized notions of the African past or latter-generation white ethnics resurrected their Irish, Italian, or Jewish identities, many assimilated Mexican Americans found solace in their newfound identity.

This new identity and the inspiration provided by men like labor leader César Chávez in California and the quixotic figure of Reies López Tijerina in northern New Mexico pushed thousands of Mexican American college and high school students into activism. In 1963, Tijerina, a former Pentecostal preacher from Texas, captured the imagination of many students when he established La Alianza Federal de Mercedes, the Federal Alliance of Land Grants. La Alianza was organized to reclaim lost properties for the descendants of Spanish and Mexican land grantees. While at first Tijerina fought his battle in the courts, by the late 1960s his movement had resorted to violence. He based his claims on the provisions of the Treaty of Guadalupe Hidalgo, which he argued guaranteed the conquered Mexicans the rights to their land, language, and culture. His emphasis on land and language influenced the tenor of the emerging Chicano nationalism.

According to F. Arturo Rosales, "Every Tijerina proclamation, even if untenable, helped to fix ideological goals for the *movimiento.*"[20]

If Tijerina, whose crusade sociologist Nancie L. González later called "a nativistic cult movement," was the Chicano Movement's earliest ideologue, then César Chávez was its Moses.[21] Many student activists were drawn to his image as much as to his cause. Dark-skinned, humble, a pious Catholic man who worked the land, Chávez represented for many young Mexican Americans the very image of the social righteousness and cultural rootedness they sought for themselves. Texas student activist José Angel Gutiérrez described Chávez as "the embodiment of a Chicano. Chicanos see themselves in César: clothes, personal style, demeanor and commitment."[22] Chávez and the United Farm Workers marched behind the standard of La Virgen de Guadalupe. They fought for better wages and improved working conditions for the most downtrodden of laborers. The national media positioned Chávez alongside Martin Luther King, Jr., in the pantheon of minority leaders. The head of a small farmworkers union was transformed into the symbolic leader of an ethnic group that was overwhelmingly urban.

Chávez's movement benefited from his newly acquired stature, but he nonetheless "distrusted the very Chicano nationalism he inspired."[23] As a believer in nonviolence and not "behaving hatefully," Chávez feared the potential divisiveness of ethnic nationalism.[24] "We oppose some of this La Raza business," he said, referring to the rhetoric of solidarity preferred by activists. "We know what it does. When La Raza means or implies racism, we don't support it. But if it means our struggle, our dignity, or our cultural roots, then we're for it."[25] Indeed, according to one Mexican American writer, Chávez "subscribed to something like the melting-pot concept, and he was faithfully leading his movement of poor, downtrodden, and alien followers toward prosperity, equality, and assimilation."[26]

By the mid-1960s, as the black civil rights movement became more militant and the campaign against the Vietnam War intensified, Mexican American student activists became more aggressive both in voicing their grievances and in proclaiming their ethnic pride. The college students who were drawn to the movement usually represented the most assimilated young Mexican Americans, those who had "significantly outstripped the levels of education and employment their parents had been able to attain."[27] As a result, they often had higher expectations of life than did their parents. In the 1960s more Mexican Americans attended college than ever before. Particularly in California, "much of the motivation for the early student movement participants was derived largely from intellectual perceptions of oppression rather than a personal daily contact with severe discrimination and prejudice."[28] The newfound governmental and academic interest in minority groups, poverty, and inequality gave rise to a slew of new studies that highlighted the many challenges that Mexican Americans faced. These studies routinely included bleak statistics about Mexican American educational levels, juvenile delinquency, drug addiction, and infant mortality rates. They highlighted employment discrimination, police brutality, and cultural, social, and educational deprivation. In a short time, Mexican Americans went from being a mostly ignored minority to one principally defined by its hardships and the discrimination it suffered. In 1960, 20 percent of Mexican Americans in Bexar County, Texas, had never completed even a year of school.[29] While 75 percent of the county's welfare recipients were Mexican American in 1970, only 50 percent of the Welfare Department's employees were Mexican American, and less than one-third were in supervisory positions.[30] In California, Mexican Americans made up 33 percent of school dropouts and 17 percent of juvenile delinquents.[31] In 1970, the U.S. Commission on Civil Rights began releasing a series of reports documenting the discrimination that Mexican Americans suffered at the hands of the American justice system. The most poignant statistics, however, derived from the casualty lists from Vietnam. While Mexican Americans constituted about 10 percent of the population in the Southwest, in 1967 they represented almost 20 percent of those killed in the war.[32] Acutely aware of the social inequities Mexican Americans faced, Chicano student activists worked—and presumed to speak—on behalf of all Mexican Americans. But while it did garner some community support, the *movimiento* was a "mainly student-led collective [that] saw itself as a revolutionary vanguard which knew best what its people needed."[33]

According to Chicano activist and historian Rodolfo Acuña, in the

1960s, "An awareness of discrimination increased among Chicanos, and many, for the first time, recognized it."[34] Indeed, militant activists encouraged this type of awareness. The new consciousness was then "reinforced and spread through" newly created "Chicano controlled media and arts."[35] While the previous generation had used ethnic-based politics in an effort to integrate into the mainstream and to reform the system, Chicano Movement activists employed it to seek "alternative models of social change in post-industrialized America."[36] They were determined to foster the revolutionary spirit by nurturing a sense of outrage as well as by enforcing the idea of ethnic solidarity, a characteristic for which neither Mexican Americans nor Mexican American organizations were known.

In a paper first published in 1966, scholar Paul M. Sheldon concluded that unlike Jewish organizations that may not get along with one another, yet are still "able to present a strong front for the betterment of the Jewish people," or black organizations that may have "radical internal differences" but nonetheless work together, Mexican American groups had not demonstrated an ability to work "for the common welfare of their own group."[37] According to Sheldon, their very heterogeneity kept Mexican Americans from forging a "mass voice to promote the common good of the group." He argued that Mexican Americans were "in fact *not* a group; they do not speak with a common voice; they do not have a mutual agreement; they are fragmented first by their heterogeneity and second by the tradition of individualism."[38] To illustrate his point he noted the difficulty one group of Mexican American conferees had in answering the question "Who are we?" At a Mexican American youth conference held in Los Angeles in 1963, the largest number of participants signed up for the discussion group on self-definition. After several hours of discussion, one in the morning and another in the afternoon, the students reported that they "cannot agree on a single definition of Mexican-Americans. Objectively, it is determined by the attitudes of the dominant community; subjectively, it is the totality of each individual, or how each person conceives of himself."[39] Consequently, the distinctions in class, geography, and levels of acculturation had made it difficult for Mexican Americans "to develop strong leadership, and to form organizations through which this large group may express its needs and desires and make itself felt in the political, economic, and social life of the broader community."[40]

In their groundbreaking essay submitted to the Ford Foundation in December 1966, three of the most prominent contemporary Mexican American scholars—Ernesto Galarza, Herman Gallegos, and Julian Samora—came to a similar conclusion. Mexican Americans may "give the outward appearance of a solid bloc," they wrote, but they were far from it.[41] In fact, they concluded, Mexican Americans had to be categorized in three segments, the "*puro Mexicano* [pure Mexican]; those who consider themselves Americans of Mexican ancestry; and those who feel they are simply Americans of Hispanic lineage. The Spanish language eludes the second and third generations, whose use of their 'mother tongue' is confined to a variable mix of isolated words and phrases and highly inventive syntax."[42] "These characteristics," the authors continued, "represent difficulties of approach to the ethnic minority as a whole because it is not a whole, either as its constituents think of themselves, or as they stratify as aliens and migrants. Distance between these strata within the minority is as important to explain their political powerlessness in the face of the burdens of existence which they bear in common, as the distance between the minority itself and the surrounding society."[43]

The authors addressed the crucial distinctions between the historical experiences of the African American and the Mexican American that contributed to their different levels of social cohesion. They concluded that the "historical conditions for solidarity [between the two groups] do not exist."[44]

> The Mexican American has had his share of discrimination and segregation, but the Southwest has never been the Deep South. The centuries of brutal social affronts that humiliated equally the Negro sharecropper, the Negro businessman, the Negro laborer and the Negro intellectual, solidifying them emotionally if not tactically, were the mainspring of their current revolt. In Mexican American society this has not been so. No overwhelming and collective revulsion against the Anglo exists that would mass all brown men against him, much less rally them all in support of the Negro. The new militancy of the young . . . does not and probably never will have the unanimous support of the Mexican American community.[45]

Needless to say, Chicano militants had little use for these findings. They proceeded with their campaign of refashioning Mexican Americans into Chicanos. They defined the boundaries of proper Chicano behavior and thinking by labeling dissenters the equivalent of race traitors. This strategy was particularly effective when employed against older Mexican American politicians who found Chicano rhetoric offensive. "Increasingly, Chicano militants ritualistically hurled the *vendido* (sellout) epithet at Mexicans in power and retaliated harshly if they did not comply to their demands."[46] While they rarely managed to oust their elders from positions of influence, activists learned how to intimidate them into a "silent compromise."[47] Pressure from the Chicanos ultimately forced mainstream groups like LULAC to become more nationalistic in their rhetoric. Some mainstream Mexican American politicians who recognized that activists had developed a vocal and organized following began acting on militants' demands. It was in this way that Chicano activism began to eclipse the previous generation and ultimately alter the political landscape.

One prominent Mexican American politician who refused to bend to militant rhetoric was San Antonio Democrat Representative Henry González. In the late 1960s, González labeled Chicano activists as "professional Mexicans" who were trying "to stir up the people by appeals to emotion [and] prejudice in order to become leader[s] and achieve selfish ends."[48] He considered the ideology of *Chicanismo* little more than the "politics of hatred" and "racism in reverse."[49] He particularly despised the Chicano Movement leaders' attempt to portray Mexican Americans as a one-dimensional caste and then presume to speak for them. "I don't claim to represent so many millions of my people like so many others are doing," he said. "I don't think that's possible to do. Our people are a pluralistic group—diverse, not homogenous. The so-called movement is imitative, a takeoff of the Negroes in other sections of the country. I don't want to be the Moses of the Mexican American people. I don't pretend to be. I don't have that ambition, and I don't think any one person can say he represents all the Mexican Americans in this country."[50] Accordingly, José Angel Gutiérrez, the Chicano student activist in Texas who would later help found the ethnically based political party La Raza Unida, accused

Representative González of "holding gringo tendencies" and of contributing to the oppression of his people by promoting integration.[51]
To Gutiérrez and other militants, Chicanos needed to liberate themselves by becoming "masters of their destiny, owners of their resources,
both human and natural, and a culturally separate people from the
gringo."[52]

Militant activists on and off campus thought assimilation and integration were acts of betrayal. They believed that collective "advancement in the face of what they considered a hostile Anglo society
depended on their ability to develop a countervailing power that
would require its own organizational structure and leadership—
Chicano power. They felt that assimilation was self-defeating in its
present token form because it dissipated Chicano militancy, absorbed
Chicano talent, and dimmed Chicano consciousness, while giving little substantive return to the Chicano masses."[53] This belief, combined with their identification with the downtrodden and a leftist
distrust of capitalism, made many activists wary of middle-class
Mexican Americans. Their hypersensitivity to poverty and discrimination led many Chicanos to assume that all Mexican Americans
were equally "impoverished, uneducated and powerless. The rhetoric
of the movement tended to encourage this kind of overgeneraliza-
tion."[54] Movement ideologues promoted the impression that only the
poor and working class were "real Chicanos." Meantime, they considered middle-class Mexican Americans or those who aspired to
move up the social ladder "sellouts," "Tío Tomases" (Uncle Toms),
or "Oreo Cookies" (brown on the outside and white on the inside).[55]

Like the militant black activists of the late 1960s, Chicanos
adopted both inspiration and ideology from the anti-colonial movements of the Third World. They argued that since the Southwest had
once been a part of Mexico, Mexican Americans, even the vast
majority of them who arrived in the twentieth century, were not
members of an immigrant group. In *Occupied America*, Rodolfo
Acuña's widely read 1972 survey of Chicano history, the activist
historian argued that Mexican Americans were a colonized people.
He contended that their migration northward was an involuntary
process. "Most Mexicans became part of the United States either
because of the Anglo conquest or because they were brought here by

economic forces over which they had little control. The uprooted Mexican was torn from his homeland 'like a nail torn from its finger.' "[56]

The Chicano portrayal of Mexican Americans as a unified, downtrodden people preternaturally loyal to their ancestral culture was astonishingly similar to the way Anglo racists had been characterizing Mexican Americans for more than a hundred years. Racists had long enjoyed portraying Mexicans as a race apart, unassimilable, and, in a phrase, being "all the same." A Mexican was a Mexican was a Mexican. The major difference in the Chicano telling was that in their version Mexican Americans had purportedly resisted the gringo all the while. Activist historians like Acuña were intent on scouring history and refashioning it to prove "that the movement did not begin in the 1960s."[57] One of their primary objectives was to destroy "myths of Mexican docility."[58] Ironically, the ideologues' obsession with resistance and their adoption of an oppositional "us versus them" worldview revealed how thoroughly they had assimilated the binary, Anglo-American conception of race.

Still, as F. Arturo Rosales concluded, "None of the Chicano Movement cultural or political pronouncements became part of an unchangeable dogma."[59] Many Mexican Americans "refused to accept a Chicano self-identity, much less the ethnic separatism espoused by the militants."[60] Historian David Gutiérrez observed that despite the heightened rhetoric of the 1960s and early 1970s, "a great many Mexican Americans continue to subscribe to some version of the melting-pot theory in their everyday lives."[61] In 1971, sociologist Celia S. Heller concluded that Mexican Americans generally continued to combine their "ethnic status with the status of American in a way as to broaden and redefine the latter: to reduce 'both the inner dilemma and the outward contradiction' of the two statuses."[62] Nor was the Chicano Movement ever able to achieve an enduring sense of ethnic Mexican unity. As Harvard historian John Womack wrote in 1972, the Chicano Movement was "at its bitterest a threat not to integrate which cannot stop the integration."[63] As evidence that their integrationist actions spoke louder than their separatist words, several prominent Chicano scholars, academicians, and activists married Anglos.[64] Despite their emphasis on ethnic unity, even the activist class was plagued by factionalization. By the early 1970s, militant Chicanos began to dismiss César Chávez as a tool of the establishment. For his part, Chávez never placed ethnic solidarity above his cause of organizing farmworkers. He continued to call for an immediate halt to illegal immigration. In October 1974 the United Farm Workers Union even organized a "wet line" along a 125-mile stretch of the Arizona-Sonora border in order to stop illegal immigrants entering into the United States.

One of the movement's biggest institutional achievements was to demand the creation of more than fifty Chicano Studies departments in universities throughout the Southwest.[65] The first generation of scholars, particularly the historians, were "closely tied to the political spirit of the Chicano Movement, which stressed alienation from American life and distance from American values."[66] As historian Manuel Gonzales wrote in 1999, "the ideal Chicano Studies professor has been, and continues to be, the activist-scholar."[67] Consequently, while the core *movimiento* activists had spent most of their passion by the early 1970s, the contours of their rhetoric would endure for decades, particularly in the realms of academia and politics.

The movement itself was multifaceted but generally "described those individuals who shared a commitment to end the injustices of racism, the war in Vietnam, the sufferings of the poor, and the degradations of farm workers."[68] In rural South Texas the movement even "accelerated the dismantling of . . . Jim Crow."[69] Throughout the Southwest, however, its most important achievement was to awaken Mexican Americans to a recognition of their ability to combat longstanding inequities in American life. The movement also stimulated an ethnic catharsis. Despite the progress of the postwar years, Mexican Americans were still too often made to feel ashamed of their heritage or the color of their skin. The Chicano Movement may not have ended that phenomenon, but it succeeded in fostering a sense of ethnic and racial pride, particularly among young people. The uproar activists created also helped draw the government's attention to the needs of a previously ignored population. Ironically, their militancy ultimately served to enhance the bargaining power of moderate Mexican American politicians and activists.

In 1968, the Ford Foundation concluded, with the help of the essay they had commissioned from Ernesto Galarza, Herman Gallegos, and Julian Samora, that "Mexican Americans were the most disorganized and fragmented minority in American life and that they needed national organization to serve their social, economic, and political needs."[70] With a $630,000 grant, Ford played an instrumental role in the founding of the Southwest Council of La Raza—which became national in 1972—an organization dedicated to organizing and providing a national platform for smaller local community action groups. That same year, Ford granted $2.2 million to help found the Mexican American Legal Defense and Education Fund (MALDEF), along the lines of the NAACP Legal Defense Fund. Calling itself the "legal arm" of the Chicano Movement, within five years MALDEF had filed hundreds of lawsuits challenging the "vestiges of segregation and discrimination throughout the Southwest."[71] They took on cases involving everything from civil rights litigation to police brutality complaints and school desegregation. MALDEF adopted a considerably broader view of its constituency than did Mexican American civil rights organizations in the pre-1960s era. In 1982, its attorneys successfully argued the case of *Plyler v. Doe* before the U.S. Supreme Court, which ruled that the children of illegal immigrants had a right to free public schooling.

Its earliest victories, however, were aimed at eliminating barriers to integration and political participation. In 1972, in *White v. Register,* MALDEF successfully argued that at-large elections politically disenfranchised Mexican Americans. From 1970 to 1973, much of MALDEF's energy went toward gaining acceptance of Mexican Americans as an "identifiable minority group." Only when such a determination was made by the courts could Mexican Americans avail themselves of the desegregation remedies afforded by the U.S. Supreme Court's ruling in *Brown v. Board of Education.* In 1971, a U.S. District Court ruled in the landmark case of *Cisneros v. Corpus Christi Independent School District* that for the purposes of desegregation Mexican Americans constituted an identifiable minority group. Two years later, the U.S. Supreme Court agreed. After decades of seeking to position Mexican Americans as "the other white race," activists now portrayed their constituents as "the other minority." "By granting official recognition of Mexican Americans as a disadvantaged minority, the court undoubtedly helped to encourage the trend among Mexican American activists to pursue political reform as part of an organized ethnic lobby."[72]

Despite its revolutionary and separatist rhetoric, the Chicano

Movement's most enduring institutional legacy was largely integrationist and reformist in nature. Still, moderate Mexican American politicians and integrationist institutions like MALDEF did not entirely discard the *movimiento*'s legacy of cultural nationalism. After the Supreme Court had determined the legal status of Mexican Americans in 1973, MALDEF turned its attention to issues of educational equality. It began to promote bilingual education as the solution to the special educational needs of the children of new immigrants. "By 1975, a quasi-schism had emerged in judicial decisions: some required the dispersal of Mexican American students for desegregation purposes while others required the concentration of such students for bilingual education purposes. The 1974 Supreme Court ruling in favor of bilingual education in the *Lau* [*v. Nichols*] case especially appeared to clash with rulings which established a constitutional basis for desegregation."[73] While on the one hand, MALDEF argued that Mexican Americans were "a victimized minority group whose deprivation could be remedied only by eliminating segregated schools," on the other hand they were demanding bilingual education, a program that required "increased concentration of teachers and grouping of students on the basis of language and national origin."[74] MALDEF officials and others may not have admitted the conflict of visions, but it was there.

But just as Chicano Generation activists, the federal government, and the courts began to grapple with Mexican Americans' new status as a minority group not unlike African Americans, a massive wave of immigration from Mexico would once again put into question what it meant to be Mexican American. While for the next several decades Chicano scholars would continue to argue that the movement was the culmination of Mexican American history, millions of new immigrants—both legal and illegal—would gradually undermine not only the demographic calculus that gave rise to the ethnic tumult of the 1960s but many of the institutional responses that emerged from it.

The global economic recession of the mid-1970s once again made immigration a national political issue in the United States. "In 1976 Congress completed the logic of formal equality [in U.S. immigration policy] by imposing country quotas of 20,000 on the Western Hemisphere. Again, that step put the greatest pressure on Mexico and Canada, the largest sending countries in the hemisphere."[75] This meant that between 1968 and 1976, "the number of visas accessible to Mexicans dropped from an unlimited supply to just 20,000 per year," not including the relatives of U.S. citizens who were eligible to join their families in the U.S.[76] According to Douglas S. Massey, Jorge Durand, and Nolan J. Malone, "If pre-1965 policies had remained in force, it is likely that the flow of Mexicans would simply have shifted from bracero to resident alien visas and Mexican immigration would have continued apace under a different name."[77]

But as it was, the number of illegal immigrants rose steadily from the late 1960s onward. "The sharp reduction in the accessibility of legal visas coincided with a time of rapid population growth and declining economic fortunes in Mexico."[78] In 1964, the United States finally terminated the bracero guest worker program, but its demise clearly did not signal the end of northward migration. In its twenty-three years of existence, "hundreds of thousands of braceros were able to familiarize themselves with U.S. employment practices, become comfortable with U.S. job routines, master American ways of life, and learn English. As a result of this new knowledge . . . the costs and risks of taking additional trips dropped and potential benefits rose."[79] These migrants then shared their experiences and networks in the United States with their families and friends back home, which "in turn reduced the costs and risks of their own international movement and increased their access to U.S. employment."[80] The bracero program had set in motion a self-perpetuating cycle of migration.

In 1968, 151,000 undocumented Mexican migrants were deported from the U.S. By 1976, the year the twenty-thousand-per-nation quota was imposed, the number of deportees reached 781,000.[81] All told, about 28 million Mexicans entered the United States as undocumented migrants between 1965 and 1986. However, most of this migration was circular. Of those 28 million, 23.4 million are believed to have returned to Mexico, which means that 4.6 million illegal Mexican immigrants settled in the U.S. during that period.[82] But even as the number of available visas diminished, due to provisions allowing for family reunification, Mexicans also gradually became the largest single share of legal immigrants. While Mexicans made up only 5.9 percent of all legal immigrants to the U.S. in the 1940s, they were 14.2 percent of the total in the 1970s and 22.6 percent in the 1980s.[83]

In the 1970s and 1980s, Mexico's economic troubles "encouraged northbound migration from sectors of Mexican society previously not drawn to the U.S."[84] Undocumented migration began to originate in states that had not traditionally sent people to the U.S. In 1973, almost half of the undocumented Mexicans apprehended in the San Diego, California, area had come from just two states: Jalisco and Michoacán. By 1987, a sampling of apprehended migrants revealed that only 28.7 percent had arrived from those two states.[85] In 1982, Mexico's inflation nearly exceeded 100 percent and the nation's long-term economic crisis began to "cut into real wages of urban workers, professionals, government employees, and middle-class entrepreneurs."[86] Consequently, a growing number of migrants came from "large industrial urban centers without traditions of northbound migration, such as Puebla and [Mexico City], and began to include more people from the urban middle and working class."[87] By 1987, "at least one out of ten Mexican migrants entering the United States clandestinely" came from the nation's capital.[88]

Once in the U.S., a growing number of migrants began to cluster in new urban destinations, finding jobs in such enterprises as construction firms, furniture factories, and foundries. By the 1980s, "no more than 10 to 15 percent of the Mexican immigrants (legals and illegals) in California, Texas, and Arizona" were employed in agriculture.[89] As a result of this shift to urban employment, Mexican migrants were much more visible to the general public than they had been before.

Beginning in the mid-1960s, a growing number of undocumented Mexican migrants began to extend their stays in the U.S. "Whereas in the 1940s and 1950s they had generally been target earners, seeking to earn as much money as possible, as quickly as possible . . . and return home, by the 1960s their perceptions and motivations had changed. Sustained access to high U.S. wages had created new standards of material well-being and instilled new ambitions for upward mobility that involved additional trips and longer stays."[90] The combination of a deteriorating economy and political instability in

Mexico and the rapid economic growth of the American Southwest provided both the push and the pull for large-scale immigration northward.

During the bracero era, many workers—legal and illegal—were able to acquire permanent alien status and then send for their families. But in the post-bracero era, a growing number of women and children ventured northward without papers. While undocumented men generally migrated on a moment's notice, "typically when a letter arrived one day, or a return migrant uncle or brother appeared," the more risky enterprise of female and family migration involved more planning and signaled a more long-term stay in the United States.[91] The arrival of women and children helped further root male migrant workers to life in the U.S. While the men are usually the pioneers, it is often the women who "create important linkages with bureaucratic institutions, such as schools, medical offices, and other public and private organizations" as well as "weave webs of interpersonal social ties among themselves and their families."[92] In other words, women are often the agents who transform sojourning families into settlers.

Nonetheless, the Mexican migrants of the late twentieth century were often as reluctant to acknowledge that the United States was their home as the millions who had preceded them. As sociologist Pierrette Hondagneu-Sotelo wrote, "Settlement has [had] a funny way of creeping up on immigrant workers who intend to stay only a short while."[93] Arturo Barrios, a janitor from Northern California, summed up the experiences of many Mexicans residing in the U.S.: "When they first come, everyone is thinking, 'I'm going to go earn some capital, or buy a ranch,' or whatever, but practically without exception, they don't accomplish this. Because you come here, and later you like it, and later you are always saying that you're going [back to Mexico], but you never leave. . . . So in reality, it's a big illusion."[94] Similarly, flower vendor Margarita Cervantes, who had resided in the U.S. for twelve years, described how permanent settlement had caught up to her:

I came in 1975 just to stay for a spell, at least that's what I thought. One thinks that it's so easy to come, make a little money, and then return to Mexico to put up a little store and maintain oneself with that—that was my thinking when my sister invited me to join her. I wanted to get out from my father's thumb, to make something for myself, but my idea was not to leave forever or to stop helping the family. But once here, it was initially difficult for me to find work, and later I became locked up in the routine of work at the motel. And at first I did not want to learn English out of fear that immigration authorities would catch us, but yes, eventually I did learn English. Now I have my little business, but it is here, not in Mexico. I have my husband, and most of my brothers and sisters are here too. My life, my sorrows and my joys, they are all here now.[95]

Among post-1965 migrants, married women have been more likely to express their desire to remain in the U.S. than both single and married men. Though they suffer similar hardships as men, particularly in the early years, women tend to prefer to remain in the north primarily for the benefit of their children. Asked if she ever considered returning to Mexico, Marisela Ramírez de Hernández, a young mother of three boys, responded:

Of course we would like to . . . as it is our country . . . *but* I only have to think if we were to go to Mexico, there we don't have what we have here. Here, with one week's pay we can buy shoes for all three children, clothes, pants, or whatever we need, and being there [in Mexico], no, we can't. With what [my husband] earns here in one day we can eat for an entire week, and we can always have the refrigerator full of milk. Also, the milk over there is not as good as it is here. If you are going to take your children from a place where they are better off to take them elsewhere, where they will suffer more, where they will have few opportunities to study for a career, it's difficult, it's very difficult.[96]

In the late 1970s and early 1980s, it was unclear to many American sociologists how this new wave of Mexican immigrants would integrate into U.S. society. Some believed that the newcomers and their children would simply adopt the oppositional identity of the Chicanos. In fact, at the height of the Chicano Movement in the early 1970s, many academics wondered whether the political ferment of the era hadn't forever altered the assimilation patterns of Mexican Americans. In 1971, at the end of a study concluding that Mexican Americans were increasingly adopting the "American ideology of advancement," sociologist Celia Heller concluded that the long-term effects of Chicano militancy "on the mobility pattern of Mexican Americans" were as yet unknown.[97] Within the span of three years, one sociologist felt compelled to overhaul his entire interpretation of the Mexican American experience. In 1970 Fernando Peñalosa wrote, "Recent changes among the Mexican American population in southern California and elsewhere have made necessary the modification or even invalidation of certain conclusions arrived at by the author in an article published . . . three years ago."[98] While in 1967, Peñalosa concluded that there was no such " 'thing' as Mexican American culture" and that "The group [was] fragmentized socially, culturally, ideologically, and organizationally," in 1970 he described a rising sense of community and cultural cohesion.[99]

By 1980, however, opinion surveys indicated that the term "Chicano," and presumably its attendant ideology, had not actually filtered down to many average Mexican Americans. One 1979 survey of 991 people of Mexican descent in five states found that only 7 percent of respondents called themselves Chicanos.[100] Another survey of U.S. citizens of Mexican descent conducted three years later in California and Texas also found that 7 percent of respondents referred to themselves as Chicanos, 1 percent higher than the number who called themselves Hispanics.[101] Not surprisingly given its origins in an ethnic American youth movement, 0 percent of Spanish monolingual respondents labeled themselves Chicanos. Two-thirds of those who used the term were younger than thirty-six years old. Yet another survey published in 1981 echoed the findings that the term "Chicano" was most popular among the young and U.S.-born. Significantly, the survey also found that those who called themselves Chicanos were more likely to have had attended or graduated from college than those who preferred other ethnic labels.[102]

By the 1980s, "the most visible vestige of the [Chicano Movement was] to be found in academia in the many university Chicano studies programs and departments" that had been established in the late 1960s and early 1970s.[103] These programs generally "had multiple objectives: research, teaching, consciousness raising, and political mobilization."[104] Particularly in California, these departments served as "safe havens for activists less as students than as professors."[105] They were "virtually monopolized by scholars who [identified] themselves with the *movimiento*."[106]

While relatively few Mexican Americans may have employed the term, the Chicano presence in universities ensured that the most educated Mexican Americans were exposed to *Chicanismo* and that the Chicano label was "often used by journalists, social scientists, and politicians."[107] Indeed, from the 1970s until the early 1990s, *Chicanismo* dominated both the academic and the journalistic interpretations of the Mexican American experience. Chicano scholars promoted the argument that Mexican Americans "experienced American society as a racial [as opposed to an ethnic] group" and that their story was more akin to that of African Americans than European Americans.[108] In the United States, racial groups have traditionally been understood as being defined by outsiders on the basis of physiological characteristics. The boundaries of ethnic groups, on the other hand, have been thought to be drawn internally by a shared history, language, or religion. While race has been considered a biologically determined—and therefore permanent—category, ethnicity has been understood to be less innate and therefore subject to change and adaptation over time. For most of American history, ethnic differences have been more successfully negotiated than racial ones.

Chicano Generation scholars generally held to the notion that "race define[d] the Mexican-origin experience, and that rigid racial boundaries endure[d] to influence all people of Mexican origin, both native and foreign born."[109] They reasoned that unlike an ethnic group whose experience is "characterized by the progressive integration into American society from one generation to the next and a fading of the obstacles to integration with each passing generation," Mexican Americans were "blocked from intergenerational mobility by the harsh realities of racial subjugation."[110]

Historians, in particular, adopted what University of California–Berkeley scholar Alex M. Saragoza called a "them-versus-us approach" to Mexican American history in which assimilation was treated with "intrinsic disapproval" and "separation and conflict" between Anglos and Mexicans were emphasized.[111] According to Saragoza, activist historians " 'used' history as an ideological base for concerted action."[112] Their search for historical precedent to the Chicano Movement was part and parcel of a broader "search for a means to organize Chicanos into a viable and coherent political force."[113] Thus, even though the "unity to which early Chicano writers appealed was not necessarily grounded in the past," historians, the most influential of whom was Rodolfo Acuña, interpreted Mexican American history as if it had been an organized collective struggle against Anglo oppression.[114] According to other critics, these scholars "depicted Mexicans (or Chicanos) as a monolithic, internally undifferentiated population."[115] Their emphasis on "group solidarity tended to minimize, deliberately or not, any concern with the [internal] variation" of the Mexican-origin population.[116]

In the 1980s, mainstream Mexican American politicians, particularly those who called themselves Hispanics, did not "share the same ethnic fervor or radical perspective as the Chicanos."[117] In Texas, Chicano Movement activism did provide "invaluable training for a new generation of leaders, individuals who [later] applied their experience and vision in other efforts."[118] But by and large Chicano activists "had long since dropped out of sight, [and were] typically involved in small businesses or Democratic Party politics."[119] In 1981, San Antonio became the first major American city to elect a Mexican American mayor. Councilman Henry G. Cisneros made history by forging an alliance "between Anglo urban businessmen and middle class Mexican Americans."[120] "By personifying the collective aspirations of his hometown," Cisneros was able to "bridge the deep chasm between Anglos and Mexicans."[121]

By 1980 the occupational distribution of the Texas Mexican population was the inverse of what it had been a half-century earlier. In 1930, "unskilled rural and urban workers comprised two-thirds of the Texas Mexican labor force."[122] Fifty years later, the number with unskilled jobs dropped to 29 percent, with the remaining 71 percent in white-collar or skilled occupations.[123] According to sociologist David Montejano, the rise of a stable Mexican American middle class facilitated the emergence of a moderate and inclusive political agenda. "In the 1980s, with the weakening of racial divisions as an issue, broadly defined class interests determine[d] the arena of political discussion and debate. In contrast to the activities of the 1970s, the most active Mexican American organizations express[ed] and pursue[d] class issues rather than explicit ethnic interests."[124] The demise of the segregationist era allowed middle-class Mexican Americans to focus their attention on issues like "education, housing conditions, sanitation, and matters of public service" in a "nonethnic manner."[125] Without this convergence of Anglo and Mexican American political interests, Henry Cisneros could not have built his electoral coalition.

The Mexican American middle class was growing even faster in California. Despite the sharp increase in the number of foreign-born during the 1970s, the percentage of Mexican-origin workers in white-collar jobs nearly tripled between 1950 and 1980.[126] During the 1980s, the percentage of U.S.-born Latinos with a college degree increased by more than 25 percent in Southern California.[127] Ironically, however, the increased access to higher education helped prolong the life span of *Chicanismo* in the state's Mexican American political circles. "If Chicano activists in Texas . . . disappeared into the Democratic Party, in California they . . . largely retreated into the state's far flung system of higher education."[128] While most Mexican American college graduates in California did not become politically radicalized, many were exposed to Chicano cultural and political rhetoric.

Nine

Mongrel America
and the New Assimilation

In the 1970s, multiculturalism, the ideology that promotes the coexistence of separate but equal cultures and essentially rejects the idea of assimilation, became dominant in academic circles. In the universities, this new ideology effectively validated and institutionalized the counterculturalism of *Chicanismo*. Together, they forged a "critique of American society sustained by two contradictory beliefs: first, that [the United States] is a racist society that won't permit Chicanos to assimilate; and second, that assimilation into the mainstream is an inexorable and insidious process that must be resisted at all costs."[1] That the university was the place where Mexican Americans came into contact with anti-assimilationist rhetoric was not without its irony. Throughout the 1970s and 1980s, it was "often the most socially, economically, and culturally assimilated Mexican Americans who espouse[d] the fiercest opposition to 'assimilation.' "[2]

California's universities also provided a refuge for more than a few aging Chicano Generation activists. Indeed, it was mostly "Marxist academics," along with "union militants," and other "unaffiliated leftists" who kept Chicano activism alive into the 1990s.[3] While their numbers were small, these activists generally had an easy time attracting the attention of the mainstream media, which had long considered self-appointed Chicano "community leaders" legitimate spokespeople for the entire Mexican American population. This visibility enabled the activists to influence mainstream Mexican American elected officials. They usually did so by attacking them publicly and accusing them of ignoring their constituencies.

Yet as much as Mexican American officials found Chicano activists annoying, some found them useful in promoting their own agendas. Activists were more effective at focusing attention on issues and creating pressure for change than politicians were by themselves. Furthermore, the presence of angry protesters sometimes strengthened the negotiating hand of moderate Mexican American officials in their dealings with other members of the establishment. According to one Mexican American politician in Los Angeles, "There is nothing better than people out there complaining when you're trying to push an issue on the inside."[4]

For all the differences—both ideological and stylistic—between Chicano activists and Mexican American politicians in California, in the early 1980s they both generally shared the belief that racism was the most pressing problem facing Mexican Americans. Although historically discrimination in California was rarely as severe as it had been in Texas or Arizona, California's Mexican American political elites considered fighting racism their highest priority. By contrast, "Elites in Arizona and Washington [D.C., saw political] apathy as their greatest concern, while . . . Texans, Coloradoans, and New Mexicans [viewed] educational issues as most salient."[5] Similarly, though younger political elites were less likely to have faced harsh anti-Mexican prejudice and discrimination than were their older counterparts, Mexican American politicos under forty-five were more likely to consider racism a primary concern. In a 1982 survey of 241 Mexican American political elites nationwide, "respondents 46 or over [did] not see racism as a major issue."[6]

This generational difference in outlook was probably due to the fact that younger political elites were likely to have been either involved in or influenced by the Chicano and the broader civil rights movements. It was also a likely by-product of a fundamental shift in American political culture since the 1960s. According to sociologist Peter Skerry, the emergence of race-based solutions such as affirmative action and the Voting Rights Act "offered Mexican Americans increased incentives to define themselves in racial terms."[7] As such, the new political system encouraged Mexican American advocates to view racism as the primary obstacle to social and economic advancement.

After the social upheaval of the 1960s, the federal government established what amounted to a race-based spoils system in which minority groups were encouraged to highlight their oppression and dysfunction to qualify for assistance. As a result, an increasing number of Mexican American politicians, as well as spokespeople for the inside-the-Beltway advocacy group, the National Council of La Raza, often found themselves vying with African Americans for the dubious title of being the most downtrodden minority in America. In a perverse twist, under this regime, a minority's weaknesses became its most salient source of political power. Activists were therefore loath to acknowledge the existence of the burgeoning Mexican American middle class lest it divert attention from their assessment of the group's problems and needs.

Both local and national advocacy groups routinely relied on academics and researchers to provide data to prove Mexican American disadvantage. According to Kenneth Prewitt, a political scientist who later became director of the U.S. Census Bureau, "More than any group in American political history, Hispanic Americans have turned to the national statistical system as an instrument for advancing their political and economic interests, by making visible the magnitude of social and economic problems they face."[8] However, the aggregate statistics from the census have sometimes been as nebulous as they were illuminating. Even though Mexican Americans experienced unprecedented mobility into the middle class in the 1980s, activists could say with a measure of truth that "by 1990 Latinos were collectively even worse off than they had been in 1980."[9] While in 1980, 12 percent of Latino families lived below the poverty line, that number had risen to 16 percent by the end of the decade. What these activists rarely pointed out, however, was that one-half of the Latino population growth—which increased by 34 percent in the 1980s—resulted from the arrival of millions of poor immigrants.[10] High poverty rates for newcomers had the effect of pushing down overall Latino statistics and eclipsing the socioeconomic progress of long-established immigrants and latter-generation Mexican Americans. In 1989, the National Council of La Raza released a study that pointed to the deepening hardship faced by Latino families and children over the previous decade. Ignoring the effect of new immigrants on Hispanic population data, the study's authors blamed the rise in the poverty rate squarely on "continuing discrimination in education and jobs."[11] In a newspaper article entitled "Lost Ground in '80s, Hispanics Say," the head of NCLR, Raúl Yzaguirre, was quoted saying,

"I can't look at any institution, I can't look at any aspect of America, and say, 'This is where we've made progress.' "[12]

Success as an organized ethnic lobby encouraged advocates to portray their minority groups as homogenous and united. The notion of sameness facilitated a politics of racial brokerage in which elite, national "race leaders" purportedly pursued the unified interests of their people as if they were corporate CEOs. It also allowed scores of local activists and ethnic ideologues to presume to speak for a single-minded, millions-strong "Latino community." But to evoke an image of a homogenous ethnic experience, activists had to portray American society as uniformly hostile to people of Latin American descent, no matter their generation, class, sex, skin color, education, or place of residence. "It doesn't matter whether you are a recent immigrant or somebody like me whose family came to Texas in 1721," said Raúl Yzaguirre, who resided in a predominantly Anglo suburb of Washington, D.C. "The public doesn't distinguish between us. All of us suffer the same levels of discrimination."[13]

In the early 1970s, just as ethnic political movements had emerged among Mexican Americans on the West Coast and Puerto Ricans in the East, "a national focus began to coalesce the larger Hispanic world."[14] The unprecedented "public awareness—at the federal and national levels—of the existence of populations of Latin American descent" inspired politicians to find common cause with other Americans of Latin American origin in order to raise their collective national profile.[15] This shift from grassroots activism to national electoral politics appeared to require a term that could bridge regional distinctions. In 1975, at the midterm Democratic conference in Kansas City, a group of politicians founded the National Association of Latino Elected and Appointed Officials (NALEO). "By using the term 'Latino,' " NALEO was, "in effect, the first coalition of Mexican Americans, Puerto Ricans, Cubans, and other Hispanics represented by political leaders."[16] A year later, "four Democratic members of the House of Representatives from Texas, California, and New York joined with the resident commissioner-elect of Puerto Rico to form a Congressional Hispanic Caucus."[17] Despite the "great difference[s] between conservative Texas rural districts and urban New York barrios," caucus members attempted to forge a common agenda and in 1978 "began to meet with President Jimmy Carter to discuss issues of [mutual] concern, such as Hispanic underrepresentation in the federal bureaucracy, education issues, and employment opportunities."[18]

By the early 1980s, the "national print media also began using the Hispanic label," and a greater number of Mexican American political elites felt obliged to adopt the term.[19] Some lawmakers, even those who considered the term misleading, found "Hispanic" politically useful. "Some people believe that Hispanics are a political force that has to be dealt with, that they're a voting bloc," said one prominent elected official, "and that's not necessarily true. But as long as we can give that impression and make them deal with us on that basis, hey, it's politically wise for us to do it."[20] Other activists, particularly those who "saw themselves as competing with African Americans for government services and jobs under antipoverty and affirmative action programs," were perfectly willing to lump "Mexican Americans in with Puerto Ricans, Cuban Americans and others simply because it increased their numbers, and presumably, their clout."[21] The emergence of the generic terms "Latino" and "Hispanic" meant that even as people of Mexican descent became a larger share of the U.S. population, the term "Mexican American" would virtually disappear from the media.

Despite the ethnic maneuvering and dire rhetoric of many vocal ethnic advocacy organizations, most of the Mexican American political elite shared a "positive view of American socio-political structures."[22] The 1982 survey of elites revealed that, nationally, "Elected officials and community leaders" considered Mexican American political apathy to be "a more significant problem than racism. Implicitly they . . . seem[ed] to be saying that [Mexican Americans had] it within their power to overcome racist obstacles."[23] Subsequent polls of the Mexican American population revealed similarly nuanced attitudes. The Latino National Political Survey, which was conducted from August 1989 to April 1990, found that 38.8 percent of Mexican American respondents had experienced discrimination because of ethnicity.[24] At the same time, Mexican Americans voiced "greater trust in the government than Anglos" did.[25]

Still, the complexity of Mexican American public opinion was generally eclipsed by the print and electronic media's penchant for seeking out activists to speak on behalf of millions of their co-ethnics. Throughout the 1980s and into the early 1990s, ethnic political grievance served as the dominant narrative for the Mexican American experience. In the 1980s, however, a new competing narrative arose out of the corporate sector's growing interest in the so-called Hispanic market. "When Latinos were fewer and without much money to spend, major corporations were not interested in them. But with information provided by the 1980 U.S. Census in their brief-cases, the sales staffs of [Spanish-language] media could argue that there was money to be made: Latinos earned over $50 billion a year."[26] In response, corporate and advertising managers "generated a good deal of survey research to investigate the buying habits of Latinos and how they could best exploit this fast-growing group."[27] According to writer Earl Shorris, "Awareness of their existence as a market was a sign to many Latinos that they had entered the main-stream: To be a consumer was to be wanted; to be wanted was to be equal; to be equal was to be an American at last."[28] And indeed, "the Hispanic marketing industry . . . played a central role in raising His-panics' visibility in public life. No other sector in society [was] as invested in emphasizing the increasing size of this population."[29] So while the political narrative of racial grievance focused on social dys-function while downplaying socioeconomic mobility, the consumer market narrative emphasized the increase in disposable income and the social desirability of Latinos. When courting advertisers, execu-tives for the burgeoning Spanish-language media "repackaged" Lati-nos "into images that render[ed] them more pleasing to corporate clients."[30] By 1989, "The collective buying power of Latinos grew to over $171 billion," increasing by 10 percent a year.[31]

The defining characteristic and raison d'être of the so-called His-panic market was the Spanish language. In addition to chronicling the growth of the Spanish-speaking consumer base, researchers for the Spanish-language media and advertising industry routinely released studies proving that "Spanish [was] the preferred language for all Hispanics" and "that the best way of reaching and connecting with them [was] through 'their language.' "[32] To ensure the future viability of this linguistically segregated consumer market, Spanish-language marketers also sought to convince mainstream corporations that Latinos would continue to speak Spanish no matter how many generations their families live in the United States. According to one Cuban American vice president for research in the Hispanic division of BBDO Worldwide, a major U.S. advertising firm, "Latinos don't assimilate and will not assimilate. With the advances in communications, they are constantly undergoing the process of cultural refueling. They are constantly going back to their countries and recharging their culture and values. The only ones that can't go back are the Cubans, but everyone else always goes back, and that's why we don't assimilate."[33]

Univision, the largest Spanish-language television network in the U.S., had the most to gain in convincing corporations that the terms "Hispanic" and "Spanish" were synonymous. In the 1990s, the media company's marketing brochure proclaimed that their audience "grows as the Hispanic population grows."[34] At one point, Univision's marketing materials also claimed that the company had an 87 percent prime-time share of Hispanic households nationwide. The truth, however, was that the 87 percent share was "not based on the total Hispanic market but on the percentage of Hispanic viewers watching Spanish television, which according to the Nielsen ratings, [ranged] from 25 percent to 40 percent depending on the season."[35] By ignoring the existence of U.S.-born English-dominant Latinos, Univision and other Spanish-language media marketers generalized about the entire Hispanic population on the basis of its Spanish-speaking part. According to one business writer in the early 1980s, "the hypothetical 'Hispanic consumer' currently being transacted in the media trade journals as well as in the ad and media shops alike, is that of the inner-city arrival."[36] Market research surveys conducted in high-density immigrant neighborhoods produced the consumer profile of "a tradition-bound Spanish-speaking recent arrival who eats a lot, is suicidally brand loyal, prefers audio-visual media, has a large family, does not venture beyond his ghetto-like environment and really gets turned on by 'his culture.' "[37]

At the very time that the rest of the American consumer market was being fragmented into smaller and smaller categories, Spanish-language marketers had a vested interest in lumping millions of Latinos into one culturally static and permanently foreign market segment. "For, in contrast to 'women' or 'teenagers,' who [were] simultaneously segmented according to lifestyles, age, tastes, or race, 'His-panics' remain[ed] a protected segment by their mere definition as a homogenously bounded, 'culturally defined' niche."[38] Anthropolo-gist Arlene Dávila concluded that Hispanic marketers prefer "fixity and authenticity" over "fluidity and hybridity."[39] Their ideal Hispanic market would be like the island of Puerto Rico, "Spanish-dominant, authentic, and contained."[40]

What few Spanish-language media executives were willing to admit, however, was that "the appearance of high language loyalty [among Mexican Americans was] due largely to the direct effect of continuing mass immigration."[41] While surveys found that Mexican Americans generally expressed a desire to pass on the Spanish lan-guage to succeeding generations, there was no evidence that they were willing to spend the time and money to establish the educational infrastructure required to maintain language fluency over time. Nor did the desire that their children maintain Spanish language fluency indicate a resistance to learning English. A 1987 national survey of Mexican American parents found that 75 percent of respondents said it was important for children to speak Spanish well.[42] The same sur-vey revealed that 97 percent of Mexican American parents thought it was "very important" for their children to speak English well.[43]

Surveys also found that Mexican Americans supported bilingual education. But it was never clear how many Americans of any back-ground actually understood the program's objectives. In 1968, when Congress passed the Bilingual Education Act, it neither defined the term "nor stated the purpose of the act, other than to provide money for local districts 'to develop and carry out new and imaginative ele-mentary and secondary school programs' to meet the special needs of non–English speaking children."[44] According to education scholar Diane Ravitch, the legislation was intentionally vague. Even the prin-cipal sponsor of the bill, Senator Ralph Yarborough of Texas, admit-ted, "Every time people ask me, 'What does bilingual education mean?' I reply that it means different things to different people."[45] For the next several decades, it wasn't clear to many Americans whether "the purpose of bilingual education [was] to provide a tran-sition to the regular English-language school program or . . . to main-tain the language and culture of non-English-speaking children."[46]

On the ground, however, the vast majority of bilingual programs in the United States used the "early-exit transitional" method, "in which students [were] expected to make a transition into 'mainstream English' classes after three or four years of instruction in their primary language. Early-exit programs [were] designed to teach children how to read and write in their native language in the belief that they [would] be better able to learn a second language, in this case English."[47] In other words, transitional bilingual education did not "anticipate the student becoming fully literate in his or her native language" and therefore was not designed to promote true bilingualism.[48] In fact, before 1998, when California voters approved a ballot initiative that all but abolished bilingual programs, guidelines for the state Department of Education stated clearly that "The primary goal of all [bilingual] programs is, as effectively and efficiently as possible, to develop in each child fluency in English."[49]

Not all Mexican American children received or were even eligible for bilingual education. The implementation of the program varied widely from district to district. Where the programs did exist, they generally enrolled only children who resided in immigrant households in which Spanish was the dominant language. Furthermore, the rapid growth of the Spanish-speaking population made it impossible for any school district to keep up with the demand for bilingual teachers. By the late 1990s, California, home to more children of immigrants than any other state, needed more than twenty thousand additional teachers to adequately staff its bilingual programs.[50] By then only 30 percent of the state's 1.4 million limited-English students were enrolled in bilingual classes.[51]

In any case, despite predictions to the contrary, linguistic assimilation among Mexican Americans continued apace. In 1978, sociologist David E. López concluded that Mexican immigrants in Los Angeles were "moving to English at rates only marginally slower than European immigrants probably did during the era of mass immigration."[52] While the use of Spanish did persist among U.S.-born Mexican Americans, particularly among those who lived in border regions, it clearly did not retard the acquisition of English. In 1990, 85 percent of U.S.-born Mexican American adults who lived in border regions spoke at least some Spanish at home. That percentage dropped "to about 70 percent for those who lived elsewhere in a border state" and to less than 50 percent for those who resided in the U.S. interior.[53] However, "for proficiency in English, proximity to the border [made] little difference: more than 95 percent of the U.S.-born Mexican Americans in each geographic zone [could] speak English well."[54]

According to sociologist Richard Alba, "bilingualism is very difficult to maintain in the U.S., and by the third generation it is extraordinarily difficult to maintain."[55] Among third-generation Mexican American children, the ability to speak Spanish varies considerably according to place of residence. While a majority of those who lived near the border in 1990 were bilingual, the opposite was true for the much larger number of children who lived farther inland. Overall, by 1990, fully 64 percent of third-generation Mexican American children spoke only English.[56]

However, even among latter-generation Mexican Americans who are bilingual, Spanish tends to serve more a colloquial than a formal function; used more in private than in public. In other words, Spanish is generally not the language in which they feel most comfortable conducting business. Likewise, many business owners find the "kitchen Spanish" of many latter-generation Latinos insufficient to "write a memo or close a deal."[57] For instance, in the creative departments of the Spanish-language marketing industry, "demands for 'perfect language skills' bar most U.S.[-born Latinos]" from employment.[58] Instead, the industry is dominated by foreign-born Latin Americans, "who have relocated to the United States as adults, often to pursue advanced studies, or who have had previous experience in the advertising and marketing industries" in their native countries.[59] Likewise, since its inception, Spanish-language television has either relied heavily on imported programming from Latin America or drawn its talent from "specific Latin American countries, where 'authentic' Spanish speakers are often recruited to work in the United States."[60] The same goes for the staffs of Spanish-language newspapers.

Like with language, cultural assimilation continued to occur in the 1980s, also in a nonlinear fashion. As had occurred with previous waves of Mexican immigrants and their children, newcomers experienced both cultural "change *and* ethnic persistence . . . simultaneously."[61] According to one 1987 study, "Certain traditional traits, such as an orientation toward Mexico as one's homeland or passing on folktales and folk remedies, seem to decline within a generation, and in some ways, there is a gradual replacement with American cultural traits. For example, American holidays quickly replace Mexican ones, and English fluency is more common than Spanish fluency."[62] At the same time, however, ethnic traits, such as extended familism, religiosity, and a liking for Mexican food, remained strong over generations. Even after four generations, "cultural replacement is not complete."[63] Anthropologist Susan E. Keefe and psychologist Amado M. Padilla concluded that "in some ways Mexican culture adapts to the American experience by producing new forms or functions, such as the development of a new and separate identity as [Mexican American]. In any case, it is clear that Mexican culture persists in the U.S., perhaps changing in character, but such is the fate of culture in general."[64]

Keefe and Padilla found that by the late 1980s "most [latter-generation] Mexican Americans [did] not live in barrios."[65] Indeed, for a generation, increasing numbers of Mexican Americans in the Southwest had "steadily moved out of poor neighborhoods when they could afford to move to middle class settings."[66] Typically, however, their "parents and some of their siblings remained" in the old neighborhood while Mexican immigrants often moved in.[67] In Southern California, still home to more people of Mexican origin than any place in the United States, traditional barrios were becoming "Mexicanized."[68] In Texas, however, many recent Mexican immigrants were bypassing heavily Mexican American South Texas and heading for "the large, fast-growing cities" of Houston and Dallas "because of superior job opportunities and less competition."[69] That explains why in the early 1980s a Texas survey found that 43 percent of Mexican American respondents said "they had no contact with undocumented workers, and 72 percent indicated that Mexican immigrants had no impact on their daily lives."[70]

In Texas, the attitudes of Mexican Americans toward Mexicans varied widely, according to class background and the extent of their interaction. Perhaps not surprisingly, lower-working-class Mexican Americans, those most likely to live near—and compete with—immigrants, tended to view the newcomers most negatively. For instance, it was not uncommon to hear lower-class Mexican Americans refer condescendingly to undocumented Mexicans as *pobrecitos* (poor little ones) or *mojados* (wetbacks).[71] They also often viewed the newcomers as backward country cousins whose willingness to take on even the most dangerous of jobs for meager pay undercut Mexican American wages.

For their part, undocumented Mexicans often viewed lower-class Mexican Americans as lazy. Illegal immigrants took "a large measure of pride in their reputation as hard workers and believe[d] that [Mexican Americans did] not make the same effort."[72] Though they were not materially well-off themselves, undocumented immigrants sometimes looked down on working-class Mexican Americans for not having worked their way up the socioeconomic ladder despite their legal status and their ability to speak English. Recent immigrants also found reason to blame Mexican Americans for not effectively controlling and disciplining their children. "This criticism extend[ed] to U.S. families in general, but the negative appraisal of [Mexican Americans lay] in the fact that there seem[ed] to be different expectations for [Mexican Americans] than for Anglos."[73]

Middle-class Mexican Americans, who had less intimate contact with newcomers than did the working class, tended to be more sympathetic toward the undocumented. To the extent that they did have contact, it was "in the form of segmented roles wherein the [undocumented were] treated as clients or as patients."[74] Mexican American entrepreneurs, many of whom operated businesses in the old barrios and had the most contact with immigrants, particularly as customers and employees, had the most complex relationship with newcomers. According to a 1982 survey of Mexican American businessmen who ran enterprises in the barrios of Austin, Texas, 90 percent of respondents considered undocumented immigrants to be an important part of the consumer base for Mexican American–owned businesses.[75] By the early 1980s, immigration—both legal and illegal—"contributed greatly to the success of the [Mexican American] business community by providing inexpensive labor and an expanded ethnic clientele."[76] This symbiotic relationship was built upon both cultural and economic ties.

But despite such critical links between the two groups, new immigrants generally lived in separate social spheres from Mexican Americans. By and large, the two groups functioned "in distinctive structural situations, and, as a result, there [was] an absence of large-scale interaction, especially at the level of personal relationships."[77] One 1986 study of immigrants in Texas found that while newcomers sometimes did rely on Mexican Americans to provide social and economic resources, the vast majority of immigrants "satisfied needs such as transportation, loans, and job information" within the immigrant community.[78] Accordingly, immigrant communities became more self-sufficient as they increased in size.

Of course, commonalities of language and culture could sometimes bridge the gap between Mexicans and Mexican Americans, but not always. Immigrants sometimes "reported that they could not approach any [Mexican American] with the assurance that the latter could speak Spanish."[79] Even when a Mexican American did speak Spanish, the use of Anglicisms and other north-of-the-border idioms sometimes made it difficult to communicate with immigrants, particularly within the workplace. For example, while Mexicans used the word *herramientas* to mean tools, Texas Mexicans often said *fierros*. "Similarly, the former used the words *grua* and *chispas* for wrecker and spark plugs while the latter used *reca* and *plogues*."[80] Not surprisingly, Mexican and Mexican American workers exhibited "few signs of ethnic solidarity."[81]

In the 1990s, a similar dynamic of cooperation and conflict could be found in Californian communities that had recently become home to large numbers of Mexican immigrants. For example, the Los Angeles suburb of La Puente, which "[h]istorically ... had a substantial Mexican American population," was 37 percent foreign-born in 1990.[82] There, some Mexican Americans felt antagonistic toward the newcomers, primarily because they were seen to be resisting assimilation. "[They] come here, impose their language on us, impose their attitudes," said one fifty-five-year-old Mexican American woman. "They don't keep it within their home. They spread them around so you can't walk into a store and make a purchase without being spoken to in Spanish ... they should clean up their act and mainstream and be more this country than their own because they're not in their own."[83] Roberta Zavala, a forty-seven-year-old La Puente resident, concurred: "People came because they wanted to immigrate for whatever reason. I have no problem as long as [they] maintain our values. You want to assimilate. . . . You have to come in . . . with an attitude, 'I come here to work. I come here to follow the rules. I come here to be a good citizen, respecting the country, respecting my neighbors.' "[84]

According to one case study, some Mexican Americans in La Puente resented immigrants for ridiculing their inability to speak Spanish fluently. "[They] have a very low opinion of what I think they call the 'Pochos' because we don't know their language," said a sixty-two-year-old Mexican American woman.[85] Some Mexican Americans feared that the growing presence of recent immigrants encouraged Anglo Americans to question the "Americanness" of all people of Mexican origin. "Realizing that members of the dominant society may not differentiate among the heterogeneous Mexican-origin community, some individuals express[ed] concern that no matter how much they [had] acculturated they [were] perceived as immigrants."[86]

For other Mexican American residents, however, the increase in the number of Spanish-speaking neighbors and co-workers made them feel "remorse, embarrassment, or guilt for not speaking Spanish 'fluently.' "[87] "I wish I knew Spanish that well [like my mother] . . . to be able to talk to people," said one third-generation Mexican American. "Even at work, the majority of the plant employees speak Spanish, and so, I feel . . . frowned on . . . because I don't say 'Hello' to them."[88] Hoping to better communicate with their neighbors and co-workers, some latter-generation Mexican Americans began practicing their Spanish "with their family and friends, attending Spanish masses, and taking Spanish classes."[89]

In Santa Paula, California, north of Los Angeles, anthropologist Martha Menchaca found a deeper rift between the native- and foreign-born. Mexican Americans often saw immigrants—and their public expression of Mexican culture—as "a source of embarrassment."[90] According to Roger Aranda, a latter-generation Mexican American attorney, "There is social snobbery between the native-born and the rest of the Hispanic community. Many of the native-born do not want to associate with the immigrants because they think immigrants are rancheros [peasants]. . . . You see social distance in the restaurants and clubs. . . . For example, there are two baseball leagues. One is composed of Mexican immigrants and the other of native-born."[91]

According to Menchaca, since Mexican Americans "had acquired many of the tastes, norms, and prejudices" of Anglo American culture, "they expected the Mexican immigrants to conform to certain cultural expectations and downplay their [Mexicanness] in public."[92] While some adult immigrants sought "to escape the stigma of being foreigners by acculturating," others refused to "change their ethnic identity" and limited their interaction with the native-born.[93] The children of immigrants, however, were much more likely to "demonstrate a receptive attitude toward the new cultural norms."[94] In school, this second generation "acquire[d] the tastes, norms, and lifestyle of the Mexican Americans. Furthermore, because many children of immigrant parents also form[ed] close friendships with their native-born peers, Mexican students develop[ed] personal ties with non-immigrant families. The common outcome [was] that, upon leaving school and becoming young adults, Americanized Mexicans prefer[red] to be identified as members of the more prestigious native-born social networks."[95] Acquiring a Mexican American identity also gave the children of immigrants greater social latitude as they came of age. "In rural communities like Santa Paula, the label 'Mexican' [was] synonymous with being a farm worker, whereas the terms 'native-born,' 'Chicano,' and 'Mexican American' [had] no strict accompanying occupational classifications."[96]

By the mid-1980s, the growing presence of Mexican immigrants in the United States once again made immigration a hot-button political issue. In 1986, Congress passed the Immigration Reform and Control Act (IRCA), which included three major provisions. "To eliminate the attraction of U.S. jobs, it imposed sanctions on employers who knowingly hired undocumented workers. To deter people from trying to enter the United States illegally in the first place, it allocated additional resources to expand the Border Patrol. To wipe the slate clean and begin afresh, it authorized an amnesty for undocumented migrants who could prove continuous residence in the United States after January 1, 1982."[97] While IRCA succeeded in stemming undocumented immigration for a few years, by 1990 it was obvious that the law had failed. In fact, "rather than discouraging illegal immigration,

IRCA actually promoted it."[98] The legalization of previously illegal immigrants gave "individuals who had already built social and human capital in the U.S. a legal basis for remaining abroad. Their newfound legal status strengthened the social capital embedded in their networks, and made crossing the border easier for other migrants. Furthermore, legalized Mexicans had greater freedom to travel to new immigrant gateways where, as pioneering migrants, they established new locales to which subsequent migrants could travel."[99] Amnesty also led to an increase in legal immigration as "spouses and dependents of IRCA-legalized migrants suddenly qualified for visas" under the family-unification provision of U.S. immigration law.[100]

Heightened border enforcement failed to deter illegal migrants from attempting to enter the United States. Blockades set up in El Paso or San Diego channeled migrants to less conspicuous areas along the two-thousand-mile border. Ironically, increased border enforcement also discouraged what otherwise would have been circular migrants from returning to Mexico. "The end result of a border buildup [was] typically longer trip durations, lower probabilities of return migration, and a shift toward permanent settlement."[101] In other words, the increased cost of crossing the border illegally—both in practical and in monetary terms—effectively kept illegal immigrants in the U.S. rather than out. Nonetheless, "between 1986 and 1996 the U.S. Congress, three presidents, and several states undertook a remarkable series of actions to reassure citizens that they were working to 'regain control' of the Mexico-U.S. border."[102] They did this at the very time that the United States and Mexico were adopting policies designed to further integrate the two nations economically. In January of 1994, the United States, Mexico, and Canada entered into the North American Free Trade Agreement, which removed barriers to free trade among the three nations. As immigration scholars Douglas Massey, Jorge Durand, and Nolan Malone wrote, "In time-honored fashion, the United States sought to have its cake and eat it too—to move headlong toward a consolidation of markets for capital, goods, commodities, and information, but simultaneously to pretend that North American labor markets would remain separate and distinct."[103]

During the deep recession of the early 1990s, anti-immigrant sentiment swept the nation. Nowhere was it felt more than in California, the state that had received nearly two-thirds of all Mexican migrants who arrived in the U.S. in the late 1980s.[104] In 1994, a grassroots movement called "Save Our State" that had emerged a year earlier in Orange County, California, successfully placed a referendum on the November ballot that sought to deny public schooling and non-emergency health care to illegal immigrants as well as require police officers, teachers, and health care workers to report anyone they suspected of being undocumented. Proponents of the measure, which was known as Proposition 187, argued that illegal immigrants were not only at the root of the state's economic ills but were eroding the Golden State's quality of life.

Two months before voters went to the polls, California Republican governor Pete Wilson, who was up for reelection, officially endorsed the controversial ballot initiative. He and other backers of Proposition 187 acknowledged that what they really wanted was a change in national immigration policy, which was the exclusive domain of the federal government. "Proposition 187, the Save Our State initiative, is the 2-by-4 we need to . . . finally force Washington to accept its responsibility for illegal immigration," Wilson said in an address to the Republican state convention.[105] Two weeks prior to the election, the Wilson campaign released an ad on illegal immigration that urged Californians to vote yes on the ballot measure. Using video footage of illegal Mexican immigrants dashing into traffic in an attempt to cross the border, a narrator ominously intoned, "They keep coming. Two million illegal immigrants in California. The federal government won't stop them at the border, yet requires us to pay billions to take care of them."[106]

As late as September 1994, a *Los Angeles Times* poll revealed that Latino voters in California, the vast majority of whom were latter-generation Mexican Americans, were supportive of Proposition 187 by a margin of 52 percent to 42 percent.[107] While the *Times* poll did not take into account generational differences, a 1984 California survey indicated that the political opinions of first-, second-, and third-generation Latinos differed significantly. For instance, on issues like bilingualism and immigration reform, "third generation Latinos were more like the rest of the population . . . than first generation Latinos were. The best example of this [was] the amnesty issue: 74 per-cent of first generation Latinos favored amnesty for illegal aliens as compared to 49 percent of the third generation" and 44 percent of Anglos.[108]

As election day neared in 1994, the generational divisions between California's Latino voters lessened. As the campaign gained momentum, many legal immigrants and latter-generation Mexican Americans began to feel as if they, too, were being targeted in some way. Indeed, the increasingly nasty, racially charged rhetoric coming from some Proposition 187 supporters made it clear that the fervor surrounding the initiative was not exclusively about the exorbitant costs of illegal immigration. While some supporters may have viewed the issue as essentially one of economics or law and order, others clearly understood that "the measure—and the campaign that surrounded it—carried an implicit cultural message as well."[109] Mervin Field, the founder of the Field Poll, one of the oldest opinion research firms in the state, thought that "the greater driving force [behind the measure], particularly in Southern California, was the cultural clash that [had] been occurring there day by day. How can you stop culture? How can you stop people from speaking the Spanish language, or posting signs in Spanish? Here was a way to stop it at the ballot box."[110]

In other words, while Proposition 187 may indeed have been an electoral response to illegal immigration, it was also an attempt to put a halt to far-reaching demographic trends in the nation's most populous state. By 1990, it was clear that immigration—both legal and illegal—was changing the cultural, ethnic, and racial landscape of California. During the 1980s, the Latino population had grown by 69 percent, while the Asian portion increased by 127 percent.[111] The state's Anglo population continued to grow—by 8 percent—but it did so at a dramatically lower rate than that of the rest of the population.[112] Consequently, while Anglos made up 76 percent of Californians in 1980, they were only 57 percent in 1990.[113] For the first time in California history, the urban black population began to decline. Latinos, on the other hand, now made up one in four Californians. Eighty percent of them were of Mexican origin.[114]

The demographic transition was most dramatic in the southern half of the state. In Los Angeles County, home to one-third of California's population, the Latino percentage rose from 11 percent to 36 percent between 1960 and 1990, while the Asian percentage jumped from 2 percent to 11 percent.[115] More significantly, the 1990 census revealed that Latinos were on the verge of overtaking Anglos as the county's largest demographic group. Meanwhile, the public became aware of the enormity of this demographic shift during a particularly bad time in the state's history. As if a severe recession was not enough, Los Angeles was also hit by wildfires, floods, a devastating earthquake, and a deadly urban riot in the first half of the 1990s. In the booming 1980s, city officials had dubbed Los Angeles the capital of the Pacific Rim. By 1991, more and more people feared that the city was becoming, in the words of author David Rieff, the capital of the Third World. According to Rieff, "It was too easy to grow accustomed to the way white Angelenos would speak of aliens 'pouring' into the country, the hypertrophied rhetoric, at times grotesquely biblical in character, of 'floods,' 'waves,' and 'invasions.' And yet most peculiar of all, in a way, was that all this apocalyptic thinking was occurring in Los Angeles, precisely the place where people had for so long prided themselves on being beyond history, beyond ethnicity."[116]

Mexican Americans were no better prepared for this massive demographic shift than were Anglos. But they were not as comfortable demonizing and blaming the new immigrants—legal or illegal—for the state's ills. As Richard Estrada, a *Dallas Morning News* columnist and immigration reform advocate, pointed out, Mexican Americans were able to disapprove of illegal immigration without feeling any antipathy for the immigrants themselves. Yet, as one *Los Angeles Times* reporter noted, among Proposition 187's "grassroots supporters, there [was] a barely concealed layer of antagonism toward illegal immigrants."[117] At public rallies, Save Our State advocates were not shy about characterizing Mexican migrants as "violent and parasitic."[118] In 1993, a freshman Republican assemblyman, William J. "Pete" Knight, circulated a poem entitled "I Love America" to his colleagues in the state legislature. The five-stanza ditty, which Knight said he received from a constituent, parodied "immigrant slang as it [told] of a fictional immigrant crossing into the United States, receiving welfare . . . [and] asking other immigrants to join him and ridiculing Americans for paying taxes to support them."[119] "Sent for family, they just trash! But they all draw more welfare cash," said one stanza. "Everything is mucho good—soon we own the neighborhood. We have a hobby, it's called breeding, welfare pay for baby feeding."[120]

As the rhetoric became more rancorous, the distinctions between illegal and legal immigrants and even between foreign- and U.S.-born Latinos began to blur. Consequently, when supporters of Proposition 187 spoke of "taking back America for Americans," Mexican American citizens were no longer certain which side they were considered to be on.[121] Thus, despite the many social and cultural distinctions between them, Mexican Americans closed ranks with illegal Mexican immigrants, and on election day, 77 percent of Latino voters rejected the initiative.[122] Though Mexicans and Mexican Americans had always shared a loose sense of kinship, their sense of peoplehood hardened during this time of strong anti-Mexican sentiment. As Martha Menchaca wrote, "In their everyday life, ethnic differences generate social cleavages, but during crisis periods [Mexicans and Mexican Americans] are able to temporarily suspend their differences and act as a cohesive group."[123]

But Mexican American opposition to Proposition 187 had less to do with solidarity than it did with self-defense. Many realized that they were not immune from the ill will being directed at illegal immigrants. Indeed, according to sociologist Tomás Jiménez, this type of nativism is often "couched in racial terms and seemingly directed at all people of Mexican descent."[124] Others surely remembered times in which they themselves were mistaken for immigrants. One Mexican American woman in La Puente described instances in which her U.S.-born husband had been treated like a foreigner. "[We are] driving along, and someone will cut us off . . . [my husband] does his little cursing thing . . . and that other person . . . if it's a White person . . . they've even called [my husband] a wetback . . . because [of] the way he looks. He looks Mexican. They'll call him a wetback in the process of their arguing. I don't think of him that way. I think of him as an American."[125] According to Jiménez, it is in moments like these that Mexican Americans experience U.S. society as more a racial than an ethnic group. Even though the social distance between Anglos and

Mexican Americans diminishes over generations, campaigns against unassimilated immigrants of the same ethnicity can raise the specter of being "mistaken for Mexican immigrants and treated as foreigners."[126]

Proposition 187 passed by a margin of three to two. Asian voters narrowly voted against it; as did African Americans. Anglo voters, on the other hand, approved the measure overwhelmingly, 63 percent to 37 percent.[127] Needless to say, its passage did not halt California's demographic transformation. In fact, the measure never became law. In March 1998, a U.S. District Court judge declared Proposition 187 unconstitutional because it improperly asserted state control over immigration policy, which is the province of the federal government. But even if the ballot measure had somehow managed to end all Latin American immigration—legal and illegal—on election day 1994, high Latino birth rates, coupled with a virtual zero population growth for Anglos, would have given California a Latino majority within fifty years.[128] While Latino population growth nationwide was due largely to immigration during the 1970s and 1980s, by the 1990s, it was being driven more by procreation than migration.[129]

Shortly before the polls closed on election day, Councilman Raúl Pérez of Huntington Park, California, the city in the United States with the highest percentage of Mexican-born residents, predicted that if the ballot measure won, "immigrants will get the message that they can't continue to sit on the fence." He believed that they needed to "make up their mind that this is their country and that they're here for good."[130] He was right. Politically, Proposition 187 accelerated the Latinization of California. Even before election day 1994, large numbers of Mexican permanent resident aliens, who historically had the lowest rate of naturalization of any immigrant group, began enrolling in citizenship classes throughout the state. In the 1994–95 school year, enrollment in citizenship classes in the Los Angeles Unified School District, the largest provider of such courses in the nation, was three times higher than the previous year and one hundred times higher than the average for the previous eight years.[131]

Faced with the possibility, however remote, of losing their right to remain in the United States, hundreds of thousands of Mexican permanent resident aliens sought security in American citizenship. Between 1992 and 1996, the number of citizenship applicants in California rose by 500 percent. By April 1995, the Los Angeles district office of the Immigration and Naturalization Service was receiving 2,200 applications for citizenship a day.[132] Fifty-eight-year-old Juan Aguilar, who was born on a ranch in La Constancia, Jalisco, had been coming to work in the U.S. since 1957 and received his Green Card, which conferred permanent resident status, in 1987. Not until the Proposition 187 campaign began did he feel a need to apply for U.S. citizenship. "Well, we were a little scared," he said. "[The Green Card] they give us is only borrowed because whatever day they want to they can take it away and throw us out." Proposition 187 also made Aguilar, who worked in a lead refinery, reconsider his relationship to Mexico. "I came here and brought my whole family, my mother, my father, and I've buried three siblings here. . . . So I told my wife, you know what, we're getting old. Everyone is here. Our girl, the oldest, who is twenty-one years old, she speaks lousy Spanish. All garbled. I told my wife that we were going to become citizens, because the truth is we have nobody [in Mexico]."[133]

Aguilar's wife, forty-four-year-old Marta, who was born in the tiny pueblo of La Barca, Jalisco, came to the same conclusion. Asked why she wanted to become an American citizen, she replied, "because my life has been made here, not in Mexico. You go to Mexico for fifteen days, eight days, and you want to go back [to the United States]. That is what happens to me. I miss it here. I am happy here. . . . It's that here a person has more comfort. I've always said, [between being] rich in Mexico or poor in the United States, a thousand times [I'll take being] poor here."[134]

The political success of Proposition 187 also inspired a national campaign to curb government spending on legal immigrants. Within weeks after Congress passed the proposition, House Republicans drafted legislation to exclude most legal immigrants from sixty federal programs. News of the proposal hit the front page of *La Opinión*, L.A.'s largest Spanish-language daily, on Christmas morning 1994. What resulted was "the greatest rush to citizenship" in U.S. history.[135] Mexicans certainly weren't the only immigrants to seek security in naturalization, but at nearly one-quarter of new citizens, Mexico had become the leading country of origin for naturalized immigrants. In 1996, there was a 212 percent increase in Mexican immigrant naturalizations over the previous year. [136]

While some Mexican Green Card holders applied for citizenship simply to secure their right to remain in the U.S., others wanted to gain a political voice. Thirty-four-year-old Miguel Estrada, a machine operator who was born in Los Reyes, Michoacán, said his primary reason for naturalizing was "to have the right to vote. That's the most important thing for me, because I've lived in this country longer than I lived in Mexico."[137] Although Estrada, who lived in Southern California, saw the anti-immigrant campaigns as a "blow to the head," he also believed that it was a blessing in disguise. "It's good that Proposition 187 passed, [because] it was a push . . . it pushed people to become citizens and find out what their rights are." In the wake of Proposition 187, Estrada described the mood among Mexican immigrants as "sad," but he was not alone in expressing an emerging sense of ethnic confidence. "We're becoming the majority," he said. "And we're going to have more rights. . . . There will be more Latinos representing us . . . More Latinos in the [House of Representatives], the Senate, and that way we'll have more confidence."[138]

In the early 1990s, sociologist David E. Hayes-Bautista concluded that Latinos in Southern California—both U.S.- and foreign-born— had reached critical mass and lived in a very different cultural ecology than did previous generations of Mexicans and Mexican Americans. Despite the ugly anti-immigrant rhetoric of the early 1990s, Mexican and other Latin American immigrants were enjoying a heightened confidence not only in their ethnic identity but in the behaviors, attitudes, and beliefs they brought to the United States. Momentum, numbers, and an increasing proximity to the homeland—both via electronic media and airplanes—allowed them to connect their past and present in ways not available to previous generations of immigrants. In addition to finding comfort, continuity, and useful social networks in the presence of large numbers of their *paisanos* (compatriots), Mexican immigrants also benefited from middle-class Mexican American political networks. In the mid- to late 1990s, the National Association of Latino Elected and Appointed Officials played a key role in efforts to naturalize immigrants. Likewise, the Southwest Voter Registration Education Project registered large numbers of newly naturalized immigrants to vote. During the anti-immigrant campaigns, many Mexican American elected officials found themselves—sometimes reluctantly—defending the rights of immigrants.

After the 1992 riots in Los Angeles the Mexican American political establishment sought to identify the still largely unknown immigrant population and to discuss why there had been no organized Latino response to the civil unrest. Elected officials, activists, and business-people began to acquaint themselves with new immigrants and to grapple with what it meant to be Mexican American in the wake of mass immigration. Not only was the Hispanic population now more foreign-born that it had been at any time since the 1920s, it was now more diverse. After 1979, political turmoil in Central America pushed thousands of refugees northward. By 1993, "the total number of Central Americans in Los Angeles [was] estimated at 500,000 to over 1 million."[139] "At the beginning we were Chicanos," said Raúl Granados, the president of the Mexican American Bar Association, in 1993. "But the reality of this city is changing. Now we have increasing numbers of Salvadorans, Nicaraguans, Guatemalans. Who are Latinos and where are they?"[140]

By the early 1990s, the generic terms "Latino" and "Hispanic" became more than abstractions and gained local currency. Though Mexicans were numerically dominant, the influence of other national origins was felt both in immigrant neighborhoods and in the Spanish-language media. L.A.'s most popular Spanish-language, drive-time radio program featured a Peruvian disc jockey, a Puerto Rican news-man, and a Mexican traffic reporter. But the emergence of a loose pan-ethnic identity didn't mean that national origin distinctions had been erased. By 2002, a poll by the Pew Hispanic Center found that while the vast majority of Latinos in the U.S. sometimes used the terms "Latino" or "Hispanic" to identify themselves, the tie to the countries of origin was ultimately "much more salient than any pan-ethnic or 'Latino/Hispanic' identity."[141] By then the term "Chicano" had lost its political connotation and had become simply a synonym for Mexican American.

Particularly in large gateway regions like Southern California, mass immigration altered the dynamics of the Mexican American experience. "While in 1970 only one in five Latinos in Los Angeles County was an immigrant, [by 1990] slightly over half was foreign-born."[142] Among adult Latinos in Southern California, fully two-thirds were born outside the United States.[143] According to one survey, by 1992 only 12 percent of adult Latinos in California were third-generation Americans.[144] For many latter-generation Mexican Americans, the presence of large numbers of immigrants offered an opportunity to "replenish the content of Mexican American ethnic identity."[145] Similar to the "hardening" effect caused by the upsurge in anti-Mexican sentiment, their ethnic identities became " 'thicker' as a result of their interaction with Mexican immigrants."[146] Of course, in the post–civil rights era, Americans were generally much more tolerant of ethnic and racial diversity. The soft multiculturalism of the times even encouraged non–Anglo Americans to nurture their own ethnic identities. But more significantly, the emergence of an immigrant-driven "Hispanic market" and electorate had changed the politics of assimilation.

By the mid-1990s, a growing number of upwardly mobile and middle-class Mexican Americans had discovered that their ethnicity and heritage could be an advantage in both the marketplace and the political arena. Suddenly Hispanic cultural attributes and the Spanish language were no longer perceived as potentially inviting discrimination by employers. Large corporations were seeking middlemen they hoped could connect them to the growing Hispanic market. Bilingualism was believed to be an "invaluable asset for a successful career in virtually any field."[147] Some employees even received "additional pay for being designated as bilingual in their workplace."[148] More than a few executives—both in the private and in the public sector—considered the hiring of Latinos—whether they were bilingual or not—as part of their Hispanic marketing plan. According to sociologist Tomás Jiménez, "the large population of immigrants . . . helped to improve the social position of Mexican Americans by creating a demand for people of Mexican descent" in a variety of political positions and occupations.[149]

By the late 1990s, a growing number of Mexican American politicians were either brushing up on their Spanish-language skills or learning the language in order to better reach naturalized immigrant voters. In 1998, California assemblyman Gil Cedillo, who represented a heavily immigrant district in downtown Los Angeles, spent two weeks in Cuernavaca, Mexico, at the Bilingual Institute, enrolled in an intensive language course. But as Mexico's cultural and linguistic influence waxed, official Mexico did not attempt to assert itself within emigrant communities the way it had during the great wave of migration in the early twentieth century.

For decades, Mexico disowned its migrants as renegades who had turned tail on their country and culture. They were *pochos* (watered-down Mexicans) who had cashed in their souls for material possessions. Although Mexico benefited from the escape valve that allowed it to lose large numbers of unemployed and underemployed citizens, the migrants were glaring symbols of their homeland's failures. Although Mexico usually condescended to its kin north of the border, it would occasionally intervene on their behalf whenever it appeared that their mistreatment harmed Mexico's national pride.

Until 1979, when President Jimmy Carter appointed Los Angeles college professor Julian Nava as U.S. ambassador, Mexico had refused to accept a Mexican American. Like other nations, Mexico wanted to exert influence in the U.S. and therefore expected that "American representatives assigned to Mexico [would] have a status sufficient to facilitate communications with the White House and the State Department. Since [Mexican Americans were] not powerful domestic actors as a group, and since no [Mexican American] had intimate personal ties to any president . . . Mexico considered it a slight to have a [Mexican American] appointed as ambassador."[150] It was only when Mexican Americans began making progress politically and economically that Mexico began to take a more sympathetic view of its diaspora.

Beginning in the late 1970s, and then intensifying under President Carlos Salinas de Gortari in the late 1980s, Mexico developed a two-pronged public relations strategy to capitalize on Mexican American progress. To reach U.S.-born Mexican Americans, Mexico courted Latino organizations and granted heritage awards to accomplished Mexican Americans. To appeal to emigrants, Mexican consulates strengthened their community outreach efforts and encouraged newcomers in the U.S. to demand their rights. In so doing, Mexico aimed to nurture sympathetic views toward itself in the Mexican American electorate and to urge migrants to keep sending money to relatives in the homeland.

In 1997, President Ernesto Zedillo signed a law allowing migrants who become naturalized U.S. citizens to retain their Mexican nationality. Responding to the enormous increase in applications for U.S. citizenship by immigrants, Mexico sought to preserve the connections of those migrants to their homeland by proclaiming that U.S. citizenship would no longer be considered cultural treason. Despite Mexico's generous invitation, after five years of the dual nationality law only 1.6 percent of those eligible availed themselves of the opportunity to claim Mexican nationality.[151]

By 2000, migrants were remitting an estimated $8 billion annually back home and were reshaping the popular image of Mexican Americans in Mexico. In many villages, U.S.-based migrants attained social and political influence by virtue of their generosity. In his inaugural speech of December 2000, President Vicente Fox referred to emigrants as "our beloved migrants, our heroic migrants."[152] Like his predecessors, Fox also pledged that Mexican consulates would become "the best allies of immigrants' rights."[153]

In a November 2000 speech to a Mexican American civil rights group, President Fox went further than any previous Mexican official to validate not only the dreams but the political loyalties of naturalized and U.S.-born Mexican Americans. "Mine will be the first Mexican administration to sincerely honor the ties that bind people of Mexican descent to the United States," he pledged.

> Mine will be the first administration team to understand that their greatest desire is to become loyal, productive citizens of a country that has welcomed them, opened doors for them, and enabled them to create opportunities for progress and prosperity. Like migrants from other countries, Mexicans who have come to stay want to belong. They want their children to learn English, they want to graduate from college, they want to live in integrated neighborhoods, they want to dream the American dream and wake up as citizens. I share those hopes. My administration wants Mexicans to prosper in the United States. We have no desire to interfere in the powerful processes that tie Mexican immigrants to this nation.[154]

But fresh from the civics lesson of Proposition 187, Mexican immigrants did not need Mexico's blessing. By the late 1990s the rush to naturalization had translated into an increase in Latino voter registration and turnout at the polls in California. According to a study by the Field Poll, during the 1990s, "Latino voters represent[ed] the fastest growing segment of the California electorate. Between 1990 and 2000 about 1 million Latinos [were] added to the state's voter rolls, representing nearly all of the 1.1 million increase in the state's . . . voter population."[155] These new voters altered the profile of the Mexican American electorate. Fully 44 percent of Latinos who registered to vote between 1994 and 2000 were foreign-born, compared to just 12 percent of Latinos who were registered prior to 1994.[156]

"With each passing election Latinos [became] a larger part of the overall state's electorate, increasing from 5 percent of voters [at the start of the decade] to 14 percent in 1998."[157] That year, Mexican American candidates across California won historic victories. In Los Angeles, a Mexican American Republican, Lee Baca, was elected county sheriff, while in San Jose, Ron Gonzales, a former manager at Hewlett-Packard who dubbed himself a "high-tech Mex," became "the first [Mexican American] mayor of a major California city since statehood."[158] Most significantly, Assemblyman Cruz Bustamante, who just two years prior had become the state's first Mexican American speaker of the assembly, was elected lieutenant governor, making him the first Mexican American statewide officeholder in more than one hundred years. By 2000, "twenty of the eighty seats in the state assembly, and seven in forty of the seats in the state senate were held by Latinos."[159]

While there was no doubt that the growing Latino electorate was partly responsible for the successful candidacies of these Mexican American politicians, the fact was that the majority of votes for Bustamante, Baca, and Gonzales were cast by non-Latinos. By 1998, surveys showed that though "Californians were keenly aware of the rapid demographic change occurring in the state . . . they were taking it in stride."[160] By 2000, according to opinion polls by the Public Policy Institute of California, "only a handful of residents named race and ethnic relations as the most important problem facing the state. Eight in ten Californians thought that racial and ethnic groups were getting along very well or somewhat well."[161] In June 2002, a three-judge federal district court panel dismissed a voting rights case brought by MALDEF against the state of California. In a historic ninety-one-page opinion, Judge Stephen Reinhardt of the U.S. 9th

Circuit Court of Appeals and U.S. District judges Christina A. Snyder and Margaret M. Morrow insisted that while it was not their "view that racial discrimination no longer affects our political institutions or motivates any portion of the electorate of Los Angeles County . . . election returns . . . reveal that in Los Angeles County, whites and other non-Latinos are currently far more willing to support Latino candidates for office than in the past. In short, at the outset of the 21st century, the data in the record before us paints a far more encouraging picture of racial voting attitudes than" it had a decade earlier.[162]

Among Mexican American voters, particularly naturalized immigrants, shared ethnicity did "constitute an important determinant of vote choice when a Latino candidate [was] on the ballot."[163] As was the experience of newcomers from the last great wave of European immigration, Mexican Americans were now able to leverage ethnic political solidarity as a means to catapult co-ethnic candidates into the American mainstream. But ethnic mobilization did not translate into ideological solidarity. Indeed, as the number of Mexican American elected officials multiplied, so did the diversity of leadership styles and political viewpoints. The strength of the state legislature's Latino Caucus lay less in its unity than in its members' ability to network with well-placed colleagues on a variety of committees. In 1996, the California Latino Legislative Caucus adopted the slogan "Latino Issues Are California Issues."[164] According to a 1997 survey, Latino political elites in Los Angeles no longer considered the once emotionally charged topic of bilingual education to be among the top five cutting-edge issues. Instead, the broader imperative of "improving public education" outranked all other issues in order of importance.[165] In another survey of Latino city council members in Southern California, two-thirds of respondents said that they had no "Latino political agenda" and 100 percent agreed with the statement that "once elected, Latinos do not fight for Latinos in their cities in the same way" as African American politicians.[166]

"When you gain power, responsibility, coalition building and lawmaking force you to have agendas that appeal to a broader base," said political scientist Fernando Guerra in 1999.[167] In fact, while many Mexican American candidates leveraged ethnicity during their campaigns, once in Sacramento most sought to avoid being pigeon-holed as "Latino politicians." In his campaigns for mayor of Los Angeles in 2001 and 2005, former speaker of the California Assembly Antonio Villaraigosa asked journalists and editors to stop applying the adjective "Latino" each time they published his name. Villaraigosa's meteoric political rise was a metaphor for the maturation of Mexican American politics. Once a militant campus Chicano activist, Villaraigosa morphed into a decidedly establishmentarian politician as his status and ambition grew. In 1998, during his swearing-in for his second term as assembly speaker, Villaraigosa went out of his way to reject what he called "the politics of protest." He quoted his late mother's admonition that it is "not enough to always be against. When you grow up, you must also be for something."[168]

While ethnicity may have played a key role in candidate selection for Mexican American voters in the 1990s, the Latino electorate was decidedly "not fertile ground for an ethnic political movement."[169] Indeed, both in California and nationally, "Hispanic political power is converging toward the national mean, not splitting away from it."[170] According to political scientist Louis DeSipio, "like the foreign-born, citizen Latinos do not show an ethnically driven dissatisfaction with the U.S. political system."[171] In fact, in California, where eight in ten Latinos are of Mexican origin, Latino voters "are bringing a more positive outlook toward government to a state where voters are notoriously cynical about politics."[172] Otherwise, however, according to pollster Mark Baldassare, "the evidence suggests that Latinos are very similar to whites in their views about California policies."[173] In 2000, Baldassare concluded that "there is no reason to think that increased participation by Latinos in the political process will result in significant shifts in citizens' policy preferences. . . . Whites and Latinos hold the same views about the state policy issues that are considered important. They think alike with regard to how state funds should be spent. They generally agree on what needs to be done to improve the state's public school system."[174]

The pace of naturalizations began to slow in the late 1990s. But the annual number of new Mexican-born U.S. citizens remained six times higher than the average between 1980 and 1993.[175] While the urgency may have waned, there was little doubt that legal Mexican immigrants had learned an important lesson on the value of U.S. citizenship. In the meantime, more Mexican immigrants arrived in the United States in the 1990s than in any previous decade, most of them illegally. However, immigrants were no longer the fastest growing segment of the Latino population. The foreign-born portion peaked in the mid-1990s at a little over 40 percent.[176] According to projections, for the next half-century, the first generation will decline as a percentage of all Latinos, Mexican Americans included. The fastest growing segment of the Latino population will be the third generation, which is projected to triple by 2040. The second generation, meanwhile, will double. As in the 1930s and 1940s, large numbers of the U.S.-born children and grandchildren of Mexican immigrants will come of age, and once again shift the cultural balance of Mexican America from immigrant to ethnic American culture.

Despite the growth in the Spanish-language media in Los Angeles, during the 1990s Spanish-language movie theaters were going out of business. "You hear about music and dance and soap operas in Spanish, but it doesn't translate into the motion picture market," said Bruce Corwin, chairman of Metropolitan Theaters, the largest operator of Spanish-language theaters in Los Angeles. "The market, quite frankly, will not be around five years from now."[177] Similar to the population at large, "Latino movie-goers are primarily teens and young adults," who "prefer mainstream Hollywood blockbusters, especially action flicks with big-name stars."[178] In a 2004 study, sociologist Richard Alba found that "despite the extensive media infrastructure that has arisen to deliver programming in Spanish and the many communities in the U.S. where Spanish is spoken on a daily basis in homes and on the streets, the language assimilation of Mexican American children did not weaken" in the 1990s.[179] Even though bilingualism had become more common, the third generation's tendency to speak only English strengthened. "In 1990, 64 percent of third-generation Mexican-American children spoke only English at home; in 2000, the equivalent figure had risen to 71 percent."[180] While the value of Spanish may have increased in the 1990s, the pull of English had not diminished.

The allure of English and acculturation in general have a profound influence on ethnic identification. While the ethnic identity of Mexican immigrants is largely ascribed, the identity of U.S.-born "Mexican Americans is fluid, situational, and at least partly voluntary."[181] Traditionally, the "pattern for most previous immigrant groups was to pass through a period of political behavior based on ethnicity, but then to lose these bonds and act on other interests."[182] Despite the many differences between Mexican and European immigration, the same general pattern should hold true for Mexican Americans. But, in contrast to the experience of many European immigrant groups, Hispanic identity is not likely to disappear in the United States. Even as the Census Bureau was poised to announce that Hispanics had become the largest minority group in the United States, Mexican Americans were already either the single largest group or the absolute majority in a growing number of cities and counties of the Southwest. Consequently, the boundaries of both Mexican American cultural and political identity were not disappearing, but expanding. Mexican Americans in the Southwest are challenging long-held notions of what it means to be a minority in America.

As Mexican Americans continued to mature politically, 1960s-style calls for ideological discipline and ethnic solidarity became more difficult to sustain. Both the growth in the number of Mexican American elected officials and the advent of Latino public opinion surveys undercut the role of civil rights advocacy groups as spokespeople for the entire Mexican origin population. The Latinization of the Southwest also undermined the viability of the civil rights–era approach to Latino social ills. Indeed, in predominately Mexican American cities of the Southwest, class began to replace race as the primary political preoccupation. According to New Mexico–based Democratic political consultant Armando Gutiérrez, Mexican Americans are "beginning to see that 'Hispanic issues' are more class issues than ethnic issues."[183] Just as the rise of Mexican American political power rendered the politics of victimhood obsolete, the growing presence and acknowledgment of a viable Latino middle class undermined the notion that Mexican Americans are a uniformly discriminated-against caste. Beginning in the late 1990s, the public portrayal of the Latino population became more complex. In October 1996, the publication of a study on the emergence of a Latino middle class in Southern California made the front page of the *Los Angeles Times*. In

2001, a Latino think tank that had never published a major study on socioeconomic mobility since it was founded in 1985 announced the existence of "a substantial and prosperous Latino middle class in the United States, which grew significantly in the 1990s."[184] Neither of these studies was intended to deny the very real poverty that many people of Mexican origin still experience. Changing demography did not eradicate the traditional obstacles that immigrants still encounter in the United States. But in heavily Latino areas of the Southwest, the recognition of the internal diversity of the Mexican American population ensured that political battles would be fought increasingly along economic rather than ethnic lines.

Weeks before the 2001 mayoral race in El Paso, Texas, a city nearly three-quarters Mexican American, Pat O'Rourke, a former county commissioner, declared that all longtime El Pasoans were culturally Latino. "We are all Mexicans in the valley," he wrote. "What causes resentment among groups today is not ethnicity, but economic differences."[185] Only a year prior, in McAllen, Texas, which is 80 percent Mexican American, a coalition of churches and schools working to combat the city's socioeconomic ills successfully championed a ballot measure that changed the at-large election system to create single-member political districts. Although it was opposed by the town's mayor on the grounds that it would dilute Latino voting power, both Anglo and Mexican American activists argued that ethnicity was no longer as important as geography or class.

In heavily Mexican American South and West Texas, even immigration was losing some of its ethnic overtones. In 1994, a poll conducted by the *El Paso Times* found that 78 percent of Mexican American respondents said they were generally in favor of Operation Hold the Line, the labor-intensive strategy to prevent illegal immigration along the El Paso border, while only 17 percent were opposed.[186] In 1996, El Paso's overwhelmingly Mexican American electorate sent Democrat Silvestre Reyes, a former high-ranking official of the U.S. Border Patrol and architect of Operation Hold the Line, to the House of Representatives. A decade later, a growing number of prominent Mexican American officials were confronting the issue of illegal immigration without demonizing the immigrants themselves. In August 2005, Bill Richardson, the Mexican American governor of New

Mexico, who supported the issuing of driver's licenses to illegal immigrants, declared a state of emergency on the border in order to funnel more money to local governments and law enforcement to cope with increasing border crime and problems related to illegal immigration. That same month, Fabián Núñez, speaker of the California Assembly, urged his state's governor to declare a state of emergency. "For Latino [elected officials] to be taken seriously, we can't say 'Open the borders,' " he said. "We have to treat our immigrants with respect, but we have to do something."[187]

In California, changing demography also affected domestic minority policy. Mass Mexican immigration undermined the racial calculus that once made affirmative action politically viable among whites. In the early 1970s, the inclusion of Mexican Americans in affirmative action programs was largely justifiable on the grounds that a majority of them were third-generation Americans and many, particularly in Texas, had suffered from a legacy of school segregation. But in the early 1970s, no one could have imagined how a generation of large-scale immigration would redefine the Mexican American experience. By the 1980s, a program that had been designed to remedy past discrimination was increasingly benefiting recently arrived immigrants and their children.

The wholesale inclusion of Latinos in the category of "protected minority" meant that by 1990 more than a third of the residents of California benefited from traditional affirmative action programs. Predictably, as the "underrepresented minority" population grew, whites' view of affirmative action soured. In 1996, Anglo voters overwhelmingly supported California's Proposition 209, which eliminated state-sponsored affirmative action programs, because many of them felt that the playing field had begun to tilt against them. Though polls show that whites generally supported programs that aimed to remedy the effects of discrimination, they withdrew their support once they believed that those programs threatened the opportunities of their own families.

Affirmative action wasn't the only program affected by the demographic shift. Other 1970s-era policies designed to integrate minorities into the mainstream now served to help Anglos, the new minority. In the Los Angeles Unified School District, whose student body is more than 70 percent Hispanic, Latinos' majority status actually puts them at a disadvantage when applying for the city's select magnet school program. Whites' newfound minority status now gives them an advantage when applying to magnet schools. Though the district is only 9 percent white, 22 percent of its magnet students are white. The racial formula designed to balance the racial makeup of the magnets also ensures that blacks and Asians are overrepresented, while Latinos can make up no more than 40 percent of students.[188] Ironically, a policy designed to open doors for minorities now serves as a glass ceiling.

In 2001, just days after the Census Bureau announced that California had become the first large state where Anglos were in the minority, the San Diego City Council banned the term "minority" from official documents and discussions. Arguing that the word was outmoded and demeaning, council members pushed the debate over the meaning of "minority" into the national spotlight. In 2005, news that whites had become a minority in Texas renewed discussion over the usefulness of the term. "Twenty or 30 years ago, we saw the country as a majority-white country with a black minority," said Roderick J. Harrison, a demographer at the Joint Center for Political and Economic Studies, "but now you have places where that is a woefully poor description of what is going on."[189]

For many Mexican Americans in heavily Latino regions, the term "minority" has become too confining and parochial to describe their reality. Mexican American elected officials, in particular, were no longer content to define themselves as protectors of minority interests and were eager to assume responsibility and leadership for the larger society. "Now that we are no longer banging on the door to get in, but are seated at the table," said Los Angeles City Council president Alex Padilla, "we have the responsibility to address broader issues that affect the entire city, state, and country. The Latino agenda becomes safer communities, good schools, jobs—in other words, non-ethnic considerations."[190] The assumption of broader responsibility also changed political rhetoric. "You get to a certain level and you have to represent a wider constituency and that tends to moderate things," said one top aide to the head of California's Latino Legislative Caucus. "You can't be as strident. You no longer represent just your community. You have to sit down and bargain with [other stakeholders]."[191]

At the same time that Mexican Americans were outgrowing the minority category in the Southwest, they and other Hispanic Americans were also calling into question the validity of the nation's racial category system. In 1977, in order to "meet the needs created by legislation passed to protect civil rights monitoring and enforcement," the Office of Budget and Management issued Directive No. 15: "Race and Ethnic Standards for Federal Statistics and Administrative Reporting."[192] The document established a pentagonal ethnic/racial scheme by which Americans would be categorized. The four designated races were White; Black; American Indian or Alaskan Native; and Asian or Pacific Islander. Just as they had since 1910, census officials included a "Some Other Race" category for those respondents who did not fit into the primary four. Hispanics were officially classified as an ethnic and not a racial group.

In 1980, for the first time, the Census Bureau added the Hispanic origin question to the decennial short form questionnaire, which was mailed to all American households. Since Hispanics had been deemed an ethnic group, they "were also instructed to identify on the census with one of the primary race groups."[193] Yet because the federal government had been counting "all Mexicans, Puerto Ricans and other persons of 'Latin descent' . . . as 'White' unless they were 'definitely Negro, Indian or some other race (as determined by observation),' " census officials assumed that most Hispanics would select white as their race.[194] What resulted, however, was a tenfold increase in the number of Americans who classified themselves as "other race."[195] Ninety-five percent of those "others" were Latinos.[196]

Concluding that significant numbers of Hispanics didn't properly understand the difference between race and ethnicity, census officials adjusted the 1990 census questionnaire to clarify that "other" meant race. Thus, the 1990 questionnaire listed the word "race" no fewer than four times in reference to the "other" option. " 'If other race, print race,' the form commanded, with an arrow to a blank box, under which the form repeated for emphasis, 'Other race (print race).' "[197] But despite these changes, "the number of racial others jumped by 45 percent between 1980 and 1990, making that category the second fastest growing racial group in the country. Again Latinos drove the increase: 97.5 percent of those choosing 'other race' identified as Hispanics."[198] In 1990, fully 43 percent of Latinos nationally chose the "other race" category.[199] In California, where people of Mexican origin make up a higher percentage of the Hispanic population than in the nation at large, that figure rose to 51 percent in 1990 and again in 2000.[200]

After the 1990 census, it became clear that both immigration and intermarriage were posing a challenge to the government's racial/ethnic scheme. The Latino-driven increase in the "Some Other Race" category highlighted the growing number of Americans—both Hispanic and non-Hispanic—who did not feel comfortable labeling themselves one of the four races. At first, census officials continued to insist that Hispanics simply did not comprehend the difference between race and ethnicity. Presumably they feared that the growing number of Americans who selected "none of the above" undermined the validity of all the other racial categories. In 1992, one bureau official publicly complained of the growing number of Hispanics who "failed to respond correctly to the question on race."[201] But by the late 1990s there was a growing recognition that many Latinos simply did not view race in the same way as the U.S. government. "In Latin America, there are a greater number of racial terms for 'intermediate' categories," read one government report. "In contrast, the emphasis in the United States has been on constructing 'pure' races (e.g., Black and White, and not biracial or multiracial terms). Conceptions of race in Latin America result in the use of more categories since they are based more on ethnicity, national origin, and culture than appearance."[202] The report went on to note that "Hispanics tend to see race as a continuum" and that "Latin American countries tend to have a more social view of race as compared with the genealogically based view in the United States."[203]

In 1993, Ohio Congressman Tom Sawyer, chairman of the House Subcommittee on Census, Statistics, and Postal Personnel, called for a series of hearings on federal measurements of race and ethnicity. "A record number of Americans are foreign-born, and fully one-quarter of us are people of color," said Representative Sawyer. "Traditional measurements of ethnicity and race may no longer reflect that growing diversity."[204]

Seven years later, the Census Bureau, which had been successfully lobbied by the likes of Carlos Fernández and the Association of MultiEthnic Americans, allowed people to identify themselves with more than one race. The results were decidedly mixed. Gone were the tidy mutually exclusive racial categories, and because a racially mixed person could effectively be counted more than once, demographic data no longer always added up to 100 percent.

While leading demographers like William Frey of the Brookings Institution agreed that the multiple-race option allowed for a more accurate portrait of America, they also conceded that it opened up a Pandora's box. "[It's] a statistical mess," Frey said. "[But] because we're a melting pot country, we have to keep thinking of ourselves differently in terms of our race."205

Acknowledgments

Perhaps the hardest thing about writing this book was that even while my mind was mired in the sixteenth or the eighteenth centuries, the world around me kept moving forward. I am grateful to the many people who helped me bridge the gap and hold my life together in the here and now. I could not have completed this book without them.

In one way or another, I had been preparing to write this book since I moved back to Los Angeles from New York in 1992. I am grateful to David E. Hayes-Bautista for his mentoring and to his wife, María, for her generosity. My mother, Emilie Cacho, provided me with room and board for two years, bought me an oak computer desk, and found me a part-time job running an after-school program so that I could spend the rest of my time writing. Nina Aguayo Sorkin gave me that job, which I will never forget.

Richard Rodríguez was kind enough to introduce me to Sandy Close, who became the first person to actually pay me to write. Joel Kotkin gave me an important early boost in my career. My editors—past and present—at the *Los Angeles Times* have nurtured me since I wrote my first op-ed piece fifteen years ago. I owe an enormous debt of gratitude to the late Frank del Olmo, Gary Spiecker, Allison Silver, Janet Clayton, Nick Goldberg, Susan Brenneman, and Andrés Martinez.

Yolanda Chávez understood the thesis of this book long before I did. I will always be grateful. Raquelle de la Rocha, Bob Duran, Amanda Rounsaville, Oscar Garza, Margaret Leal-Sotelo, Tara Taylor, Frank McRae, Ernie Powell, Teresa Lara, and Jonathan Behr provided key support when I needed it most, as did Marie Rodríguez and Marcos Frommer. I could always rely on Marie Louise Condron to egg me on and cheer me up. Tamar Jacoby, Mike Madrid, and Thomas Tseng never failed to remind me that there was light at the end of the tunnel.

I had a lot of research help along the way. Mira Geffner did an extraordinary job digging up sources at UCLA libraries. Swati Pandey stoically endured bus rides to Georgetown and the Library of Congress to find crucial last-minute material. Zachariah Mampilly and María Elena Guadamuz bravely took on the formidable task of fact-checking the final manuscript.

Particularly during the final stages, Annette Kleiser was an endless source of inspiration, sound judgment, and critical insight. She saw the method in the madness whenever I could not. Adrian Wooldridge connected me to my agent, Sarah Chalfant, who has been a tremendous advocate on my behalf. Erroll McDonald of Pantheon lived up to his reputation as a visionary editor. Altie Karper and Robin Reardon imposed order on the chaos.

I have had the distinct pleasure of being a fellow at the New America Foundation since its inception in 1999. I am grateful to Ted Halstead and the New America team—past and present—particularly Sherle Schwenninger, Rachel White, Simone Frank, David Lesher, and Gordon Silverstein. I also owe thanks to Jim Canales and Amy Domínguez-Arms of the James Irvine Foundation.

Finally, as he has been throughout my life, my father, Manuel Henry Rodríguez, was a constant source of support, both intellectual and emotional. I dedicate this book to him.

Koreatown, Los Angeles
June 5, 2007

Notes

PREFACE

1. Carlos A. Fernández, "Testimony of the Association of MultiEthnic Americans Before the Subcommittee on Census, Statistics, and Postal Personnel of the U.S. House of Representatives," June 30, 1993.
2. Ibid.
3. Carlos A. Fernández, "La Raza and the Melting Pot: A Comparative Look at Multiethnicity," in *Racially Mixed People in America,* ed. Maria P. P. Root (Thousand Oaks, Calif.: Sage, 1992), 139.
4. Ibid., 133.
5. Ernesto Galarza, Herman Gallegos, and Julian Samora, *Mexican-Americans in the Southwest* (Santa Barbara: McNally & Loftin, 1969), 19.
6. Ernesto Galarza, "Mexicans in the Southwest: A Culture in Process," in *Plural Society in the Southwest,* eds. Edward H. Spicer and Raymond H. Thompson (New York: Interbook, 1972), 271.
7. Ibid., 296.
8. Manuel A. Machado, Jr., *Listen Chicano: An Informal History of the Mexican-American* (Chicago: Nelson Hall, 1978), 150.
9. Ibid.
10. Federico A. Sánchez, "Raíces Mexicanas," *Grito del Sol* 1, no. 1 (October–December 1976): 85.
11. Ibid., 75.
12. Carlos G. Vélez-Ibáñez, "Through the Eyes of an Anthropologist," in *The Chicanos: As We See Ourselves,* ed. Arnulfo Trejo (Tucson: University of Arizona Press, 1979), 47–48.
13. Roberto R. Bacalski-Martínez, "Aspects of Mexican American Cultural Heritage," in *The Chicanos: As We See Ourselves,* ed. Arnulfo D. Trejo (Tucson: University of Arizona Press, 1979), 19.
14. James Diego Vigil, *From Indians to Chicanos: The Dynamics of Mexican American Culture* (Prospect Heights, Ill.: Waveland, 1984), 202.
15. Richard Rodríguez, *Days of Obligation: An Argument with My Mexican Father* (New York: Viking, 1992), 24.
16. Gregory Rodriguez, "Forging a New Vision of America's Melting Pot," *New York Times,* February 11, 2001, Sect. 4; 1.
17. John Phillip Santos, "An Elegy for Identities: Who We Are in a Globalized World," Zócalo "Public Square" Lecture Series, May 5, 2004.

18. Alan Riding, *Distant Neighbors: A Portrait of the Mexicans* (New York: Vintage, 2000), 4.

19. Enrique Krauze, *Mexico: Biography of Power, A History of Modern Mexico, 1810–1996* (New York: Harper Perennial, 1997), xiv.

20. Agustín Basave Benítez, *México mestizo: Análisis del nacionalismo mexicano en torno a la mestizofilia de Andrés Molina Enríquez* (Mexico City: Fondo de Cultura Económico, 1992), 141.

21. Octavio Paz, *The Labyrinth of Solitude: Life and Thought in Mexico*, trans. Lysander Kemp (New York: Grove, 1961), 87.

22. Ibid., 20.

23. Alan Knight, "Racism, Revolution, and *Indigenismo*: Mexico, 1910–1940," in *The Idea of Race in Latin America, 1870–1940*, ed. Richard Graham (Austin: University of Texas Press, 1990), 86.

24. Manuel Gamio, *Forjando patria* (Mexico City: Editorial Porrúa, 1960), 98. Passage translated by Manuel H. Rodríguez.

25. Ibid., 6.

26. Ibid., 86.

27. José Vasconcelos, "The Latin-American Basis of Mexican Civilization," in *Aspects of Mexican Civilization* (Chicago: University of Chicago Press, 1926), 83.

28. Ibid., 99.

29. Ibid., 93.

30. Riding, *Distant Neighbors*, 3.

31. Claudio Lomnitz-Adler, *Exits from the Labyrinth: Culture and Ideology in the Mexican National Space* (Berkeley: University of California Press, 1992), 280.

32. Ibid., 279.

33. Gloria Anzaldúa, *Borderlands, La Frontera: The New Mestiza*, 2nd ed. (San Francisco: Aunt Lute, 1999), 101.

34. Roberto R. Ramírez and G. Patricia de la Cruz, "The Hispanic Population in the United States: March 2002, Current Population Reports," P20-545, U.S. Census Bureau, Washington, D.C.

35. Michael J. Rosenfeld, "Measures of Assimilation in the Marriage Market: Mexican Americans 1970–1990," *Journal of Marriage and Family* 64, no. 1 (2002), 160.

36. David E. Hayes-Bautista and Gregory Rodriguez, "L.A. County's Answer to Racial Tensions: Intermarriage," *Los Angeles Times*, May 5, 1996, M6.

37. Ibid.

38. Sonya M. Tafoya, "Check One or More . . . Mixed Race and Ethnicity in California," *California Counts: Population Trends and Profiles*, Public Policy Institute of California, Vol. 1, No. 2, January 2000, 6.

39. Sharon Lee and Barry Edmonston, "Hispanic Intermarriage, Identification, and U.S. Latino Population Change," unpublished paper, July 22, 2005, 4.

40. Gregory Rodriguez, "Mongrel America," *Atlantic Monthly*, January–February 2003, 95.

41. Ibid.

42. Rodriguez, "Forging a New Vision of America's Melting Pot," 1.

43. Milton M. Gordon, *Assimilation in American Life: The Role of Race, Religion, and National Origins* (New York: Oxford University Press, 1964), 106.

44. Rodolfo O. de la Garza with Fujia Lu, "Explorations into Latino Voluntarism," in *Nuevos Senderos: Reflections on Hispanics and Philanthropy,* eds. Diana Campoamor, William A. Díaz, and Henry A. J. Ramos (Houston: Arte Público, 1999), 74.

45. Rodolfo O. de la Garza, Louis DeSipio, F. Chris García, and Angelo Falcón, *Latino Voices: Mexican, Puerto Rican, and Cuban Perspectives on American Politics* (Boulder: Westview, 1992), 135–36.

46. Amy Goldstein and Roberto Suro, "A Journey in Stages: Assimilation's Pull Is Still Strong, but Its Pace Varies," *Washington Post,* January 16, 2000, A1.

47. Antonio Villaraigosa, "Inaugural Address," July 1, 2005. (Passage translated by Gregory Rodriguez.)

48. J. Hector St. John de Crèvecoeur, *Letters from an American Farmer and Sketches of 18th-Century America* (New York: Penguin, 1986), 70.

49. Israel Zangwill, "Afterword," in *The Melting-Pot: Drama in Four Acts* (New York: Macmillan, 1923), 207.

ONE: THE BIRTH OF A PEOPLE

1. Hugh Thomas, *Conquest: Montezuma, Cortés, and the Fall of Old Mexico* (New York: Simon & Schuster, 1993), 162.

2. Ibid., 164.

3. Bernal Díaz, *The Conquest of New Spain* (New York: Penguin, 1963), 60.

4. Ibid.

5. Ibid., 61.

6. Ibid.

7. Díaz del Castillo, *Historia verdadera de la conquista de la Nueva España* (Barcelona: Editorial Planeta, 1992), 74.

8. Thomas, *Conquest,* xiii.

9. Lewis Hanke, *The Spanish Struggle for Justice in the Conquest of America* (Boston: Little, Brown, 1965), 7.

10. Ibid.

11. Sarah Cline, "The Spiritual Conquest Reexamined: Baptism and Christian Marriage in Early Sixteenth-Century Mexico," *Hispanic American Historical Review* 73, no. 3 (1993), 455.

12. Lewis Hanke, *Aristotle and the American Indians* (London: Hollis and Carter, 1959), 19.

13. Thomas, *Conquest,* xii.

14. C. E. Marshall, "The Birth of the Mestizo in New Spain," *Hispanic American Historical Review* 19, no. 2 (May 1939): 162.

15. Thomas, *Conquest,* 158.

16. R. C. Padden, *The Hummingbird and the Hawk: Conquest and Sovereignty in the Valley of Mexico, 1503–1541* (New York: Harper Torchbooks, 1970), 229.

17. Thomas, *Conquest,* 170.
18. Díaz, *The Conquest of New Spain,* 80.
19. Ibid., 82.
20. Frances Karttunen, "Rethinking Malinche," in *Indian Women of Early Mexico,* eds. Susan Schroeder, Stephanie Wood, and Robert Haskett (Norman: University of Oklahoma Press, 1997), 302.
21. Julia Tuñón Pablos, *Women in Mexico: A Past Unveiled* (Austin: University of Texas Press, 1999), 17.
22. Frances Karttunen, "La Malinche and *Malinchismo,*" in *Encyclopedia of Mexico: History, Society and Culture,* ed. Michael S. Werner (Chicago: Fitzroy Dearborn, 1997), 776.
23. James Lockhart, *Nahuas and Spaniards: Postconquest Central Mexican History and Philology* (Stanford: Stanford University Press; and Los Angeles: UCLA Latin American Center, 1991), 9.
24. Karttunen, "Rethinking Malinche," 304.
25. Tzvetan Todorov, *The Conquest of America: The Question of the Other* (Norman: University of Oklahoma Press, 1999), 58.
26. Ibid.
27. Díaz, *The Conquest of New Spain,* 108.
28. Ibid.
29. Thomas, *Conquest,* 113.
30. Díaz, *The Conquest of New Spain,* 121.
31. Ibid.
32. Ibid.
33. Ibid.
34. Ibid.
35. Ibid., 122.
36. Thomas, *Conquest,* 213.
37. Díaz, *The Conquest of New Spain,* 125.
38. Ibid.
39. Diego Muñoz Camargo, *Historia de Tlaxcala* (Mexico City: Oficina Tipográfica de la Secretaría de Formento, 1892), 190 (passage translated by Manuel H. Rodríguez).
40. Ibid., 191.
41. Ibid.
42. Díaz, *The Conquest of New Spain,* 176.
43. Ibid., 178.
44. Thomas, *Conquest,* 255.
45. Díaz, *The Conquest of New Spain,* 186.
46. Pedro Carrasco, "Indian Spanish Marriages in the First Century of the Colony," in *Indian Women of Early Mexico,* eds. Susan Schroeder, Stephanie Wood, and Robert Haskett (Norman: University of Oklahoma Press, 1997), 90.
47. Muñoz Camargo, *Historia de Tlaxcala,* 192.
48. Asunción Lavrin, "Women in Colonial Mexico," in *The Oxford History of Mexico,* eds. Michael C. Meyer and William H. Beezly (New York: Oxford University Press, 2000), 250.

49. Díaz, *The Conquest of New Spain,* 108.
50. Magnus Mörner, *Race Mixture in the History of Latin America* (Boston: Little, Brown, 1967), 14.
51. Lavrin, "Women in Colonial Mexico," 250.
52. Michael Meyer and William Sherman, *The Course of Mexican History,* 5th ed. (New York: Oxford University Press, 1995), 208.
53. Lavrin, "Women in Colonial Mexico," 249.
54. Meyer and Sherman, *The Course of Mexican History,* 209.
55. Padden, *The Hummingbird and the Hawk,* 230.
56. Richard Konetzke, "El mestizaje y su importancia en el desarrollo de la población hispano-americana durante la época colonial," *Revista de Indias* 7, no. 23 (1946): 27.
57. Ibid., 28.
58. Ibid.
59. Mörner, *Race Mixture in the History of Latin America,* 27.
60. Ramón Eduardo Ruíz, *Triumphs and Tragedy: A History of the Mexican People* (New York: W. W. Norton, 1992), 47.
61. Richard F. Townsend, *The Aztecs,* rev. ed. (London: Thames & Hudson, 2001), 24.
62. Thomas, *Conquest,* 264.
63. Miguel León-Portilla, ed., *The Broken Spears: The Aztec Account of the Conquest of Mexico* (Boston: Beacon, 1969), 41.
64. Thomas, *Conquest,* 271.
65. Townsend, *The Aztecs,* 28.
66. Díaz, *The Conquest of New Spain,* 214.
67. Hernán Cortés, *Letters from Mexico,* trans. and ed. Anthony Pagden (New Haven: Yale University Press, 1986), 101–2.
68. León Portilla, *The Broken Spears,* xix.
69. Thomas, *Conquest,* 11.
70. Colin M. MacLachlan and Jaime E. Rodríguez O., *The Forging of the Cosmic Race: A Reinterpretation of Colonial Mexico* (Berkeley: University of California Press, 1980), 62.
71. Townsend, *The Aztecs,* 116.
72. Ross Hassig, "The Collision of Two Worlds," in *The Oxford History of Mexico,* eds. Michael C. Meyer and William H. Beezley (New York: Oxford University Press, 2000), 80.
73. Meyer and Sherman, *The Course of Mexican History,* 91.
74. Díaz, *The Conquest of New Spain,* 219.
75. Hassig, "The Collision of Two Worlds," 94.
76. Thomas, *Conquest,* 305.
77. Padden, *The Hummingbird and the Hawk,* 229.
78. Díaz, *The Conquest of New Spain,* 254.
79. Thomas, *Conquest,* 436.
80. José Pérez de Barradas, *Los mestizos de América* (Madrid: Espasa-Calpe, 1976), 129 (passage translated by Manuel H. Rodríguez).
81. Ibid.

82. Díaz, *The Conquest of New Spain*, 310.

83. Pérez de Barradas, *Los mestizos de América*, 129.

84. Thomas, *Conquest*, 473.

85. Ibid., 444.

86. Ruiz, *Triumphs and Tragedy*, 52.

87. Hassig, "The Collision of Two Worlds," 112.

88. Thomas, *Conquest*, 528.

89. Díaz, *The Conquest of New Spain*, 408.

90. Ibid., 409.

91. Carrasco, "Indian Spanish Marriages in the First Century of the Colony," 88.

92. Ibid.

93. Ibid.

94. Meyer and Sherman, *The Course of Mexican History*, 208.

95. Ibid.

96. Richard Konetzke, "El mestizaje y su importancia en el desarrollo de la población hispano-americana durante la época colonial," 215–16.

97. Mörner, *Race Mixture in the History of Latin America*, 37.

98. Pérez de Barradas, *Los mestizos de América*, 91.

99. Ibid.

100. Mörner, *Race Mixture in the History of Latin America*, 37.

101. Ibid.

102. Lavrin, "Women in Colonial Mexico," 250.

103. Carrasco, "Indian Spanish Marriages in the First Century of the Colony," 102.

104. Pérez de Barradas, *Los mestizos de América*, 132.

105. Mörner, *Race Mixture in the History of Latin America*, 25.

106. Konetzke, "El mestizaje y su importancia en el desarrollo de la población hispano-americana durante la época colonial," 218.

107. Mörner, *Race Mixture in the History of Latin America*, 25.

108. Ibid.

109. Marshall, "The Birth of the Mestizo in New Spain," 174.

110. Thomas, *Conquest*, 577.

111. Meyer and Sherman, *The Course of Mexican History*, 131.

112. Marshall, "The Birth of the Mestizo in New Spain," 173.

113. Meyer and Sherman, *The Course of Mexican History*, 205.

114. Charles Gibson, *Spain in America* (New York: Harper & Row, 1966), 116.

115. Marshall, "The Birth of the Mestizo in New Spain," 175.

116. Juan de Solórzano Pereira, "The Mestizo," in *Readings in Latin American Civilization, 1492 to the Present*, ed. Benjamin Keen (Boston: Houghton Mifflin, 1967), 125.

117. Marshall, "The Birth of the Mestizo in New Spain," 174.

118. J. I. Israel, *Race, Class and Politics in Colonial Mexico, 1610–1670* (London: Oxford University Press, 1975), 61–62.

119. Ibid., 62.

120. Ibid.

121. R. Douglas Cope, *The Limits of Racial Domination: Plebeian Society in Colo-*

nial Mexico City, 1660–1720 (Madison: University of Wisconsin Press, 1994), 14–15.

122. Peggy K. Liss, *Mexico Under Spain, 1521–1556: Society and the Origins of Nationality* (Chicago: University of Chicago Press, 1975), 136.

123. Pérez de Barradas, *Los mestizos de América*, 133.

124. Gibson, *Spain in America*, 116, footnote.

125. Cope, *The Limits of Racial Domination*, 16.

126. Israel, *Race, Class and Politics in Colonial Mexico*, 65.

127. MacLachlan and Rodríguez O., *The Forging of the Cosmic Race*, 216–17.

128. Israel, *Race, Class and Politics in Colonial Mexico*, 66.

129. Ibid., 64.

130. Cope, *The Limits of Racial Domination*, 13.

131. MacLachlan and Rodríguez O., *The Forging of the Cosmic Race*, 218.

132. Marshall, "The Birth of the Mestizo in New Spain," 172.

133. Mörner, *Race Mixture in the History of Latin America*, 38.

134. MacLachlan and Rodríguez O., *The Forging of the Cosmic Race*, 221.

135. Marshall, "The Birth of the Mestizo in New Spain," 173.

136. Patricia Seed, *To Love, Honor, and Obey in Colonial Mexico: Conflicts over Marriage Choice, 1574–1821* (Stanford: Stanford University Press, 1988), 23–24.

137. Israel, *Race, Class and Politics in Colonial Mexico*, 63.

138. Liss, *Mexico Under Spain*, 142.

139. Ibid., 142–43.

140. Ibid., 142.

141. Cope, *The Limits of Racial Domination*, 15.

142. Ibid.

143. Israel, *Race, Class and Politics in Colonial Mexico*, 60.

144. Ibid., 66.

145. Ibid.

146. Eric R. Wolf, *Sons of the Shaking Earth* (Chicago: University of Chicago Press, 1959), 238.

147. Gibson, *Spain in America*, 116.

148. Wolf, *Sons of the Shaking Earth*, 238.

149. Ibid.

150. Ibid., 239.

151. MacLachlan and Rodríguez O., *The Forging of the Cosmic Race*, 217.

152. Pérez de Barradas, *Los mestizos de América*, 134.

153. Cope, *The Limits of Racial Domination*, 15.

154. Magnus Mörner and Charles Gibson, "Diego Muñoz Camargo and the Segregation Policy of the Spanish Crown," *Hispanic American Historical Review* 42, no. 4 (November 1962): 560.

155. Cope, *The Limits of Racial Domination*, 15.

156. Marshall, "The Birth of the Mestizo in New Spain," 182.

157. Ibid., 179.

TWO: THE RISE AND FALL OF THE
SPANISH COLONIAL RACIAL SYSTEM

1. Jacques Lafaye, *Quetzalcóatl and Guadalupe: The Formation of Mexican National Consciousness, 1531–1813* (Chicago: University of Chicago Press, 1976), xviii.

2. Antonio Valeriano, "Nican Mopohua: Narración de las apariciones guadalupanas," translated into Spanish by Primo Feliciano Velázquez, 2. This is a pamphlet.

3. Ibid.

4. Stafford Poole, C.M., *Our Lady of Guadalupe: The Origins and Sources of a Mexican National Symbol, 1531–1797* (Tucson: University of Arizona Press, 1997), 27.

5. Charles Gibson, *The Aztecs Under Spanish Rule: A History of the Indians of the Valley of Mexico, 1519–1810* (Stanford: Stanford University Press, 1964), 133.

6. Enrique Florescano, *Memory, Myth, and Time in Mexico: From the Aztecs to Independence* (Austin: University of Texas Press, 1994), 132.

7. Ibid., 144.

8. Lafaye, *Quetzalcóatl and Guadalupe*, xix.

9. Florescano, *Memory, Myth, and Time in Mexico*, 143.

10. Ibid.

11. Ibid., 133.

12. Lafaye, *Quetzalcóatl and Guadalupe*, 216.

13. Florescano, *Memory, Myth, and Time in Mexico*, 231.

14. Virgilio Elizondo, *Galilean Journey: The Mexican-American Promise* (Maryknoll, N.Y.: Orbis, 1983), 12.

15. Lafaye, *Quetzalcóatl and Guadalupe*, 288.

16. James Lockhart, *Nahuas and Spaniards: Postconquest Central Mexican History and Philology* (Stanford: Stanford University Press; and Los Angeles: UCLA Latin American Center, 1991), 21.

17. Hugo G. Nutini and Betty Bell, *Ritual Kinship: The Structure and Historical Development of the Compadrazgo System in Rural Tlaxcala*, Vol. 1 (Princeton: Princeton University Press, 1980), 290–91.

18. Linda Curcio-Nagy, "Faith and Morals in Colonial Mexico," in *The Oxford History of Mexico*, eds. Michael C. Meyer and William H. Beezly (New York: Oxford University Press, 2000), 159.

19. J. Jorge Klor de Alva, "Spiritual Conflict and Accommodation in New Spain: Toward a Typology of Aztec Responses to Christianity," in *The Inca and Aztec States, 1400–1800: Anthropology and History*, eds. George A. Collier, Renato I. Rosaldo, and John D. Wirth (New York: Academic Press, 1982), 353.

20. Robert Ricard, *The Spiritual Conquest of Mexico* (Berkeley: University of California Press, 1966), 97.

21. Woodrow Borah, "Discontinuity and Continuity in Mexican History," *Pacific Historical Review* 48, no. 1 (1979): 12.

22. Ricard, *The Spiritual Conquest of Mexico*, 291.

23. Michael Meyer and William Sherman, *The Course of Mexican History*, 5th ed. (New York: Oxford University Press, 1995), 149.

24. Curcio-Nagy, "Faith and Morals in Colonial Mexico," 155.

25. Magnus Mörner, *Race Mixture in the History of Latin America* (Boston: Little, Brown, 1967), 46.

26. Ibid., 47.

27. Magnus Mörner and Charles Gibson, "Diego Muñoz Camargo and the Segregation Policy of the Spanish Crown," *Hispanic American Historical Review*, 42, no. 4 (November 1962): 562.

28. George Kubler, *Mexican Architecture of the Sixteenth Century*, Vol. 1 (New Haven: Yale University Press, 1948), 66.

29. Ibid., 49.

30. Florescano, *Memory, Myth, and Time in Mexico*, 112.

31. Ibid., 113.

32. Mörner and Gibson, "Diego Muñoz Camargo and the Segregation Policy of the Spanish Crown," 562.

33. Mörner, *Race Mixture in the History of Latin America*, 31.

34. Borah, "Discontinuity and Continuity in Mexican History," 11.

35. Eric R. Wolf, *Sons of the Shaking Earth* (Chicago: University of Chicago Press, 1959), 196.

36. Colin M. MacLachlan and Jaime E. Rodríguez O., *The Forging of the Cosmic Race: A Reinterpretation of Colonial Mexico* (Berkeley: University of California Press, 1980), 202.

37. Mörner, *Race Mixture in the History of Latin America*, 12.

38. J. I. Israel, *Race, Class and Politics in Colonial Mexico, 1610–1670* (London: Oxford University Press, 1975), 13.

39. Kubler, *Mexican Architecture of the Sixteenth Century*, Vol. 1, 50.

40. Enrique Krauze, *Mexico: Biography of Power: A History of Modern Mexico, 1810–1996* (New York: HarperCollins, 1997), 53.

41. Israel, *Race, Class and Politics in Colonial Mexico*, 13.

42. MacLachlan and Rodríguez O., *The Forging of the Cosmic Race*, 202.

43. Ibid., 168.

44. Ibid., 202.

45. Israel, *Race, Class and Politics in Colonial Mexico*, 56.

46. Woodrow Borah, *New Spain's Century of Depression* (Berkeley: University of California Press, 1951), 41.

47. Israel, *Race, Class and Politics in Colonial Mexico*, 41.

48. James Lockhart, *The Nahuas After the Conquest: A Social and Cultural History of the Indians of Central Mexico, Sixteenth Through Eighteenth Centuries* (Palo Alto: Stanford University Press, 1992), 431.

49. Ibid.

50. Borah, *New Spain's Century of Depression*, 41–42.

51. R. Douglas Cope, *The Limits of Racial Domination: Plebeian Society in Colonial Mexico City, 1660–1720* (Madison: University of Wisconsin Press, 1994), 91.

52. Cope, *The Limits of Racial Domination*, 92.

53. Israel, *Race, Class and Politics in Colonial Mexico,* 57.

54. Cope, *The Limits of Racial Domination,* 92.

55. Ibid.

56. Ibid.

57. Israel, *Race, Class and Politics in Colonial Mexico,* 56.

58. Ibid., 56–57.

59. Marvin Harris, *Patterns of Race in the Americas* (New York: Walker, 1964), 38.

60. Ibid., 38–39.

61. Lockhart, *The Nahuas After the Conquest,* 433.

62. Borah, "Discontinuity and Continuity in Mexican History," 11.

63. Mörner, *Race Mixture in the History of Latin America,* 31.

64. Lockhart, *The Nahuas After the Conquest,* 434–35.

65. J. Ignacio Dávila Garibi, "Posible influencia del nahuatl en el uso y abuso del diminutivo en el español de México," *Estudios de Cultura Nahuatl* 1 (1959): 94.

66. Hugh Thomas, *Conquest: Montezuma, Cortés, and the Fall of Old Mexico* (New York: Simon & Schuster, 1993), 44.

67. Krauze, *Mexico: Biography of Power,* 58.

68. MacLachlan and Rodríguez O., *The Forging of the Cosmic Race,* 200.

69. Ilona Katzew, *Casta Painting: Images of Race in Eighteenth-Century Mexico* (New Haven: Yale University Press, 2004), 39.

70. Cope, *The Limits of Racial Domination,* 23.

71. Ibid., 20.

72. Ibid., 24.

73. Asunción Lavrin, "Women in Colonial Mexico," in *The Oxford History of Mexico,* eds. Michael C. Meyer and William H. Beezly (New York: Oxford University Press, 2000), 251.

74. Cope, *The Limits of Racial Domination,* 24.

75. Mörner, *Race Mixture in the History of Latin America,* 58.

76. Katzew, *Casta Painting,* 51.

77. Ibid., 93.

78. Lavrin, "Women in Colonial Mexico," 251.

79. Patricia Seed, *To Love, Honor, and Obey in Colonial Mexico: Conflicts over Marriage Choice, 1574–1821* (Stanford: Stanford University Press, 1988), 231.

80. Cope, *The Limits of Racial Domination,* 161.

81. Lavrin, "Women in Colonial Mexico," 252.

82. Cope, *The Limits of Racial Domination,* 25.

83. Lavrin, "Women in Colonial Mexico," 262.

84. Thomas Calvo, "The Warmth of the Hearth: Seventeenth-Century Guadalajara," in *Sexuality and Marriage in Colonial Latin America,* ed. Asunción Lavrin (Lincoln: University of Nebraska Press, 1989), 292.

85. Cope, *The Limits of Racial Domination,* 84–85.

86. Ibid., 78.

87. Dennis Nodin Valdés, "The Decline of the Sociedad de Castas in Mexico City" (Ph.D. diss., University of Michigan, 1978), 188.

88. Ibid.
89. Mörner, *Race Mixture in the History of Latin America,* 69.
90. Cope, *The Limits of Racial Domination,* 24.
91. Ibid.
92. Ibid., 52–53.
93. Ibid., 53.
94. Ibid.
95. Valdés, "The Decline of the Sociedad de Castas in Mexico City," 182.
96. Ibid.
97. Cope, *The Limits of Racial Domination,* 53.
98. Valdés, "The Decline of the Sociedad de Castas in Mexico City," 185.
99. Ibid., 184.
100. Calvo, "The Warmth of the Hearth: Seventeenth-Century Guadalajara," 297.
101. Seed, *To Love, Honor, and Obey in Colonial Mexico,* 98.
102. Cope, *The Limits of Racial Domination,* 89.
103. Ibid., 120.
104. MacLachlan and Rodríguez O., *The Forging of the Cosmic Race,* 201.
105. Seed, *To Love, Honor, and Obey in Colonial Mexico,* 151.
106. Ibid., 146.
107. Ibid., 147.
108. Ibid.
109. Ibid.
110. Lavrin, "Women in Colonial Mexico," 254.
111. Ibid.
112. Seed, *To Love, Honor, and Obey in Colonial Mexico,* 221.
113. Ibid.
114. Pierre L. van den Berghe, *Race and Racism: A Comparative Perspective* (New York: John Wiley & Sons, 1967), 53.

THREE: THE SPANIARDS VENTURE NORTH

1. Herbert E. Bolton, *The Spanish Borderlands* (Albuquerque: University of New Mexico Press, 1996), 171.
2. David J. Weber, *The Spanish Frontier in North America* (New Haven: Yale University Press, 1992), 77.
3. John F. Bannon, *The Spanish Borderlands Frontier, 1513–1821* (Albuquerque: University of New Mexico Press, 1979), 39.
4. Bolton, *The Spanish Borderlands,* 178.
5. Ramón A. Gutiérrez, *When Jesus Came, the Corn Mothers Went Away: Marriage, Sexuality, and Power in New Mexico, 1500–1846* (Stanford: Stanford University Press, 1991), 103–4.
6. Ibid., 103.
7. Ibid.
8. Ibid.
9. Ibid., 152.

10. Ibid., 156.

11. Weber, *The Spanish Frontier in North America*, 332.

12. Oakah L. Jones, Jr., *Los Paisanos: Spanish Settlers on the Northern Frontier of New Spain* (Norman: University of Oklahoma Press, 1979), 132.

13. Frances V. Scholes, "Civil Government and Society in New Mexico in the 17th Century," *New Mexico Historical Review* 10, no. 2 (April 1935): 98.

14. Weber, *The Spanish Frontier in North America*, 327.

15. Ibid., 332.

16. Antonio Ríos-Bustamante, "New Mexico in the Eighteenth Century: Life, Labor and Trade in the Villa de San Felipe de Albuquerque, 1706–1790," *Aztlán* 7 (Fall 1976): 380.

17. James E. Officer, *Hispanic Arizona, 1536–1856* (Tucson: University of Arizona Press, 1987), 41.

18. Martha Menchaca, *Recovering History, Constructing Race: The Indian, Black, and White Roots of Mexican Americans* (Austin: University of Texas Press, 2001), 104.

19. Andrés Tijerina, *Tejanos and Texas Under the Mexican Flag, 1821–1836* (College Station: Texas A&M University Press, 1994), 8.

20. Menchaca, *Recovering History, Constructing Race*, 66.

21. Weber, *The Spanish Frontier in North America*, 327.

22. Ibid., 247.

23. Ibid.

24. Douglas Monroy, *Thrown Among Strangers: The Making of Mexican Culture in Frontier California* (Berkeley: University of California Press, 1990), 81.

25. Ibid., 83.

26. Antonia I. Castañeda, "Engendering the History of Alta California, 1769–1848: Gender, Sexuality, and the Family," in *Contested Eden: California Before the Gold Rush*, eds. Ramón A. Gutiérrez and Richard J. Orsi (Berkeley: University of California Press, 1998), 239.

27. Ibid., 241.

28. Charles E. Chapman, *A History of California: The Spanish Period* (New York: Macmillan, 1928), 303.

29. Jack D. Forbes, "Black Pioneers: The Spanish-Speaking Afroamericans of the Southwest," *Phylon: The Atlanta University Review of Race and Culture* 27, no. 3 (Fall 1966): 236.

30. Weber, *The Spanish Frontier in North America*, 327.

31. Jack D. Forbes, "Black Pioneers: The Spanish-Speaking Afroamericans of the Southwest," 236.

32. Ibid.

33. Weber, *The Spanish Frontier in North America*, 307.

34. William Mason, "Indian-Mexican Cultural Exchange in the Los Angeles Area, 1781–1834," *Aztlán* 15, no. 1 (Spring 1984): 129.

35. Ibid.

36. Ibid., 131.

37. Ibid., 133–34.

38. Ibid., 135.

39. Monroy, *Thrown Among Strangers,* 106.

40. Menchaca, *Recovering History, Constructing Race,* 141–42.

41. Manuel G. Gonzales, *Mexicanos: A History of Mexicans in the United States* (Bloomington: Indiana University Press, 1999), 46.

42. Weber, *The Spanish Frontier in North America,* 265.

43. Forbes, "Black Pioneers: The Spanish-Speaking Afroamericans of the Southwest," 25.

44. Richard H. Dana, *Two Years Before the Mast: A Personal Narrative of Life at Sea* (New York: Modern Library, 2001), 87.

45. Menchaca, *Recovering History, Constructing Race,* 157–59.

46. D. A. Brading, *The Origins of Mexican Nationalism* (Cambridge, U.K.: Centre of Latin American Studies, 1985), 3.

47. Gutiérrez, *When Jesus Came, the Corn Mothers Went Away,* 193.

48. David J. Weber, *The Mexican Frontier, 1821–1846: The American Southwest Under Mexico* (Albuquerque: University of New Mexico Press, 1982), 162.

49. Rebecca McDowell Craver, *The Impact of Intimacy: Mexican-Anglo Intermarriage in New Mexico, 1821–1846* (El Paso: Texas Western Press, 1982), 27–28.

50. Eugene C. Barker, "Native Latin American Contributions to the Colonization and Independence of Texas," *Southwestern Historical Quarterly* 46, no. 3 (January 1943): 328–29.

51. Weber, *The Mexican Frontier,* 176.

52. David J. Weber, ed., *Foreigners in Their Native Land: Historical Roots of the Mexican Americans* (Albuquerque: University of New Mexico Press, 1973), 81.

53. Jane Dysart, "Mexican Women in San Antonio, 1830–1860: The Assimilation Process," *Western Historical Quarterly* 7, no. 4 (October 1976): 370.

54. Weber, *The Mexican Frontier,* 239.

55. Ibid., 166.

56. Craver, *The Impact of Intimacy,* 75.

57. Ibid., 2.

58. Ibid., 8.

59. Ibid., 9.

60. Ibid., 46.

61. Weber, *The Mexican Frontier,* 183.

62. Monroy, *Thrown Among Strangers,* 163.

63. Weber, *The Mexican Frontier,* 204.

64. Ibid.

65. Alan Rosenus, *General Vallejo and the Advent of the Americans* (Berkeley: Urion, 1999), 41.

66. Weber, *The Mexican Frontier,* 239.

67. Ibid., 240.

68. Menchaca, *Recovering History, Constructing Race,* 209.

FOUR: MEXICANS AND THE LIMITS OF SLAVERY

1. Colin M. MacLachlan and Jaime E. Rodriguez O., *The Forging of the Cosmic Race: A Reinterpretation of Colonial Mexico* (Berkeley: University of California Press, 1990), 218.

2. David J. Weber, ed., *Foreigners in Their Native Land: Historical Roots of the Mexican Americans* (Albuquerque: University of New Mexico Press, 1973), 17.

3. Eugene C. Barker, *Mexico and Texas* (Dallas: P. L. Turner, 1928), 86.

4. Randolph B. Campbell, *An Empire for Slavery: The Peculiar Institution in Texas, 1821–1865* (Baton Rouge: Louisiana State University Press, 1989), 21.

5. David J. Weber, *The Mexican Frontier, 1821–1846: The American Southwest Under Mexico* (Albuquerque: University of New Mexico Press, 1982), 213.

6. Ibid., 214.

7. Ibid.

8. Ibid., 214–15.

9. Campbell, *An Empire for Slavery,* 42.

10. Ibid.

11. Frederick Law Olmsted, *A Journey Through Texas, Or a Saddle-Trip on the Southwestern Frontier* (Austin: University of Texas Press, 1982), 65.

12. Ibid., 163.

13. Paul Schuster Taylor, *An American-Mexican Frontier: Nueces County, Texas* (Chapel Hill: University of North Carolina Press, 1934), 33.

14. Campbell, *An Empire for Slavery,* 63–64.

15. Taylor, *An American-Mexican Frontier,* 37.

16. Arnoldo de León, *They Called Them Greasers: Anglo Attitudes Toward Mexicans in Texas, 1821–1900* (Austin: University of Texas Press, 1983), 50.

17. Ibid., 52.

18. Ibid.

19. Campbell, *An Empire for Slavery,* 219.

20. Olmsted, *A Journey Through Texas,* 456.

21. Campbell, *An Empire for Slavery,* 64.

22. Ibid., 180.

23. Rosalie Schwartz, *Across the Rio to Freedom: U.S. Negroes in Mexico* (El Paso: Texas Western Press, 1975), 26.

24. Ibid.

25. Olmsted, *A Journey Through Texas,* 325.

26. John Hope Franklin and Alfred A. Moss, Jr., *From Slavery to Freedom: A History of African Americans,* 7th ed. (New York: McGraw Hill, 1994), 149.

27. Thomas R. Hietala, *Manifest Design: Anxious Aggrandizement in Late Jacksonian America* (Ithaca: Cornell University Press, 1985), 33–34.

28. Ibid.

29. Ibid.

30. Gerald M. Capers, *John C. Calhoun: Opportunist: A Reappraisal* (Chicago: Quadrangle, 1969), 233.

31. Ralph Waldo Emerson, *The Journals and Miscellaneous Notebooks of Ralph*

Waldo Emerson, Vol. 9, 1843–1847, ed. Ralph H. Orth and Alfred R. Ferguson (Cambridge: Harvard University Press, 1971), 430.

32. David M. Potter (completed and edited by Don E. Fehrenbacher), *The Impending Crisis, 1848–1861* (New York: Harper Colophon, 1976), 19.

33. Ibid., 20.

34. Bernard DeVoto, *The Year of Decision, 1846* (New York: St. Martin's Griffin, 2000), 297–98.

35. Potter, *The Impending Crisis,* 22.

36. James M. McPherson, *Battle Cry of Freedom: The Civil War Era* (New York: Ballantine, 1989), 50.

37. Transcript, Speech of Mr. Fowler of Massachusetts, Delivered in the House of Representatives, March 11, 1850, 8.

38. McPherson, *Battle Cry of Freedom,* 57.

39. DeVoto, *The Year of Decision, 1846,* 298–99.

40. Transcript, Speech of Mr. Jas. Wilson, of N. Hampshire on The Political Influence of Slavery, and the Expediency of Permitting Slavery in the Territories Recently Acquired from Mexico, Delivered in the House of Representatives, February 16, 1849, 15.

41. McPherson, *The Battle Cry of Freedom,* 76.

42. Oscar J. Martínez, *Troublesome Border* (Tucson: University of Arizona Press, 1988), 80.

43. Reginald Horsman, *Race and Manifest Destiny: The Origins of American Racial Anglo-Saxonism* (Cambridge: Harvard University Press, 1981), 238.

44. Ibid., 243–44.

45. Hietala, *Manifest Design,* 155.

46. Horsman, *Race and Manifest Destiny,* 241.

47. Ibid., 246.

48. Hietala, *Manifest Design,* 163.

49. Horsman, *Race and Manifest Destiny,* 241.

50. Ibid., 239.

51. Hietala, *Manifest Design,* 155.

52. Weber, *Foreigners in Their Native Land,* 135.

53. Ibid., 137.

54. Ibid.

55. Ibid., 135.

56. Horsman, *Race and Manifest Destiny,* 276.

57. Ibid., 213.

58. Ibid., 247.

59. Neil Foley, *The White Scourge: Mexicans, Blacks and Poor Whites in Texas Cotton Culture* (Berkeley: University of California Press, 1999), 21.

FIVE: THE ANGLOS MOVE WEST

1. Michael C. Meyer and William L. Sherman, *The Course of Mexican History,* 5th ed. (New York: Oxford University Press, 1995), 345.

2. John S. D. Eisenhower, *So Far from God: The U.S. War with Mexico, 1846–1848* (New York: Anchor, 1989), 369.

3. Manuel G. Gonzales, *Mexicanos: A History of Mexicans in the United States* (Bloomington: Indiana University Press, 1999), 79.

4. George I. Sánchez, *Forgotten People: A Study of New Mexicans* (Albuquerque: Calvin Horn, 1967), 16.

5. Robert J. Rosenbaum, *Mexicano Resistance in the Southwest: The Sacred Right of Self-Preservation* (Austin: University of Texas Press, 1981), 9.

6. Patricia Nelson Limerick, *The Legacy of Conquest: The Unbroken Past of the American West* (New York: W. W. Norton, 1987), 231.

7. James Officer, "Historical Factors in Interethnic Relations in the Community of Tucson," *Arizoniana* 1, no. 3 (Fall 1960): 13.

8. Ibid.

9. David J. Weber, ed., *Foreigners in Their Native Land: Historical Roots of the Mexican Americans* (Albuquerque: University of New Mexico Press, 1973), 131.

10. Ibid., 130–31.

11. Richard Griswold del Castillo, *The Los Angeles Barrio, 1850–1890: A Social History* (Berkeley: University of California Press, 1979), 27.

12. Rosenbaum, *Mexicano Resistance in the Southwest*, 14.

13. Ibid.

14. Richard Griswold del Castillo and Arnoldo de León, *North to Aztlán: A History of Mexican Americans in the United States* (New York: Twayne, 1997), 32.

15. Rosenbaum, *Mexicano Resistance in the Southwest*, 27.

16. Paul S. Taylor, *An American-Mexican Frontier: Nueces County, Texas* (Chapel Hill: University of North Carolina Press, 1934), 65.

17. S. Dale McLemore and Ricardo Romo, "The Origins and Development of the Mexican American People," in *The Mexican American Experience: An Interdisciplinary Anthology*, eds. Rodolfo O. de la Garza, Frank D. Bean, Charles M. Bonjean, Ricardo Romo, and Rodolfo Alvarez (Austin: University of Texas Press, 1985), 11.

18. Gonzales, *Mexicanos*, 108.

19. Ibid., 109.

20. Rosenbaum, *Mexicano Resistance in the Southwest*, 153.

21. Ibid., 151.

22. Manuel G. Gonzales, *The Hispanic Elite of the Southwest* (El Paso: Texas Western Press, 1989), 18.

23. Ibid., 19.

24. Weber, *Foreigners in Their Native Land*, 125–27.

25. Gonzales, *The Hispanic Elite of the Southwest*, 14.

26. David Montejano, *Anglos and Mexicans in the Making of Texas, 1836–1986* (Austin: University of Texas Press, 1997), 27.

27. Leonard Pitt, *The Decline of the Californios: A Social History of the Spanish-Speaking Californians, 1846–1890* (Berkeley: University of California Press, 1970), 278.

28. Weber, *Foreigners in Their Native Land,* 163–64.

29. Tomás Almaguer, *Racial Fault Lines: The Historical Origins of White Supremacy in California* (Berkeley: University of California Press, 1994), 70.

30. Weber, *Foreigners in Their Native Land,* 148.

31. Pitt, *The Decline of the Californios,* 42.

32. Almaguer, *Racial Fault Lines,* 65.

33. Ibid., 48.

34. Martha Menchaca interview with Gregory Rodriguez, July 2001.

35. Griswold del Castillo and de León, *North to Aztlán,* 23.

36. Weber, *Foreigners in Their Native Land,* 151.

37. Albert Camarillo, *Chicanos in a Changing Society: From Mexican Pueblos to American Barrios in Santa Barbara and Southern California, 1848–1930* (Cambridge: Harvard University Press, 1996), 25.

38. Ibid., 53.

39. Griswold del Castillo, *The Los Angeles Barrio,* 105.

40. Pitt, *The Decline of the Californios,* 169.

41. Griswold del Castillo, *The Los Angeles Barrio,* 113.

42. Pitt, *The Decline of the Californios,* 174.

43. Ronald C. Woolsey, "Rites of Passage? Anglo and Mexican-American Contrasts in a Time of Change: Los Angeles, 1860–1870," *Southern California Quarterly* 69, no. 2 (Summer 1987): 82.

44. Martha Menchaca, *Recovering History, Constructing Race: The Indian, Black, and White Roots of Mexican Americans* (Austin: University of Texas Press, 2001), 223.

45. Griswold del Castillo, *The Los Angeles Barrio,* 75.

46. Richard Griswold del Castillo, *La Familia: Chicano Families in the Urban Southwest, 1848 to the Present* (Notre Dame: University of Notre Dame Press, 1984), 66–67.

47. Pitt, *The Decline of the Californios,* 125.

48. Ibid., 125.

49. Ibid., 269.

50. Almaguer, *Racial Fault Lines,* 71.

51. Griswold del Castillo, *The Los Angeles Barrio,* 124.

52. Ibid., 134.

53. Ibid., 151.

54. Ibid.

55. Ibid., 152–53.

56. Griswold del Castillo and De Leon, *North to Aztlán,* 33.

57. Darlis A. Miller, "Cross-Cultural Marriages in the Southwest: The New Mexico Experience, 1846–1900," in *New Mexico Women: Intercultural Perspectives,* eds. Joan M. Jensen and Darlis A. Miller (Albuquerque: University of New Mexico Press, 1986), 100.

58. Ibid., 106.

59. Ibid., 100.

60. Rosenbaum, *Mexicano Resistance in the Southwest,* 26.

61. Sarah Deutsch, *No Separate Refuge: Culture, Class, and Gender on an Anglo-Hispanic Frontier in the American Southwest, 1880–1940* (New York: Oxford University Press, 1987), 27.

62. Ibid., 103.

63. Howard Roberts Lamar, *The Far Southwest, 1846–1912: A Territorial History* (New York: W. W. Norton, 1970), 149.

64. Ibid., 198.

65. John R. Chávez, *The Lost Land: The Chicano Image of the Southwest* (Albuquerque: University of New Mexico Press, 1991), 74.

66. Deutsch, *No Separate Refuge*, 38.

67. Linda Gordon, *The Great Arizona Orphan Abduction* (Cambridge: Harvard University Press, 1999), 52.

68. Griswold del Castillo and de León, *North to Aztlán*, 43.

69. Gordon, *The Great Arizona Orphan Abduction*, 52.

70. Deutsch, *No Separate Refuge*, 27.

71. Robert W. Larson, *New Mexico's Quest for Statehood, 1846–1912* (Albuquerque: University of New Mexico Press, 1968), 148.

72. Weber, *Foreigners in Their Native Land*, 254–55.

73. Montejano, *Anglos and Mexicans in the Making of Texas*, 31.

74. Jane Dysart, "Mexican Women in San Antonio, 1830–1860: The Assimilation Process," *Western Historical Quarterly* 7, no. 4 (October 1976): 370.

75. Ibid.

76. Montejano, *Anglos and Mexicans in the Making of Texas*, 37.

77. Ibid., 84.

78. Ibid.

79. Ibid., 8.

80. Ibid., 34.

81. Paul S. Taylor, *Mexican Labor in the United States, Dimmit County, Winter Garden District, South Texas* (Berkeley: University of California Press, 1930), 434.

82. Taylor, *An American-Mexican Frontier*, 302.

83. Griswold del Castillo, *The Los Angeles Barrio*, 171.

84. Ibid., 172.

85. Arnoldo de León, *Mexican Americans in Texas: A Brief History*, 2nd ed. (Wheeling, Ill.: Harlan Davidson, 1999), 45.

86. Kenneth L. Stewart and Arnoldo de León, *Not Room Enough: Mexicans, Anglos, and Socioeconomic Change in Texas, 1850–1900* (Albuquerque: University of New Mexico Press, 1993), 97–98.

87. Montejano, *Anglos and Mexicans in the Making of Texas*, 95.

88. Mario T. García, *Desert Immigrants: The Mexicans of El Paso, 1880–1920* (New Haven: Yale University Press, 1981), 229.

SIX: CAUGHT BETWEEN NORTH AND SOUTH

1. Neil Foley, *The White Scourge: Mexicans, Blacks, and Poor Whites in Texas Cotton Culture* (Berkeley: University of California Press, 1997), 24.

2. Robert F. Heizer and Allan F. Almquist, *The Other Californians: Prejudice and Discrimination Under Spain, Mexico, and the United States to 1920* (Berkeley: University of California Press, 1977), 97.

3. Ibid.

4. Ibid., 98.

5. Ibid.

6. Ibid.

7. Tomás Almaguer, *Racial Fault Lines: The Historical Origins of White Supremacy in California* (Berkeley: University of California Press, 1994), 550.

8. Heizer and Almquist, *The Other Californians*, 98.

9. Almaguer, *Racial Fault Lines*, 55.

10. Ibid., 55.

11. Ibid.

12. Martha Menchaca, *Recovering History, Constructing Race: The Indian, Black, and White Roots of Mexican Americans* (Austin: University of Texas Press, 2001), 222.

13. Ibid., 3.

14. F. Arturo Rosales, *¡Pobre Raza!: Violence, Justice, and Mobilization Among México Lindo Immigrants, 1900–1936* (Austin: University of Texas Press, 1999), 4.

15. David Montejano, *Anglos and Mexicans in the Making of Texas, 1836–1986* (Austin: University of Texas Press, 1987), 115–16.

16. Rosales, *¡Pobre Raza!*, 2.

17. Jovita González de Mireles, "Latin Americans," in *Our Racial and National Minorities*, eds. Francis J. Brown and Joseph S. Roucek (New York: Prentice Hall, 1937), 501.

18. Jovita González, "America Invades the Border Towns," *Southwest Review* 15, No. 4 (Summer 1930). 472.

19. Ibid., 473.

20. Sarah Deutsch, *No Separate Refuge: Culture, Class, and Gender on an Anglo-Hispanic Frontier in the American Southwest, 1880–1940* (New York: Oxford University Press, 1987), 94.

21. Linda Gordon, *The Great Arizona Orphan Abduction* (Cambridge: Harvard University Press, 1999), 122.

22. Paul S. Taylor, *An American-Mexican Frontier: Nueces County, Texas* (Chapel Hill: University of North Carolina Press, 1934), 315.

23. Albert Camarillo, *Chicanos in a Changing Society: From Mexican Pueblos to American Barrios in Santa Barbara and Southern California, 1848–1930* (Cambridge: Harvard University Press, 1996), 183.

24. Ibid., 189.

25. Ibid.

26. Oscar J. Martínez, "On the Size of the Chicano Population: New Estimates, 1850–1900," *Atzlán* 6, no. 1 (Spring 1975): 55.

27. Gordon, *The Great Arizona Orphan Abduction*, 22.

28. Mario T. García, *Desert Immigrants: The Mexicans of El Paso, 1880–1920* (New Haven: Yale University Press, 1981), 14.

29. Douglas S. Massey, Jorge Durand, and Nolan J. Malone, *Beyond Smoke and Mirrors: Mexican Immigration in an Era of Economic Integration* (New York: Russell Sage Foundation, 2003), 27.

30. Mark Reisler, *By the Sweat of Their Brow: Mexican Immigrant Labor in the United States, 1900–1940* (Westport, Conn: Greenwood, 1976), 6.

31. Ibid., 7.

32. Manuel G. Gonzales, *Mexicanos: A History of the Mexicans in the United States* (Bloomington: Indiana University Press, 1999), 122.

33. Taylor, *An American-Mexican Frontier*, 105.

34. Reisler, *By the Sweat of Their Brow*, 8.

35. Foley, *The White Scourge*, 44.

36. Douglas Monroy, *Rebirth: Mexican Los Angeles from the Great Migration to the Great Depression* (Berkeley: University of California Press, 1999), 99.

37. García, *Desert Immigrants*, 57.

38. Arnoldo de León, *Mexican Americans in Texas: A Brief History*, 2nd ed. (Wheeling, Ill.: Harlan Davidson, 1999), 54.

39. Reisler, *By the Sweat of Their Brow*, 12.

40. Foley, *The White Scourge*, 43.

41. García, *Desert Immigrants*, 106.

42. Monroy, *Rebirth*, 99.

43. Reisler, *By the Sweat of Their Brow*, 13.

44. Ibid., 4.

45. Foley, *The White Scourge*, 40.

46. Ibid., 154.

47. Ricardo Romo, "Work and Restlessness: Occupational and Spatial Mobility Among Mexicanos in Los Angeles, 1918–1928," *Pacific Historical Review* 26, No. 2 (May 1977): 157–80.

48. Massey, Durand, and Malone, *Beyond Smoke and Mirrors*, 29.

49. Reisler, *By the Sweat of Their Brow*, 14.

50. Paul S. Taylor, *A Spanish-Mexican Peasant Community: Arandas in Jalisco, Mexico* (Berkeley: University of California Press, 1933), 51.

51. David G. Gutiérrez, *Walls and Mirrors: Mexican Americans, Mexican Immigrants, and the Politics of Ethnicity* (Berkeley: University of California Press, 1995), 70.

52. Gordon, *The Great Arizona Orphan Abduction*, 138–39.

53. Richard A. García, *The Mexican American Mind: A Product of the 1930s, in History, Culture and Society: Chicano Studies in the 1980s* (Ypsilanti, Mich.: Bilingual Press, 1983), 75.

54. Emory Bogardus, "Second Generation Mexicans," *Sociology and Social Research*, No. 13 (January–February 1929), 283.

55. García, *Desert Immigrants*, 185.

56. Ibid.

57. Ibid., 186.

58. Ricardo Romo, *East Los Angeles: History of a Barrio* (Austin: University of Texas Press, 1998), 99–100.

59. García, *Desert Immigrants,* 189.
60. Ibid., 191.
61. Ibid.
62. Romo, *East Los Angeles,* 101.
63. Ibid., 102.
64. Ibid., 103.
65. Ibid., 106.
66. Reisler, *By the Sweat of Their Brow,* 24.
67. Ibid., 24–25.
68. Ibid., 29.
69. Ibid., 30.
70. Ibid., 33.
71. Ibid., 38.
72. Ibid., 55.
73. Mae M. Ngai, *Impossible Subjects: Illegal Aliens and the Making of Modern America* (Princeton: Princeton University Press, 2004), 67.
74. George J. Sánchez, *Becoming Mexican American: Ethnicity Culture and Identity in Chicano Los Angeles, 1900–1945* (New York: Oxford University Press, 1993), 60.
75. Ngai, *Impossible Subjects,* 70.
76. Sánchez, *Becoming Mexican American,* 51.
77. Madison Grant, *The Passing of the Great Race; or, The Racial Basis of European History,* 4th rev. ed. (New York: Charles Scribner's Sons, 1923), 17.
78. Monroy, *Rebirth,* 210.
79. Ibid., 38.
80. Ibid.
81. Romo, *East Los Angeles,* 142.
82. Ibid., 141–42.
83. Ibid., 142.
84. Ibid., 161.
85. Monroy, *Rebirth,* 39.
86. Romo, *East Los Angeles,* 155.
87. Monroy, *Rebirth,* 175.
88. García, *Desert Immigrants,* 200.
89. Sánchez, *Becoming Mexican American,* 141.
90. Arthur León Campa, *Spanish Folk-Poetry in New Mexico* (Albuquerque: University of New Mexico Press, 1946), 9.
91. García, *Desert Immigrants,* 211–12.
92. Monroy, *Rebirth,* 173.
93. Sánchez, *Becoming Mexican American,* 173.
94. Douglas Monroy, "Making Mexico in Los Angeles," in *Metropolis in the Making: Los Angeles in the 1920s,* eds. Tom Sitton and William Deverell (Berkeley: University of California Press, 2001), 171.
95. Sánchez, *Becoming Mexican American,* 198.
96. Deutsch, *No Separate Refuge,* 112.

97. George I. Sanchez, *Forgotten People: A Study of New Mexicans* (Albuquerque: Calvin Horn, 1967), 26.

98. Carole E. Christian, "Joining the American Mainstream: Texas's Mexican Americans During World War I," *Southwestern Historical Quarterly* 92 no. 4 (April 1989): 559.

99. Ibid., 580–81.

100. Taylor, *An American-Mexican Frontier*, 245.

101. Ibid.

102. O. Douglas Weeks, "The Texas-Mexican and the Politics of South Texas," *American Political Science Review* 24, no. 3 (August 1930): 622.

103. Taylor, *An American-Mexican Frontier*, 263.

104. Ibid.

105. Reisler, *By the Sweat of Their Brow*, 209.

106. Mario García, *Mexican Americans: Leadership, Ideology, and Identity, 1930–1960* (New Haven: Yale University Press, 1989), 31.

107. Taylor, *An American-Mexican Frontier*, 290.

108. García, *Mexican Americans*, 30.

SEVEN: BECOMING MEXICAN AMERICAN

1. Mario T. García, *Mexican Americans: Leadership, Ideology, and Identity, 1930–1960* (New Haven: Yale University Press, 1989), 13.

2. George J. Sánchez, *Becoming Mexican American: Ethnicity Culture and Identity in Chicano Los Angeles, 1900–1945* (New York: Oxford University Press, 1993), 214.

3. Leo Grebler, Joan W. Moore, and Ralph C. Guzmán, *The Mexican American People: The Nation's Second Largest Minority* (New York: Free Press, 1970), 525.

4. Emory Bogardus, "Mexican Repatriates," *Sociology and Social Research* 17 (November–December 1933): 174.

5. Grebler, Moore, and Guzmán, *The Mexican American People*, 524.

6. Abraham Hoffman, *Unwanted Mexican Americans in the Great Depression: Repatriation Pressures, 1929–1939* (Tucson: University of Arizona Press, 1979), 86.

7. Grebler, Moore, and Guzmán, *The Mexican American People*, 524.

8. Sánchez, *Becoming Mexican American*, 216.

9. Douglas Monroy, *Rebirth: Mexican Los Angeles from the Great Migration to the Great Depression* (Berkeley: University of California Press, 1999), 210–11.

10. Sánchez, *Becoming Mexican American*, 216.

11. Hoffman, *Unwanted Mexican Americans in the Great Depression*, 136.

12. Ibid.

13. Sánchez, *Becoming Mexican American*, 212.

14. Bogardus, "Mexican Repatriates," 170.

15. Sánchez, *Becoming Mexican American*, 218.

16. Francisco E. Balderrama and Raymond Rodríguez, *Decade of Betrayal: Mexi-*

can Repatriation in the 1930s (Albuquerque: University of New Mexico Press, 1996), 212.

17. Manuel Gamio, *Mexican Immigration to the United States* (Chicago: University of Chicago Press, 1930), 236.

18. Mae N. Ngai, *Impossible Subjects: Illegal Aliens and the Making of Modern America* (Princeton: Princeton University Press, 2004), 72.

19. Manuel G. Gonzales, *Mexicanos: A History of Mexicans in the United States* (Bloomington: Indiana University Press, 1999), 148.

20. Ibid.; Sánchez, *Becoming Mexican American*, 12.

21. Neil Foley, *The White Scourge: Mexicans, Blacks, and Poor Whites in Texas Cotton Culture* (Berkeley: University of California Press, 1997), 175.

22. Grebler, Moore, and Guzmán, *The Mexican American People*, 526.

23. Douglas S. Massey, Jorge Durand, and Nolan J. Malone, *Beyond Smoke and Mirrors: Mexican Immigration in an Era of Economic Integration* (New York: Russell Sage Foundation, 2003), 34.

24. Sánchez, *Becoming Mexican American*, 210.

25. Mark Reisler, *By the Sweat of Their Brow: Mexican Immigrant Labor in the United States, 1900–1940* (Westport, Conn.: Greenwood, 1976), 152.

26. Ibid., 153.

27. Ibid.

28. Madison Grant, *The Passing of the Great Race; or, The Racial Basis of European History,* 4th rev. ed. (New York: Charles Scribner's Sons, 1923), 17.

29. Reisler, *By the Sweat of their Brow,* 157.

30. Ibid., 156.

31. Ibid.

32. Max Sylvius Handman, "Economic Reasons for the Coming of the Mexican Immigrant," *American Journal of Sociology* 35, no. 4 (January 1930): 609–10.

33. Max Sylvius Handman, "The Mexican Immigrant in Texas," *Southwestern Political and Social Science Quarterly* 7, no. 1 (June 1926): 41.

34. Ibid., 37.

35. Glenn E. Hoover, "Our Mexican Immigrants," *Foreign Affairs* 8, no. 1 (October 1929): 99.

36. Ibid., 107.

37. Clara E. Rodríguez, *Changing Race: Latinos, the Census, and the History of Ethnicity in the United States* (New York: New York University Press, 2000), 83.

38. Remsen Crawford, "The Menace of Mexican Immigration," *Current History,* February 1930, 903.

39. Patrick Lukens Espinosa, "Mexico, Mexican Americans and the FDR Administration's Racial Classification Policy: Public Policy in Place of Diplomacy" (Ph.D. diss., Arizona State University, December 1999), 126.

40. Reisler, *By the Sweat of their Brow,* 135.

41. Ibid., 136.

42. Fernando V. Padilla, "Early Chicano Legal Recognition: 1846–1897," *Journal of Popular Culture* 13, no. 3 (Spring 1980): 570; Martha Menchaca, "Chicano

Indianism: A Historical Account of Racial Repression in the United States," *American Ethnologist* 20, no. 3 (1993), 596; Lukens Espinosa, "Mexico, Mexican Americans and the FDR Administration's Racial Classification Policy," 127.

43. Padilla, "Early Chicano Legal Recognition: 1846–1897," 571.

44. Lukens Espinosa, "Mexico, Mexican Americans and the FDR Administration's Racial Classification Policy," 143.

45. Ibid., 145.

46. Ibid., 146.

47. Ibid., 146–47.

48. Ibid., 148.

49. Ibid., 165.

50. Ibid., 165–66.

51. Ibid., 167.

52. Ibid., 168.

53. Paul Schuster Taylor, *An American-Mexican Frontier: Nueces County, Texas* (Chapel Hill: University of North Carolina Press, 1934), 268.

54. Ibid.

55. Ibid., 250.

56. Ibid.

57. Ibid., 268.

58. Ibid., 269.

59. Ibid., 267.

60. Foley, *The White Scourge*, 41.

61. Ibid.

62. Taylor, *An American-Mexican Frontier*, 257.

63. Mario T. García, "Mexican Americans and the Politics of Citizenship: The Case of El Paso, 1936," *New Mexico Historical Review* 59, no. 2 (April 1984): 191.

64. Neil Foley, "Partly Colored or Other White: Mexican Americans and Their Problem with the Color Line." Paper delivered at the Labor and Working Class History Association luncheon at the Organization of American Historians meeting, April 1, 2000, nonpaginated.

65. García, "Mexican Americans and the Politics of Citizenship: The Case of El Paso, 1936," 191.

66. Ibid., 193.

67. Ibid., 199.

68. Ibid.

69. Ibid.

70. Lukens Espinosa, "Mexico, Mexican Americans and the FDR Administration's Racial Classification Policy," 88.

71. Sánchez, *Becoming Mexican American*, 225.

72. Ngai, *Impossible Subjects*, 74.

73. Sánchez, *Becoming Mexican American*, 228.

74. García, *Mexican Americans*, 16.

75. Ibid., 15.

76. Sánchez, *Becoming Mexican American*, 228.

77. Gonzales, *Mexicanos*, 181.

78. Monroy, *Rebirth,* 258.

79. O. Douglas Weeks. "The Texas-Mexican and the Politics of South Texas," *American Political Science Review* 24, no. 3 (August 1930): 616.

80. Ibid., 622.

81. Taylor, *An American-Mexican Frontier,* 276.

82. Ibid., 275.

83. Richard A. García, *Rise of the Mexican American Middle Class: San Antonio, 1929–1941* (College Station: Texas A&M University Press, 1991), 87.

84. Sánchez, *Becoming Mexican American,* 262.

85. Monroy, *Rebirth,* 267.

86. Sarah Deutsch, *No Separate Refuge: Culture, Class, and Gender on an Anglo-Hispanic Frontier in the American Southwest, 1880–1940* (New York: Oxford University Press, 1987), 188–89.

87. John R. Chávez, *The Lost Land: The Chicano Image of the Southwest* (Albuquerque: University of New Mexico Press, 1991), 117.

88. Carlos E. Cortés, "Mexicans," in *Harvard Encyclopedia of American Ethnic Groups,* ed. Stephen Thernstrom (Cambridge: Harvard University Press, 1980), 711.

89. Richard Griswold del Castillo and Arnoldo de León, *North to Aztlán: A History of Mexican Americans in the United States* (New York: Twayne, 1997), 102.

90. Chávez, *The Lost Land,* 117.

91. Albert Camarillo, *Chicanos in California: A History of Mexican Americans in California* (San Francisco: Boyd & Fraser, 1984), 72.

92. Monroy, *Rebirth,* 260.

93. Ibid.

94. Carey McWilliams, *North from Mexico: The Spanish-Speaking People of the United States* (New York: Greenwood, 1968), 260.

95. Raúl Morín, *Among the Valiant: Mexican-Americans in World War II and Korea* (Alhambra, Calif., Borden, 1963), 10.

96. Ibid., 21.

97. Gonzales, *Mexicanos,* 164.

98. Pauline R. Kibbe, *Latin Americans in Texas* (Albuquerque: University of New Mexico Press, 1946), 226–27.

99. Chávez, *The Lost Land,* 121.

100. Ibid.

101. Morín, *Among the Valiant,* 256.

102. Ibid., 24.

103. Monroy, *Rebirth,* 261.

104. García, *Mexican Americans,* 36.

105. Monroy, *Rebirth,* 261.

106. S. Dale McLemore and Ricardo Romo, "The Origins and Development of the Mexican American People," in *The Mexican American Experience: An Interdisciplinary Anthology,* ed. Rodolfo O. de la Garza et al. (Austin: University of Texas Press, 1985), 27.

107. Morín, *Among the Valiant,* 180–81.

108. W. Lloyd Warner et al., *Democracy in Jonesville* (New York: Harper & Brothers, 1949), 288.

109. McWilliams, *North from Mexico*, 260.

110. F. Arturo Rosales, *Chicano! The History of the Mexican American Civil Rights Movement* (Houston: Arte Público, 1997), 96.

111. Chávez, *The Lost Land*, 121.

112. Daniel L. Schorr, " 'Reconverting' Mexican Americans," *New Republic* 30 (September 1946): 412.

113. Henry A. J. Ramos, *The American G.I. Forum: In Pursuit of the Dream, 1948–1983* (Houston: Arte Público, 1998), 9.

114. Ibid., 11.

115. Chávez, *The Lost Land*, 124.

116. John Burma, "The Civil Rights Situation of Mexican Americans and Spanish Americans," in *Race Relations: Problems of Theory: Essays in Honor of Robert E. Park*, eds. Jitsuichi Masuoka and Preston Valien (Chapel Hill: University of North Carolina Press, 1961), 159.

117. Griswold del Castillo and de León, *North to Aztlán*, 103.

118. Josh Sides, *L.A. City Limits: African American Los Angeles from the Great Depression to the Present* (Berkeley: University of California Press, 2003), 110.

119. Ibid.

120. Ibid., 111.

121. Ruth D. Tuck, *Not with the Fist: Mexican-Americans in a Southwest City* (New York: Harcourt, Brace, 1946), 220–21.

122. Richard Griswold del Castillo, *La Familia: Chicano Families in the Urban Southwest, 1848 to the Present* (Notre Dame: University of Notre Dame Press, 1984), 71.

123. Grebler, Moore, and Guzmán, *The Mexican American People*, 406.

124. David G. Gutiérrez, *Walls and Mirrors: Mexican Americans, Mexican Immigrants, and the Politics of Ethnicity* (Berkeley: University of California Press, 1995), 183.

125. Grebler, Moore, and Guzmán, *The Mexican American People*, 408.

126. Martha Menchaca, *Recovering History, Constructing Race: The Indian, Black, and White Roots of Mexican Americans* (Austin: University of Texas Press, 2001), 293.

127. Ibid.

128. Foley, *The White Scourge*, 205.

129. Otey M. Scruggs, "Texas, Good Neighbor?," *Southwestern Social Science Quarterly* 43, no. 2 (September 1962): 119.

130. Johnny M. McCain, "Texas and the Mexican Labor Question, 1942–1947," *Southwestern Historical Quarterly* 85, no. 1 (July 1981): 49.

131. Foley, *The White Scourge*, 207.

132. Massey, Durand, and Malone, *Beyond Smoke and Mirrors*, 36.

133. Ibid.

134. Ibid., 39.

135. Walter Nugent, *Into the West: The Story of Its People* (New York: Vintage, 2001), 304.

136. Ibid., 303.

137. Massey, Durand, and Malone, *Beyond Smoke and Mirrors*, 36.

138. Douglas Massey et al., *Return to Aztlán: The Social Process of International Migration from Western Mexico* (Berkeley: University of California Press, 1990), 55.

139. Ngai, *Impossible Subjects*, 140–41.

140. Massey, *Return to Aztlán*, 55.

141. Ngai, *Impossible Subjects*, 152.

142. Gonzales, *Mexicanos*, 176.

143. Gutiérrez, *Walls and Mirrors*, 159.

144. Ngai, *Impossible Subjects*, 150–51.

145. Ibid., 149.

146. Ibid.

147. Gutiérrez, *Walls and Mirrors*, 145.

148. Ngai, *Impossible Subjects*, 159.

149. Ibid.

150. Gutiérrez, *Walls and Mirrors*, 158.

151. Ibid.

152. Ngai, *Impossible Subjects*, 159.

153. Gutiérrez, *Walls and Mirrors*, 159.

154. Ngai, *Impossible Subjects*, 159.

155. García, *Mexican Americans*, 52.

156. Ngai, *Impossible Subjects*, 159.

157. Gutiérrez, *Walls and Mirrors*, 160.

158. Ngai, *Impossible Subjects*, 160.

159. Gutiérrez, *Walls and Mirrors*, 161.

160. Ngai, *Impossible Subjects*, 153.

161. Gonzales, *Mexicanos*, 177.

162. Gutiérrez, *Walls and Mirrors*, 164.

163. Massey, Durand, and Malone, *Beyond Smoke and Mirrors*, 37.

164. Gutiérrez, *Walls and Mirrors*, 168.

165. García, *Mexican Americans*, 42.

166. Gutiérrez, *Walls and Mirrors*, 166.

167. Ibid.

168. Rosales, *Chicano!*, 280.

169. Gutiérrez, *Walls and Mirrors*, 203.

170. Gonzales, *Mexicanos*, 193.

171. Nugent, *Into the West*, 285.

172. Bureau of the Census, "We, The Mexican Americans," in *Pain and Promise: The Chicano Today*, ed. Edward Simmen (New York: Mentor, 1972), 48.

173. Fernando Peñalosa, "The Changing Mexican-American in Southern California," *Sociology and Social Research* 51, no. 4 (July 1967): 410.

174. Ibid.

175. Fernando Peñalosa, "Recent Changes Among the Chicanos," *Sociology and Social Research* 55, no. 1 (October 1970): 49.

176. John Womack, Jr., "A Special Supplement: Chicanos," *New York Review of Books* 19, no. 3 (August 31, 1972): 13.

177. Gonzales, *Mexicanos*, 193.

EIGHT: THE CHICANO MOVEMENT

1. F. Arturo Rosales, *Chicano! The History of the Mexican American Civil Rights Movement* (Houston: Arte Público, 1997), 108.

2. John R. Chávez, *The Lost Land: The Chicano Image of the Southwest* (Albuquerque: University of New Mexico Press, 1991), 129.

3. Rosales, *Chicano!*, 108.

4. Mario T. García, *Mexican Americans: Leadership, Ideology, and Identity, 1930–1960* (New Haven: Yale University Press, 1989), 61.

5. Ibid.

6. Stephen Steinberg, *The Ethnic Myth: Race, Ethnicity and Class in America* (Boston: Beacon, 1989), 3.

7. Ibid.

8. U.S. Census Bureau, *Profile of the Foreign Born Population in the United States: 2000* (Washington, D.C.: U.S. Department of Commerce, 2001), 9.

9. Rosales, *Chicano!*, 217.

10. David G. Gutiérrez, *Walls and Mirrors: Mexican Americans, Mexican Immigrants, and the Politics of Ethnicity* (Berkeley: University of California Press, 1995), 184.

11. Tony Castro, *Chicano Power: The Emergence of Mexican America* (New York: Saturday Review Press, 1974), 134.

12. Steinberg, *The Ethnic Myth*, 3.

13. Rosales, *Chicano!*, 224.

14. Rodolfo Acuña, *Occupied America: The Chicano's Struggle Toward Liberation* (San Francisco: Canfield, 1972), 243.

15. Armando B. Rendón, *Chicano Manifesto* (New York: Macmillan, 1971), 319.

16. Ibid., 322.

17. Ibid., 325.

18. Ibid.

19. Rubén Salazar, "A Stranger in One's Land," in *Pain and Promise: The Chicano Today*, ed. Edward Simmen (New York: Mentor, 1972), 162.

20. Rosales, *Chicano!*, 154.

21. Nancie L. González, *The Spanish-Americans of New Mexico* (Albuquerque: University of New Mexico Press, 1969), 99.

22. John C. Hammerback and Richard J. Jensen, *The Rhetorical Career of César Chávez* (College Station: Texas A&M University Press, 1998), 26.

23. Chávez, *The Lost Land*, 134.

24. Richard Griswold del Castillo and Richard A. García, *César Chávez: A Triumph of Spirit* (Norman: University of Oklahoma Press, 1995), 47.

25. Chávez, *The Lost Land*, 136–37.

26. Castro, *Chicano Power*, 100.

27. Gutiérrez, *Walls and Mirrors*, 183–84.

28. Rosales, *Chicano!*, 223.

29. Acuña, *Occupied America*, 255.

30. Salazar, "A Stranger in One's Land," 178

31. Manuel H. Guerra, "The Mexican-American Child: Problems or Talents?," in *Pain and Promise: The Chicano Today*, ed. Edward Simmen (New York: Mentor, 1972), 200.

32. Griswold del Castillo and Aruoldo de León, *North to Aztlán: A History of Mexican Americans in the United States* (New York: Twayne, 1997), 132.

33. Rosales, *Chicano!*, 250.

34. Acuña, *Occupied America*, 275.

35. Ibid., 275–76.

36. García, *Mexican Americans*, 300.

37. Paul M. Sheldon, "Community Participation and the Emerging Middle Class," in *La Raza: Forgotten Americans*, ed. Julian Samora (Notre Dame: University of Notre Dame Press, 1969), 146.

38. Ibid., 127.

39. Ibid., 126.

40. Ibid., 125.

41. Ernesto Galarza, Herman Gallegos, and Julian Samora, *Mexican Americans in the Southwest* (Santa Barbara: McNally and Loftin, 1969), 58.

42. Ibid.

43. Ibid.

44. Ibid., 64.

45. Ibid., 63.

46. Rosales, *Chicano!*, 192.

47. Ibid.

48. Gutiérrez, *Walls and Mirrors*, 186.

49. Ibid.

50. Castro, *Chicano Power*, 153.

51. Gutiérrez, *Walls and Mirrors*, 186.

52. Ibid.

53. Castro, *Chicano Power*, 100.

54. Griswold del Castillo and de León, *North to Aztlán*, 135.

55. Celia S. Heller, *New Converts to the American Dream?: Mobility Aspirations of Young Mexican Americans* (New Haven: College and University Press, 1971), 244.

56. Acuña, *Occupied America*, 123.

57. Ibid., 8.

58. Ibid.

59. Rosales, *Chicano!*, 250.

60. Gutiérrez, *Walls and Mirrors*, 187.

61. Ibid., 216.

62. Heller, *New Converts to the American Dream?*, 245.

63. John Womack, Jr., "A Special Supplement: The Chicanos," *New York Review of Books* 19, no. 3 (1972), 15.

64. Edward Murguía, *Chicano Intermarriage: A Theoretical and Empirical Study* (San Antonio: Trinity University Press, 1982), 39.

65. Matt S. Meier and Feliciano Ribera, *Mexican Americans/American Mexicans: From Conquistadors to Chicanos* (New York: Hill and Wang, 1993), 232.

66. García, *Mexican Americans,* 294.

67. Manuel G. Gonzales, *Mexicanos: A History of Mexicans in the United States* (Bloomington: Indiana University Press, 1999), 1.

68. Griswold del Castillo and García, *César Chávez,* 42.

69. David Montejano, *Anglos and Mexicans in the Making of Texas, 1836–1986* (Austin: University of Texas Press, 1997), 285.

70. Castro, *Chicano Power,* 150.

71. Ibid., 58; Griswold del Castillo and de León, *North to Aztlán,* 135.

72. Gutiérrez, *Walls and Mirrors,* 187.

73. Guadalupe San Miguel, Jr., *Let All of Them Take Heed: Mexican Americans and the Campaign for Educational Equality in Texas, 1910–1981* (Austin: University of Texas Press, 1987), 184.

74. Ibid.

75. Mae N. Ngai, *Impossible Subjects: Illegal Aliens and the Making of Modern America* (Princeton: Princeton University Press, 2004), 261.

76. Douglas S. Massey, Jorge Durand, and Nolan J. Malone, *Beyond Smoke and Mirrors: Mexican Immigration in an Era of Economic Integration* (New York: Russell Sage Foundation, 2003), 43.

77. Ibid., 42.

78. Ibid., 44.

79. Ibid., 42.

80. Ibid.

81. Ngai, *Impossible Subjects,* 261.

82. Massey, Durand, and Malone, *Beyond Smoke and Mirrors,* 45.

83. Roger Daniels, *Guarding the Golden Door: American Immigration Policy and Immigrants Since 1882* (New York: Hill and Wang, 2004), 181.

84. Pierrette Hondagneu-Sotelo, *Gendered Transitions: Mexican Experiences of Immigration* (Berkeley: University of California Press, 1994), 187.

85. Wayne A. Cornelius, "From Sojourners to Settlers: The Changing Profile of Mexican Immigration to the United States," in *U.S.-Mexico Relations: Labor Market Interdependence,* eds. Jorge A. Bustamante, Clark W. Reynolds, and Raúl A. Hinojosa Ojeda (Stanford: Stanford University Press, 1992), 158.

86. Hondagneu-Sotelo, *Gendered Transitions,* 31.

87. Ibid.

88. Cornelius, "From Sojourners to Settlers," 161.

89. Ibid., 177.

90. Massey, Durand, and Malone, *Beyond Smoke and Mirrors,* 41–42.

91. Hondagneu-Sotelo, *Gendered Transitions*, 57.

92. Ibid., 202.

93. Ibid., 1.

94. Ibid., 102.

95. Ibid., 1.

96. Ibid., 100.

97. Heller, *New Converts to the American Dream?*, 251.

98. Fernando Peñalosa, "Recent Changes Among Chicanos," *Sociology and Social Research* 55, no. 1 (October 1970): 47.

99. Fernando Peñalosa, "The Changing Mexican-American in Southern California," *Sociology and Social Research* 51, no. 4 (July 1967): 405–06; Peñalosa, "Recent Changes Among Chicanos," 47.

100. Rogelio Saenz and Benigno E. Aguirre, "The Dynamics of Mexican Ethnic Identity," *Ethnic Groups*, Vol. 9 (1991), 26.

101. Rodolfo O. de la Garza and Robert R. Brischetto, *The Mexican American Electorate: A Demographic Profile*, The Mexican American Electorate Series, Hispanic Population Studies Program, Occasional Paper No. 1 (San Antonio: Southwest Voter Registration Education Project; and Austin: Center for Mexican American Studies, University of Texas, 1982), 14.

102. John A. García, "Yo Soy Mexicano . . .: Self-Identity and Sociodemographic Correlates," *Social Science Quarterly* 62, no. 1 (March 1981): 91.

103. Rosales, *Chicano!*, 253.

104. Harley L. Browning and Rodolfo O. de la Garza, "Introduction," in *Mexican Immigrants and Mexican Americans: An Evolving Relation*, eds. Harley L. Browning and Rodolfo O. de la Garza (Austin: Center for Mexican American Studies, University of Texas at Austin, 1986), 3.

105. Peter Skerry, *Mexican Americans: The Ambivalent Minority* (New York: Free Press, 1993), 260.

106. Manuel G. Gonzales, *Mexicanos: A History of Mexicans in the United States* (Bloomington: Indiana University Press, 1999), 1.

107. García, "Yo Soy Mexicano . . . ," 90.

108. Tomás R. Jiménez, "Replenished Identity: Mexican Americans, Mexican Immigrants and Ethnic Identity" (Ph.D. diss., Harvard University, December 2004), 20.

109. Ibid., 21.

110. Ibid., 21–22.

111. Alex M. Saragoza, "Recent Chicano Historiography: An Interpretive Essay," *Aztlán: A Journal of Chicano Studies* 19, no. 1 (1988–1990): 9.

112. Ibid., 39.

113. Ibid.

114. Ibid.

115. David G. Gutiérrez, "Significant to Whom?: Mexican Americans and the History of the American West," *Western Historical Quarterly* 24, no. 4 (November 1993): 530.

116. Browning and de la Garza, "Introduction," 3.

117. Juan Gómez-Quiñones, *Chicano Politics: Reality and Promise, 1940–1990* (Albuquerque: University of New Mexico Press, 1990), 184.

118. Montejano, *Anglos and Mexicans in the Making of Texas,* 290.

119. Skerry, *Mexican Americans,* 49.

120. David Montejano, *Anglos and Mexicans in the Twenty-first Century* (East Lansing: Julian Samora Research Institute, Michigan State University, 1992), 10.

121. Skerry, *Mexican Americans,* 34.

122. Montejano, *Anglos and Mexicans in the Making of Texas,* 298.

123. Ibid., 299.

124. Ibid.

125. Ibid., 299–300.

126. Montejano, *Anglos and Mexicans in the Twenty-first Century,* 10.

127. Gregory Rodriguez, *The Emerging Latino Middle Class* (Malibu, Calif.: Pepperdine Institute for Public Policy, 1996), 13.

128. Skerry, *Mexican Americans,* 260.

NINE: MONGREL AMERICA
AND THE NEW ASSIMILATION

1. Peter Skerry, *Mexican Americans: The Ambivalent Minority* (New York: Free Press, 1993), 364.

2. Ibid., 29.

3. Ibid., 258.

4. Ibid., 266.

5. Rodolfo O. de la Garza, "Public Policy Priorities of Chicano Political Elites," working paper, U.S.-Mexico Project Series, No. 7 (Washington, D.C.: Overseas Development Council, 1982), 9.

6. Ibid., 10.

7. Skerry, *Mexican Americans,* 11.

8. Kenneth Prewitt, "Public Statistics and Democratic Politics," in *The Politics of Numbers,* eds. William Alonso and Paul Starr (New York: Russell Sage Foundation, 1987), 271.

9. Richard Griswold del Castillo and Arnoldo de León, *North to Aztlán: A History of Mexican Americans in the United States* (New York: Twayne, 1997), 151.

10. David Savage, "Asians, Latinos Surge in U.S. Growth Rates," *Los Angeles Times,* March 2, 1990, A4.

11. Knight Ridder Newspapers, "Lost Ground in '80s, Hispanics Say," *Chicago Tribune,* December 17, 1989, C11.

12. Ibid.

13. Michelle Mittelstadt, "La Raza's Hispanic America Report Shows Education, Job Problems," Associated Press, February 6, 1992.

14. Joan Moore and Harry Pachón, *Hispanics in the United States* (Englewood Cliffs: Prentice Hall, 1985), 194.

15. Suzanne Oboler, *Ethnic Labels, Latino Lives: Identity and the Politics of*

(Re)Presentation in the United States (Minneapolis: University of Minnesota Press, 1995), 83.

16. Moore and Pachón, *Hispanics in the United States,* 197.

17. William Petersen, "Politics and the Measurement of Ethnicity," in *The Politics of Numbers,* eds. William Alonso and Paul Starr (New York: Russell Sage Foundation, 1987), 229.

18. Moore and Pachón, *Hispanics in the United States,* 197.

19. Laura E. Gómez, "The Birth of the 'Hispanic' Generation: Attitudes of Mexican American Political Elites Toward the Hispanic Label," *Latin American Perspectives* 19, no. 4 (Fall 1992): 45.

20. Ibid., 52.

21. Frank del Olmo, "Cuban in Congress Spells End of Hispanic," *Los Angeles Times,* September 5, 1989, B7.

22. De la Garza, "Public Policy Priorities of Chicano Political Elites," 9.

23. Ibid., 8.

24. Rodolfo O. de la Garza, Louis DeSipio, F. Chris García, and Angelo Falcón, *Latino Voices: Mexican, Puerto Rican, and Cuban Perspectives on American Politics* (Boulder: Westview, 1992), 92.

25. Ibid., 15.

26. Earl Shorris, *Latinos: A Biography of a People* (New York: W. W. Norton, 1992), 230.

27. Griswold del Castillo and de León, *North to Aztlán,* 152.

28. Shorris, *Latinos,* 231.

29. Arlene Dávila, *Latinos Inc.: The Making and Marketing of a People* (Berkeley: University of California Press, 2001), 86.

30. Ibid., 4.

31. Griswold del Castillo and de León, *North to Aztlán,* 152.

32. Dávila, *Latinos Inc.,* 71.

33. Ibid., 79.

34. Gregory Rodriguez, "The Rising Language of Latino Media: English," *Los Angeles Times,* May 4, 1997, M1.

35. Dávila, *Latinos Inc.,* 72.

36. C. Carlos Balkan, "The Crisis in Hispanic Marketing," *Hispanic Business,* December 1982, 25.

37. Ibid., 24.

38. Dávila, *Latinos Inc.,* 8.

39. Ibid., 237.

40. Ibid., 77.

41. David E. López, "Chicano Language Loyalty in an Urban Setting," *Sociology and Social Research* 62, no. 2 (January 1978): 276.

42. Joan Baratz-Snowden, Donald Rock, Judith Pollack, and Gita Wilder, *Parent Preference Study* (Princeton: Educational Testing Service, 1988), 49.

43. Ibid.

44. Diane Ravitch, *The Troubled Crusade: American Education, 1945–1980* (New York: Basic, 1983), 273.

45. Ibid.

46. Ibid.

47. Gregory Rodriguez, "English Lesson in California," *Nation,* April 20, 1998, 16.

48. Little Hoover Commission, *A Chance to Succeed: Providing English Learners with Supportive Education* (Sacramento: Little Hoover Commission, 1993), 22.

49. Gregory Rodriguez, "An Opportunity for Latino Lawmakers to Take the Lead," *Los Angeles Times,* November 30, 1997, M1.

50. Rodriguez, "English Lesson in California," 16.

51. Gregory Rodriguez, "The Bilingualism Debate Remakes California Politics," *Washington Post,* February 8, 1998, C2.

52. López, "Chicano Language Loyalty in an Urban Setting," 276.

53. Richard Alba and Victor Nee, *Remaking the American Mainstream: Assimilation and Contemporary Immigration* (Cambridge: Harvard University Press, 2003), 226.

54. Ibid., 226–227.

55. Gregory Rodriguez, "The Overwhelming Allure of English," *New York Times,* April 7, 2002, Sect. 4,3.

56. Alba and Nee, *Remaking the American Mainstream,* 225.

57. Sarah Tully Tapia, "English Isn't the Issue in Miami," *Arizona Daily Star,* April 11, 2000.

58. Dávila, *Latinos Inc.,* 34–35.

59. Ibid., 34.

60. Ibid., 28.

61. Susan E. Keefe and Amado M. Padilla, *Chicano Ethnicity* (Albuquerque: University of New Mexico Press, 1987), 191.

62. Ibid., 116.

63. Ibid., 195.

64. Ibid., 116.

65. Ibid., 8.

66. Joan Moore and James Diego Vigil, "Barrios in Transition," in *In the Barrios: Latinos and the Underclass Debate,* eds. Joan Moore and Raquel Rinderhughes (New York: Russell Sage Foundation, 1993), 47.

67. Ibid.

68. Ibid., 45.

69. Harley Browning and Ruth M. Cullen, "The Complex Demographic Formation of the U.S. Mexican Origin Population, 1970–1980," in *Mexican Immigrants and Mexican Americans: An Evolving Relation,* eds. Harley L. Browning and Rodolfo O. de la Garza (Austin: Center for Mexican American Studies, University of Texas, 1986), 49.

70. Rodolfo O. de la Garza, "Mexican Americans, Mexican Immigrants, and Immigration Reform," in *Clamor at the Gates,* ed. Nathan Glazer (San Francisco: Institute for Contemporary Studies, 1985), 103.

71. Nestor Rodríguez and Rogelio T. Núñez, "An Exploration of Factors That Contribute to Differentiation Between Chicanos and Indocumentados," in *Mexican Immigrants and Mexican Americans: An Evolving Relation,* eds. Harley L.

Browning and Rodolfo O. de la Garza (Austin: Center for Mexican American Studies, University of Texas, 1986), 140.

72. Ibid., 141.

73. Ibid.

74. Ibid., 142.

75. Gilberto Cárdenas, Rodolfo O. de la Garza, and Niles Hansen, "Mexican Immigrants and the Chicano Ethnic Enterprise: Reconceptualizing an Old Problem," in *Mexican Immigrants and Mexican Americans: An Evolving Relation,* eds. Harley L. Browning and Rodolfo O. de la Garza (Austin: Center for Mexican American Studies, University of Texas, 1986), 169.

76. Cárdenas, de la Garza, and Hansen, "Mexican Immigrants and the Chicano Ethnic Enterprise: Reconceptualizing an Old Problem," 159.

77. Rodríguez and Núñez, "An Exploration of Factors That Contribute to Differentiation Between Chicanos and Indocumentados," 139.

78. Ibid., 144.

79. Ibid., 150–151.

80. Ibid., 151.

81. Rodolfo O. de la Garza, "Chicanos as an Ethnic Lobby: Limits and Possibilities," in *Chicano-Mexicano Relations,* eds. Tatcho Mindiola, Jr., and Max Martínez (Houston: Mexican American Studies, University of Houston, 1992), 40.

82. Gilda Laura Ochoa, "Mexican Americans' Attitudes Toward and Interactions with Mexican Immigrants: A Qualitative Analysis of Conflict and Cooperation," *Social Science Quarterly* 81, no. 1 (March 2000): 90.

83. Ibid., 91.

84. Ibid.

85. Ibid., 92.

86. Gilda L. Ochoa, *Becoming Neighbors in a Mexican American Community: Power, Conflict, and Solidarity* (Austin: University of Texas Press, 2004), 128.

87. Ochoa, "Mexican Americans' Attitudes Toward and Interactions with Mexican Immigrants," 91–92.

88. Ibid., 94.

89. Ibid.

90. Martha Menchaca, *The Mexican Outsiders: A Community History of Marginalization and Discrimination in California* (Austin: University of Texas Press, 1997), 207.

91. Ibid., 209.

92. Ibid.

93. Ibid., 207.

94. Ibid.

95. Ibid.

96. Ibid., 208.

97. Douglas S. Massey, Jorge Durand, and Nolan J. Malone, *Beyond Smoke and Mirrors: Mexican Immigration in an Era of Economic Integration* (New York: Russell Sage Foundation, 2003), 90.

98. Ibid., 91.

99. Tomás R. Jiménez, "Replenished Identity: Mexican Americans, Mexican Immigrants and Ethnic Identity" (Ph. D. diss., Harvard University, December 2004), 48.

100. Massey, Durand, and Malone, *Beyond Smoke and Mirrors*, 91.

101. Ibid., 129.

102. Ibid., 89.

103. Ibid., 73

104. Ibid., 106.

105. Bill Stall and Dave Lesher, "Stressing GOP Unity, Wilson Backs Prop. 187," *Los Angeles Times,* September 18, 1994, A3.

106. Massey, Durand, and Malone, *Beyond Smoke and Mirrors*, 89.

107. Paul Feldman, "62% Would Bar Services to Illegal Immigrants," *Los Angeles Times,* September 14, 1994, A1.

108. Bruce Cain and Roderick Kiewiet, "California's Coming Minority Majority," *Public Opinion,* February–March 1986, 51–52.

109. Paul Hefner, "Prop. 187 Exposed Cultural Clash," *Los Angeles Daily News,* November 14, 1994, N1.

110. Ibid.

111. Frank Clifford and Anne C. Roark, "Census Finds Ethnic Boom in Suburbs, Rural Areas," *Los Angeles Times,* February 26, 1991, A1.

112. Ibid.

113. Ibid.

114. Kevin Roderick, "Anglos Rank Highest in Home Ownership," *Los Angeles Times,* May 11, 1991, A21.

115. Georges Sabagh and Mehdi Bozorgmehr, "Population Change: Immigration and Ethnic Transformation," in *Ethnic Los Angeles,* eds. Roger Waldinger and Mehdi Bozorgmehr (New York: Russell Sage Foundation, 1996), 87.

116. David Rieff, *Los Angeles: Capital of the Third World* (New York: Simon & Schuster, 1991), 127.

117. Patrick J. McDonnell, "Prop. 187 Turns Up Heat in U.S. Immigration Debate," *Los Angeles Times,* August 10, 1994, A1.

118. Gregory Rodriguez, "The Browning of California," *New Republic,* September 2, 1996, 18.

119. John Chandler, "Latinos Fail to Change Knight's Viewpoint," *Los Angeles Times,* May 24, 1993, B1.

120. *San Francisco Examiner,* "Poem Gets Legislator in Trouble," *Orlando Sentinel,* May 21, 1993, A5.

121. Gregory Rodriguez, "Reverse Assimilation: How Proposition 187 Hastened the Latinization of California," *LA Weekly,* August 9–15, 1996, 27.

122. *Los Angeles Times* poll, "A Look at the Electorate," November 18, 1994, 2.

123. Menchaca, *The Mexican Outsiders,* 218.

124. Jiménez, "Replenished Identity," 25.

125. Ochoa, "Mexican Americans' Attitudes Toward and Interactions with Mexican Immigrants," 97–98.

126. Jiménez, "Replenished Identity," 25.

127. *Los Angeles Times* poll, "A Look at the Electorate," 2.

128. David E. Hayes-Bautista and Gregory Rodriguez, "A Rude Awakening for Latinos," *Los Angeles Times,* November 11, 1994, B7.

129. Roberto Suro and Jeffery S. Passell, *The Rise of the Second Generation: Changing Patterns in Hispanic Population Growth* (Washington, D.C.: Pew Hispanic Center, October 2003), 3.

130. Hayes-Bautista and Rodriguez, "A Rude Awakening for Latinos," B7.

131. Rodriguez, "The Browning of California," 19.

132. Seth Mydans, "The Latest Big Boom: Citizenship," *New York Times,* August 11, 1995, A12.

133. Interview with Juan and Marta Aguilar by Gregory Rodriguez. December 16, 1994. Translation by Gregory Rodriguez.

134. Ibid.

135. Mydans, "The Latest Big Boom: Citizenship," A12.

136. Gregory Rodriguez, *From Newcomers to New Americans: The Successful Integration of Immigrants into American Society* (Washington, D.C.: National Immigration Forum, July 1999), 14.

137. Interview with Miguel Estrada by Gregory Rodriguez. December 16, 1994. Translation by Gregory Rodriguez.

138. Ibid.

139. Norma Chinchilla, Nora Hamilton, and James Loucky, "Central Americans in Los Angeles: An Immigrant Community in Transition," in *In the Barrios: Latinos and the Underclass Debate,* eds. Joan Moore and Raquel Pinderhughes (New York: Russell Sage Foundation, 1993), 53.

140. David E. Hayes-Bautista and Gregory Rodriguez, *Latino South Central* (Los Angeles: Alta California Policy Research Center, 1994), 6.

141. Mollyann Brodie, Annie Steffenson, Jaime Valdez, Rebecca Levin and Roberto Suro, 2002 *National Survey of Latinos* (Washington, D.C.: Pew Hispanic Center; and Menlo Park: Kaiser Family Foundation, December 2002), 23.

142. Hayes-Bautista and Rodriguez, "Latino South Central," 2.

143. Gregory Rodriguez, *The Emerging Latino Middle Class* (Malibu, Calif.: Pepperdine Institute for Public Policy, 1996), 3.

144. Aída Hurtado, David E. Hayes-Bautista, R. Burciaga Valdez and Anthony C. R. Hernández, *Redefining California: Latino Social Engagement in a Multicultural Society,* California Identity Project (Los Angeles: UCLA Chicano Studies Research Center, 1992), 9.

145. Jiménez, "Replenished Identity," 112.

146. Ibid.

147. Ibid., 132.

148. Ibid., 132.

149. Ibid., 223.

150. De la Garza, "Chicanos as an Ethnic Lobby: Limits and Possibilities," 40.

151. Gregory Rodriguez, "When Votes Cross the Line Between Lands," *Los Angeles Times,* June 1, 2004, B11.

152. Gregory Rodriguez, "Vicente Fox Blesses the Americanization of Mexico," *Los Angeles Times,* December 10, 2000, M1.

153. Ibid.

154. Vicente Fox, Transcript of Speech by Mexican President Elect, November 9, 2000, Los Angeles, 26th Annual Awards Dinner of Mexican American Legal Defense and Education Fund.

155. Mark DiCamillo and Mervin Field, "The Expanding Latino Electorate," Field Poll, May 1, 2000, 1.

156. Ibid., 3.

157. Ibid., 2.

158. Héctor Tobar, "In Contests Big and Small, Latinos Take Historic Leap," Los Angeles Times, November 5, 1998, A1.

159. Mark Baldessare, A California State of Mind: The Conflicted Voter in a Changing World (Berkeley: University of California Press; and San Francisco: Public Policy Institute of California, 2002), 168.

160. Ibid., 149.

161. Ibid.

162. Hon. Stephen Reinhardt, Hon. Christina A. Snyder, and Hon. Margaret M. Morrow, United States District Court Central District of California, Cano v. Davis, Opinion and Order Granting Defendants' Motions for Summary Judgment, June 12, 2002, 63.

163. Matt A. Barreto, "The Role of Latino Candidates in Mobilizing Latino Voters: Revisiting Latino Vote Choice," prepared for Latino Politics: The State of the Discipline (College Station: Texas A&M University Press, 2004), 31.

164. Gregory Rodriguez, "The Bilingualism Debate Remakes California Politics," Washington Post, February, 8, 1998, C2.

165. Center for the Study of Los Angeles, "City of Los Angeles Latino Leader Survey," Spring 1997, Loyola Marymount University, 2.

166. Louis F. Moret, "The Latino Political Agenda in Southern California Municipalities," Doctor of Public Administration diss., School of Organizational Management, Department of Public Administration, University of La Verne, August 1998, 82, 87.

167. Gregory Rodriguez, "Latino Leadership Matures," Los Angeles Times, February 5, 1999, B9.

168. Gregory Rodriguez, "From Minority to Mainstream, Latinos Find Their Voice," Washington Post, January 24, 1999, B1.

169. Louis DeSipio, Counting on the Latino Vote: Latinos as a New Electorate (Charlottesville: University Press of Virginia, 1998), 179.

170. Robert A. Levine, "Assimilation, Past and Present Waves of Immigration," Public Interest 159 (March 22, 2005): 93.

171. DeSipio, Counting on the Latino Vote, 179.

172. Mark Baldessare, California in the New Millennium: The Changing Social and Political Landscape (Berkeley: University of California Press; and San Francisco: Public Policy Institute of California, 2000), 134.

173. Ibid., 127.

174. Ibid.

175. Massey, Durand, and Malone, Beyond Smoke and Mirrors, 138.

176. Interview with Barry Edmonston by Gregory Rodriguez, August 29, 2005.

177. Jennifer Netherby, "Spanish Cinemas Dying Out in LA," *Los Angeles Business Journal,* October 4, 1999, 1.

178. Ibid.

179. Richard Alba, *Language Assimilation Today: Bilingualism Persists More than in the Past, but English Still Dominates* (Albany, N.Y.: Lewis Mumford Center for Comparative Urban and Regional Research, University of Albany, November 2004), 9.

180. Ibid., 1.

181. Brian Duncan and Stephen J. Trejo, "Ethnic Identification, Intermarriage, and Unmeasured Progress by Mexican Americans," IZA Discussion Paper No. 1629 (Bonn: Institute for the Study of Labor [IZA], June 2005), 6.

182. DeSipio, *Counting on the Latino Vote,* 178.

183. Rodriguez, "From Minority to Mainstream, Latinos Find Their Voice," B1.

184. Frank D. Bean, Stephen J. Trejo, Randy Capps, and Michael Tyler, "The Latino Middle Class: Myth, Reality and Potential" (Claremont, Calif.: Tomás Rivera Policy Institute, 2001), 3.

185. Gregory Rodriguez, "Where the Minorities Rule," *New York Times,* February 10, 2002, Sect. 4, 6.

186. Gregory Rodriguez, "We're Patriotic Americans Because We're Mexicans," *Salon.com,* February 24, 2000.

187. Sam Enríquez, "Núñez Trip Hits Heavy Resistance," *Los Angeles Times,* August 27, 2005, A1.

188. Rodriguez, "Where the Minorities Rule."

189. Erin Texeira, " 'Minority' Criticized as Outdated, Inaccurate as Nation's Demographics Change," Associated Press, August 18, 2005.

190. Rodriguez, "Where the Minorities Rule."

191. Vincent J. Schodolski, "Latino Politicians Gain Power, Subdue Tone in California," *Chicago Tribune,* August 10, 1997, 1, 7.

192. Clara Rodríguez, *Changing Race: Latinos, the Census, and the History of Ethnicity in the United States* (New York: New York University Press, 2000), 153–154.

193. Kenneth Prewitt, "Racial Classification in America: Where Do We Go from Here?" *Daedalus* 134, no. 1 (January 1, 2005), 5.

194. Office of Management and Budget, "Recommendations from the Interagency Committee for the Review of the Racial and Ethnic Standards to the Office of Management and Budget Concerning Changes to the Standards for the Classification of Federal Data on Race and Ethnicity," Part 2, July 9, 1997, 36909.

195. Ian Haney López, "Race on the 2010 Census: Hispanics & the Shrinking White Majority," *Daedalus* 134, no. 1 (January 1, 2005), 42.

196. Peter Skerry, *Counting on the Census?* (Washington, D.C.: Brookings Institution Press, 2002), 62.

197. Haney López, "Race on the 2010 Census: Hispanics and the Shrinking White Majority," 42.

198. Ibid.

199. Clara Rodríguez, *Changing Race,* 135.

200. Sonya M. Tafoya, "Latinos and Racial Identification in California," Public Policy Institute, California Counts: Population Trends and Profiles, Vol. 4, No. 4, May 2003, 4.

201. David E. Hayes-Bautista and Gregory Rodriguez, "Latinos Are Redefining Notions of Racial Identity," *Los Angeles Times,* January 13, 1993, B7.

202. Office of Management and Budget, "Recommendations from the Interagency Committee for the Review of the Racial and Ethnic Standards to the Office of Management and Budget Concerning Changes to the Standards for the Classification of Federal Data on Race and Ethnicity," 36909–10.

203. Ibid., 36909.

204. Marilyn Lewis, "U.S. Government Rethinks Its Official Racial Categories," *San Jose Mercury News,* April 13, 1993, A1.

205. Haya El Nasser, "Census to Define Multiracial in Myriad Ways," *USA Today,* February 28, 2001, D8.

Index